JOHN CATT'S

W
S

2

Which school? for
Special Needs

2018/19

Directorate of
Education & Leisure
Cyfadran Addysg
a Hamdden

27th Edition
Editor: Jonathan Barnes

JOHN
CATT
EDUCATIONAL
LIMITED

Published in 2018 by
John Catt Educational Ltd,
12 Deben Mill Business Centre,
Woodbridge, Suffolk IP12 1BL UK
Tel: 01394 389850   Fax: 01394 386893
Email: enquiries@johncatt.com
Website: www.johncatt.com
© 2015 John Catt Educational Ltd

**A CIP catalogue record for this book is available from the
British Library.**

ISBN: 978 1 911382 79 9

Contacts
Editor
Jonathan Barnes

Advertising and School Profiles
Tel: +44 (0) 1394 389850
Email: sales@johncatt.com

Distribution/Book Sales
Tel: +44 (0) 1394 389863
Email: booksales@johncatt.com

Contents

How to use this guide

Here are some pointers on how to use this guidebook effectively

Which School? for Special Needs is divided into specific sections:

1. Editorial

This includes articles, written by experts in their fields, explaining various aspects of special needs education. There are also case studies and other interesting articles.

2. Profiles

Here the schools and colleges have been given the opportunity to highlight what they feel are their best qualities in order to help you decide whether this is the right school for your child. They are presented in sections according to the needs they specialise in:

- social interaction difficulties (autism, ASC & ASP)
- emotional, behavioural and/or social difficulties.
- learning difficulties (including dyslexia/SPLD)
- sensory or physical impairment

Within these sections, schools and colleges are listed by region in alphabetical order.

3. Directory

Here you will find basic up-to-date information about every independent or non-maintained special needs school and college, and further education colleges, in England, Northern Ireland, Scotland and Wales, giving contact details, size of school and which specific needs are catered for. (You will find a key to the abbreviations at the start of each directory section) The directory is divided into four sections:

- social interaction difficulties (autism, ASC & ASP)
- emotional, behavioural and/or social difficulties.
- learning difficulties (including dyslexia/SPLD)
- sensory or physical impairment

Within these sections, each establishment is listed by region in alphabetical order and those that have entries in the profiles section are cross-referenced to allow you to find further detailed information. Against each entry you will find a number of symbols indicating any SEN speciality, including an icon to indicate if the school is DfE approved.

4. Useful associations and websites

In this section we provide a list of useful organisations and websites relevant to special educational needs, which may be useful to parents looking for specific help or advice.

5. Maintained schools

Here we have included basic details of all maintained special schools in England, Northern Ireland, Scotland and Wales. They are listed according to their Local Authority.

6. Index

Page numbers preceded by a D indicate a school appearing in the directory, those without will be found in the profiles section.

How to use this guide effectively
John Catt's *Which School? for Special Needs* can be used effectively in several ways according to the information you are looking for. For example, are you looking for:

A specific school? If you know the name of the school but are unsure of its location simply go to the index at the back of the guide where you will find all schools listed alphabetically.

A particular type of school? Both the profiles and directories are divided into sections according to the type of provision. **See also the appendix on page 185**, which lists specific special needs and the schools that cater for them.

A school in a certain region? Look first in the relevant directory. This will give you the basic information about the schools in each region, complete with contact details and which specific needs are catered for. More detailed information can be found in the profiles section for those schools who have chosen to include a full entry.

More information on relevant educational organisations? At the end of the directories you will find a list of useful organisations and websites relevant to special educational needs.

Please note: regional divisions
To facilitate the use of this guide, we have included the geographical region 'Central & West'. This is not an officially designated region and has been created solely for the purposes of this publication.

One final thing, on the next page you will find a list of commonly used SEN abbreviations. This list can be found repeated at various points throughout the guide.

Abbreviations – a full glossary can be found at page 319

ADD	Attention Deficit Disorder	LD	Learning Difficulties
ADHD	Attention Deficit and Hyperactivity Disorder	MLD	Moderate Learning Difficulties
		MSI	Multi-sensory Impairment
ASC	Autistic Spectrum Conditions	OCD	Obsessive Compulsive Disorder
ASD	Autistic Spectrum Disorder	PD	Physical Difficulties
ASP	Asperger Syndrome	PH	Physical Impairment
AUT	Autism	Phe	Partially Hearing
BESD	Behavioural, Emotional and Social Difficulties	PMLD	Profound and Multiple Learning Difficulties
		PNI	Physical Neurological Impairment
CCD	Complex Communication Difficulties	SCD	Social and Communication Difficulties
CLD	Complex Learning Difficulties	SCLD	Severe to Complex Learning Difficulties
CP	Cerebral Palsy	SEMH	Severe Emotional and Mental Heath Needs
D	Deaf		
DYS	Dyslexia	SEBN	Social, Emotional and Behavioural Needs
DYSP	Dyspraxia	SLD	Severe Language Difficulties
EBD	Emotional and Behavioural Difficulties	SLI	Specific Language Impairment
EPI	Epilepsy	SPLD	Specific Learning Difficulties
GLD	General Learning Difficulties	SP&LD	Speech and Language Difficulties
HA	High Ability	VIS	Visual Impairment
HI	Hearing Impairment		

From Isolation to Independence

TCES Group schools provide LA funded education for pupils aged 7-19 years whose Social, Emotional or Mental Health (SEMH) needs or Autism Spectrum Condition (ASC) has made it difficult for them to achieve success in a mainstream school. Pupils' co-morbid needs can be complex. Undiagnosed speech, language and communication needs (SLCN), sensory difficulties or learning difficulties can create barriers to learning that must be addressed before the pupil can settle into education. Our integrated approach to education, health and care takes each pupil on an individual journey that encourages a love of learning. We offer two types of provision according to the needs of the pupil:

Day School Provision

For pupils with SEMH needs or an ASC for whom the expectation is that they will be able to thrive in and integrate easily into a small group learning environment, which would include an internal induction period as standard. Once in school full time, the pupil would be supported by TCES Group's Team Around the Child approach.

There may be exceptional circumstances where a pupil may need additional support over a specified period to ensure they are able to engage with and thrive in their placement.

Day school services are delivered and managed by the Leadership Teams in each of our schools – Head and Deputy Head Teachers and Inclusion Managers – in conjunction with Head of Clinical Services, Clinical and Therapy Team and our School Improvement Team.

Create Service

For pupils with SEMH or an ASC for whom integration into a class-based school placement is not indicated, which may be for a number of reasons. At best they will need a graduated programme into a small group learning environment. They may need 1:1 support in the medium to long term in tandem with TCES Group's Team Around the Child approach.

Pupils with SEMH or an ASC who either present high risk to themselves or others or who are extremely vulnerable and are therefore at high risk. Pupils' complex and additional needs (across education, health and care) negate their ability to be educated in any group setting.

Create Services are delivered and managed by Head Teachers, Case Co-ordinators, Teachers and Tutors as a parallel service to that of our schools, in conjunction with our Head of Clinical Services, Clinical and Therapy Team and School Improvement Team. Therapeutic education, assessment and monitoring is delivered through a highly specialised case co-ordination model. Pupils may attend one of Create's Therapeutic Hubs, be educated in safe community spaces or, in some cases, their own homes.

East London
Independent School

North West London
Independent School

www.tces.org.uk
020 8543 7878

Essex Fresh Start
Independent School

Create Service
Personalised Therapeutic Education

Giving your child the best opportunity to be an effective student

There is now more choice than ever, writes Philip Garner, but with that comes a responsibility to ensure that you find the best fit

Choosing a school for any child is one of the most important aspects of parenting. When a child has additional or special educational needs or disabilities (SEND) this process can be a challenging one – although the choice available to parents is now greater than it has ever been. Schools in the UK education system comprise either mainstream or special schools. The former can be administered by a local authority or function as private/independent establishments, or as an academy, a school within an 'academy trust' or a 'free school'. Special schools are often free-standing schools, which cater exclusively for either a single type of SEND or a more diverse range of needs. Often, in any given location, mainstream and special schools work quite closely together: this is a positive feature of provision, and one that brings benefits to both schools.

The choices you make will be informed in large part by the information you gather about the school system and the options that individual schools provide alongside your own knowledge and insight about your child's learning needs; this combination will best ensure that you can identify the school which offers your child the greatest opportunity to be an effective student, at whatever age or level.

In the UK, there has been considerable discussion for almost 40 years now about the relative merits of inclusive mainstream education and separate specialist provision. These conversations can be summarised in the so-called 'inclusion debate'. The idea of educational inclusion was that all students should be in a mainstream school; some still regard this as the only way that children who have any learning difficulties or SEND should be educated. However, an alternative view is that 'inclusion' is not defined simply by 'place'; it is argued that it is more about meeting learning and developmental needs in an environment where everyone respects the differences in individuals.

Thus, 'inclusive practice' is apparent in both specialist and mainstream settings. Mainstream schools can meet even complex needs, providing effective SEND provision is regarded by all teachers as a core feature of the school's role. Equally, special schools can be 'inclusive' in that they can enable even those students with complex needs to thrive and to reach their full potential as learners. In the face of such choices, parents need be comprehensive and structured in the way that they assemble information about the best place for their child learn, so that they can be happy and contented learners at a level appropriate to their needs.

Fortunately, there is now more choice than ever in the UK for parents seeking an appropriate education of their child with SEND. Each of the schools identified in this Guide is fully registered and regularly inspected, not only by the Office for Standards in Education (OfSTED) but also by the Care Quality Commission. Many excel in addressing specific learning needs, and in curricular areas which are innovative and distinctive. Ultimately, however, they form an index, a starting point in identifying the type of school that will best meet the needs of your child. Utilising the information contained in the Guide, alongside other resources, will equip you to make an effective, informed and student-centred choice.

> The choices you make will be informed in large part by the information you gather about the school system and the options that individual schools provide alongside your own knowledge and insight about your child's learning needs; this combination will best ensure that you can identify the school which offers your child the greatest opportunity to be an effective student, at whatever age or level.

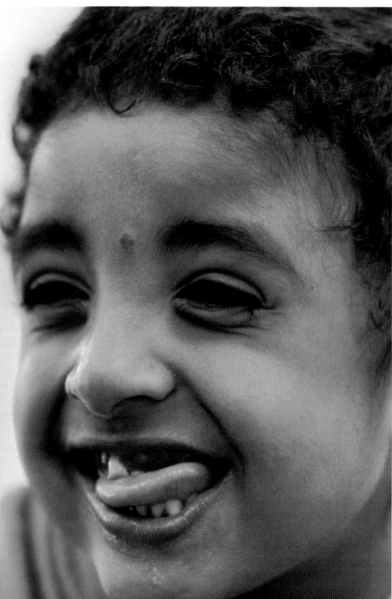

This Guide will be a welcome resource for those parents who are embarking on such a decision-making journey. It provides a compendium of information from which you can start this process. Not only does it comprise a comprehensive gazetteer of schools, according to their provision, but it also gives expert insights to assist you in decision-making. Having some insider knowledge can make all the difference when you come to make those vital school visits, starting with a clear understanding of current legislation as it applies to SEND. Visits to schools are those occasions when you can develop critical insights about a school's vision, its policies and organisation and the way that the curriculum is structured and taught. This is best done by reading the school's literature for parents, alongside relevant sections in this Guide, and then ensuring that your queries receive responses that you feel are satisfactory. And although it gives you a detailed picture of national provision

In England, the Code of Practice (2014) sets out the statutory arrangements for the education of children and young people right up to 25 years. More than ever before there is now a focus on the views, wishes and feelings of your child and their input to any decision that affects them. The information you obtain from this Guide can be made accessible to them, adapted as appropriate; their questions should be at the heart of the process. Ultimately, choosing a school to meet the special educational needs of your child is a team effort. Though the child is at the centre, your role as a mediator of key information about SEND will be essential to reaching a successful outcome. This Guide should be viewed as an essential companion or support in this effort.

Philip Garner BA, PGCE, MA (Ed), Dip.Res, PhD is Professor of Education at The University of Northampton

*Philip Garner is among the contributors to **Great Expectations: Leading an Effective SEND Strategy in School**, edited by David Bartram OBE.*

This book features leading educationalists and school leaders with a track record of improving outcomes for children and young people with additional needs discussing and highlighting the significant role that school leaders play in shaping effective practice in SEND.

Available for £15 from www.johncatt.com

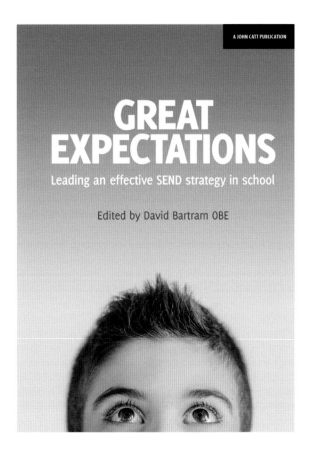

For more information about NAS schools, see page 59

Supporting autistic pupils for over 50 years

The National Autistic Society outlines its strategy for working with young people

Autism is a development disability that affects people for their whole lives from childhood through to adulthood. If you're autistic, you might experience the world differently and can sometimes find communicating and relating to others challenging. It's like you're getting too much information and it can make daily life overwhelming. There are around 700,000 people including children in the UK living with autism – that's more than 1 in 100.

An estimated 140,000 school-aged children in the UK are on the autism spectrum. It affects each child differently and can make school life very difficult. For instance, some children are so sensitive to light or sound that a bright overhead light or humming computer can be physically painful and make it almost impossible to follow a lesson. For others, a small change to the day's schedule, like the school bus turning up late or a sudden change to the seating plan, can feel like the end of the world.

The National Autistic Society is here to transform lives, challenge perceptions and build a society that works for autistic people. We started providing autism-specific education over fifty years ago in 1965, we have developed our education offer into a diverse network of independent and free schools, and programmes which are relied upon by hundreds of people across the UK. There are eight thriving National Autistic Society autism-specific schools all which are highly rated. Ofsted has rated six of our schools in England as 'Good' or 'Outstanding'.

"The principal, governors and trust (at Church Lawton) have, in a short space of time, created an inclusive and caring ethos. The principal and staff are passionate about making a difference to the lives of pupils." The National Autistic Society Church Lawton School Ofsted report

We are specialists providing support and education for young people on the autism spectrum and we are focused on their progress. MyProgress® is the name of the overall strategy for working with your child that The National Autistic Society's schools offer. With MyProgress®, your child will have the best start in life because every aspect of their care and education will be tailor-made for them.

Everything our schools does is centred on your child, we make sure that our curriculum meets their specific needs and out multidisciplinary team will closely support their learning in communication, social, behavioural, emotional, sensory, physical and self-help skills.

MyProgress® will comprise of:

- A MyAbility Profile, which provides a summary of the initial assessment showing the young person's strengths and areas for development.

- MyProgress® meetings identifies what the school and family can do to build on the young person's strengths and interests. Achievements are celebrated, progress is evaluated and targets are recommended for any areas for development. Collaboration with parents is central to improving outcomes for young people. Induction sessions are provided for all parents of new students to explain MyProgress®. Personalised goals are developed collaboratively between the young person, their parents, commissioners and the school through MyProgress® meeting soon after the placement starts.

- MyProgress® plans set out academic, social and independence targets and says how the curriculum and timetable are going to be tailored to meet the student's needs. A student's MyProgress® plan is the cornerstone of the personalised educational programme tailored to meet the specific needs of an individual student.

- MyProgress® file provides evidence of achievement of key milestones. The evidence may be a piece of work or a photo with the date and objective.

- MyProgress® Report provides a brief highlight of what's working well and action plan to address areas not working so well. The report also clearly present progress against targets agreed in the MyProgress® Plan. The report is sent to all stakeholders ahead of the termly MyProgress® meeting.

MyProgress® guarantees that your child will use approaches that we have tried and tested over many years: we know that they make a difference.

"The National Autistic Society's MyProgress system tracks what children can do. This helps to celebrate their achievements, such as taking part in small group activities and joining in with lessons." The National Autistic Society Robert Ogden School Ofsted report

In addition to running eight specialist schools, we challenge society's perceptions by campaigning nationally and working with businesses and policy-makers to change laws and deliver services that work better for autistic people.

In November 2017, The National Autistic Society and the All Party Parliamentary Group on Autism published a report on autism and education. It found that autistic children and young people in England are being let down and held back from achieving their potential by the education system. Together with Ambitious About Autism, we have launched our Held Back campaign. We want the Government to make sure no children are held back from meeting their potential because they're autistic.

The National Autistic Society has a pioneering, innovative and flexible approach to education. When delivered by our experienced staff and tailored to each person's needs, we can transform a young person's life.

"My child is extremely happy at the school. I think the teachers genuinely care about the development of every single child in the school. My child has progressed very well. I cannot praise the school enough." Parent

Our unique education provision is facilitated by our passionate and highly-trained staff, who take great care to create a path for each pupil, helping them through their early years on to secondary school, higher education and beyond. Find out more about our strategy and our schools here: www.autism.org.uk/schools.aspx

Moving forwards

Douglas Silas, of Douglas Silas Solicitors, casts an expert's eye over the latest developments in the SEND sector

So that's it then? We have now completed the transitional phase from the old SEN framework to the new SEN framework brought in by the Children and Families Act 2014 (which began on 1st September 2014 and was meant to be completed by 31st March 2018). But some would say that actually the real work starts now, as we now need to move forward.

As people say that you tend to predict the future by looking at the past, let me look at things that seem to have happened (or not happened) during the past year in the world of SEND (Special Educational Needs and Disability).

It is important for me to reiterate from the outset the now well-known and often used phrase: 'Law Trumps Policy' and point out the still lack of enough joined-up working (not only the Children and Families Act, but also the Children Act 1989 and the Care Act 2014).

There have again been continuing difficulties with a lack of specificity in Education, Health and Care (EHC) Plans and I would also criticise the formats of some EHC Plans. For example, some are still not linking provisions to outcomes or following the correct order of sections (i.e. A-K). Others are still grouping sections together and using tabulated/landscape formatting, which is quite cumbersome to follow or work with.

And do not even get me started on how long EHC plans seem to have become generally, compared to Statements of SEN – what happened to the new requirement for them to now be clear, concise, accessible and easy to understand!?

From the parents' perspective, there have been some arguably unlawful transfers, due to some Local Authorities (LAs) not giving sufficient notice of the commencement of the transfer process (i.e. sometimes not calling a Transfer Review meeting or telling parents after the event that an Annual Review meeting was a Transfer Review meeting). Or some LAs not undertaking a lawful EHC needs assessment, by not seeking updated advice and information (i.e. making unilateral decisions to use existing evidence to draw up an EHC plan, even when it's very out of date);

From the LA's perspective, we seem to have become over-reliant on EHC plans, which they argue are expensive, bureaucratic and often add little value. They say that perhaps we should start thinking about using models where resources can be guaranteed to more schools.

From the perspective of the SEND Tribunal, they submit that they are still often finding unclear reasons for LA decisions, or a lack of evidence from EHC needs assessments. They have also stressed the importance of getting up to date and correct evidence. They have also highlighted (again) difficulties with the format of EHC Plans.

From the Department for Education's (DfE) perspective, there seems to be improvement in attainment for children and young people with SEND in the past year, compared to the year before; but they say that the quality of EHC Plans still seems to vary too widely between LAs and the outcomes on them are still often too general (according to Ofsted and CQC). They acknowledge that some health and care advice/provision is still not being sought properly in assessments, with the result that some EHC Plans produced have not been good. Additionally, they also say that there are now more young people with SEND going on to post-16 education, training and employment.

> From the LA's perspective, we seem to have become over-reliant on EHC plans, which they argue are expensive, bureaucratic and often add little value. They say that perhaps we should start thinking about using models where resources can be guaranteed to more schools.

The DfE have also said that co-production of EHC plans have been working more now for many young people and parents, but that there are still challenges for a few LAs and there are some LAs who are doing things more successfully than others which we all need to learn from them.

So what does the next year hold?

The SEND Tribunal are bringing in a few procedural changes, such as revised bundle guidance, which will cap the number of pages of evidence each party can submit in an appeal (in addition to a 'core' bundle, which will include the EHC plan itself, with its accompanying documents). The SEND Tribunal will also be revising their guidance for professional witnesses, so that expert reports are clearer about issues and recommending the provision that a child or young person with SEND needs.

Importantly for us all, the SEND Tribunal are introducing a National Trial (which has now already started for decisions about children/young people with SEN from 3 April 2018), which gives them additional powers to allow them to make recommendations relating to social care and health, as well as educational decisions.

The type of issues they now expect in these cases (following a pilot) are:

- Where there is a lack of social care evidence and therefore a lack of specification in social care evidence re identified need or specification of support (i.e. no social care assessment or the response from Social Care being 'not known to this service');

- The need for residential care based on social care evidence;

- The lack of identification/evidence from CAMHS (the Children and Adolescent Mental Health Service) – for example, the need for CBT (Cognitive Behavioural Therapy).

They argue that this should allow for more positive working between SEN and social care teams within LAs and therefore for a more holistic view of the child or young person. They also say (again, from the pilot's findings) that health issues raised have not been significant or clinical, but have been particularly relevant for post-school or residential placements, where there may seem at first to be no educational need.

Finally, from my perspective, although it is argued that parental confidence has now been improved in the whole SEND system, I still think that it is important for us to recognise that we still need to continually move forward and build on good practices.

I also think that we need to remember that we need to look more holistically at a child or young person's overall SEND needs.

For more information about Douglas Silas Solicitors, visit www.specialeducationalneeds.co.uk

Securing the best outcome for your child

Hayley Mason, Senior Solicitor and Business Development Lead at SEN Legal Ltd, on the steps to an effective Education and Health Care Plan (EHC)

Many parents will have seen Nadhim Zahawi MP – the current Children and Families Minister, talking on BBC Breakfast on 30th March 2018 about how the SEND reforms are a 'huge success' and claiming that he hasn't seen an EHC Plan that is not worth the paper it is written on. Many parents will have also been left scratching their heads as to why Mr Zahawi's experience is so different to their own – claiming that he is living in a parallel universe.

When pressed on the current difficulties faced by parents of children/young persons with special educational needs (SEN) – in terms of delays, lack of funding and limited special educational provision being provided, Mr Zahawi stated that the government will "continue to look at the statistics to understand why a handful of Local Authorities are having problems."

It did not take long before vast numbers of parents took to social media to air their concerns – calling for an audit of the data supplied and highlighting the difficulties each of them have faced in their respective Local Authority areas. These personal accounts covered the length and breadth of the UK.

Whilst the government have pledged to invest £6 billion in special educational needs and disabilities by 2018/19, the question remains as to the usefulness of such funding if the government's basic understanding of the difficulties parents face is so wholly misunderstood.

One of the issues that Mr Nahawi did recognise was that the rate of children with SEN being excluded from mainstream school is disproportionately high. He sought to reassure parents by announcing a set of reviews which will look into why this is. My question therefore is why can't Mr Nahawi put 2 + 2 together to get 4?

Children with 'poor' EHC Plans, which do not specify the child's specific special educational needs and do not quantify the proper amount of provision that those needs require, often result in the child's genuine difficulties being wrongly categorised as 'bad behaviour' for which they are excluded. This appears to be because mainstream schools do not generally have the resources or the funding to provide above the level of provision specified in the child's EHC Plan and the level of disruption is easier remedied by way of exclusion (whether that exclusion is lawful or not is a whole other matter).

Every child with SEN is entitled to a properly specified and quantified EHC Plan so that it is visible at first glance of the EHC Plan by any professional, what that child's specific needs are and how best to support them. The special educational provision detailed should be what the child's SEN require – not simply what their Local Authority is willing to provide. There is no 'if we afford it' clause in any of the legislation.

Mr Nahawi proudly states "I have got EHC Plans on my desk which I would certainly be proud of if that was my child" but is the minister too far removed to know what a 'good' EHC Plan looks like?

Far too many parents are led to believe they have a 'good' EHC Plan because they are comparing theirs against another child's, who is often in the same Local Authority – constrained by that particular Local Authority's policy or funding guidelines. For example, you may think that your child has a 'good' EHC Plan if Section F states that your child requires 1:1 support and no other child has 1:1 support stated in their EHC Plan. The real question is

> Every child with SEN is entitled to a properly specified and quantified EHC Plan so that it is visible at first glance of the EHC Plan by any professional, what that child's specific needs are and how best to support them. The special educational provision detailed should be what the child's SEN require – not simply what their Local Authority is willing to provide. There is no 'if we afford it' clause in any of the legislation.

what does 1:1 support really mean? Effectively nothing.

Written in this way, 1:1 support could be from the class teacher, teaching assistant, midday supervisor or even a peer. It could be for 2 minutes per week, 2 hours per week or 35 hours per week including structured and unstructured times (i.e. lunch and break times). Without specification and quantification, EHC Plans are open to interpretation by the reader as to the amount of provision to be provided and when considering budget cuts, what is provided is often towards the lower end. The amount of provision provided can vary hugely from one Local Authority to another.

Some real life but 'poor' examples of EHC Plans I have seen include:

- No reference to a diagnosis of Autism, despite the child having the diagnosis for many years;

- Special educational provision being included in Sections C, D, G, H1 or H2 rather than Section F which means that the provision is not legally enforceable;

- Historical and outdated information being included, such as references to the child's nursery setting which they have not attended for ten years plus;

- Wording such as 'access to,' 'opportunities for' and 'to provide'; and

- Therapy input only being provided by 'school staff.'

Mr Nahawi claims that "no one has said to me that the EHC plans aren't worth the paper they're written on" – I see many every day in my line of work and would be happy to tell him so myself.

Here at SEN Legal, we specialise in advising parents and securing the best possible outcomes and provision for their children, as defined by the child's particular special educational needs and not on the basis of what the Local Authority are willing to provide. If you have any doubt about the legality of your child's EHC Plan, or whether it is legally 'good' or not, we offer an EHCP Health Check service for a one-off fee of just £300 (+VAT).

The good news is EHC Plans are relatively easily amended to something much more specific, quantified and useful going forward – you just need to know where to look.

For more information about SEN Legal Ltd, visit www.senlegal.co.uk

Coping with transition

Hesley Group schools recognise that moving between different stages of education and life are transformative events

Transition is an essential part of our lives and our experiences during different transitions are formative in our approach to future transitional experiences.

When we transition from school to adulthood, this is a time of excitement and celebration but also one of challenge and change. We may be fortunate to have good family and friendships to support us during this navigation into adulthood. This time can though be difficult for all of us and impacts both positively and negatively on our future life choices and experiences.

As a young person in a "Looked After" care situation those transitions are highly significant to their life experience, self-worth and esteem.

When you consider that many young people moving into Adult Provisions are at high risk of exclusion, feeling marginalised and having poorer outcomes, their transitional life experiences have surely impacted on this. Transition can be a time of risk, poor transition can raise anxiety and result in difficulties for the young and already vulnerable young person. What works for one young person may not work for another because of their developmental maturity and needs.

Every young person that enters a care experience in their life also experiences a significant number of varied transitions.

Transitions come in varied forms for the young person, new peers, new schools, new adults as well as different living arrangements whether short or long term. The anxiety young people may feel during that initial transition into a care situation will be variable but for each young person this is a significant life experience and as care providers one we must work to get right.

Each transition stage can bring further feelings of confusion and dislocation from their prior experiences – when you consider many young people have multiple transitions in their life in a care setting, it is imperative that we have a child centred approach and review the young person's experience so they are enabled and supported, with the right skills, to make positive transitions through those usually tricky next stages of their life, through puberty, teenage years and into adulthood.

When considering the transitional experience we need to see the whole journey. A young person entering a care setting should have an initial plan and outcomes for leaving care identified at the transition into care and not just wait until the formal transitional planning commences, or is recommended, in NHS guidance, to

commence, at ages 14-16. This sounds far simpler than it is in reality, but if we are all truly committed to enabling young people's development and to support them to fulfil their potential, this step and starting point is intrinsic to the outcome success for each young person.

Education, Support and Care providers must understand and be committed to a positive experience for all children, young people and adults. This starts, for providers, at the point of receiving a referral. A positive provider approach will consider transitional support as significant to ensure the success for the person/child. Assessment, of the care/education and support needed, will inform the transitional support and enable a clear, child/person centred approach to the transition pathway. Positive providers will avoid "too quick" referral to admission turnarounds. Transitions need a period of time to build some level of familiarity and trust and this may include visits and some stay overs to build some connection with the setting. However there are those times when "quick" is in the best interest of the person or child due to urgency or safeguarding concerns.

When an urgent and swift transition is needed, an assessment is still required, providers can't easily make decision from "on the scene crisis calls" and pick up young people there and then. However with robust information sharing from the social work or health team involved, Providers can, if they have the resources available at the

time, make fairly swift decisions that would enable a safer environment for a child or young/person. The providers can then undertake more robust assessments and still undertake a varied transitional pathway in situ of the new care setting.

Within Hesley we support transitions throughout peoples changing lives, whether that be moving into our Childrens Homes, accessing our schools or moving on at various ages to new providers settings or going home to their families or moving into their new home as an adult.

We are committed to ensuring each transition is positive for all involved and feedback and involvement from families, friends and other stakeholders is valuable during this time and whilst we support and care for the young person.

We identify from initial assessment, the indicative outcomes for the young person to leave our establishments and we plan how we can support that young person to achieve that and then work together to develop those skills and confidence.

We can measure success in different areas with different outcomes.

- Young people leaving to attend main stream school with SEN support.

- Young adults leaving our school to live in one of our flats and attend college or vocational programmes.

- Young adults feeling excited about meeting the adult services social worker and starting to really form their future plans.

- Young adults and young people coming to the service and having support from 2 staff 24/7 and after a year this support reducing to 1:1 support.

- Young people accessing work placements and experience during school to equip them with vital life skills.

Transitional pathways are as unique as the young person planning and experiencing them.

Our role, at Hesley, as a provider, is to ensure young people are not dependent on us, we really don't want to be their home for life, we want more than anything to equip them and where applicable, their loved ones with the skills to have more independent lifestyles – however that may look for them personally.

If you would like to find out more about the services offered by Hesley Group please visit www.hesleygroup.co.uk or call 0800 055 6789. For more information on Hesley Group schools, see page 54

**Outcomes
First Group**
innovators in care and education

Shared goals and exceptional outcomes

The clinical and education teams at Outcomes First Group create vocational and educational programmes around the individual – all focused on achieving the best quality of life

Outcomes First Group is a leader in the provision of outcomes-led learning, life skills, and therapeutic care for children and adults with autism, complex and social, emotional and mental health needs. We have a national network of special schools and therapeutic care homes through our Hillcrest and Options Autism divisions, working with the majority of commissioning authorities. We offer personalised education plans, vocational training, stable care settings and high quality clinical and therapeutic support from our in-house multidisciplinary clinical teams.

At Outcomes First Group we place the people we support at the centre of everything we do. Our schools provide a range of vocational programmes designed to help the people we support to build educational attainment, self-confidence and a lifelong interest in self-development. This person centred approach ensures that both the academic and pastoral needs of the children are met, which in turn has a positive impact on learning. The average attendance rate for SEN pupils during the academic year 2016/2017 was 90.3% in comparison to an attendance rate of 92.45% for schools across the Outcomes First Group. This is a reflection of the quality and engagement of the education service being offered.

Supported by our embedded clinical team, we use best practice alongside our own innovative and robust evidence based models to deliver exceptional outcomes for the people we support. Our integrated clinical approach recognises that all the people we support are individual and our provisions are tailored to meet their needs and wishes from the point of admission and throughout their placement with us.

The journey starts with a comprehensive assessment of our young people's strength and weakness, across a wide range of areas, including: cognitive, academic, adaptive, behavioural, social, emotional, sensory and communicative domains. The output of this wide ranging assessment is the production of a comprehensive clinical report which then feeds into our Person Centred Planning (PCP) process.

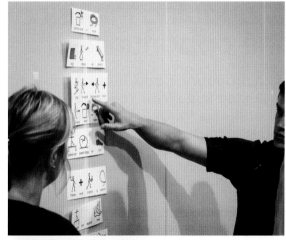

At this point our integrated clinical approach uses information from the educational and residential services, to support the development of person centred quality of life goals for each individual. Quality of Life is our central focus, and in order to ensure we capture the many aspects of this, we have adopted the Kids Life Scale. Kids Life allows us to capture a wide array of domains important to ensuring our young people are thought about from their perspective in a comprehensive way, including: Emotional Wellbeing, Physical Wellbeing, Material Wellbeing, Rights, Self-Determination, Personal Development, Social Inclusion and Interpersonal Relationships.

Once we have formed appropriate goals within our Quality of Life Framework, which provides the basis for joint working across all of our services, our various interventions are planned and delivered via clinical care plans, residential consistent support tools, and educational learning intentions.

In order to monitor the effectiveness of our collective interventions, our quality of life goals are constructed in line with a Goal Attainment Scaling Process. This enables us to measure outcomes and ensure that both the clinical and education teams are working towards the same aims for the young people that we support.

Outcomes First Group currently have 98% of services rated Good, Outstanding or Fully Compliant with the respective registering body, compared to a national average of around 80%. As well as this we have been recognised by the Education Investor Awards – School Operator Private Schools Group, for the innovative way in which the Group's in-house clinical team supports the education team in delivering shared goals.

To find out more about Outcomes First Group, visit: www.outcomesfirstgroup.co.uk or call 01789 767800. You can find out more about our Options Schools for children with autism, complex needs, learning disabilities and our Hillcrest schools for children with social, emotional and mental health needs on pages 71, 72, 81, 82, 87, 90, 92, 93, 99, 100, 103, 104

Managing the risk and maximising the opportunities

Ann Bradbury, Head Teacher at St John's Catholic School for the Deaf in Boston Spa, West Yorkshire, looks at positive risk management and its potential for building resilience, confidence and enhanced learning experiences

In any learning environment, risk is at the top of everyone's list: 'Can we do that?','Have we completed a risk assessment?','We'll never be able to do that, the risks are too great.'

Sometimes the thought and fear of what could possibly go wrong might hamper the chances of an event or trip happening at all or ultimately dictate which children may be able to take part.

In specialist school settings such as ours, the risks might naturally be perceived as being even greater, for example, where young people may have additional support or complex health needs. But should that mean they don't get the opportunities offered to their peers in mainstream environments?

The reality is that trips away from school, opportunities to learn outside the classroom, community-based activities and other potentially 'risky' activities are a vital part of all young people's education. The positive impact they have on a young person's overall well-being, sense of achievement, resilience and confidence is clear to see.

As a school which offers both day places and residential support for young people who are deaf or who may have multi-sensory impairment as well as, in some cases, physical difficulties, St John's Catholic School for the Deaf, looks carefully at the risks associated with just these sorts of activities and supports our students to take part in as many of them as possible.

Many of the pupils at St John's use a cochlear implant as many will need additional support. The school aims to make as many activities and opportunities to learn outside the classroom to be accessible for as many pupils as possible, both in the Primary and Secondary areas of the school.

Within the Primary Department, we are very aware that children's experiences and relationships in their early years have a profound effect on their later academic, social and emotional development.

It is vitally important to provide a rich and appropriate curriculum to support children's growth in all these areas and some of these curricular activities may have risk associated with them.

Our pupils participate in regular enrichment experiences such as horse riding, sporting events, drama and music, many of these outside of our school setting.

We are a partner school in the Wharfe Valley Learning Partnership which is an Educational Trust of nine high-achieving local schools that work together to enhance the quality of learning for all our pupils. This provides many opportunities for our pupils to work with their local peers. Students also visit local universities and take part in climbing, swimming and other adventurous activities.

Within our Secondary department, we again embrace positive risk management and both day and residential pupils take part in a huge range of activities outside and inside of school.

What we would never do is discount something out of hand the possibility of our young people taking part in what some might consider to be 'risky' activities just because they may have additional support or health needs or complexities.

We absolutely see, and have seen over many, many years the wonderful experiences young people at the school have enjoyed and which might be considered to carry risk and how that has positively impacted on their resilience and ability to move forward in life with less fear and more confidence.

A prime example of a potentially 'high risk' activity is the school's yearly trip to Rome, a highlight of the annual calendar looked forward to by the children and staff alike. There are also regular skiing trips.

Travelling with any group of young people abroad obviously brings with it inherent risk but there may be additional risks for young people who are deaf or who have multi-sensory or other communication difficulties alongside, in some cases, physical disabilities, all of which adds an increased vulnerability.

We are of course aware that the young people at St John's may be additionally vulnerable due to their difficulties and we obviously look very carefully at whether it is safe and appropriate for a young person to travel abroad. But wherever we can develop solutions

and support frameworks to help that happen, we do.

For example, one young person who uses a wheelchair wanted to go to Rome and we were, through careful planning and liaison between their family, the young person themselves, the care and education teams, able to find ways to facilitate that. We want as many of our students to be able to experience as many different things as possible before they leave us and move on in the world.

The school's approach to positive risk management was praised by Ofsted who said: 'The school curriculum is enriched with a myriad of visitors and visits away from the classroom. These experiences bring learning to life for pupils. For example, skiing trips and trips to Rome and France widen pupils' horizons and understanding of the world, which contribute to their spiritual, moral, social and cultural understanding.'

We absolutely agree, and this is why, although the risks may be perceived to be higher, we offer these opportunities. For us it is about setting the right framework around each pupil and each activity they want to do. Obviously, looking closely at the risks but looking also at the benefit to the young person.

For us, positive risk management is part of day to day life here at St John's and while we obviously take risk very seriously, giving as wide a range of opportunities to our young people as possible is part of our role and, we believe, helps furnish them with a range of skills and experiences to stand them in the best possible stead for a successful future.

For more information about St John's Catholic School for the Deaf, see page 140

Celebrating our 'Outstanding' success

Catherine Garton, Headteacher of Kirby Moor School in Cumbria, reflects on the school's achievements

My staff team are experienced in working with pupils who have encountered negative experiences at previous educational settings. Positive encouragement and learning experiences are reinforced in every area of the school to enable every young person to feel included and very much a part of our school. It is important that we instil a sense of pride and belonging for every young person to encourage a positive experience in education and give them aspirations and goals to achieve both now and in the future.

We work with students who benefit from a much smaller setting, with greater predictability and more intensive support available, pupils may have one or more of the following: autism, attachment disorders, anxiety issues, learning difficulties & SEMH needs. Our aim is to achieve academic, social and emotional progress. We want to prepare our students for future independent lives.

We believe that education is about developing the whole person, by meeting the physical, emotional, spiritual and social, as well as their academic learning needs. We are committed to making a positive impact on young people's lives and helping them to become the person they want to be. Planning engaging activities helps our pupils develop knowledge and skills, resulting in more self-confident pupils ready for more independent futures.

Assessment is a very important tool in ensuring the individual pupils are making good progress and any areas of difficulty are quickly addressed. The teachers here are very adept at using a large variety of assessment tools, which minimise any stress to the pupils but ensure a very clear picture is created of each pupil, their strengths and areas we need to address or support. Pupils are supported by individual programmes and planning. This ensures that our pupils are always being taught at the level which leads them to thrive. We have an active elected school council, football and cross-country teams.

"Teachers make sure that older pupils gain qualifications as they move through the school so they are well equipped for their next steps at whatever point they move on. For younger pupils, the school works intensively with them to unpick and address presenting issues. This helps teachers to identify the most suitable next steps for these pupils." – Ofsted Outstanding.

Recent Developments

- Field studies trips to enhance Key Stage 3&4 Geography and History.
- Specialising the Herdley Bank centre for pupils to "get ready to learn and to engage through creative approaches to the National Curriculum".

Our therapeutic model is based upon:

- The Whole Brain Child approach of Dan Sigal.
- Staff support pupils adopting the PACE approach: Patience, Acceptance, Curiosity and Empathy.
- Therapeutic Parenting.

This blend encourages pupils to: think, understand emotional based responses, make new choices and it aids emotional regulation. A team of psychotherapists can offer 1:1 play, art, drama and equine therapy for our young people.

Post 16 transitions

The school has links with local colleges. We work closely on transition programs for our young people. We work closely with our young people and the student support teams in the colleges to ensure the pupils are as prepared as they can be for the move. The process for our staff starts when the pupils are in year 9. We ensure we are planning for the pupils at a level which they are capable of achieving. Meetings with the Pastoral Lead and career advisor sessions help to focus our young people on achievable yet challenging goals for their futures.

The practical process usually begins in year 10 where the pupils visit colleges and talk about the courses they may enjoy. They then look at the requirements for entry and which support they would continue to need once at college.

In year 11 we look at a series of visits, then college sessions (in lesson and social times), talks with student support teams and the more formal requests for support through EHCP. For those pupils who are moving back to their own Local areas away from Cumbria we mirror the same support. We arrange a series of meetings to coordinate with home contact at weekends.

Outdoor education

Pupils enjoy outdoor education throughout the year. The days are planned with individual ability and fitness taken into account but the main focus is placed on fun and team building. Each pupil has one day of outdoor education per half term, going out in small groups. Activities include: mountain biking, climbing, orienteering, bush craft, dry ski slope skiing and hill walking.

Kirby Moor School gained Outstanding by Ofsted in December 2017, in all areas:

Effectiveness of leadership and management:

"The headteacher sets exceptionally high standards for both pupils and staff. The increased focus on academic performance is paying dividends. Parents are delighted by the positive difference the school has made to their children."

Quality of teaching, learning and assessment:

"Teachers know their pupils very well. They plan tasks which engage and enthuse pupils. Comprehensive assessments when pupils join the school help teachers accurately identify gaps in pupils' learning."

Personal development, behaviour and welfare:

"Leaders make sure that the curriculum provides a wealth of opportunities for pupils to learn how to keep themselves safe. The pastoral manager works closely with every pupil to prepare meticulously for their next steps."

Outcomes For Pupils:

"Kirby Moor succeeds with pupils where many other schools have failed. Teachers are adept at developing personalised pathways for pupils so that they fill gaps and acquire knowledge and skills relevant to their own circumstances."

For more information on Kirby Moor School, see page 98

How sport can benefit young people with an ASD diagnosis

Sarah Sherwood, Director of SEN at LVS Oxford and LVS Hassocks, looks at the benefits of exercise

A focus on social and emotional wellbeing is a key area in which schools can enhance the development of students with autism, with access to outdoor space for sport and exercise something that can be of huge benefit.

Studies have shown…

A number of studies have found that physical exercise reduces the levels of cortisol in the body. The adrenaline rush that causes the fight/flight/freeze response in autistic individuals is maintained if the individual has high cortisol levels, therefore extending the period of behaviours of concern. This, along with the other more obvious health benefits, such as maintaining a healthy weight and reducing the likelihood of depression, indicates that regular physical exercise should be a component part of any programme for an individual with ASD.

Just 20 minutes or more of aerobic exercise at least 3 times a week can result in a decrease of stereotypic behaviours and other behaviours of concern. A prime example of this is Marcus, 15, at LVS Oxford. He has Attention Deficit Hyperactivity Disorder (ADHD) and requires regular movement breaks to aid his concentration in lessons, using the outdoor trampoline and trim trail during these breaks. He also plays football, rugby, hockey, tennis, javelin and badminton. Marcus said: "Sport helps me feel calmer and better able to focus on my studies. I really enjoy all the sports we do in school".

Taking on the sporting challenge

Participation in physical exercise may be a challenge for some individuals with ASD due to motor planning difficulties, low motivation and sensory differences all of which impact on ability to participate. However, skills for physical education can be taught in the same way that any new skill is taught, by breaking it down into smaller parts and rewarding successful achievement of each component. At LVS Oxford and LVS Hassocks, both schools for students with autism, staff adopt this approach along with other autism strategies to ensure each individual is able to participate.

What schools can do

For some activities, visuals are used to indicate where a student should stand, or larger balls or bats are used to ensure success when co-ordination may be a challenge. The sessions are broken down for students (e.g. warm up, individual skills practice, pack away equipment), so they can monitor their progress through the activity. Staff use clear, precise language and allow extra processing time for students due to the additional demands of the session. A range of physical activities are offered at the schools and for those that do not enjoy team games, swimming, running and trips to the gym are offered as they require fewer social cues.

Sports Day

Sports Day allows students to try different things, with the activities catering for varying abilities. Interschool events are also valuable in offering students opportunities to compete against other young people with similar challenges to themselves, raising the confidence and self-esteem of participants.

A future through sport?

For those with a real passion for sport, it can even provide a focus for future careers. LVS Oxford helped Ben secure a work placement at a local gym where he supported members with their personal exercise programmes and helped staff with the day-to-day running of the gym. Ben said: "My work experience helped me learn about the gym equipment and the exercise programmes offered. I'm now working hard on my maths, English and other subjects so I can gain qualifications and hopefully get an apprenticeship in a gym or a place on a sports course at college."

For more information go to www.lvs-oxford.org.uk or www.lvs-hassocks.org.uk or see pages 68 and 75

LVS Oxford student Ben (left) on his work placement at a local gym

Positive change, new responsibilities and increased confidence

Some inspiring stories from students at RNIB College Loughborough

At RNIB College Loughborough we offer specialist support to people with vision impairment, as well as those with other disabilities.

We're a small, friendly day and residential college where each staff member wants to empower you to achieve your full potential. We can help you to move on to your next step.

Our Further Education offers you opportunities to:

- develop your independence
- prepare for work, volunteering or training
- build your personal life skills
- learn about looking after yourself
- get out into the local community.

You can either learn through our enterprise-based programme or study for a mainstream course at Loughborough College, located next door.

Enterprises programme

If you follow our enterprises programme, you'll learn practical skills and gain work experience in our enterprises. These are our student-led businesses where you'll be doing meaningful jobs in real settings:

- Bell Bar café
- conference centre
- eBay shop
- arts centre
- craft studio
- shop
- college office

Charlie's story

"Charlie is in his third year at RNIB College and I have nothing but high praise for them and the help they have given to him.

"Charlie was a very anxious young man when he first started. The college worked with us and listened to Charlie's concerns. They immediately put one-to-one support in place to help Charlie settle in and overcome his worries.

"Charlie has an Autistic Spectrum Condition (ASC) and tends to isolate himself, especially when anxious. His teacher and I worked together and with some gentle persuasion we were able to encourage Charlie to mix more with his peers and not sit on his own as much. He now has more confidence and staff at the RNIB College know how to reassure him so he can get on with his day.

"The College is helping Charlie to become more independent. He's developed many skills and has gained some qualifications. He has worked in the College office and the eBay shop with staff that encourage and push him to reach his full potential. Not an easy task when Charlie would prefer to be relaxing, reading or playing on the computer!

"Charlie is now in his final year and is on a Supported Internship programme out of the college setting. He is fully supported by RNIB and learning more new skills.

"I would recommend the RNIB College to others in an instant. It is a warm, calm and friendly atmosphere as soon as you enter the building. They understand Charlie and meet his needs, whilst doing their utmost to help him strive for a promising future and becoming a valid member of society."
Diane – Charlie's mum

"Anna, my teacher, has helped me with my problems at college. I have learnt new skills in the college office and the eBay shop. I enjoy going on the karaoke at lunch time and singing my favourite songs. I have met some nice friends there too like Pete, Lewis, Jamal, Alisha, Libby and my old friend Nathan. I also worked in Sip & Surf and am now working at Diam in reception with help from Naomi, Doris and Louise."
Charlie

Mainstream courses

We offer the opportunity to develop essential life skills at RNIB College alongside a qualification through Loughborough College.

Loughborough College has a wide range of academic and vocational programmes available from Foundation Learning to A Levels and equivalent. Courses could include:

- GCSE Maths and English
- AS and A2 Level qualifications
- Vocational courses at Level 1, 2 and 3.

You will have a dedicated personal tutor at RNIB College to support you. We offer a range of specialist services and advice to help you with things like accessing curriculum materials.

We can also build additional activities around your mainstream course to make a full-time programme of study.

Needs we support:

- Vision impairment
- Learning difficulties and disabilities
- Autistic Spectrum Conditions (ASC)
- Physical disabilities
- Communication difficulties
- Mild hearing problems
- Additional healthcare needs, such as epilepsy
- Additional emotional and behavioural difficulties

For more information about RNIB College Loughborough, see page 132 and visit www.rnibcollege.ac.uk

Lauren's story

Lauren struggled at school, but her prospects changed when she came to live and study at RNIB College Loughborough.

Lauren says: "It was because of the emotional support from staff, Learning Support Assistants, teachers, tutors, that I was able to move on from where I was, and think 'Do you know what? I can do it'."

"I like the fact that they promote independence, but with support if and when you need it, so you have the chance to develop. They are great because they teach you a load of different skills and prepare you for the real world."

Lauren qualified in Health and Social Care and continues her studies independently at university today. She hopes to specialise in working with children and young people who have been through abuse and trauma.

"They are great because they teach you a load of different skills and prepare you for the real world."

Jamal's story

Jamal started with us in 2015 and wanted to build his confidence as he was a little apprehensive in his new environment. We focused on giving him opportunities to communicate with other students. Jamal's long term goals were to get involved in the community and to do some voluntary work. He loves animals so in the first year he secured a work placement at Manor Farm which helped him develop his work skills. Jamal got on really well here and received great feedback and gradually took on more tasks.

Jamal enjoyed working in our café, the Bell Bar, both in the kitchen and front of house hospitality work. He gained a range of transferrable skills to use in other work places. He was able to make hot drinks, serve customers and keep the café clean.

Jamal is now able to do more tasks independently. He has built up his reading, writing and numeracy skills which in turn helped his confidence. He enjoyed wrapping the parcels in our eBay shop and going out to the post office to send the parcel. Jamal has attended activities at the local leisure centre, particularly enjoying tennis and step aerobics.

Our transitions team worked with the local McDonalds to develop a Supported Internship for Jamal. The Supported Internship is an education programme based for two days with an employer and for one day in College. Jamal has made a great start and is really enjoying it. He's working in a hospitality host role, keeping the restaurant clean and tidy and greeting customers, following on from his Bell Bar café experience. On Wednesdays when they are not in College the Interns get out in the community for independent travel training and have been practising travelling by bus and train to Leicester.

Thinking about his Internship, Jamal said "I like doing the maths lessons as it helps me count the money for the bus. I like trips on the bus and train."

"I have noticed a positive change in Jamal and feel he has developed a great deal since coming to the RNIB College. He seems to be really enjoying the supported internship at McDonald's. Every time I ask him what he likes about College and his Internship, he says, 'I love it'! What more could you want?!' – Rosie, Jamal's mum

How to support your child's speech, language and communication

Six essential tips from leading charity I CAN, which runs two specialist schools

Did you know though that the size of a child's vocabulary at age five is an indicator of later attainment and that early language skills at two years old predicts later emotional and behavioural ability? It's easy when busy to let talk slip but supporting communication in the home will help your child speak to their teacher in nursery, read and make friends in school and later on be successful in GCSEs and the workplace.

There are several ways you can make the most of talking with your child whatever their age. Although a lot of language development happens between 0-5, continuing to nurture and support language is just as important for older children and young people. Some top tips include:

1. Join in with the things your child is interested in. This will show that you value them, help build their attention skills and encourage them to talk more.

2. Develop their vocabulary by helping them learn and remember new words. Talking about what words mean as well as thinking about the different sounds in the word will help increase the number of words they know and understand. Use new words more repetitively and in lots of different situations to help your child remember them.

3. Build on what your child says: if they are a toddler, repeat what they've said to you but add extra words. If they are an older child include more complex phrases, e.g. "I'm going to buy grandad

I CAN – The children's communication charity

Our vision is a world where all children have the communication skills they need to fulfil their potential.

1.4 million children in the UK have severe communication difficulties, and in some areas over 50% of children start school with delayed language.

We work directly with the people who educate, care for, support and advise children, young people and families.

Help us ensure no child is left out or left behind because of a difficulty speaking or understanding.

www.ican.org.uk

some socks", "Yes you're going to buy Granddad some socks in order to keep his feet warm".

4. Comment and prompt rather than ask questions and try to ask questions that require more than a yes/no answer, e.g rather than "Are you making some cakes?" say "What would you like to bake?"

5. Keep language clear so your child knows what you're asking them to do. Give your child enough time to think about what you are saying. Sometimes it can take a few seconds for a child to process the words that you've used.

6. Finally make learning language fun. Enjoy talking and sharing experiences. Transitioning between settings adds lots of additional opportunities for discussing the impact and importance of decisions in a gentle way.

I CAN is the leading charity for children and young's people's speech, language and communication. We provide effective, practical evidenced based solutions that support all children's communication development. For more information about I CAN visit www.ican.org.uk

If you have concerns about our child's speech, language and communication you can talk to or email an I CAN speech and language therapist through the I CAN Help enquiry service. Call 020 7843 2544 or visit https://www.ican.org.uk/how-we-support-children/

For more information I CAN schools, see page 56

School life without labels: breaking down barriers for SEN pupils

CEO and Schools' Proprietor Thomas Keaney shares TCES Group's unique approach to integrating pupils with autism spectrum conditions (ASC) and social, emotional and mental health (SEMH) needs

Parents and families who have children with special educational needs often tell of the struggle that they face to receive a diagnosis. We've all heard stories about the challenges some people have obtaining a Statement of Special Educational Needs (SEN) or an Education, Health and Care Plan for their child.

A statement or plan is seen as a passport to support and it does play a role in ensuring access; however, at TCES Group we believe that labels should not define a pupil.

TCES Group is a leading provider of specialist education for children or young people who have been excluded or for whom mainstream schools are unable to provide the necessary support. Many of our pupils have experienced multiple school placement rejections and, on average, have been out of full-time education for 18 months before joining us. The progression of their social, emotional and communication skills is often impaired or delayed by their experiences or condition.

We believe that every pupil should be given the opportunity to thrive and we pride ourselves on never permanently excluding any child or young person. We support pupils to learn from each other and have created school communities that are inclusive, thriving, and socially and emotionally healthy. Uniquely, we integrate pupils with autism spectrum conditions and social, emotional and mental health needs. We do not separate and segregate pupils because of their support needs. Instead we educate them together in specially adapted state-of-the-art autism friendly environments that work well for both typical and atypical pupils.

Our radical approach to inclusion involves twice-weekly whole school pupil meetings in each of our schools. These Group Process sessions provide a forum for young people to reflect on their experience of difference in themselves and others. The results we've witnessed by empowering pupils to have a voice have been both moving and surprising.

Through Group Process, pupils describe in detail how they have internalised these experiences and concluded that they do not and cannot 'belong' in any social institution. We work with the internalised damaging outcomes of these rejections and support our pupils to redefine and rebuild a personal identity that is strengths-based and supports their self-esteem and well-being in the long term.

Group Process allows pupils to develop self-reflection, empathy, self-esteem, listening and speaking skills, communication skills, and social and independence skills. We encourage them to play an active part in their school community but to use their voice to communicate their needs in pro-social and emotionally healthy ways.

Pupils have discussed wide-ranging issues including gender differences, homophobia, race, class, disability, and rejection. They learn to acknowledge and understand the impulse that they may have to exclude, demean or diminish others. These impulses often have their roots in their own experience of social exclusion and stem from their personal fears, anxieties and concern about their identity.

We work with our pupils to acknowledge their own experiences of social isolation, hopelessness and despair, and to discover new opportunities to take part in a school community in which they feel they 'truly belong'. Pupils describe being at one of our schools as 'like a family'. I am inspired by the courage and integrity that they bring to the Group Process.

All pupils are encouraged to have a voice, and those on our Student Councils particularly have expressed how much value they gain from the process. Our pupils' journey starts in the development of healthy functioning of pupil groups, starting with the Student Councils. Here, opportunities are offered to pupils who struggle to have a voice, to join a democratic Student Council where their voices are both heard and acted upon. Pupils who would not normally be seen as positive influences across their school are transformed by being given an opportunity to join. They are given a real say and, as importantly, are seen by peers as champions of other pupils' wishes and feelings around the running of a democratically empowering school.

In our experience, SEMH pupils often struggle with

> All pupils are encouraged to have a voice, and those on our Student Councils particularly have expressed how much value they benefit from the process.

shyness, emotional sensitivity, embarrassment, shame, and impulsivity. Their ASC peers may bring opposite but equally difficult experiences of social deficits, including mild disinhibition or limits in self-awareness and the inability to deliberate and think on their experiences of self and others.

Through Group Process, our ASC pupils have developed a greater sensitivity to others and they are more receptive to the rhythm of a group dialogue. They are more able to link the discussion to their own experience, learning skills of social adjustment and discovering in their own kindness and care for others a new shared identity of respect and mutual support, and empowerment of self and others. Similarly, our SEMH pupils have discovered a greater receptivity to others, increased ability to tolerate others, and a new understanding of their own sensitivity and ability to listen and be receptive towards others' experience.

Our Group Process meetings instil hope and develop pupils' understanding of universal human experiences of isolation, rejection and exclusion, which are understood and transformed into a major recommitment to engage both in learning and with their school community.

Group Process requires skilled facilitation and support skills from our staff teams and group leaders. We have a team of experts including psychotherapists and motivational and leadership coaches, and we engage with research teams to explore the impact of our Group Process as a way of building healthy whole school communities and accelerating social skills development for all.

Thomas Keaney has 25 years' experience of educating children and young people with the most complex and wide-ranging special educational needs. Operating as a Social Enterprise, TCES Group runs three independent schools in London and the South East, plus Therapeutic Hubs for its parallel service, Create, for young people with multiple overlapping and complex needs who need more intensive adult and clinical support in a range of non-school settings.

How can I find a school that is a good fit for my DME child?

Julie Taplin, Chief Executive of Potential Plus UK, offers some expert advice

Dual and Multiple Exceptionality (DME) describes children and young people that have both high ability and one or more special education needs. In other parts of the world, such as in the US and Australia, it is termed Twice Exceptionality or 2e. According to the Department for Education in England, about 2 to 10 children out of every 100 who are highly able also have a special education need. This can make it difficult for parents and carers to find a school environment that understands and provides for both sides of this coin; ensuring that the ability is identified and challenged whilst the need is acknowledged and supported.

So how can parents start to find a school that is a good fit for their DME child?

A good place to start is the school's Inclusion Policy. This might be on the school website or parents can request a copy. It might be a stand-alone document or it might be included within another school policy. Regardless of the terminology that is being used, parents can look for information about how the school aims to identify the strengths and abilities of its learners and how these will be provided for; as well as the school's details about its recognition and support for those with special education needs. This provides a starting point to aid parents in any discussions with the school about how they can identify and meet the needs of their DME child.

How can schools identify DME learners?

One of the best ways is for schools to take a multi-dimensional approach. Teachers work together, across specialisms and departments. In most cases the Lead Teacher for high ability learners works together with the SENDCO (Special Educational Needs and Disabilities Coordinator). They consider the whole profile of the learner, looking for discrepancies between attainment in different subjects and/or the required skills in those areas.

When DME is suspected some schools use psychological tests that consider the ability (as opposed to the attainment) of a learner. This would look at verbal and non-verbal reasoning, and teachers can compare the results with the attainment levels of the learner in a variety of school subjects to see if they are comparable or whether there are significant discrepancies. Many DME children display a 'spiky' profile with significant highs and lows.

One very appropriate approach to the identification of DME children is through provision in the classroom. Opportunities are provided for the whole class for challenge, problem-solving, higher order thinking, divergent thinking, team building, leadership, and so on. These might range from short 10-minute lesson starters to full day challenges. Teachers observe the outcomes of such activities, such as the level of thinking that learners demonstrate, and use this information about the learners' area of strength or interest to better understand the learning profile of the child and put appropriate provision in place.

My child has been identified as DME, what does appropriate provision in the classroom look like?

The child's needs as a DME learner must be given full consideration. There should be an emphasis on their areas of ability and strength, ensuring meaningful challenge in the classroom and beyond; whilst providing coping strategies for weaker areas and opportunities for the development of a wide range of skills. Teachers should ask the question: "What will it take for this child to succeed here?"

At the same time there may be a need for ongoing monitoring of any specific difficulties linked to the special education need, but it should all be done within a supportive environment that develops strengths and helps the child to learn how to self-advocate.

Provision in the classroom can be aided through the development of an IEP (Individual Education Plan) or ILP (Individual Learning Plan), which highlights the child's areas of strength that need to be challenged and how suitable provision can be put in place. At the same time it addresses the special education need and how to support it. It is a document that can be shared by both the school and the parent, and, dependent on the age and stage of the child, they may also have significant input into the plan.

An example plan could cover the following aspects:

- Strengths might include curiosity, rapidity of learning, making connections, mathematical ability or verbal reasoning.

- Areas for development could be gross or fine motor skills, the ability to work with others, spelling, or something specifically linked to the special education need.

- Needs might cover opportunities to work with similar ability peers in a specific subject, help overcoming explicit barriers to learning, or a more individualised programme of learning.

- Provision could require content from other areas of the curriculum, regular opportunities to work at depth in specific subjects, or subject mentoring.

- Experiences beyond the curriculum might include debating clubs, university taster courses, or opportunities for expression in the arts.

- Targets can be agreed together with the learner, aiding the development of SMART goal setting.

For some children it would be appropriate for an EHCP (Education, Health and Care Plan) to form the basis for this support.

All of this should help parents and carers have an idea of what can be provided in school and the extent to which the school understands the needs of the DME learner and how to provide for the whole child.

Potential Plus UK is an educational charity that supports children and young people with high learning potential, including those that have both exceptional abilities and special education needs. We offer support to families and schools through our information and advice service, which includes webchat, telephone advice and online resources. We aid understanding and provision through parent workshops and professional development for teachers. Our events provide a community of families to reduce the isolation often experienced by these children and their parents. For more information visit our website www.potentialplusuk.org, or email amazingchildren@potentialplusuk.org or call us on 01908 646433.

Fun and adventure – an integral part of the timetable

Cruckton Hall School in Shropshire is entering an exciting phase, writes Mary Owen

Following an OFSTED Inspection in May 2017 Cruckton Hall School was graded 'Good' in both Education and Care. All teams within school have worked hard to ensure that this grade is reflective of the quality of our provision and the progress the pupils make.

In the recently published 2016-17 DfE Performance Tables, Cruckton Hall School pupils gained an Attainment 8 score which is amongst the highest in the country for specialist schools with a similar cohort of pupils.

The hard work and bespoke support offered to our pupils has allowed them to flourish and prepare them for their next steps in learning. Some have moved on to 'A' Level programmes which they access at local mainstream colleges with support from Cruckton Hall staff; others are experiencing continued success in our new Post 16 educational classrooms, further developing their skills for work and independent life.

The key to our success with our pupils is built on the foundation of solid working relationships and an unconditional positive regard for all. Working with the young person we develop a bespoke curriculum, linked heavily to the child's Education Health and Care Plan, which is supported by a variety of therapies (including Forest School, LEGO Therapy, Music Therapy and Drama Therapy), and a very successful outdoor education programme which is accessed by our pupils in one of two ways:

1. Timetabled sessions including Duke of Edinburgh Award Scheme and off site learning activities.
2. Referral from staff to work towards specific outcomes linked to their individual needs.

Outdoor activities include mountain biking, climbing, walking, trekking, taking on challenges such as The Three

Peaks, camping trips and educational visits to a variety of places to name just a few!

Research has found that outdoor education programmes can produce the following outcomes for students:

- Improved Communication
- Increased Motivation
- Improved Cognition and Learning
- Development of Friendships
- Leadership and Responsibility
- Increased Self-esteem
- Resilience
- Improved Health
- Improved Self-regulation

The majority of our pupils have a diagnosis of ASD and also have experienced several unsuccessful educational placements in a variety of settings. As part of the initial assessment and admissions process we can find that, because of past experiences, pupils are not ready to learn and could not manage to be within a classroom environment. At Cruckton Hall School we firmly believe that a different approach is needed. As a starting point some of our pupils respond well to our nurturing environment and individualised bespoke timetable.

Our initial assessments give a detailed account of developmental and nurture needs as a starting point for an individual's timetable and curriculum offer. On analysing this information, we can ascertain areas of development that need to be addressed. Due to life experiences up to the point of admission, many of our pupil's struggle with attachment and the ability to develop and form positive emotional regulatory relationships with others around them. With this in mind, we focus on the child' emotional security in the work we do across all aspects of life at Cruckton.

To enable this to happen we carefully plan for a small staff team to be in place around each child. This is to provide the support needed so that our pupils feel safe and secure with those around him. As part of the drive to increase educational progress and engagement we regularly review the wider therapy sessions on offer to our pupils. From this we know that our pupils experience success in a wide range of academic and therapeutic learning areas. These include off-site learning and educational visits, Forest School, Outdoor Education, Dog Therapy, Equine Therapy and Music. Through this approach we are able to engage our most complex pupils with incidental and incremental learning which is enjoyable and increases pupil progress.

> Learners are given high-quality careers advice and guidance, complemented by effective support during transition to the next stage of their education, training or employment.
>
> Ofsted, May 2017

One of our recent additions to the range of strategies we have at Cruckton is the use of the SCERTS framework. SCERTS stands for Social Communication, Emotional Regulation and Transactional Support. This provides a clear framework of detailed assessment to unpick what skills a pupil has and needs to develop. When our children and young people are able to communicate in a socially appropriate way, they then have the skills to be able to regulate their emotions. One of our tools for the development of this is increasingly through the delivery and use of 'Zones of Regulation' with our pupils. This gives them the vocabulary and framework to be able to express how they feel and also the strategy they need to use to emotionally regulate.

Cruckton Hall School is entering an exciting phase, as we continue to build on the progress already made on our journey to Outstanding. We are particularly excited by our upcoming developments with a wider range of pupil needs, and also our new learning pathways which provide constant development and progression for all our children from 8 to 19 and beyond to 25 as part of our local adult services.

For more information about Cruckton Hall School see page 78

Sensory rooms – essential tools or white elephant?

Kevin Wheatley, managing director of AmbiSpace Ltd, looks at the essential requirements

Multi-sensory therapy is an activity which usually takes place in a dedicated room where patients experience a range of unpatterned visual, auditory, olfactory and tactile stimuli. These rooms are designed to create a feeling of comfort and safety, where the individual can relax, explore and enjoy the surroundings. (Baker et al, 1997).

Sensory rooms first appeared in the Netherlands in 1970 as a safe calming space in which neurologists could observe mental health patients while they explored their surroundings using their senses. From this start the idea of a relaxing space capable of delivering multi and specific sensory stimulus evolved and expanded beyond healthcare and in to special needs education.

This evolution over the next 30 years came from a very narrow base and although it spread quickly there was limited innovation of products and design as suppliers largely grew in number by existing companies splitting

and replicating what had been done before. Sometimes they did this very well and sometimes not so well.

I personally have visited many sensory rooms up and down the country, usually as a result of them reaching the end of their productive life and in need of updating. I have seen very good examples and some that left me with a sense of despair. What I have gained from all the places I have visited is the insight that a well designed sensory room is an extremely valuable resource for the people who use them on a daily basis.

There are two key factors that decide if a sensory room is an essential tool or a white elephant:

1. Control
It would be easy to think control is simply about how a sensory room can be interacted with, big button remotes, tablet apps and simple switches. Whilst these are essential access points within a room there is a larger control factor that is often overlooked.

A few years ago, I was involved in a project at a specialist educational establishment were a young man with severe physical and mental disabilities was prone to going in to violent crisis three times a day for up to 20 minutes at a time. During these episodes he would self-harm, which meant three members of staff needed to hold him down on a foam mat to reduce the risk of injury. A modern multi-sensory room was designed and installed within the unit in to which he was taken at regular times throughout the day. The result was his crisis episodes reduced to one every eight days.

This was attributed by the staff to the ability to create a personalised environment around him that reduced his anxiety and frustration levels. In addition to this calming effect the staff observed that although he had been statemented as completely blind and totally deaf, he was tracking the moving lights and turning his head in the direction of sounds. This enabled them to modify his personal management program resulting in a further reduction in the incidences of challenging behaviour.

The key to this was that the sensory room created a safe, controlled and therefore predictable environment outside of the normal world, that could be adapted to the very specific requirements of the individual. This intervention at key times allowed him to relax. From this relaxed state and free from everyday interferences, different sensory inputs could be introduced in a controlled measurable manner that uncovered the young man's previously obscured true abilities. His life was improved and so was that of the staff who cared for him. The sensory room was the difference that enabled this young man to stay in the educational establishment he was in.

2. Inclusive by Design

Traditional sensory rooms are often heavily stacked towards visual and low ability provision. This in large part evolved due to the low level nature of technology initially available to suppliers creating the early sensory favourites such as bubble tubes. Often it is the accidental result of picking individual products on their standalone merits without an overarching design in place. We tend to shop with our eyes and I personally have visited many sensory rooms where this is evident to the point of sensory overload.

For a sensory room to be an essential tool it needs to be inclusive by design. With the range of technology available today it is an entirely achievable goal to create a single space that will meet the needs of all from very low to high functioning disabilities. It works best when the project starts with a brief that says,

"We don't need a sensory room, we need a controllable space that shuts out the immediate World and creates an alternative personalised one. We need an adaptable environment that will influence the mood of occupants on their individual personal terms. We need accessible sensory experiences available to everyone who enters".

Then you will have an essential sensory room that creates multisensory experiences, supports personal wellbeing and delivers differentiated educational experiences.

Kevin is an award winning sensory and immersive specialist who designs rooms and pods to deliver technology driven experiences for special needs and education. He has previously taught young people with SEN and successfully recovered from the debilitating condition M.E., an experience that strongly influences his work today.

Beamsley makes memories

Holiday accommodation that offers self-catering breaks for groups of people with extra needs

The Skipton area of Yorkshire has recently been voted as the best place to live in the UK. Not everyone is lucky enough to live here but many people visit on a regular basis. The Beamsley Project is an ideal base for you to explore the Yorkshire Dales, relax or enjoy group activities.

We have been welcoming groups of people with extra needs since 1996 and continue to improve our services. If you need space we have it. Housed in a converted chapel we provide first class facilities so that you can enjoy your stay.

In the main centre there are six ground floor bedrooms and two ensuite rooms on the first floor accessed by a lift. In total we can sleep 24 people in the centre with a further 6 in the adjoining cottage. Our bedrooms have single beds not bunks and the costs include bed linen. There are excellent social facilities with a large first floor hall with TV, table tennis and pool table and a cosy ground floor lounge with smart TV and calming bubble tower. There is WIFI in many parts of the building.

There are ample showers and toilets and a bathroom with an adult nursing table and ceiling hoist. We have a range of special equipment including mobile hoists, commodes, shower chairs and special cutlery. You will have sole use of the Centre, although there may be a group in the nearby Cottage, as we do not take multiple bookings. This ensures your safety and peace of mind. You are welcome to discuss your needs with our friendly staff before booking or why not visit us to plan your visit?

Our catering style kitchen and adjacent dining room are ideal for group meals or for independence training exercises. The hobs and sinks are all height adjustable and there are fridges, freezers, water boiler, micro wave, toasters, filter coffee machine and dishwasher. If you prefer to have your meals made, no problem, as we have excellent outside caterers who will tailor make a package to suit your needs. They can provide anything from one meal to all meals. If you enjoy the outside life you can make use of our BBQ.

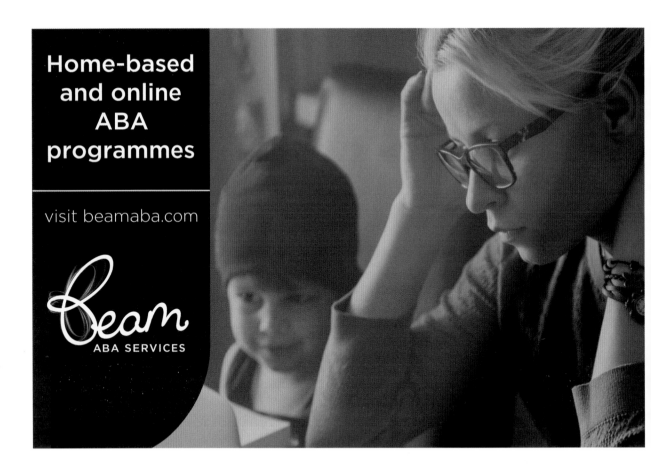

Beamsley helps you to enjoy your stay but we know that sometimes there are chores too. So, we provide washing machines and tumble driers to help with these tasks.

From the grounds there are extensive views to Beamsley Beacon and into the Dales. The gardens are safe and relaxing with wheel chair access and space to play. There is a large field for games and space to chill.

We are easy to find being on the side of the A59 Skipton to Harrogate road and parking is plentiful and safe. The area is stunning with lots to do, from the steam railway about 5 minutes away to canal boat trips in nearby Skipton or farm visits to Thornton Hall Farm Country Park or Hesketh Farm Park. Beamsley Project is on the Bolton Abbey Estate and there are great accessible

river side walks, forest trails and several cafes all within a few minutes of your base. The Yorkshire Dales makes a great and memorable holiday and provides excellent opportunities to make the National Curriculum live for everyone.

The coast is also easy to reach either to the west with Blackpool, St. Anne's and Southport within an hour's drive. Eastwards you are soon in Harrogate and York and Scarborough & Whitby make exciting day visits. If you prefer the sophistication of city life Leeds and Bradford provide shops, theatres, museums, and a wide variety of eating and drinking places. The National Railway Museum in York and the Royal Armouries in Leeds make fascinating free visits. Our staff can help with your planning to make a memorable and exciting holiday or group training session.

Northcott Special School in Hull has organised annual residentials to Beamsley for many years, including one year with an OFSTED inspector in tow. Other groups have included outdoor pursuits groups, craft & drama groups, canoeing, hand cycling, independence training… you name it, the facilities at Beamsley are flexible and welcoming for many types of activities. Our staff are ready to provide advice and take your booking. We are open all year round because there is always lots to do. Please give us a call on 01756 710 255 or email us at info@ beamsleyproject.org

You can see more photographs and information such as a room plan and risk assessments at www. beamsleyproject.org

OUR SERVICES FOR SCHOOLS

Potential
Plus | Discover.
UK | Nurture.
| Succeed.

SCHOOL PARTNERSHIP BENEFITS

- Online teacher resources
- Best practice sharing
- Discounts on CPD Training and Parents' Workshops
- Support for all parents of identified pupils:
  - Online parent resources
  - Monthly updates
  - Access to online community
  - Discounts on national events

CPD TRAINING

Topics include:

- Identifying Able, Gifted & Talented Learners
- Classroom Strategies to Provide Challenge
- Tackling Underachievement
- Fostering Resilience in the Classroom

PARENTS' WORKSHOPS

Topics include:

- Parenting an Able, Gifted & Talented Child
- Creative and Critical Thinking
- Extending Your Child's Learning at Home
- Supporting Your Child's Social and Emotional Needs

UNDERACHIEVEMENT ASSESSMENTS

We provide assessments to identify reasons for underachievement in seemingly able children covering cognitive ability, working memory, processing, sensory issues and social/emotional issues.

Potential Plus UK works with schools and parents to support able, gifted & talented children and help them achieve excellence. We can help you identify able learners, understand their capabilities, tailor provision to ensure they make progress, support underachievers and Dual or Multiple Exceptional learners (those who have high ability and a learning difficulty).

FOR MORE INFORMATION
go to   www.potentialplusuk.org
call us on   **01908 646433**
or email   amazingchildren@potentialplusuk.org
CHARITY REGISTRATION NO 313182

How good is your provision for dyslexic pupils?

We offer:

For your school a visit by a dyslexic expert

For parents a free Register of schools approved for their dyslexia provision

Contact CReSTeD via email: admin@crested.org.uk
www.crested.org.uk

Registered charity no. 1052103
Council for the Registration of Schools Teaching Dyslexic Pupils

Introducing CReSTeD

Exploring the work of the Council for the Registration of Schools Teaching Dyslexic Pupils

Introduction

The Council for the Registration of Schools Teaching Dyslexic Pupils (CReSTeD) is a charity set up to help parents and those who advise them choose schools for children with Specific Learning Difficulties (SpLD) of which the main difficulty is dyslexia. There is however a general recognition that dyslexia rarely exists in isolation and latest research demonstrates a high level of co-occurrence with other difficulties. These include Dyspraxia, Dyscalculia, ADD, as well as Pragmatic and Semantic Language Difficulties.

CReSTeD acts as a source of information which can help parents making a placement decision about a child with SpLD. CReSTeD is a valuable resource for parents, educational advisers and schools.

CReSTeD was established in 1989 and publishes and maintains a list of schools and centres accredited for their SpLD provision – the Register – annually. The schools and centres listed within the Register cover all levels of provision for SpLD pupils and include both state and independent provision. The vast majority of schools on the Register are mainstream, offering a wide range of teaching styles, environment and facilities.

The Register

CReSTeD's main activity is to produce and supply to parents, free of charge, a Register of schools and centres which provide for pupils with one or more SpLD. The levels of provision is divided into six broad categories, five for schools: Dyslexia Specialist Provision (Category DSP), Specialist Provision Schools (Category SPS), Dyslexia Unit (Category DU), Withdrawal System (Category WS) and Maintained Sector (Category MS) and one for centres: Teaching Centres (Category TC). Children have different requirements and personalities; the categories are a way of helping match each child to the type of provision at the school or centre. A report from an Educational Psychologist or a specialist teacher who holds an Assessment Practising Certificate should offer guidance as to the level of provision relevant to the child.

A child at the severe end of the dyslexia spectrum may require a Dyslexia Specialist Provision school, whereas a child with, for example, only some slowness in spelling skills may be suitably provided for in a school from Category Withdrawal System. The categories offer this guidance. Note that the Maintained sector is only open to local authority schools and not to Independent schools.

The Register includes a checklist to help parents decide if a school or centre can meet their child's education needs in relation to SpLD. It also provides a geographical index of schools.

CReSTeD Criteria and Visits

Every school and centre on the CReSTeD list has been independently verified for SpLD provision by CReSTeD consultants which is not the case in all other lists.

The first stage of any registration is for the school to complete the CReSTeD registration form and to provide supporting documentation, such as policies for dyslexia. This form covers staff development, admission policy, organisation of the school week, specific arrangements for SpLD pupils, examination results for the whole school and for SpLD pupils in particular, resources and a list of parents' names so that the Consultant may check parents' feelings about the school or centre.

These criteria include the provision of relevant and high quality information technology resources, Joint Council for Qualifications (JCQ) approved training qualifications for teachers, awareness of the needs of dyslexic pupils by the non-specialist staff, and arrangements to obtain and provide special provision for examinations.

Consultants, who look to see if this information is accurate and that the school or centre meets the criteria set by CReSTeD Council for the particular category, visit the schools.

Schools and centres are visited on a three yearly cycle, with possible earlier visits if there are substantial changes, which should always be swiftly communicated to CReSTeD. If the Head of a CReSTeD school changes, we require the school to inform us and ask the new Head to confirm that the school intends to continue with the SpLD provision in accordance with the criteria set by CReSTeD (at the agreed category level). This enables us to retain the school's details in the Register without the need for an extra visit.

CReSTeD Council will initiate 'responsive' visits if it has any cause for concern about a particular school.

Information

The Register is published annually and is obtainable from the CReSTeD Administrator. To encourage accuracy, Council require schools and centres to inform it of significant changes which impact on provision for SpLD pupils.

The CReSTeD website: www.crested.org.uk contains all the information that is in the Register. It is updated as new information is received, or new schools approved, and contains links to the websites of all registered schools and centres as well as to other websites that may be of assistance to parents of children with one or more SpLD.

CReSTeD Council

Council includes representatives from a wide area of SpLD provision including Dyslexia Action, the British Dyslexia Association, Helen Arkell Dyslexia Centre, the Dyslexia-SpLD Trust and schools.

Categories

Categories are used to explain the type of provision given by a school. One category should not be seen as 'better' than another, but as a guide to the provision required by the student.

There are six categories within our criteria according to the type of provision:

- Dyslexia Specialist Provision (DSP) schools established primarily to teach pupils with Dyslexia.

- Dyslexia Unit (DU) schools offer a designated unit that provides specialist tuition on a small group or individual basis, according to need.

- Maintained Schools (MS) local authority schools able to demonstrate an effective system for identifying pupils with dyslexia.

- Specialist Provision (SPS) schools are specifically established to teach pupils with dyslexia and other related specific learning difficulties.

- Teaching Centre (TC) designated centre providing specialist tuition on a small group or individual basis, according to need.

- Withdrawal System (WS) schools help dyslexic pupils by withdrawing them from appropriately selected lessons for specialist tuition.

Conclusion

CReSTeD was founded to help parents. It has had, and will continue to have, influence on the standards of provision for pupils with SpLD's. Council is grateful for the support of the British Dyslexia Association, Dyslexia Action, Helen Arkell Dyslexia Centre, the Dyslexia-SpLD Trust, the schools on the Register and parents.

For further information contact us via email: admin@crested.org.uk

Or visit our website: www.crested.org.uk

Accessible activity adventures

Calvert Trust Exmoor create inclusive opportunities for students of all ages and abilities

'Outdoor adventures' and 'disability' aren't phrases that often get put together, but at Calvert Trust Exmoor accessible and inclusive activity adventures are the norm; pupils of all ages with all types of disability take part in adventure activities like climbing, archery, horse riding, wheelchair abseil, carriage driving and canoeing alongside their peers.

Calvert Trust Exmoor offers a unique opportunity for students of any age and any ability to experience exciting and challenging residential adventure activities in a safe, accessible environment.

Many guests are surprised by how much they can do at Calvert Trust Exmoor. As recent guests JFK School put it; "Calvert Trust Exmoor in the only activity centre that could cater for the needs of all of our students. I've taught one of the students for a year, but I really didn't know him the way I do now. He is able to do things we simply didn't know about! The bond between the students has grown, and we've gained so much from supporting our young people in this incredible environment."

The fully catered accessible accommodation is five star rated by VisitEngland and accredited by the National Accessible Scheme. You can read all about their accessibility from the accessibility statement on their website; www.calvert-trust.org.uk/access

A break with Calvert Trust Exmoor includes a structured programme of exciting accessible activities, which are specifically designed and equipped to cater for all. Within each activity session these activities are then tailored to the specific needs of the particular pupils taking part.

Rob Lott, Head of Communications for the Trust explains; "Our philosophy is 'it's what you CAN do that counts'; our experienced instructors tailor the activities they are delivering to best enable every single one of our guests to be able to take part. We are all about 'can'!"

The accommodation consists of ensuite single, twin and triple bedrooms including some with H-track ceiling hoists, as well as a number of apartments with open plan kitchen and living space, which can be booked on

either a self- catered or fully inclusive basis. They also offer mobile hoists, shower chairs, electric beds, trembler pads, and other free of charge loan equipment to make your stay more comfortable regardless of your disability.

Other facilities on site included a fully accessible hydrotherapy swimming pool with high needs changing facilities, a Jacuzzi, games room, bar, sensory room and the Acland room, which is a fully glazed, elevated, communal area with fantastic views to the south west across Wistlandpound Reservoir, down the valley of the river Yeo and into South Devon.

Whatever your age or ability, a visit to Calvert Trust Exmoor will provide a life changing experience; building new skills, making friends and having fun. For many students the positive effects are both immediate and long lasting. Spring West Academy said; "We've visited on several occasions, student success and independence was significantly and positively impacted on. You provide opportunities students would not usually have, respite for families, and team development. One of our students, who's permanently in a wheelchair, conquered his fear of taking part in the abseiling activity. He was so elated completing the task that he took part again the following day, twice!

Another one of our young people who has very difficult home circumstances has returned from the trip with a renewed sense of self-worth and belief, and relationships with staff and fellow students have significantly improved."

The centre is open all year round and welcomes schools and colleges to visit for three, four or seven night breaks, or even just for the day.

Fully inclusive residential breaks at the centre start from as little as £210 per person. You can find out more from www.calvert-trust.org.uk/schools , by finding them on Facebook and Twitter, and by contacting them on exmoor@calvert-trust.org.uk or 01598 763221.

School groups

Hesley Group

Central Services, Hesley Hall
Tickhill, Doncaster, DH11 9NH
Tel: +44 (0)1302 866906
Fax: +44 (0)1302 861661
Email: enquiries@hesleygroup.co.uk
Website: www.hesleygroup.co.uk

Autism | Learning Disabilities | Complex Needs

Fullerton House College

Tickhill Square, Denaby, Doncaster, South Yorkshire DN12 4AR
Tel: 01709 861663
Fax: 01709 869635
Email: enquiries@hesleygroup.co.uk
Website: www.hesleygroup.co.uk
FOR MORE INFORMATION SEE PAGE 85

Fullerton House School

Tickill Square, Denaby, Doncaster, South Yorkshire DN12 4AR
Tel: 01709 861663
Fax: 01709 869635
Email: enquiries@hesleygroup.co.uk
Website: www.fullertonhouseschool.co.uk
FOR MORE INFORMATION SEE PAGE 84

Wilsic Hall College

Wadworth, Doncaster, South Yorkshire DN11 9AG
Tel: 01302 856382
Email: enquiries@hesleygroup.co.uk
Website: www.hesleygroup.co.uk
FOR MORE INFORMATION SEE PAGE 85

Wilsic Hall School

Wadworth, Doncaster, South Yorkshire DN11 9AG
Tel: 01302 856382
Email: enquiries@hesleygroup.co.uk
Website: www.wilsichallschool.co.uk
FOR MORE INFORMATION SEE PAGE 88

Hillcrest Children's Services

Regional office Midlands:
Turnpike Gate House, Alcester Heath
Alcester, Warwickshire B495JG
Email: info@hillcrestcs.co.uk
Website: www.hillcrestchildrensservices.co.uk

Hillcrest Glebedale School

Grove Road, Heron Cross, Stoke-on-Trent, Staffordshire ST4 3AY

Tel: 01782 320773

Email: info@hillcrestcs.co.uk

Website: www.hillcrestchildrensservices.co.uk

FOR MORE INFORMATION SEE PAGE 103

Hillcrest Jubilee School

84-86 Jubilee Road, Waterlooville, Hampshire PO7 7RE

Tel: 02392 250963

Email: info@hillcrestcs.co.uk

Website: www.hillcrestchildrensservices.co.uk

FOR MORE INFORMATION SEE PAGE 99

Hillcrest New Barn School

The Long Barn, Welford, Newbury, West Berkshire RG20 8HZ

Tel: 01488 505145

Email: info@hillcrestcs.co.uk

Website: www.hillcrestchildrensservices.co.uk

FOR MORE INFORMATION SEE PAGE 92

Hillcrest Park School

Southcombe, Chipping Norton, Oxford, Oxfordshire OX7 5QH

Tel: 01608 644621

Email: info@hillcrestcs.co.uk

Website: www.hillcrestchildrensservices.co.uk

FOR MORE INFORMATION SEE PAGE 93

Hillcrest Shifnal School

Lamledge Lane, Shifnal, Shropshire TF11 8SD

Tel: 01952 468220

Email: info@hillcrestcs.co.uk

Website: www.hillcrestchildrensservices.co.uk

FOR MORE INFORMATION SEE PAGE 104

Hillcrest Slinfold School

Stane Street, Slinfold, Horsham, West Sussex RH13 0QX

Tel: 01403 790939

Email: info@hillcrestcs.co.uk

Website: www.hillcrestchildrensservices.co.uk

FOR MORE INFORMATION SEE PAGE 100

I CAN

**31 Angel Gate (Gate 5), Goswell Road
London EC1V 2PT
Tel: 0845 225 4073
Fax: 0845 225 4072
Email: info@ican.org.uk
Website: www.ican.org.uk**

helps children communicate

I CAN'S Dawn House School

Helmsley Road, Rainworth, Mansfield,
Nottinghamshire NG21 0DQ
Tel: 01623 795361
Fax: 01623 491173
Email: dawnhouse@ican.notts.sch.uk
Website: www.dawnhouseschool.org.uk
FOR MORE INFORMATION SEE PAGE 110

I CAN's Meath School

Brox Road, Ottershaw, Surrey KT16 0LF
Tel: 01932 872302
Fax: 01932 875180
Email: meath@meath-ican.org.uk
Website: www.meathschool.org.uk
FOR MORE INFORMATION SEE PAGE 113

Kisimul

**The Old Vicarage, 61 High Street,
Swinderby, Lincoln,
Lincolnshire LN6 9LU
Tel: 01522 868279
Email: enquiries@kisimul.co.uk
Website: www.kisimul.co.uk**

Cruckton Hall

Cruckton, Shrewsbury, Shropshire SY5 8PR

Tel: 01743 860206

Fax: 01743 860941

Email: robert.arrowsmith@cruckton.com

Website: www.cruckton.com

FOR MORE INFORMATION SEE PAGE 78

Kisimul School

The Old Vicarage, 61 High Street, Swinderby,
Lincoln, Lincolnshire LN6 9LU

Tel: 01522 868279

Fax: 01522 866000

Email: admissions@kisimul.co.uk

Website: www.kisimul.co.uk

FOR MORE INFORMATION SEE PAGE 108

Kisimul School – Woodstock House

Woodstock Lane North, Long Ditton, Surbiton, Surrey KT6 5HN

Tel: 020 8335 2570

Fax: 020 8335 2571

Email: admissions@kisimul.co.uk

Website: www.kisimul.co.uk

FOR MORE INFORMATION SEE PAGE 114

Kisimul Upper School

Acacia Hall, Shortwood Lane, Friesthorpe,
Lincoln, Lincolnshire LN3 5AL

Tel: 01673 880022

Fax: 01673 880021

Website: www.kisimul.co.uk

LVS Hassocks
and LVS Oxford

West Sussex and Oxfordshire
Tel: 01344 884440
Email: admissions@lvs-hassocks.org.uk

LVS Hassocks

London Road, Sayers Common, Hassocks, West Sussex BN6 9HT
Tel: 01273 832901
Email: office@lvs-hassocks.org.uk
Website: www.lvs-hassocks.org.uk
FOR MORE INFORMATION SEE PAGE 75

LVS Oxford

Spring Hill Road, Begbroke, Oxfordshire OX5 1RX
Tel: 01865 595170
Email: enquiries@lvs-oxford.org.uk
Website: www.lvs-oxford.org.uk
FOR MORE INFORMATION SEE PAGE 68

NAS

393 City Road
London EC1V 1NG
Tel: +44 (0)20 7833 2299
Fax: +44 (0)20 7833 9666
Email: nas@nas.org.uk
Website: www.nas.org.uk

The National Autistic Society

NAS Anderson School

Luxborough Lane, Chigwell, Essex IG7 5AB
Email: theandersonschool@nas.org.uk
Website: www.andersonschool.org.uk
FOR MORE INFORMATION SEE PAGE 69

NAS Church Lawton School

Cherry Tree Avenue, Church Lawton, Stoke-
on-Trent, Staffordshire ST7 3EL
Tel: 01270 877601
Email: church.lawton@nas.org.uk
Website: www.churchlawtonschool.org.uk
FOR MORE INFORMATION SEE PAGE 80

NAS Daldorch House School

Sorn Road, Catrine, East Ayrshire KA5 6NA
Tel: 01290 551666
Fax: 01290 553399
Email: daldorch@nas.org.uk
Website: www.daldorchhouseschool.org.uk
FOR MORE INFORMATION SEE PAGE 89

NAS Daldorch Satellite School

St Leonards, East Kilbride, South Lanarkshire G74
Tel: 01355 246242
Fax: 01290 553399
Email: daldorch@nas.org.uk
Website: www.daldorchhouseschool.org.uk

NAS Helen Allison School

Longfield Road, Meopham, Kent DA13 0EW
Tel: 01474 814878
Email: helen.allison@nas.org.uk
Website: www.helenallisonschool.org.uk
FOR MORE INFORMATION SEE PAGE 76

NAS Radlett Lodge School

Harper Lane, Radlett, Hertfordshire WD7 9HW
Tel: 01923 854922
Fax: 01923 859922
Email: radlett.lodge@nas.org.uk
Website: www.radlettlodgeschool.org.uk
FOR MORE INFORMATION SEE PAGE 70

NAS Robert Ogden School

Clayton Lane, Thurnscoe, Rotherham, South Yorkshire S63 0BG
Tel: 01709 874443
Fax: 01709 870701
Email: robert.ogden@nas.org.uk
Website: www.robertogdenschool.org.uk
FOR MORE INFORMATION SEE PAGE 86

NAS Sybil Elgar School

Havelock Road, Southall, Middlesex UB2 4NY
Tel: 020 8813 9168
Fax: 020 8571 7332
Email: sybil.elgar@nas.org.uk
Website: www.sybilelgarschool.org.uk
FOR MORE INFORMATION SEE PAGE 73

NAS Thames Valley School

Conwy Close, Tilehurst, Reading, Berkshire RG30 4BZ
Tel: 0118 9424 750
Email: thames.valley@nas.org.uk
Website: www.thamesvalleyschool.org.uk
FOR MORE INFORMATION SEE PAGE 77

Options Autism and Learning Difficulties

Regional office Midlands:
Turnpike Gate House, Alcester Heath
Alcester, Warwickshire B495JG
Email: info@optionsautism.co.uk
Website: www.optionsautism.co.uk

innovators in care and education

Baston House School

Baston Road, Hayes, Bromley, Kent BR2 7AB
Tel: 020 8462 1010
Email: info@bastonhouseschool.org.uk
Website: www.bastonhouseschool.org.uk
FOR MORE INFORMATION SEE PAGE 71

Hillingdon Manor School

The Manor, Harlington Road, Hillingdon, Middlesex UB8 3HD
Tel: 01895 813679
Email: enquiries@hmschool.org.uk
Website: www.hillingdonmanorschool.org.uk
FOR MORE INFORMATION SEE PAGE 72

Options Barton

Barrow Road, Barton-upon-Humber, Lincolnshire DN18 6DA
Tel: 01652 631280
Email: info@optionsautism.co.uk
Website: www.optionsautism.co.uk
FOR MORE INFORMATION SEE PAGE 87

Options Higford

Higford Hall, Higford, Shifnal, Shropshire TF11 9ET
Tel: 01952 630600
Email: info@optionsautism.co.uk
Website: www.optionsautism.co.uk
FOR MORE INFORMATION SEE PAGE 81

Options Kinsale

Kinsale Hall, Llanerch-y-Mor, Holywell, Flintshire CH8 9DX
Tel: 01745 562500
Email: info@optionsautism.co.uk
Website: www.optionsautism.co.uk
FOR MORE INFORMATION SEE PAGE 90

Options Trent Acres

Alrewas Road, Kings Bromley, Staffordshire DE13 7HR
Tel: 01543 473772
Email: info@optionsautism.co.uk
Website: www.optionsautism.co.uk
FOR MORE INFORMATION SEE PAGE 82

Options West London Community College

The Courtyard Campus, Church Rd, Hayes, Middlesex UB3 2UH
Tel: 0208 573 7419
Email: info@wlcc-uk.com
Website: www.optionsautism.co.uk

part of the

Outcomes First Group

RNIB
**105 Judd Street
London WC1H 9NE
Tel: 0303 123 9999
Email: helpline@rnib.org.uk
Website: www.rnib.org.uk**

RNIB College Loughborough

Radmoor Road, Loughborough, Leicestershire LE11 3BS

Tel: 01509 611077

Fax: 01509 232013

Email: enquiries@rnibcollege.ac.uk

Website: www.rnibcollege.ac.uk

FOR MORE INFORMATION SEE PAGE 132

RNIB Pears Centre for Specialist Learning

Wheelwright Lane, Ash Green, Coventry, West Midlands CV7 9RA

Tel: 024 7636 9500

Fax: 024 7636 9501

Email: pearscentre@rnib.org.uk

Website: www.rnib.org.uk/pearscentre

FOR MORE INFORMATION SEE PAGE 138

RNIB Sunshine House School

33 Dene Road, Northwood, Middlesex HA6 2DD

Tel: 01923 822538

Fax: 01923 826227

Email: sunshinehouse@rnib.org.uk

Website: www.rnib.org.uk/sunshinehouse

FOR MORE INFORMATION SEE PAGE 133

TCES Group

**Park House, 8 Lombard Road, Wimbledon
London SW19 3TZ
Tel: +44 (0)20 8543 7878
Fax: +44 (0)20 8543 7877
Email: referrals@tces.org.uk
Website: www.tces.org.uk**

East London Independent School (ELIS)

Stratford Marsh, Welfare Road, , London E15 4HT

Tel: 020 8555 6737

Email: referrals@tces.org.uk

Website: www.tces.org.uk

FOR MORE INFORMATION SEE PAGE 95

Essex Fresh Start Independent School (EFS)

Church Street, Witham, Essex CM8 2JL

Tel: 01376 780088

Email: referrals@tces.org.uk

Website: www.tces.org.uk

FOR MORE INFORMATION SEE PAGE 94

North West London Independent School (NWLIS)

85 Old Oak Common Lane, Acton, , London W3 7DD

Tel: 020 8749 5403

Email: referrals@tces.org.uk

Website: www.tces.org.uk

FOR MORE INFORMATION SEE PAGE 96

School profiles

Schools and colleges specialising in social interaction difficulties (Autism, ASC & ASP)

Prior's Court School

(Founded 1999)

Hermitage, Thatcham,
West Berkshire RG18 9NU
Tel: 01635 247202/245914
Fax: 01635 247203
Email: mail@priorscourt.org.uk
Website: www.priorscourt.org.uk
Director of Education and Learning:
Sue Piper

Appointed: September 2011
School type: Independent Special School
Age range of pupils: 5–19
No. of pupils enrolled as at 01/01/2018: 65
Boys: 51 **Girls:** 14 **Sixth Form:** 23
No. of boarders: 60
Fees per annum as at 01/01/2018:
On application

Prior's Court School is an independent special school for students with autism aged from 5 to 19 years. The School offers day, weekly and termly places with 38, 44 and 52 week options. Students are on the autistic spectrum have moderate to severe learning difficulties and complex needs. They may have additional associated diagnoses. Some students exhibit challenging behaviours. All are working within P scales to lower national curriculum levels.

The School was opened in 1999. It is managed by Prior's Court Foundation, a registered, non-profit making charity which also runs a young adult provision and specialist autism training centre on the same site.

As an autism-specific school, Prior's Court is able to focus on meeting the special needs of its students in the most effective and consistent way to support their learning:

- A meaningful and functional curriculum with individualised learning programmes used throughout the waking day is built around students' interests and skills.
- The environment is adapted to meet students' needs – it is highly structured, calm, low-arousal, safe and secure with space and physical exercise a key feature providing opportunities to learn, exercise, socialise and relax onsite. Set in over 50 acres, facilities include a stable yard and paddocks for animal husbandry, a walled garden with greenhouse and polytunnel for horticulture, sensory swimming pool, trampolines, trim trail, zip wire, swings, activity track and outdoor gym.
- The school's strong focus on training means that staff are experienced in using a range of methodologies and strategies to support each individual's needs and development in all settings throughout the waking day.
- A large onsite multi-disciplinary team including Occupational therapy, Speech & Language therapy, Clinical Psychologists and Nurses as well as dedicated horticulture, animal husbandry, swimming, activities and ICT instructors provide support through-

out the school day and in residential settings as well as out in the community where appropriate. All staff (education, residential, night, multi-disciplinary and therapeutic team) are trained from induction onwards ensuring the highest levels of knowledge and expertise. These dedicated staff work closely with families and professionals to create a co-ordinated and consistent programme of education and care whose success is recognised worldwide.

By combining autism expertise and best practice with a person-centred approach, the school aims to achieve the highest level of progress for each individual enabling them to self-manage behaviour, communicate, manage transitions, develop independent living and social skills, make choices and advocate and progress to building vocational skills and undertaking work-placement activities. Skills once taught and practiced onsite can then be generalised and undertaken successfully offsite. Frequent access to the nearby villages, towns and community facilities enable students to work towards inclusion as far as possible.

"I am absolutely delighted with the progress being achieved. Teaching and house staff are superb, broadening our child's skills and experience. Improvement in speech and language has been very impressive, as has the ability to self-manage behaviour."
Parent at Prior's Court School

LVS Oxford

A unique, positive education for young people on the autism spectrum

Spring Hill Road, Begbroke, Oxfordshire OX5 1RX
Tel: 01865 595170
Email: enquiries@lvs-oxford.org.uk
Website: www.lvs-oxford.org.uk

Head Teacher: Mrs Louisa Allison-Bergin
School type: Coeducational Day
Age range of pupils: 11–19
No. of pupils enrolled as at 01/01/2018: 58

LVS Oxford is an SEN school providing a unique, positive education for young people on the autism spectrum aged 11 to 19.

As students with communication, socialisation and imagination difficulties all have different skills and attributes, we offer a specialist curriculum that recognises young people on the autism spectrum as individuals. Our approach is focused on educational achievement and building life skills to give students a greater chance of living more independently when they leave.

At LVS Oxford our students learn a range of relevant academic and vocational skills in a vibrant and stimulating environment. Supported by their teachers, the ongoing assessment can lead to a range of nationally recognised qualifications.

Opened in 2014, LVS Oxford offers an ever growing range of qualifications including A-level, GCSE, AQA and OCR entry level and BTECs. Five students sat our first ever GCSEs in 2016, with 100% achieving A*-C grades.

Older students and those in weekly residential are given a real focus on developing their independent living skills. They take responsibility for many day-to-day activities from cleaning their bedrooms and doing their own washing to planning and preparing meals.

Supported by excellent pastoral care, we encourage independence, wellbeing and healthy lifestyles, with students learning life skills outside the classroom in a safe and secure environment. There are on-site speech, language and occupational therapists, a school nurse

and a child psychotherapist supporting our students.

We recognise that one of the biggest concerns is what will happen when a young person with a diagnosis on the autism spectrum leaves school at 19. We prepare young people with autism spectrum disorders for life in the workplace, so when students leave us they have the skills and knowledge to get a job and sustain work. They are given the opportunity to engage in work based training either on site, working in the grounds or kitchen, as well as off site for experience in their chosen area, such as Blenheim Palace or the gym.

Whilst we have a criteria and policy for admissions, we also recommend you contact us to discuss the individual's needs or attend one of our open days.

Anderson School

NAS Anderson School
Luxborough Lane, Chigwell, Essex, IG7 5AB
E: theandersonschool@nas.org.uk
www.andersonschool.org.uk

Principal: Gary Simm

School type: mixed free school with day placements for children and young people on the autism spectrum

Catchment area: Essex, East London and neighbouring authorities
Age range: 11-19
Capacity: 78
Established: 2017

Anderson School opened in September 2017 to children and young people on the autism-spectrum.

It is part of the National Autistic Society's Enterprise Campus situated on a 13-acre site, the campus hosts an Enterprise Centre and the National Inclusion and Development Centre. This is in addition to our sixth form centre, workshop and training facilities and indoor and outdoor sports facilities.

Our ambition is to transform the lives of autistic young people with the aspiration that all students leave the school ready for further education, employment or training.

As with all The National Autistic Society schools, the pedagogy of Anderson School is informed by the National Autistic Society's **MyProgress®** methodology. This has been developed through over 50 years' of experience and research to ensure best practice in teaching young autistic people. The school works in partnership with our other seven schools and the wider organisation to strengthen and develop expertise and innovative thinking.

MyProgress® guarantees that children will use tried and tested approaches that we have developed and used in our network of schools over many years: we know they make a difference. In addition to this we will take opportunities to pilot new and innovative interventions to facilitate the development of social understanding, resilience and independence.

Placements are funded by your local authority.

The National Autistic Society

"My ultimate aim for this campus is that every child that leaves school will go into meaningful paid employment or other activity."

Mark Lever, CEO, The National Autistic Society

Radlett Lodge School

NAS Radlett Lodge School
Harper Lane, Radlett, Herts WD7 9HW
T: 01923 854 922 | F: 01923 859 922
E: radlett.lodge@nas.org.uk | www.radlettlodgeschool.org.uk

Principal: Jeremy Keeble

School type: mixed independent school with day, weekly and termly residential placements for children and young people on the autism spectrum

Catchment area: national
Age range: 4-19
Capacity: 55
Established: 1974

At Radlett Lodge School, we are driven by our determination to provide the highest quality education to the children in our care and do the best we can for their families. Ofsted have recognised our pursuit for excellence by rating us Outstanding for both education and care for a number of years.

We get to know every pupil well, ensuring every element of their school life is personalised to them. We use the principles of The National Autistic Society's **MyProgress®** strategy to help your child to learn, develop and prepare for adult life to the very best of their ability – and we celebrate every achievement.

Radlett Lodge School caters for early years, primary, secondary and post-16 pupils. The school and our residential lodge are located on the same site, which supports a close-knit environment and easy transitions. Strong ties with our local community mean pupils apply their learning to the outside world, particularly when approaching adulthood in our post-16 unit. We also offer flexi-boarding to our pupils, and outreach support to external pupils.

In a structured and supportive learning environment and with the help of friendly, approachable staff, students develop social relationships and receive a broad and balanced education.

Placements are funded by your local authority.

The National Autistic Society

"The care and welfare of pupils is at the heart of the school's work."

Ofsted, 2017

Ofsted
Outstanding
Provider

Baston House School

Baston Road, Hayes, Bromley,
Kent, BR2 7AB
Tel: 020 8462 1010
Email: info@bastonhouseschool.org.uk

Website: www.bastonhouseschool.org.uk
Headteacher: Mr Greg Sorrell
School type: Day
Age range of pupils: 5–19 years

Baston House School is an independent special school for children and young people aged from 5 to 19 years with autism and associated complex needs.

Our school environment supports learning and promotes the well-being of pupils and staff through a strong sense of community cohesion, and through developing social understanding, improving well-being, and enhancing academic achievement and independence.

We support learners in achieving their full potential by putting learning and well-being at the heart of everything that we do. A key factor in any child's learning and well-being is the teacher, our highly experienced, skilled, dedicated and committed teaching teams and support staff work together to provide a safe and engaging environment to meet the needs of the people that we support.

The school's designated team reflects the needs of the children and young people that learn with us, however additional support can also be accessed from other specialists within the wider Clinical Team. This enables us to be responsive to any newly identified, time limited or changing needs of a child or young person throughout their placement with us.

"Students' achievement is good. This is shown in the quality of work in their books, observations of their learning in lessons, and through the school's own information about each student's progress. This good progress from their starting points is as a result of good teaching and a carefully matched curriculum that successfully meets the students' needs." (Ofsted)

Baston House School provides effective specialist education and support to pupils with autism and to their families, enabling pupils to achieve their full potential in education and in life outside school.

Hillingdon Manor School

Primary School Address
Yiewsley Grange, High Street, Yiewsley,
Middlesex, UB7 7QP
Tel: 01895 420315
Secondary School Address
The Manor, Harlington Road, Hillingdon,
Middlesex, UB8 3HD
Tel: 01895 813679

Email: enquiries@hmschool.org.uk
Website:
www.hillingdonmanorschool.org.uk
Primary Headteacher: Mr Ciaran Walsh
Secondary Headteacher:
Mr Richard McCabe
School type: Day
Age range of pupils: 3–19 years

Hillingdon Manor School is an independent special school for children and young people with autism between 3 to 19 years of age. The School strives to provide effective, specialist education and support to pupils with autism, allowing pupils to achieve their full potential both in and outside of school.

Located over two sites for primary and secondary, the school offers a unique mix of education and support to pupils with a wide spectrum of needs and abilities. Personalised teaching and learning in an autism specific environment allows pupils' individual needs to be addressed completely and their capabilities fully realised.

At Hillingdon Manor School, we aim to provide a broad and balanced education for all of the people that we support within a happy, stimulating and healthy environment and we want each child to achieve the best they can.

The National Curriculum is tailored to the individual needs of the pupil through the use of the Equals schemes of work and is supported through a communication-centred environment.

"Students enter the school at various ages, frequently following difficult experiences of education and with negative feelings about school. Leaders enable almost all students to achieve well as they progress through the school." (Ofsted)

We value the importance of celebrating achievement to build children's self-esteem. Our Weekly Star of the Week assemblies are used formally to celebrate pupil's achievements both inside and outside of school. Parents are welcome to join us in our sharing Assemblies throughout the year. Hillingdon Manor School is also home to the Autism with Attitude street dance group. The group, which includes students from the school, made history in July 2017 when they qualified as the first special needs dance team to make it through to the finals of the United Dance Organisations (UDO) Championships.

We are proud of our school and the staff work extremely hard to make learning fun and exciting for all our pupils. We feel privileged to lead an enthusiastic and committed team; and firmly believe that when young people move on from our school they have the necessary skills and coping strategies to succeed regardless of individual needs.

Sybil Elgar School

NAS Sybil Elgar School
Havelock Road, Southall, Middlesex, UB2 4NY
T: 020 8813 9168 | F: 020 8571 7332
E: sybil.elgar@nas.org.uk | www.sybilelgarschool.org.uk

Principal: Chloe Phillips

School type: mixed independent school with day, weekly term-time and 52-week residential placements for children and young people on the autism spectrum

Catchment area: national
Age range: 4-22
Capacity: 90
Established: 1965

As the first autism-specific residential school in the world, Sybil Elgar School is a pioneer in autism education. Having paved the way in autism education for over 50 years, we have the knowledge and experience to apply the tailored education and care each young person who learns with us will receive.

We have a highly specialised curriculum, and our dedicated staff closely support the learning of each pupil in communication, social, behavioural, emotional, sensory, physical and self-help skills. Our extensive performing arts curriculum complements this. Students can discover a new passion or enhance learning in other subjects through music, art and dance. They might play the drums in the school band and even perform at an international arts festival.

Our welcoming environment extends across our three school sites, which include a post-16 department and our year-round children's home, where all staff work together to ensure the safety, wellbeing and progress of all our students.

We follow the principles of The National Autistic Society's **MyProgress**® strategy to ensure each of our students has an experience with us that is truly personalised to them, their strengths, weaknesses and ambitions. And we recognise every achievement, helping our students value their successes and celebrate them.

Placements are funded by your local authority.

The National Autistic Society

"The curriculum is creative, innovative and progressive. Pupils love learning and make outstanding progress."

Ofsted, 2018

West Kirby School and College

WEST KIRBY SCHOOL AND COLLEGE

(Founded 1881)

Meols Drive, West Kirby, Wirral,
Merseyside CH48 5DH
Tel: 0151 632 3201
Fax: 0151 632 0621
Website: www.wkrs.co.uk
Principal: Mr Iain Sim

School type:
Coeducational Day & Weekly Boarding
Age range of pupils: 5–19
No. of pupils enrolled as at 01/01/2018: 87
Fees per annum as at 01/01/2018:
On application

Changing Children's Lives, Building Better Futures

WKS is a Non-Maintained Special School for pupils with a wide range of social, communication difficulties often linked with conditions such as Autism and additional complex learning needs.

The school prides itself on being able to help some very complex young people access the National Curriculum and work towards appropriate accreditation in all subjects including Open Awards, GCSEs and AS Levels. Staff are highly skilled in the understanding of the social and emotional needs of the pupils, as well as being able to personalise the academic work accordingly and provide high levels of support.

We believe the views of the pupils are paramount to success and the school offers opportunities for this through School Council, Pupil Voice and individual discussion. Every pupil has an 'individual support plan' which they and staff contribute to. Differentiation and small classes with high levels of adult support have proven successful. We have excellent facilities, particularly for sport, music and other practical subjects.

The school has its own Clinical Service team which provides additional 'therapy' and educational support often necessary for the pupils to access the National Curriculum and fulfil their academic and personal potential. This department consists of: a Clinical Psychologist, Speech and Language Therapists, Occupational Therapist, Behaviour and Reading support specialists/teams, a Learning Mentor, a Family Liaison Officer and Pastoral Care Team.

We have the option of day only provision or flexible boarding provision with pupils staying between one and four nights per week. Residential units include two houses in the locality and all are maintained to a high standard, with individual bedrooms and common areas for dining and recreation.

We have forged strong links with schools in South Africa and China and an orphanage in India, where exchange visits have taken place over a number of years now, real experiences which most of our pupils would have considered beyond their reach. Many enrichment activities are also an important part of the school experience.

Post 16 is bespoke provision on-site. Each pupil has a study programme tailored to their individual needs, involving academic study, vocational and employability skills and further development of social and communication skills. The college has recently established supported Internships to facilitate access to college and work.

Staff are experienced at assisting pupils in the difficult process of transition from school to adult life. All pupils benefit from the strong pastoral ideal that runs through the school, to be aware both of themselves as individuals and within a group, increasing their respect for others, their self-esteem, emotional regulation and self-awareness.

Our staff are well qualified, experienced professionals. Recruitment procedures are rigorous with exemplary professional development available for all. Continued professional development is supported through an extensive range or partnerships with local schools, universities and other agencies.

'This school remains outstanding' (Ofsted 2016).

WKRS is a registered charity no. 207790.

LVS Hassocks

LVS Hassocks
A unique, positive education for young people
on the autism spectrum

London Road, Sayers Common, Hassocks,
West Sussex BN6 9HT
Tel: 01273 832901
Email: office@lvs-hassocks.org.uk
Website: www.lvs-hassocks.org.uk

Head Teacher: Ms Terry Kelly
School type:
Coeducational Day & Weekly Boarding
Age range of pupils: 11–19
No. of pupils enrolled as at 01/01/2018: 55

LVS Hassocks is an SEN school providing a unique, positive education for young people on the autism spectrum aged 11 to 19.

Our approach is focused on educational achievement and building life skills to give young people a greater chance of living more independently when they leave. Our experience shows that students, parents and supporting local authorities value our specialist care and innovative approach to helping young people reach their full potential.

Academic progress is an important area of development for students, and at LVS Hassocks young people learn a range of relevant academic and vocational skills in a vibrant and stimulating environment. Our accredited qualifications include A-levels, GCSEs, BTECs, NVQs, Functional Skills and ASDAN. LVS Hassocks enjoyed

its best ever GCSE results in 2017 with 10 students sitting 18 exams, and a record 64% of exam papers graded A*-C. 70% of students achieved all A*-D grades, with a number of them having now moved on to mainstream college places.

The spacious and comfortable rooms at LVS Hassocks help residential students to feel safe and secure, and older learners especially are encouraged to develop their independent living skills. They are given responsibility for doing many day-to-day tasks such as washing and cleaning to planning and preparing the group evening meal.

There are on-site speech, language and occupational therapists, a massage therapist, dedicated chefs and practical instructors delivering the vocational skills to help learners develop as individuals. A new sensory room which opened in 2017

provides a further calming impact and gives students the opportunity to regulate themselves.

Real world learning allows all students the opportunity to engage in work-based training either on-site or off-site with work experience placements in their chosen area, such as hairdressing, catering or retail.

One of LVS Hassocks' proudest achievements is our ability to help learners find opportunities beyond school, in further education and full and part-time work after they leave. Our 100% rate of successful placements is testimony to our ethos, helping young people with autism to build positive futures and fulfilled lives within their own communities.

Whilst we have a criteria and policy for admissions, we also recommend you contact us to discuss the individual's needs or attend one of our open days.

Helen Allison School

NAS Helen Allison School
Longfield Road, Meopham, Kent DA13 0EW
T: 01474 814 878
E: helen.allison@nas.org.uk | www.helenallisonschool.org.uk

Principal: Kim McConnell

School type: mixed independent school with day and weekly term-time residential placements for children and young people on the autism spectrum

Catchment area: London, South East and East Anglia
Age range: 5-19
Capacity: 77
Established: 1968

At Helen Allison School we deliver a high quality, relevant and enjoyable education and use our expert knowledge of autism to find the best possible way for each student to learn to the best of their ability.

Following the principles of **MyProgress®**, The National Autistic Society's strategy for working with autistic students, we ensure they get the best start in life with an education tailored to them.

We believe in preparing our students for fulfilling adult lives, so our main curriculum is enhanced with a wide range of social activities and community-based learning.

Through our hub, older students partake in work experience, pursue formal qualifications or might even organise a football tournament with other local schools and colleges.

Rated 'Outstanding' for education, and 'Outstanding' for care under the new Ofsted criteria, we are always pushing for excellence for our students, thinking creatively to adapt to their needs and aspirations.

As one of only a few schools with our own therapeutic team, your child will develop not only academically but foster strong social and communication skills so they can thrive alongside their peers.

Placements are funded by your local authority.

The National Autistic Society

"Teachers plan lessons so they build on pupils' interests to capture their enthusiasm and support likely future pathways."

Ofsted, 2017

Ofsted Outstanding Provider

Thames Valley School

NAS Thames Valley School
Conwy Close, Tilehurst, Reading, Berkshire RG30 4BZ
T: 0118 9424 750 | E: thames.valley@nas.org.uk
www.thamesvalleyschool.org.uk

Principal: David Stewart

School type: mixed free school with day placements for children and young people on the autism spectrum

Catchment area: Reading, Berkshire and neighbouring local authorities
Age range: 5-16
Capacity: 50
Established: 2013

Thames Valley School is a high-achieving specialist school for children and young people on the autism spectrum. Our school has been purpose-built for us, meaning we could design it to be perfectly suitable for our students. We have calming pods where children can relax or read, independent rooms attached to every classroom, outdoor play areas for all ages and a state-of-the-art innovation hub, opening up opportunities for pupils to take on digital projects such as coding, social media and cyber security.

We have high expectations of our pupils, and through delivering the National Curriculum at all key stages, we expect the majority of our students to attain at least the same levels as their mainstream school peers. At age 16 our pupils take national qualifications, and our aim is for most to achieve a wide range of GCSE's at A to C or equivalent vocational qualifications.

Small classes, committed and experienced specialist teachers and a wonderful learning environment all contribute to making our school an exceptional place to be. We follow the principles of The National Autistic Society's **MyProgress®** strategy to give your child an education specific to them, so they can flourish.

Placements are funded by your local authority.

The National Autistic Society

"The school has been the making of my son, he loves coming to school!"

Parent

Ofsted
Good
Provider

Cruckton Hall
(part of the Kisimul Group)

(Founded 1981)

Cruckton, Shrewsbury, Shropshire SY5 8PR

Tel: 01743 860206

Fax: 01743 860941

Email: robert.arrowsmith@cruckton.com

Website: www.cruckton.com

Head Teacher: Robert Arrowsmith

School type: Boys' Residential

Age range of boys: 8–19

No. of pupils enrolled as at 01/01/2018: 80

Fees per annum as at 01/01/2018:

On application

Curriculum

All boys at the school have an Individual Pupil Care Plan that sets out their educational and therapeutic needs in addition to care, behavioural or medical information. The curriculum offered to each boy is highly personalised to take these into account. All boys follow a broad curriculum based on the National Curriculum, but then have bespoke activities or interventions built into their timetables. All are taught towards examinations appropriate to their abilities in Maths, English and Science. There are a range of academic options up to GCSE level encompassing humanities, technology and creative subjects. Specialist rooms support the learning in these areas. In addition, we can provide tutoring to A Level where a student is gifted and talented.

Alongside traditional academic subjects, we offer Outdoor Education, including Duke of Edinburgh, our own Forest School, Equine work and a whole range of activities such as Climbing and Cycling with qualified instructors. These support mental and physical well-being and provide opportunities for boys to interact with each other in different groupings and with different adults and the public.

Sessions with Speech and Language therapists, 1-1 interventions for core subjects and work with Assistant Educational Psychologists are built into individualised timetables as needed.

Assessment and entry requirements

Entry is by interview and assessment. The multi-disciplinary team of professionals will carry out a baseline assessment on each student within the first six weeks

of admission. Cruckton has a visiting consultant child and adolescent psychiatrist who visits the boys on a regular basis, as required. The multi-disciplinary team consists of a consultant educational psychologist, a speech and language therapist and an occupational therapist. They provide a variety of interventions and therapies to minimise the anxieties and maximise the development of our young people.

The wider environment

The hall is a listed building surrounded by ten acres of gardens that include woods, playing fields and play areas. The site is located within a friendly rural community, in beautiful countryside, four miles from the market town of Shropshire. The Welsh Marches provide a stunning backdrop and a rich source of options for our regular trips and adventures. The town of Shrewsbury offers excellent amenities for the school and is now linked to the motorway network of the West Midlands, greatly improving access.

Residential environment and activities

The structure that provides success for the boys in the classroom environment is replicated in the residential area and boys have a range of recreational activities provided, which reflect their needs and encourage their specialisms. Many boys choose an active leisure programme. This can be provided by activities such as skateboarding, swimming, football and cricket, and in the summer the Adventure Camp encourages team work amongst our student group through activities such as orienteering, mountain biking, rock climbing and raft building. For the more studious, a range of activities from *Warhammer* to chess club are provided. Links with local clubs and societies include the local stables, local army

cadet force, Jiu Jitsu, Laser Quest, bowling alley, street dancing and swimming are well-established. The links between the IEP targets are shared across the 24-hour approach, both in the home and education setting, with a huge variety of enrichment activities and programmes. Forest school, Lego therapy, robotics, stable management, mountain biking and work experience are all part of the enrichment programme.

Behaviour management

It is accepted that many boys come to Cruckton Hall School exhibiting both difficult and challenging behaviour. The structural consistency of various approaches, combined with a consistent nurturing environment, has a track record of providing the boys with the ability to be accepted within social settings of their choice. The basis of the approach is to foster the following qualities: self-respect, respect for other students, respect for staff, courtesy, politeness, patience, tolerance and motivation to work. Boys will be encouraged and supported to meet as many of these expectations as is possible. Attendance at school is a non-negotiable requirement of a boy's placement at Cruckton Hall. School uniform is always worn.

Aims and philosophy

Cruckton Hall School aims to provide a warm, structured and caring learning environment in which each boy feels safe and secure, can succeed, is treated as an individual and is able to develop his skills and talents in order that he leaves school as an active participant in, and a positive contributor to, society.

"Cruckton Hall School's new curriculum has had a positive impact on improving and accelerating pupils' progress. Pupils develop the skills they need to learn effectively in lessons and to be prepared for the next stage of their education, training or employment."

Church Lawton School

NAS Church Lawton School, Cherry Tree Avenue, Church Lawton, Stoke-on-Trent, Staffordshire ST7 3EL
T: 01270 877 601 | E: church.lawton@nas.org.uk
www.churchlawtonschool.org.uk

Principal: Paul Scales

School type: mixed free school with day placements for children and young people on the autism spectrum

Catchment area: Cheshire East and surrounding authorities, including Cheshire West, Stoke-on-Trent and Staffordshire

Age range: 4-19
Capacity: 60
Established: 2015

Church Lawton School is The National Autistic Society's second free school providing tailored care for local autistic students. We opened in 2015 and offer a highly specialised learning environment to our pupils on our brand new, purpose-built site.

With large open classrooms and an average class size of six, our pupils have the space and attention they need to reach their full potential.

Combined with well-resourced classrooms our building is equipped for academic excellence, and so we aim for our pupils to perform well in different exam pathways including Entry Level, GCSEs, ASDAN, A Levels and more. We have recently received an Ofsted rating of good with outstanding features.

We follow the principles of **MyProgress®**, The National Autistic Society's overall strategy for working with children on the autism spectrum. Systematic and thorough, we work with you and your child to create the best education for them.

We equip pupils with the skills and knowledge to support them as they move into further study and adult life. They get to know their community and, as they move through the school, have the opportunity to take part in work experience or study in local colleges and universities. Above all we are dedicated to making sure every one of our pupils is given the tools they need to thrive.

Placements are funded by your local authority.

The National Autistic Society

"I have never come across a school that is as kind, caring and understanding about its pupils."
A visiting parent

Ofsted
Good
Provider

Options Higford

Higford Hall, Higford, Shifnal,
Shropshire, TF11 9ET
Tel: 01952 630600
Email: info@optionsautism.co.uk

Website: www.optionsautism.co.uk
Headteacher: Ms Anne Adams
School type: Day & Residential
Age range of pupils: 8–19 years

Options Higford is a specialist service providing care and education for children and young people aged 8 to 19 with autistic spectrum conditions (ASC), associated complex needs and challenging behaviours. We are a DfE registered school and Ofsted registered children's home, offering day and residential placements, with up to 52-week or 38-week (term-time) residential care provided within specially-adapted on-site accommodation.

Set in 28 acres of rolling Shropshire countryside, Higford provides a safe, homely environment for children and young people with ASC. Our extensive site and facilities provide the people we support with opportunities to safely exercise choice and control. We offer an exceptional range of activities and amenities designed to promote the development of life skills and apply learning across different situations.

Options Higford is specifically designed to meet the needs of individuals with autism, complex needs and associated learning disabilities as reflected in our multidisciplinary team, qualified staff, staff ratios, and purpose built specialist facilities.

Clinical support is led by the Head of Clinical Services and is delivered by a core team of clinicians to include Psychiatrists, Clinical Psychologists, Forensic Psychologists, Psychotherapists, Occupational Therapists, and Speech and Language Therapists.

"Students make good and often outstanding progress, achieving well in their academic and personal development." (Autism Accreditation)

At Higford we take a person-centred and outcomes focused approach to providing care and education that is designed to help each student exercise choice and control, increase their confidence and prepare for adulthood. We believe that education should be individually tailored and delivered in a variety of environments, with a curriculum that encourages the development of communication, social and life skills as well as academic achievement. Each student's individual learning abilities, requirements and academic progression are consistently monitored to ensure that support remains proactive, learning opportunities are maximised and every individual achievement is celebrated.

For post 19 students our transition services offer a planned, structured move-on from our schools to individually-designed residential programmes. This enables the people we support to achieve independence by further developing life, vocational and social skills.

Options Higford is an Autism Accredited provision. The accreditation is awarded by The National Autistic Society (NAS) and ensures the highest quality of standards are met based on a personalised model of support and unified standard of excellence.

Options Trent Acres

Options
innovators in care and education

Alrewas Road, Kings Bromley,
Staffordshire, DE13 7HR
Tel: 01543 473772
Email: info@optionsautism.co.uk
Website: www.optionsautism.co.uk

Headteacher:
Ms Melanie Callaghan-Lewis
School type: Day & Residential
Age range of pupils: 8–18 years

Options Trent Acres offers integrated education and therapeutic care to children and young people aged between 8 to 18 years old with autism, associated learning disabilities and complex needs. Options Trent Acres provides a highly structured environment which helps the people that we support to manage their behaviour and develop personal care, social interaction and independence skills.

Options Trent Acres is situated on a 12 acre site which provides a wide range of facilities and services within the homes and throughout the site, including indoor and outdoor riding arenas, outside sports area, outdoor play equipment and access to arts and crafts facilities.

The School has various animals on-site including; horses, alpacas, goats, donkeys, rabbits, geese, ducks and chickens which support and encourages relaxation and promotes a calm environment for students to start their therapeutic journey.

Our team reflects the needs of the children and young people that learn with us, however additional support can also be accessed from other specialists within the wider Clinical Team. This enables us to be responsive to the newly identified, time limited or changing needs of an individual throughout their placement with us.

At Trent Acres School we take a person-centred and outcomes focused approach to providing education that is designed to help each student exercise choice and control, increase their confidence and prepare them for adulthood. We believe that education should be individually tailored and delivered in a variety of environments, with a curriculum that encourages the development of functional communication, social and life skills as well as academic achievement and community access. Each student's individual learning abilities, requirements and holistic and academic progression are consistently monitored to ensure that support remains proactive, learning opportunities are maximised and every individual achievement is celebrated.

Queen Alexandra College (QAC)
A National College for People with Disabilities

Queen Alexandra College

(Founded 1847)

Court Oak Road, Harborne, Birmingham, West Midlands B17 9TG

Tel: 0121 428 5050

Fax: 0121 428 5048

Email: info@qac.ac.uk

Website: www.qac.ac.uk

Principal: Hugh J Williams

School type:
Coeducational Day & Residential

Age range of pupils: 16+

No. of pupils enrolled as at 01/01/2018: 250

QAC is a friendly Specialist College based in Birmingham. We welcome students who come to our College from all over the country – as well as many who are local to us.

The College has been at its current location since 1903. Our original purpose was to provide education for people who were blind or visually impaired.

Today, in addition to supporting people who have a visual impairment, we offer support and guidance for students on the autistic spectrum (including individuals with Asperger's syndrome), those with moderate to severe learning difficulties, students with physical disabilities and those with other needs.

Ultimately, we have a great mix of students which adds to the wonderful atmosphere here in College. Class sizes are small and support levels high.

At QAC your learning is planned around your individual needs, interests and ambitions. Our curriculum covers a wide range of programmes including entry level courses (Preparation for Life) and a range of vocational qualifications. A supported internship study programme could also be followed, which involves spending the majority of time with an employer in a real job role. We have a dedicated Employment Pathways curriculum.

The College has a team of specialists on site who are able to support students, including a Visual Impairment Training Officer, Speech and Language Therapists, a Dyslexia Tutor, Healthcare Professionals, Counsellors, Mentors, a Braille Tutor, Mobility and Travel Trainers and a Personal and Sexual Health Education (PSHE) Lead.

Enrichment programmes enhance the curriculum and help to develop self-esteem, confidence and independence. Our residential provision develops essential skills for personal development such as independent living and social skills.

Facilities include new buildings with the latest technology, a fitness centre, state-of-the-art sports hall, sports field, sensory room, onsite travel training area, library and student centre.

For more information please visit www.qac.ac.uk or call 0121 428 5041

Fullerton House School

Autism | Learning Disabilities | Complex Needs

(Founded 1990)

Tickill Square, Denaby, Doncaster,
South Yorkshire DN12 4AR

Tel: 01709 861663
Fax: 01709 869635
Email: enquiries@hesleygroup.co.uk
Website: www.fullertonhouseschool.co.uk
General Manager: Heidi Dugdale-Dawkes
Appointed: 2017
Registered Manager: Ian Oliver

Head of Education: Michael Walsh
School type: Independent Specialist Residential School
Age range of pupils: 8–19
Fees per annum as at 01/01/2018:
Available on request

A specialist residential school offering flexible education and care, principally as a 52-week service with limited capacity for day placements, for young people aged 8-19, all of whom have complex needs including behaviour that may challenge and a learning disability, often in association with autism.

Fullerton House School is situated in the heart of the village of Denaby Main, near Doncaster. Its central location provides easy access by road, rail or air. Our mission is to enhance the lives of the young people entrusted to us by focusing on their specific needs, capabilities and aspirations.

Education: Each person has a carefully designed Individual Learning Plan based on their EHCP as well as their specific needs in line with the National Curriculum, which supports their positive progress in a range of areas.

Extended learning: During evenings, weekends and school holidays a wide range of extra-curricular activities are on offer to ensure that people are fully engaged with stimulating and meaningful experiences both on and off-site.

Professional services: A dedicated on-site team including carers, teachers, tutors, communication, behaviour and occupational therapy , psychology and other specialists ensure that people have ready access to the services they require.

High-quality accommodation: Single person and small group occupancy of high-quality accommodation is provided at Fullerton House School. Each person has their own bedroom, the majority of which have en-suite bathrooms. We also have a range of on-site facilities to complement and enrich the lives of those who come to live and learn with us.

Keeping in contact: We understand that while we may offer a very positive option for the person, we may not be on your doorstep. Keeping in touch with loved ones is essential. Everyone has a plan to support optimum contact with family/carers and friends whether this be by phone, letter, email or Skype.

Specialist Colleges

Hesley Group

Autism | Learning Disabilities | Complex Needs

(Founded 2013)

Fullerton House College

Tickhill Square, Denaby, Doncaster,

South Yorkshire DN12 4AR

Tel: 01709 861663

Fax: 01709 869635

Wilsic Hall College

Wadworth, Doncaster,

South Yorkshire, DN11 9AG

Tel: 01302 856382

Fax: 01709 853608

Email: enquiries@hesleygroup.co.uk

Website: www.hesleygroup.co.uk

General Manager: Heidi Dugdale-Dawkes

Appointed: 2017

School type: Independent Specialist Residential College

Age range of pupils: 18–25

Fullerton House College Capacity: 12

Wilsic Hall College Capacity: 8

Fees per annum as at 01/01/2018:

On request

Specialist residential colleges offering flexible education care and support for up to 52 weeks per year for young people aged 18-25, who have complex needs including behaviour that may challenge and a learning disability, often in association with autism.

At Wilsic Hall College, everyone lives within a beautiful rural setting with ready community access and at Fullerton House College in the heart of the community, in an urban setting with many local facilities including a sports centre, restaurants and shops.

Mission

We have 2 pathways available for the young people attending college.

Formal Education Pathway with a focus on gaining educational qualifications, skills and experience to move on to employment opportunity and further independence in their lives.

Next Steps Pathway for young people who have completed their formal educational route and are now wishing to build vocational and independence skills for life style experience and development-including social enterprise work.

Both pathways offer accreditation in the skills and qualifications the young people achieve, but the journeys are varied and personalised to the young persons needs and outcomes at this significant life stage.

Education: Everybody has a highly personalised programme of learning, equipping them with skills they will need for adult life.

Extended learning: During evenings, weekends and college holidays a wide range of extra-curricular activities are on offer to ensure people are fully engaged with stimulating experiences both on and off site providing further, meaningful learning opportunities.

Professional services: A dedicated multi-disciplinary therapeutic team including college tutors, college support workers, consultant clinical psychologist, consultant psychiatrist, applied behaviour analysts, speech and language therapists, occupational therapists, registered manager, care and support staff work together to support each individual's progress.

High quality accommodation: College accommodation includes individualised bedrooms, quality living spaces that promote independence and progressive skills development assisted by the appropriate use of specialist/adaptive technology. We also have a range of on-site and off-site facilities that offer progressive learning opportunities for young people with a range of needs and wishes.

Keeping in contact: We work to develop relationships between staff and families that are strong, positive and mutually respectful. People are supported to be in contact with their friends and family; we welcome visits to the colleges at any time. Everyone has a plan that will include the best means for them to maintain this contact whether by 'phone, letter, email or Skype.

Robert Ogden School

NAS Robert Ogden School
Clayton Lane, Thurnscoe, South Yorkshire S63 0BG
T: 01709 874 443 | F: 01709 807 701
E: robert.ogden@nas.org.uk | www.robertogdenschool.org.uk

Principal: Lorraine Dormand

School type: mixed independent school with day, weekly term-time and 52-week residential placements for children and young people on the autism spectrum

Catchment area: national
Age range: 5-19
Capacity: 127
Established: 1976

One of the largest schools in the UK for autistic children and young people, Robert Ogden School offers an environment where students can feel safe, supported and encouraged to achieve beyond their expectations. Following the principles of **MyProgress®**, The National Autistic Society's strategy for working with your child, we create a tailor-made experience for each student so they reach their full potential.

We are autism experts, with a specialist team dedicated to providing the highest quality care and education to our students. We have two Inclusive Learning Hubs run by a highly skilled group of staff who ensure pupils with particularly complex needs, requiring a non-directive approach, get the individualised curriculum and attention they need to thrive alongside their peers.

With autism-friendly buildings and facilities, your child will comfortably settle into school life. We even have a pottery room, several sensory and soft play rooms, a purpose-built primary unit and a teaching flat for independent living skills. Our students have every opportunity to develop the skills they will need for adult life, which is why we have a student-run café and shop, an award-winning fudge making enterprise project and a partnership with local charity shops. We give our students the help they need to make the best of their strengths and build upon them.

Placements are funded by your local authority.

The National Autistic Society

"You have achieved what many others could not… I am so grateful for Robert Ogden, no wonder so many parents are fighting for a place, it truly is a magnificent school with magnificent staff."

Sarah, parent

Ofsted
Good
Provider

Options Barton

innovators in care and education

Barrow Road, Barton-upon-Humber,
Lincolnshire, DN18 6DA
Tel: 01652 631280
Email: info@optionsautism.co.uk
Website: www.optionsautism.co.uk

Headteacher: Mr Ed Watkins
School type: Day & Residential
Age range of pupils: 8–19 years

Options Barton is a specialist service providing care and education for children and young people aged 8 to 19 with autistic spectrum conditions (ASC), associated complex needs and challenging behaviours. We are a DfE registered school and Ofsted registered children's home, offering day and residential placements, with up to 52-week or 38-week (term time) residential care provided within specially adapted on-site accommodation. The school also provide day only placements.

Located near historic Barton-upon-Humber on the rolling Lincolnshire Wolds countryside, Options Barton provides a safe, homely environment for children and young people with ASC. Our extensive site and facilities provide the people we support with opportunities to safely exercise choice and control. We offer an exceptional range of activities and amenities designed to promote the development of life skills and learning.

Options Barton is specifically designed to meet the needs of individuals with autism, complex needs and associated learning disabilities as reflected in our multidisciplinary team, qualified staff, staff to student ratios, and purpose built specialist facilities. Clinical support is led by the Head of Clinical Services and is delivered by a core team of clinicians to include Clinical Psychologist, Assistant Psychologist, Speech and Language Therapists, Occupational Therapist, Nursing Team and Consultant Psychiatrist.

"The staff at Options Barton are fantastic. The child centred approach, with full understanding of autism is a paramount feature." (Autism professional)

Options Barton delivers an adapted and differentiated National Curriculum for Key Stage 2, 3 and 4 students, and a vocational-based curriculum for post-16 students. Teaching frameworks have been specially designed for children and young people with special needs. Options Barton promotes the use of a range of approaches including SPELL and TEACCH, which again are individually adapted to the needs of each student. Parents/carers play an essential role in the development and delivery of student's individual programmes, and are considered as key members of the staff team.

Options Barton takes a person-centred approach to the delivery of care and education that is designed to enable students to express their needs and wants, and to become more independent. Particular priority is given to the development of communication and interpersonal skills, and the use of regular physical activity to improve overall emotional and physical wellbeing.

For post 19 students our transition services offer a planned, structured move-on from our schools to individually-designed residential programmes in the same region. This enables the people we support to achieve independence by further developing life, vocational and social skills.

Options Barton is an Autism Accredited provision. The accreditation is awarded by The National Autistic Society (NAS) and ensures the highest quality of standards are met based on a personalised model of support and unified standard of excellence.

Wilsic Hall School

Autism | Learning Disabilities | Complex Needs

(Founded 1996)
Wadworth, Doncaster,
South Yorkshire DN11 9AG

Tel: 01302 856382
Email: enquiries@hesleygroup.co.uk
Website: www.wilsichallschool.co.uk
Head: Geoff Turner
Appointed: 2008
School type:
Independent Specialist Residential School

Age range of pupils: 11–19
Capacity: 32
Fees per annum as at 01/01/2018:
Available on request

A specialist residential school offering flexible education and care, principally as a 52-week service with limited capacity for day placements, for young people aged 11-19, all of whom have complex needs including behaviour that may challenge and a learning disability, often in association with autism.

Wilsic Hall School is situated in its own 14-acre site approximately five miles south of Doncaster. Its central location provides easy access by road, rail or air. Our mission is to enhance the lives of the people entrusted to us by focusing on their specific needs, capabilities and aspirations.

Education: Each person has a carefully designed Individual Education Plan based on their specific needs in line with the National Curriculum, which supports their positive progress in a range of areas.

Extended learning: During evenings, weekends and school holidays a wide range of extra-curricular activities are on offer to ensure that people are fully engaged with stimulating and meaningful experiences both on and off-site.

Professional services: A dedicated team including carers, teachers, tutors, behaviour, communication and occupational therapy, psychology and other specialists ensure that each person has ready access to the services they require.

High-quality accommodation: Single person and small group occupancy of high-quality accommodation is provided at Wilsic Hall School. Each person has their own bedroom, the majority of which have en-suite bathrooms. We also have a range of on-site facilities to complement and enrich the lives of those who come to live and learn with us.

Keeping in contact: We understand that while we may offer a very positive option for the person, we may not be on your doorstep. Keeping in touch with loved ones is essential. Everyone has a plan to support optimum contact with family/carers and friends whether this be by phone, letter, email or Skype.

Daldorch House School

NAS Daldorch House School
Sorn Road, Catrine, East Ayrshire, Scotland KA5 6NA
T: 01290 551 666 | F: 01290 553 399
E: daldorch@nas.org.uk | www.daldorchhouseschool.org.uk

Principal: Bernadette Casey

School type: mixed independent school with day, weekly, termly and 52-week residential placements for children and young people on the autism spectrum

Catchment area: national
Age range: 8-21
Capacity: 28 residential
Established: 1998

At Daldorch House School we work compassionately with each of our pupils, while challenging them to achieve to the best of their ability. Our 11 acre site is in a beautiful rural setting, while being only an hour from the bustle of Glasgow city centre.

Our classrooms are designed to suit the needs of all our pupils, and each lesson is arranged according to those learning in it.

Developing communication, social and life skills is at the core of our 24-hour curriculum at Daldorch, and we enrich each pupil's learning by capitalising on their interests and expanding their understanding of the world.

We also have a satellite school in East Kilbride, offering a year-round residential provision for families living in the South Lanarkshire local authority area, meaning your child can live and learn close to home in an area they know well.

Our curriculum is relevant, engaging and designed to develop each child's independence as they mature, our focus on lifelong learning strengthening as they approach adult life. With a blended approach to learning through The National Autistic Society's **MyProgress®** strategy, your child will have an education at Daldorch that is entirely personalised to them.

Placements are funded by your local authority.

The National Autistic Society

"The school has excellent systems for identifying the strengths of young people and the difficulties they face."
Education Scotland

Options Kinsale

Kinsale Hall, Llanerch-y-Mor, Holywell, Flintshire, CH8 9DX
Tel: 01745 562500
Email: info@optionsautism.co.uk

Website: www.optionsautism.co.uk
Headteacher: Mr Ian Roberts
School type: Day & Residential
Age range of pupils: 8–19 years

Options Kinsale is a specialist service providing care and education for children and young people aged 8 to 19 with a range of Complex Needs, including autism, Asperger's Syndrome, dyspraxia and ADHD, as well as impaired social or cognitive functioning due to early life trauma and attachment difficulties. We are an ESTYN registered school and CIW (Care Inspectorate Wales) registered children's home, offering day and residential placements, with up to 52-week or 38-week (term-time) residential care provided within specially adapted on-site accommodation. The school also provide day only placements.

Our extensive site and facilities provide the people we support with opportunities to exercise choice and control safely. We offer an exceptional range of activities and amenities designed to promote the development of life skills and apply learning within a range of situations and settings.

"Without the dedication and fantastic care and support of the staff, my son would not have made such positive improvements. Prior to Kinsale I would not have believed that he could have made such positive relationships with his support staff and that his self-esteem and confidence could have improved so much." (Parent)

Our team reflects the needs of the children and young people that live and learn within the school, however additional support can also be accessed from other specialists within the wider Clinical Team. This enables us to be responsive to the newly identified, time limited or changing needs of an individual throughout their placement with us.

At Options Kinsale we take a person-centred and outcomes focused approach to providing care and education designed to help each student increase their confidence and prepare

for adulthood. We believe that education should be personalised and delivered in a variety of environments, with a curriculum that encourages the development of communication, social and life skills as well as academic achievement. Each student's individual learning abilities, requirements and academic progression are consistently monitored to ensure that support remains proactive, learning opportunities are maximised and every individual achievement is celebrated.

For post 19 students our transition services offer a planned, structured move-on from our schools to individually-designed residential programmes in the same region. This enables the people we support to achieve independence by further developing life, vocational and social skills.

Schools and colleges specialising in emotional, behavioural and/or social difficulties (EBSD)

Hillcrest New Barn School

The Long Barn, Welford, Newbury, West Berkshire, RG20 8HZ

Tel: 01488 505145

Email: info@hillcrestcs.co.uk

Website: www.hillcrestchildrensservices.co.uk

Headteacher: Ms Alice Anstee

School type: Day (with satellite residential homes)

Age range of pupils: 6–16 years

No. of pupils enrolled as at 01/01/2018: 20

Hillcrest New Barn School provides education, therapy, welfare and support for children and young people aged from 6 to 16 years who have social, emotional and mental health needs.

Hillcrest New Barn offers a bespoke curriculum for every student. Its ethos is based around nurturing, making progress and helping young people feel safe and cared for.

The pupils gain a remarkable trust and rapport with the staff who support them through their personal challenges. The relaxed atmosphere allows students to concentrate on learning, developing, and becoming their own person.

As well as being a Department for Education registered Independent School, New Barn School also takes pupils from the local residential homes offered by Hillcrest Children's Services.

The school is set in the rural estate of Welford, Berkshire, five miles northwest of Newbury and 11 miles south of Wantage in a newly converted barn. The nearby Welford Park is famous for its snowdrops and for hosting the Bake Off marquee.

Our provision is tailored to each student ensuring that their educational, therapeutic and holistic needs are met, and barriers to learning are addressed.

At New Barn, students aim to arrive at similar destinations as those in more formal educational settings. They just take a different route. The School provides every student with a broad, balanced, differentiated and relevant curriculum based on the National Curriculum guidelines.

"Teaching staff are tenacious. They will do everything they can to interest the pupils and ensure that they have the opportunity to learn and succeed." (Ofsted)

Our pupils may have experienced failure in education and trauma in their personal lives which often results in low self-esteem. Hillcrest New Barn School therefore endeavours to empower its pupils through successful learning to develop their confidence and self-esteem. We involve the pupils in their learning by listening to their views and considering their choices.

Hillcrest New Barn School is committed to empowering and inspiring individuals to learn, achieve and succeed, in a bid to help reintegrate them back into mainstream settings, facilitate plans to return home or enable them to progress as individuals in their own home placements and schools.

Hillcrest Park School

Southcombe, Chipping Norton, Oxford, Oxfordshire, OX7 5QH
Tel: 01608 644621
Email: info@hillcrestcs.co.uk
Website: www.hillcrestchildrensservices.co.uk

Headteacher: Mr David Davidson
School type: Day (with satellite residential homes)
Age range of pupils: 7–18 years
No. of pupils enrolled as at 01/01/2018: 28

Hillcrest Park School is an independent special school offering a bespoke approach to education for children and young people aged from 7 to 18 years who have social, emotional and mental health needs. We pride ourselves on providing a caring and supportive environment alongside a diverse curriculum, created to raise pupil's self-esteem and provide each young person with the opportunity to reach their individual potential.

Many of our pupils have other special educational needs including specific learning difficulties, mild or moderate learning difficulties and high functioning autistic spectrum conditions (ASC) and Asperger's Syndrome.

Students may come from foster placements or from local families that need specialist provision and many of our students reside in one of the local residential homes offered by Hillcrest Children's Services.

Hillcrest Park School provides every student with a broad, balanced, differentiated and relevant curriculum based on the National Curriculum guidelines. A comprehensive 14-16 curriculum Pathway is available at Park School. This offers GCSE, BTEC, ASDAN, Functional Skills Levels 1 and 2, Number and Measure Levels 1 and 2, ICT ECDL Levels 1 and 2 and other external examinations.

The curriculum is tailored to meet all of the students' needs. For example, in the upper school, the subjects offered are directly relevant to the specific needs and ability of the individual pupil – GCSE Maths, Maths Functional Skills Level 1 and 2 and Maths Number and Measure Level 1.

Our pupils may have experienced failure in education and trauma in their personal lives which often results in low self-esteem. Hillcrest Park School therefore endeavours to empower its pupils through successful learning to develop their confidence and self-esteem. We involve the pupils in their learning by listening to their views and considering their choices, especially in the later key stages.

"Safeguarding arrangements are rigorous and pupils confirm they feel safe. Leaders establish a school culture of high expectations for all." (Ofsted)

Hillcrest Park School is committed to empowering and inspiring individuals to learn, achieve and succeed, in a bid to help reintegrate them back into mainstream settings, facilitate plans to return home or enable them to progress as individuals in their own home placements and schools.

Essex Fresh Start Independent School (EFS)

Essex Fresh Start
Independent School

(Founded 2007)
Church Street, Witham, Essex CM8 2JL
Tel: 01376 780088
Email: referrals@tces.org.uk
Website: www.tces.org.uk

Head Teacher: Cheryl Rutter
Appointed: 2007
Schools' Proprietor: Thomas Keaney
School type: Coeducational Day
Age range of pupils: 7–19 years

Essex Fresh Start (EFS) is a TCES Group school, providing LA funded day-school education for pupils aged 7-19 years whose Social, Emotional or Mental Health needs or Autism Spectrum Condition has made it difficult for them to achieve success in a mainstream school. Pupils' co-morbid needs can be complex. Undiagnosed speech, language and communication needs, sensory or learning difficulties can create barriers to learning that must be addressed before the pupil can settle into education.

Our integrated approach to education, health and care, takes each pupil on an individual journey that encourages a love of learning. We provide a well-structured routine in a safe, calm and happy environment which promotes tolerance and respect throughout our school community. We nurture ambition and work with each child to provide them with the life skills, accreditation and certification needed to achieve future careers.

Pupils are taught in groups of up to six

to ensure each individual receives an intensive level of support, with a Teacher and TA as minimum. TCES Group's Inclusion Model is embedded at EFS, delivered by the Inclusion Manager and Pastoral Co-ordinator: tutor support, key work, group process, nurture groups, leadership skills and drama therapy, speech and language intervention and clinical assessments are part of the core offer.

The school delivers TCES Group's 5 Part Curriculum, which includes access to support from the Clinical and Therapy Team on an as-needs basis. SALT, OT, Counselling, Drama and Art Therapy are delivered by our in-house team and access to Clinical Psychology and a Paediatrician at Consultant level can be arranged for pupils whose needs require further investigation.

Pupils attending EFS often need highly personalised learning programmes and can remain for Post-16 programmes of study, specialising in developing independence, preparation for adult life and life after school.

We nurture each child's ambitions by accrediting them with as many achievements as possible to help them make positive choices for their future careers. As a result, 80% of our leavers happily go straight into work, education or training.

A parallel service to our schools, TCES Group's Create Service offers therapeutic education, delivered through a case co-ordination model, to pupils who present (or are at) significant risk to themselves or others, who cannot be educated in a school setting.

To find out more about the school and its facilities please come and visit us! In the first instance please contact us on referrals@tces.org.uk or 020 8543 7878.

East London Independent School (ELIS)

East London
Independent School

Stratford Marsh, Welfare Road,
London E15 4HT
Tel: 020 8555 6737
Email: referrals@tces.org.uk
Website: www.tces.org.uk

Head Teacher: Sandra Harrison
Schools' Proprietor: Thomas Keaney
School type: Coeducational Day
Age range of pupils: 7–19 years

East London Independent School (ELIS) is a TCES Group school, providing LA funded day-school education for pupils aged 7-19 years whose Social, Emotional or Mental Health needs or Autism Spectrum Condition has made it difficult for them to achieve success in a mainstream school. Pupils' co-morbid needs can be complex. Undiagnosed speech, language and communication needs, sensory or learning difficulties can create barriers to learning that must be addressed before the pupil can settle into education.

ELIS is housed in a newly developed state-of-the-art school building, which boasts a specially designed low-arousal, autism friendly environment that suits all pupils regardless of their needs.

Our integrated approach to education, health and care, takes each pupil on an individual journey that encourages a love of learning. We provide a well-structured routine in a safe, calm and happy environment which promotes tolerance and respect throughout our school community. We nurture ambition and work with each child to provide them with the life skills, accreditation and certification needed to achieve future careers.

Pupils are taught in groups of up to six to ensure each individual receives an intensive level of support, with a Teacher and TA as minimum. TCES Group's Inclusion Model is embedded at ELIS, delivered by the Inclusion Manager and Pastoral Co-ordinator: tutor support, key work, group process, nurture groups, leadership skills and drama therapy, speech and language intervention and clinical assessments are part of the core offer.

The school delivers TCES Group's 5 Part Curriculum, which includes access to support from the Clinical and Therapy Team on an as-needs basis. SALT, OT, Counselling, Drama and Art Therapy are delivered by our in-house team and access to Clinical Psychology and a Paediatrician at Consultant level can be arranged for pupils whose needs require further investigation.

Pupils attending ELIS often need highly personalised learning programmes and can remain for Post-16 programmes of study, specialising in developing independence, preparation for adult life and life after school.

A parallel service to our schools, TCES Group's Create Service offers therapeutic education, delivered through a case co-ordination model, to pupils who present (or are at) significant risk to themselves or others, who cannot be educated in a school setting.

To find out more about the school and its facilities please come and visit us! In the first instance please contact us on referrals@tces.org.uk or 020 8543 7878.

North West London Independent School (NWLIS)

(Founded 2008)

85 Old Oak Common Lane, Acton, London W3 7DD

Tel: 020 8749 5403

Email: referrals@tces.org.uk

Website: www.tces.org.uk

Head Teacher: Katrina Medley

Schools' Proprietor: Thomas Keaney

School type: Coeducational Day

Age range of pupils: 7–19 years

No. of pupils enrolled as at 01/01/2018: 69

TCES Group's North West London Independent School (NWLIS) provides LA funded day-school education for pupils aged 7-19 years whose Social, Emotional or Mental Health needs or Autism Spectrum Condition has made it difficult for them to achieve success in a mainstream school. Pupils' co-morbid needs can be complex. Undiagnosed speech, language and communication needs, sensory or learning difficulties can create barriers to learning that must be addressed before the pupil can settle into education.

Our integrated approach to education, health and care, described by Ofsted as innovative and unique, takes each pupil on an individual journey that encourages a love of learning. We provide a well-structured routine in a safe, calm and happy environment which promotes tolerance and respect throughout our school community. We nurture ambition

and work with each child to provide them with the life skills, accreditation and certification needed to achieve future careers.

Pupils are taught in groups of up to six to ensure each individual receives an intensive level of support, with a Teacher and TA as minimum. TCES Group's Inclusion Model is embedded at NWLIS, delivered by the Inclusion Manager and Pastoral Co-Ordinator: tutor support, key work, group process, nurture groups, leadership skills and drama therapy, speech and language intervention and clinical assessments are part of the core offer.

The school delivers TCES Group's 5 Part Curriculum, which includes access to support from the Clinical and Therapy Team on an as-needs basis. SALT, OT, Counselling, Drama and Art Therapy are delivered by our in-house team and access to Clinical Psychology and a Paediatrician at Consultant level can be

arranged for pupils whose needs require further investigation. *"Pupils rapidly develop their social skills and resilience to manage their emotions through the school's unique therapeutic approach."* Ofsted 2017

Pupils attending NWLIS often need highly personalised learning programmes and can remain for Post-16 programmes of study, specialising in developing independence, preparation for adult life and life after school.

A parallel service to our schools, TCES Group's Create Service offers therapeutic education, delivered through a case co-ordination model, to pupils who present (or are at) significant risk to themselves or others, who cannot be educated in a school setting.

To find out more about the school and its facilities please come and visit us! In the first instance please contact us on referrals@tces.org.uk or 020 8543 7878.

Early Intervention Works

Therapeutic Care and Education for Younger Children

Appletree
treatment centre
growing & learning together

www.appletreetreatmentcentre.co.uk

Over 20 years' experience specialising in therapeutic care and education for girls and boys 6 to 12 years old with emotional, health, social and associated learning difficulties, who have suffered: Trauma, Neglect, Physical, Emotional, Sexual abuse.

Therapy in Action - Not Therapy in a Vacuum

Qualified, Experienced Psychologists and Therapists provide individual therapy for our children, clinical input for each childs' programme, clinical consultation and training for our care, teaching and support teams.

Therapeutic Relationships, Structured 24 hour Programme
Our therapeutically informed teams are skilled at helping our children form healthy attachments, build emotional resilience and confidence, increasing their self-esteem, helping them acquire the skills needed to succeed at home, in life and in school.

Stability and Felt Security are Key to our Children's Success
Once a child is placed with us we will not exclude them, they will only experience planned moves forward. This stability and security helps them develop meaningful relationships, build self esteem and develop resilience.

Successful reintegration to families

After an average of just 2 years and 6 months with us at least 90% of our leavers year after year are able to leave residential care/special school provision and return to families or foster families and day schools. The remaining 10% of our leavers continued in residential care to facilitate increased and appropriate contact with their families.

We work alongside adoptive, foster and birth families

All children engage in individual therapy, most continue throughout their stay with us

Close to 100% attendance in education with no unauthorized absence

Appletree

Fell House

Willow Bank

Appletree Treatment Centre has three children's homes

Appletree for up to 12 children

Fell House for up to 8 children

Willow Bank for up to 5 children

We provide high quality therapeutic care and education. We help children who are vulnerable and require a nurturing environment.

Appletree and Fell House each have their own school on site, Willow Bank children attend Appletree school

tel 015395 60253 - Natland, Kendal Cumbria LA9 7QS **- email clair.davies@appletreetc.co.uk**

Everyone within Appletree Treatment Centre has a responsibility for, and is committed to, safeguarding and promoting the welfare of children and young people and for ensuring that they are protected from harm.

Kirby Moor School

Longtown Road, Brampton,
Cumbria CA8 2AB
Tel: 016977 42598
Email: info@nlcs.uk.com

Website: www.nlcs.uk.com/our-school/
Headteacher: Mrs Catherine Garton
School type: Boys' Day
Age range of boys: 7–18

Kirby Moor School with The Herdley Bank Centre annex educates pupils aged 7-18, rated Outstanding again in December 2017. North Lakes Care-Education-Therapy operates the school sites providing therapeutic residential care and day pupil education for boys.

North Lakes has succeeded in enabling young people to make above expected progress socially, emotionally and academically. Our schools meet the needs of pupils who face Social, Emotional and Mental Health challenges. Our 2 school sites specialise in supporting and progressing those who live with: Autism spectrum conditions, attachment-based disorders, high anxiety & SEMH.

Pupils typically have an EHCP.

"Pupils make rapid progress from their starting points across the curriculum. Pupils' academic success is particularly strong in English and mathematics… Within a short space of time, pupils start to catch up with their peers nationally, in a range of subjects.." – Ofsted, Outstanding.

Key Strengths:

- We support pupils who benefit from a highly predictable daily routine, with formal and informal classroom spaces.
- Pupils achieve higher than expected rates of progress.
- The classroom learning and practical, hands-on activities are underpinned by the content of the National Curriculum.
- The facilities and teaching lead pupils to make outstanding progress academically, socially and in understanding the world around them.
- Individual robust transition programmes help support our pupils for the next stage of their education.
- The location promotes a quiet and calming environment.
- Our pupils achieve excellent attendance scores and truly re-engage with learning – including those with school phobia.

Hillcrest Jubilee School

84-86 Jubilee Road, Waterlooville,
Hampshire, PO7 7RE
Tel: 02392 250963
Email: info@hillcrestcs.co.uk
Website:
www.hillcrestchildrensservices.co.uk

Headteacher: Mr Tim Rogers
School type: Day
(with satellite residential homes)
Age range of pupils: 8–16 years
No. of pupils enrolled as at 01/01/2018: 22

Hillcrest Jubilee School provides education, therapy, welfare and support for children and young people aged from 8 to 16 years who have social, emotional and mental health needs.

A stable and caring environment combined with high staff to student ratios, ensures that every student at Jubilee School has the opportunity to develop their abilities, share new experiences and be supported in realising their future potential. Jubilee School wants education to be a positive and enjoyable experience where students are proud of their achievements and strive to do well.

Students may come from foster placements or from local families that need specialist provision and many of our students reside in one of the local residential homes offered by Hillcrest Children's Services.

Jubilee School provides every student with a broad, balanced, differentiated

and relevant curriculum based on the National Curriculum guidelines. A comprehensive 14-16 curriculum Pathway is available at Jubilee and at local colleges. This offers GCSE, BTEC, ASDAN, NVQ, DofE and other external examinations, catering for their current and future needs.

Jubilee School encourages students to develop their learning, leadership and independence skills through a well-balanced curriculum offering academic, creative, practical and physical experiences. Embedded within the fabric of Jubilee School is the Social, Moral, Spiritual and Cultural development of each student. There is a strong emphasis on learning outside of the classroom making the most of the local facilities and the South Downs. We have developed strong links within our local community with local colleges, businesses, charities and sport centres.

"Sensitive support from staff ensures that pupils make rapid progress in their personal development." (Ofsted)

Our pupils may have experienced failure in education and trauma in their personal lives which often results in low self-esteem. Hillcrest Jubilee School therefore endeavours to empower its pupils through successful learning to develop their confidence and self-esteem. We try to involve the pupils in their learning by listening to their views and considering their choices.

Hillcrest Jubilee School is committed to empowering and inspiring individuals to learn, achieve and succeed, in a bid to help reintegrate them back into mainstream settings, facilitate plans to return home or enable them to progress as individuals in their own home placements and schools.

Hillcrest Slinfold School

Stane Street, Slinfold, Horsham,
West Sussex, RH13 0QX
Tel: 01403 790939
Email: info@hillcrestcs.co.uk
Website:
www.hillcrestchildrensservices.co.uk

Headteacher: Mr John Stacey
School type: Day & Residential
Age range of boys: 11–16 years
No. of pupils enrolled as at 01/01/2018: 20

Hillcrest Slinfold School provides education, therapy, welfare and support for children and young people aged from 11 to 16 years who have social, emotional and mental health needs as well as other complex learning needs often associated with autistic spectrum conditions and ADHD.

A stable and caring environment combined with high staff to student ratios, ensures that every student at Slinfold School has the opportunity to develop their abilities, share new experiences and be supported in realising their future potential.

Students may come from foster placements or from local families that need specialist provision and many of our students reside in one of the local residential homes offered by Hillcrest Children's Services.

Slinfold School believes 'education' should be a positive and enjoyable experience where students are proud of their achievements and strive to do well.

The level of support and intervention a child receives is based upon their level of need. Work is carefully differentiated in order to meet the individual needs of students and regular assessment ensures continuity and progression.

Each student has individually tailored positive expectations for achievement. This ensures they are challenged appropriately and experience success frequently.

"Across the school, staff build warm, trusting and caring relationships with pupils that enable them to participate in lessons successfully." (Ofsted)

Hillcrest Slinfold School aims to create a centre of excellence for the education, care and personal development of the young people that we support.

Our students may have experienced failure in education and trauma in their personal lives, often resulting in low self-esteem. Our challenge is to support these young people to achieve their academic and personal potential and help to equip them with the skills they need to enjoy life.

All our students learn to experience success and develop strategies to deal with any difficulties that they may encounter. We aim to support our students to develop self-confidence and self-esteem.

Philpots Manor School

(Founded 1959)
West Hoathly, East Grinstead,
West Sussex RH19 4PR
Tel: 01342 810268
Email: info@philpotsmanorschool.co.uk
Website: www.philpotsmanorschool.co.uk
Education Co-ordinator:
Mr Darin Nobes BA (Hons), PGCE, NPQH

School type: Coeducational Boarding
Age range of pupils: 7–19
No. of pupils enrolled as at 01/01/2018: 43
Boys: 30 **Girls:** 13
Fees per annum as at 01/01/2018:
Day: £65,000
Weekly Boarding: £65,000

Founded in 1959 and set in the heart of the Sussex countryside, Philpots Manor School is an independent residential special needs school and training centre offering an academic and social education to children and young adults from 7 to 19 years of age.

The emotional, behavioural, social and communication problems that most of our students display may stem from a learning difficulty, social deprivation, abuse or from a recognised clinical condition, such as epilepsy, a development disorder or autism.

Classes usually contain a maximum of six students with one class teacher and at least one class assistant. Our residential units can accommodate either up to six or nine residential students, depending on the size of the unit. We also cater for day students. We offer a 36 week curriculum with residential children returning home at weekends. As well as offering a wide range of academic subjects we also offer horse-riding, pottery, gardening, weaving, art and music. Most pupils are entered for examination at GCSE or Entry Level in English, Maths, Science and Art at a time that is appropriate for each. Up to six GCSE subjects are offered.

OCN courses for Post-16 pupils accredit a wide range of subjects that most pupils study. Continuous assessment by the teachers avoids examinations for those pupils who least benefit from additional stress in their lives. Current courses include stable management and land-based studies.

We offer a wide range of therapies including speech and language, occupational therapy, cranial osteopathy, drama therapy and creative arts therapy.

For further information, please visit our website at:
www.philpotsmanorschool.co.uk
or telephone 01342 810268

West Heath School

WEST**HEATH**
REBUILDING LIVES THROUGH EDUCATION

(Founded 1998)

Ashgrove Road, Sevenoaks, Kent TN13 1SR
Tel: 01732 460553
Fax: 01732 456734
Email: admissions@westheathschool.com
Website: www.westheathschool.com
Principal: Mr James Nunns
Appointed: September 2016

School type: Coeducational Day & Boarding
Age range of pupils: 10–20
No. of pupils enrolled as at 01/01/2018: 135
Fees per annum as at 01/01/2018:
Day: £52,500
Residential supplement: From £35,000

Who we are

West Heath is an Ofsted Outstanding and award-winning charity set up specifically to support vulnerable children for whom maintained SEN and mainstream schools were unable to meet needs. The school designation of Social, Emotional and Mental Heath only goes a short way to describing the complexity of need of our students. We have up to 130 places, 29 of which are residential, therapeutic centre and training facilities, all based on our 32 acre site in Sevenoaks, Kent.

Who we support

Students referred to us will have seen their mainstream provision break down, some having worked their way through a number of specialist providers unable to meet need or effectively engage with the young person. Others may have come from the Health sector, having been resident in a mental health provision. The SEN diagnosis of our student group is varied, many have a diagnosis of an Austism Spectrum Condition; all our students face challenges with their social communication and interaction with the social world in which they live.

How we support

Our focus is on education, both in terms of academic and personal development. Barriers to learning and the challenges our students face are met rather than avoided, with strategies put in place to support ongoing development. We have a range of therapies on site, working directly with students to meet needs identified from professionals. Therapy is embedded into our curriculum, with Speech and Language and Self Science lessons forming part of the weekly timetable. We have created a number of different learning environments and approaches to education to enable students to successfully access provision and to make learning possible.

What can you study?

We follow the National Curriculum and have a range of options in Key Stage 4. Our facilities are extensive including a professional catering kitchen, sports facilities including tennis courts and swimming pool, expressive arts, including a studio and textiles room. We also offer options including Duke of Edinburgh, animal-based studies and Princes Trust. Study is not limited to the subjects we offer on site, students work toward studying at college with support before finally making the transition to independent study.

The environment

Our school has a number of study environments. All our class sizes are small, with a maximum of six per class in Key Stage 3 and eight in Key Stage 4. Students whom are unable to meet the challenges of a general school structure and require a higher level of support and will be based within our Therapeutic Centre, some of our students are unable to keep themselves safe and therefore will study with our offsite team until they are able to meet the challenges of their daily lives.

After West Heath

We are pleased to say that the majority of our learners have positive and successful outcomes. These may include returning to study in a mainstream environment, gaining full time employment or simply being better placed to meet the personal challenges that had previously been barriers to their becoming active members of society.

Hillcrest Glebedale School

Grove Road, Heron Cross, Stoke-on-Trent, Staffordshire, ST4 3AY

Tel: 01782 320773

Email: info@hillcrestcs.co.uk

Website: www.hillcrestchildrensservices.co.uk

Headteacher: Ms Karen Caswell

School type: Day (with satellite residential homes)

Age range of pupils: 7–19 years

No. of pupils enrolled as at 01/01/2018: 30

Hillcrest Glebedale School provides education, therapy and support for children and young people aged from 7 to 19 years with social, emotional and mental health needs.

The clinical team support the education team in developing a pupil centred curriculum which proactively promotes the children and young people's social, emotional and mental health. We aim to deliver the highest quality provision which maximises each person's quality of life and personal achievements.

The curriculum is provided in a structured and supportive environment and is planned to meet the personal, academic and pastoral needs of the pupils at each stage of their schooling. In order to support access to the curriculum, education staff work alongside clinicians in order to understand and respond therapeutically to the children learning with us.

"Students who enter the school with negative attitudes to education achieve more than they thought possible." (Ofsted)

Students may come from foster placements or from local families that need specialist provision and many of our students reside in one of the local residential homes offered by Hillcrest Children's Services.

Hillcrest Glebedale School offers an education which exposes pupils to a broad, balanced, differentiated and relevant curriculum, presents them with challenges in which creativity is fostered and which is based on the essential elements of the National Curriculum.

The School delivers a structured programme of education, tailored to each pupil's individual needs and taking into account their Education, Health Care Plan of Special Educational Needs. Where appropriate, pupils receive targeted personalised interventions both academic and/or therapeutic.

Hillcrest Glebedale School takes a multi-disciplinary and person-centred approach to the delivery of care, education and clinical services, enabling students to develop their life skills as well as progress academically. The school aims to ensure that students are well equipped to make the transition to young adult life.

Hillcrest Shifnal School

Lamledge Lane, Shifnal,
Shropshire, TF11 8SD
Tel: 01952 468220
Email: info@hillcrestcs.co.uk
Website:
www.hillcrestchildrensservices.co.uk

Headteacher: Mr David Coles
School type: Day
(with satellite residential homes)
Age range of pupils: 7–19 years
No. of pupils enrolled as at 01/01/2018: 55

Hillcrest Shifnal School provides education and support for children and young people aged from 7 to 19 years with social, emotional and mental health needs, as well as other complex needs that could be associated with autism spectrum conditions and learning difficulties.

Students may come from foster placements or from local families that need specialist provision and many of our students reside in one of the local residential homes offered by Hillcrest Children's Services.

Hillcrest Shifnal School offers an education which exposes students' to a broad, balanced, differentiated and relevant curriculum, presents them with challenges in which creativity is fostered and which is based on the essential elements of the National Curriculum. Other courses such as Outdoor Education, Duke of Edinburgh, Fishing,

Motor Mechanics and Animal Care are delivered in a mixture of onsite and offsite facilities, supporting students' interests and aspirations.

The curriculum is provided in a structured and supportive environment and is planned to meet the personal, academic and pastoral needs of the students at each stage of their schooling.

"The programme for personal, social, health and economic education supports the school in achieving its aims for the pupils and helps them develop respect for and acceptance of other people." *(Ofsted)*

The school has an excellent adult to student ratio with class sizes of up to a maximum of five students, which are taught and supported by at least two staff in every lesson. This enables us to give our

students high levels of support at all times.

Hillcrest Shifnal School strive to provide learning experiences and opportunities that will enhance the lives of all the students we educate. We are inclusive of all backgrounds and abilities with our key focus being learning through emotional intelligence and developing resilience within our students.

Our aim is to provide a balanced and bespoke curriculum which will enable students the room to grow and develop into confident, creative and well-rounded members of the community. Specialist staff work with students to develop positive working relationships and to provide a cohesive, nurturing environment within which every individual can thrive. Hillcrest Shifnal School is a place where everybody is somebody and everyone works hard to achieve this aim.

The **Roaches** School

The Roaches School

- Children Aged from 7 to 16
- Trained to support social, emotional and behavioural difficulties
- Based on two sites;
- Lower School - Roach End Farm, nestling in the Peak District
- Upper School - Satis House, located in Biddulph to support boys and girls with complex social difficulties.

Therapeutic Centre

- 24 hour therapeutic placement
- Staff are trained to meet young people's therapeutic needs.
- A member of the Community of Communities
- Young People's needs are identified and guided by qualified Psychotherapists
- Individual key workers are allocated to ensure that your child's needs are being addressed.

Testimonial

"My son has been attending the Roaches School for four years. During this time he has been in full time education where previously he had been excluded from two mainstream schools. His self esteem and confidence were very low and he had attempted suicide at 7 years old and often stated he wished he was dead. Since attending The Roaches his confidence has excelled, his behaviour has improved dramatically and he is much happier within himself. This wouldn't have happened without the Roaches staff who give regular feedback, and offer outstanding support to my son and to us as a family. I would recommend the Roaches School to any family who have a child who requires a lot of extra support with their education and their social/ emotional needs and general wellbeing."

The Roaches School has been graded as "Outstanding" by Ofsted since Oct 2010.

Schools and colleges specialising in learning difficulties (including dyslexia/SPLD)

Kisimul School

(Founded 1977)

The Old Vicarage, 61 High Street,
Swinderby, Lincoln, Lincolnshire LN6 9LU
Tel: 01522 868279
Fax: 01522 866000
Email: admissions@kisimul.co.uk
Website: www.kisimul.co.uk
Director of Education:

Mr Danny Carter BA(Hons), MA, MEd
School type: Coeducational
Independent Residential Special School
Age range of pupils: 8–19
No. of pupils enrolled as at 01/01/2018: 60
Fees per annum as at 01/01/2018:
On application

Kisimul School is one of the UK's leading independent residential special schools, offering a homely and safe environment for children who have severe learning difficulties, challenging behaviour, autism and global developmental delay.

Kisimul School offers residential education, care and leisure programmes at both our upper and lower school, for up to 52 weeks of the year, for pupils aged 8 to 19 years. The school is registered with the Department for Education and Ofsted. Limited day placements are also offered at both school sites.

The name Kisimul, pronounced 'kishmul', was taken from Kisimul Castle, which overlooks one of the safest harbours in the British Isles. Like its namesake, Kisimul School offers a safe haven, providing care and protection for its pupils whilst preparing them for the journey ahead into adulthood.

Kisimul School was founded in 1977 in a comfortable Georgian house (known today as the Old Vicarage) set in four acres within the small Lincolnshire village of Swinderby. Facilities at the Old Vicarage include an indoor heated swimming pool, large playground, soft play areas with ball pool and multi-sensory rooms for relaxation and stimulation.

In 2003, our upper school, Acacia Hall opened, offering the same standard of exceptional care and education within grounds adapted and utilised in a way to reflect the older age group. Acacia Hall offers riding stables, an adventure playground, collection of small farm animals and an area dedicated to horticulture.

Kisimul School has opened an additional school, Woodstock House, in Long Ditton, Surrey. Woodstock House received its first pupils in April 2008, and

again offers the same quality of care and education for pupils aged 8 to 19 years. Kisimul School has developed this site to be a mirror image of its existing school operations, using the same teaching methods and ethos.

Kisimul School's mission is to continuously strive for excellence in the care and education of its pupils, with a vision to have the best assisted living environment.

The school provides a caring, consistent, safe and supportive environment in which its young people can flourish and develop their skills in order to fully realise their individual potential. Residential and school staff work closely together to enable the pupils to progress in their personal development and learning. The 24-hour approach incorporates a wide range of activities to enrich the learning experiences of all pupils, helping them to learn to communicate and cooperate more effectively with others and enabling them to grow in confidence, self-esteem and independence.

The highly structured school curriculum aims to address the very specific needs of our pupils, by providing every opportunity for them to enjoy their education and develop their skills, knowledge and understanding through practical and functional learning experiences.

Classes are small and matched to learning profiles alongside the dynamics of peers. There is a high staffing ratio which reflects the complex needs of learners. The curriculum incorporates the National Curriculum (lower school) and an accreditation based vocational learning model is a feature at the upper school. An integrated therapeutic programme includes Psychology, Speech and Language, Music Therapy and Occupational Therapy (Sensory

Integration) is part of the core provision of the school.

A key priority is to develop our pupils' communication skills and since many are non-verbal we teach the alternative and augmentative systems of Makaton signing and PECS (Picture Exchange Communication System) alongside vocalisations and speech.

External accreditation is gained through a wide variety of ASDAN 'Towards Independence' programmes and the Duke of Edinburgh's Award Scheme.

Kisimul School works closely with the parents, carers and professionals from its placing authorities to ensure the highest possible standards of care and education.

Kisimul School is committed to the view that all people are entitled to equality of opportunity regardless of ability or disability, gender or chosen gender, age, status, religion, belief, nationality, ethnic origins or sexual orientation.

For further information, including exciting job opportunities within Kisimul School, please visit our website at www. kisimul.co.uk or contact us at the address above.

I CAN'S Dawn House School

I CAN

helps children communicate

(Founded 1974)

Helmsley Road, Rainworth, Mansfield, Nottinghamshire NG21 0DQ
Tel: 01623 795361
Fax: 01623 491173
Email: dawnhouse@ican.notts.sch.uk
Website: www.dawnhouseschool.org.uk
Principal: Jenny McConnell

School type:
Coeducational Day & Residential
Age range of pupils: 5–19
No. of pupils enrolled as at 01/01/2018: 79
Fees per annum as at 01/01/2018:
On request

I CAN's Dawn House School is a specialist speech, language and communication school for children and young people aged 5-19 years. We are committed to the highest quality education, therapy and care for pupils with speech and language disorder or Asperger's Syndrome and associated difficulties.

At Dawn House School the pupils receive the specialist intensive support that they need. We are able to cater for a number of other difficulties which are commonly associated with communication difficulties, including: learning difficulties,

behavioural difficulties, problems with attention and memory, motor dyspraxia, sensory difficulties, autistic spectrum difficulties and emotional problems.

Pupils' individual needs are assessed and addressed through curriculum planning and assessment and IEP planning. Speech and language therapists and teachers plan lessons that meet two sets of targets: curriculum learning objectives and specific speech and/or language aims. For pupils who need more specific focused work to develop their speech and language

skills, individual or small group sessions are timetabled during the school day.

Our school makes use of Makaton to support children's learning. The school also promotes the use of a range of voice output devices to support individual pupil's communication.

A full-time Occupational Therapist and OT assistants work within some lessons and with individual pupils on more focused, intensive work where necessary. The Family and Community Liaison Worker supports pupils' families and is a key link between home and school.

Residential Care at Dawn House School aims to ensure the emotional and physical well-being of our boarding pupils through an extended curriculum. The school can provide opportunities for non-residential young people to benefit from extended days and overnight stays. The care staff organise a range of activities out of school hours.

Dawn House was rated as an 'Outstanding' school by Ofsted in March 2014 and January 2015, its residential care inspection also gained an 'Outstanding' rating in February 2016. The inspectors found pupils at the school achieve exceptionally well and all pupils make outstanding progress whatever their individual needs or disabilities.

The Further Education department caters for students (16-19 years) who have a communication difficulty or Asperger's Syndrome. The provision is based at the Dawn House site but has very close partnerships with Vision West Notts and Portland two local FE colleges, local employers and training providers.

Dawn House School is part of I CAN, the children's communication charity (www.ican.org.uk).

The Link Primary School

(Founded 1964)
138 Croydon Road, Beddington, Croydon,
Surrey CR0 4PG
Tel: 020 8688 5239
Fax: 020 8667 0828
Email: office@linkprim.co.uk

Website: www.linkprim.co.uk
Head Teacher: Mrs Sandy Turner
School type: Coeducational Day
Age range of pupils: 4–11
No. of pupils enrolled as at 01/01/2018: 50

Part of the Orchard Hill College Academy Trust, The Link Primary School provides specialist teaching and therapy for up to 50 children aged 4 to 11 years whose primary need is speech, language and communication. Some pupils may also have additional learning, sensory or physical needs. The School has been recognised by Ofsted as 'outstanding' since 2008 and draws upon over 50 years of experience.

The School has a warm, safe, friendly and nurturing environment which helps children to learn, express their ideas, communicate, develop friendships and become confident citizens. Small classes with high adult to child ratio enable children to settle quickly, move confidently around the school and learn the daily routines which form an integral part of school life.

Children enjoy a wide range of school facilities including an ICT suite, library, fully equipped hall, food technology room, art room and quiet rooms. During playtime they have access to climbing frames, sandpit, trikes and other outdoor toys and games.

A brand new teaching block with facilities for enhanced therapy was completed in September 2015 and also provides the children with larger classrooms and additional outdoor learning opportunities including a sensory garden and kitchen allotment.

We foster close relationships with our local community to enable our children to gain valuable life experiences and encourage children to play an active role in extra-curricular activities such as dance and athletics club. A range of off-site activities are available including horse riding and swimming. Pupils also participate in regular trips to encourage social skills and to enhance their curriculum.

Establishing and developing relationships with parents and carers is a central part of our philosophy. Children learn best when the school and parents work together and we value the contribution that parents make to our school and endeavour to provide many opportunities where parents are involved in school life.

Blossom Lower School and Upper House

(Founded 1993)
1-5 Christopher Place, Chalton Street,
London, NW1 1JF
Tel: 020 7383 3834
Email:
admincp@blossomhouseschool.co.uk

Website: www.blossomhouseschool.co.uk
Principal: Joanna Burgess OBE
School type: Coeducational Day
Age range of pupils: 3–11
No. of pupils enrolled as at 01/01/2018: 17

Blossom House School is a specialist school for children with speech, language and communication difficulties. Recognised as 'outstanding' by Ofsted, the school continues to expand and now has two separate sites, one at Christopher Place in Central London and another at Motspur Park in South West London.

Blossom Lower School, Christopher Place currently has pupils aged from 3-9 years, who will be moving up through the school to year 6. Blossom House, Motspur Park has pupils from 3-19 years and includes a post 16 'college links' provision.

Although many of our pupils have some associated difficulties such as fine motor problems or poor organisational skills, all are within the broadly average range of cognitive ability. We provide an integrated, holistic programme of learning and therapies in a caring and highly supportive environment, so that each child has the opportunity to fulfil his or her potential.

Blossom House has a unique atmosphere created by a dedicated, highly competent and wonderfully caring staff. Specific strengths are acknowledged and weaknesses supported, so that each child 'blossoms' and has the opportunity

to fulfil his or her potential, whether that is remaining with us or returning to mainstream education.

The key aims of the school:

- To provide a communication centred environment where children with a range of speech, language and communication difficulties are supported in all areas of their learning.
- To provide a highly skilled team of specialist therapists, teachers and support staff who can work with the children in a range of learning environments.
- To provide support and advice for parents.

I CAN's Meath School

helps children communicate

(Founded 1982)

Brox Road, Ottershaw, Surrey KT16 0LF
Tel: 01932 872302
Fax: 01932 875180
Email: meath@meath-ican.org.uk
Website: www.meathschool.org.uk
Headteacher: Janet Dunn OBE, MA, AdvDipSpecEduc

Appointed: September 2003
School type: Coeducational Day & Residential
No. of pupils enrolled as at 01/01/2018: 60
Fees per annum as at 01/01/2018:
On request

I CAN's Meath School is a residential (weekly) and day school providing children aged 4-11 years with severe speech and language disorders, including Asperger's Syndrome/high functioning ASD. Meath School is a unique proactive specialised learning community. The school and care settings have been recognised by Ofsted as continuously 'outstanding' since 2008 and are on the Ofsted Outstanding Providers list.

Children with associated difficulties may also benefit from the provision. These include some degree of learning difficulty, attention control, fine and gross motor co-ordination problems, mild visual and/or hearing impairments, medical needs and social interaction problems.

Learning and achieving

All pupils are taught within a dynamic broad, balanced and relevant curriculum, based on the National Primary Curriculum (2014). There is a strong underpinning focus on thinking and learning skills which can be transferred throughout different subjects and into real life situations. Four levels of the curriculum are delivered at a modified pace and are highly differentiated to meet the needs of all pupils with severe and complex language needs. Strong multi-professional processes for assessment, planning, teaching and reviewing ensure that each pupil makes outstanding progress in language skills and learning.

Classes are primarily based on pupils' language comprehension levels, also taking account of curriculum attainments, learning and social needs. In this way we know behaviour and progress are maximised. Class groups can include between eight and twelve pupils, across year groups and Key Stages.

Each class has a core team of teacher, speech and language therapist and at least one learning support assistant. The speech and language therapy team and occupational therapist department are a critical and integral part of the pupils' education. Specialist teaching is offered in music, art, craft, design and PE.

Partnership with parents

Meath School staff collaborates closely with parents, sharing successes and helping with any concerns or difficulties at home. The Family Support Worker acts as a link between home and school and will visit families where needed.

The School

Meath School is housed in fine Victorian buildings and the site includes a modern teaching block, gym, music, art and cookery rooms, ICT suite, small swimming pool, school field, activity play areas and a woodland park with bike track. The school has a programme of lunch clubs, after school clubs, trumpet tuition and a summer holiday club.

Meath School is part of I CAN, the children's communication charity (www.ican.org.uk), and is an integral part of the I CAN Centre in Surrey. The Centre offers holistic multi-disciplinary independent two day specialist assessment services, training and outreach programmes.

Kisimul School – Woodstock House

(Opened 2008)

Woodstock Lane North, Long Ditton,
Surbiton, Surrey KT6 5HN
Tel: 020 8335 2570
Fax: 020 8335 2571
Email: admissions@kisimul.co.uk
Website: www.kisimul.co.uk
Director of Education:
Mr Danny Carter BA(Hons), MA, MEd

School type: Coeducational
Independent Residential Special School
Age range of pupils: 8–19
No. of pupils enrolled as at 01/01/2018: 40
Fees per annum as at 01/01/2018:
On application

Kisimul School is one of the UK's leading independent residential special schools, offering a homely and safe environment for children who have severe learning difficulties, challenging behaviour, autism and global developmental delay.

Kisimul School offers residential education, care and leisure programmes at both our upper and lower school, for up to 52 weeks of the year, for pupils aged 8 to 19 years. The school is registered with the Department for Education and Ofsted. Limited day placements are also offered.

The name Kisimul, pronounced 'kishmul', was taken from Kisimul Castle, which overlooks one of the safest harbours in the British Isles. Like its namesake, Kisimul School offers a safe haven, providing care and protection for its pupils whilst preparing them for the journey ahead into adulthood.

The original Kisimul School was founded in 1977 in a comfortable Georgian house (known today as the Old Vicarage) set in four acres within the small Lincolnshire village of Swinderby. Facilities at the Old Vicarage include an indoor heated swimming pool, large playground, soft play areas with ball pool and multi-sensory rooms for relaxation and stimulation.

In 2003, our upper school, Acacia Hall opened, offering the same standard of exceptional care and education within grounds adapted and utilised in a way to reflect the older age group. Acacia Hall offers riding stables, an adventure playground, collection of small farm animals and an area dedicated to horticulture.

Woodstock House received its first pupils in April 2008, and again offers the same quality of care and education for pupils aged 8 to 19 years. Kisimul School has developed this site to be a mirror image of its existing school operations, using the same teaching methods and ethos.

Woodstock House is situated within 8.1 acres of tranquil countryside, offering space to develop in a safe and secure environment. Woodstock House is within easy access from the M25 via the A3.

Kisimul School's mission is to continuously strive for excellence in the care and education of its pupils, with a vision to have the best assisted living environment.

The school provides a caring, consistent, safe and supportive environment in which its young people can flourish and develop their skills in order to fully realise their individual potential. Residential and therapy staff work closely together to enable the pupils to progress in their personal development and learning. The 24-hour approach incorporates a wide range of activities to enrich the learning experiences of all pupils, helping them to learn to communicate and cooperate more effectively with others and enabling them to grow in confidence, self-esteem and independence.

The highly structured school curriculum aims to address the very specific needs of our pupils, by providing every opportunity for them to enjoy their education and develop their skills, knowledge and understanding through practical and functional learning experiences.

Classes are small and matched to learning profiles alongside the dynamics of peers. There is a high staffing ratio which reflects the complex needs of learners. The curriculum incorporates the National Curriculum and features an accreditation based vocational learning model. An integrated therapeutic programme includes Psychology, Speech and Language, Music Therapy, Aromatherapy and Occupational Therapy (Sensory Integration) is part of the core provision of the school.

A key priority is to develop our pupils' communication skills and since many are non-verbal we teach the alternative and augmentative systems of Makaton signing and PECS (Picture Exchange Communication System) alongside vocalisations and speech.

External accreditation is gained through a wide variety of ASDAN 'Towards Independence' programmes.

Kisimul School works closely with the parents, carers and professionals from its placing authorities to ensure the highest possible standards of care and education.

Kisimul School is committed to the view that all people are entitled to equality of opportunity regardless of ability or disability, gender or chosen gender, age, status, religion, belief, nationality, ethnic origins or sexual orientation.

For further information, including exciting job opportunities within Kisimul School, please visit our website at www.kisimul.co.uk or contact us at the address above.

Moor House School & College

Mill Lane, Hurst Green, Oxted,
Surrey RH8 9AQ
Tel: 01883 712271
Email:
information@moorhouseschool.co.uk
Website: www.moorhouseschool.co.uk
Principal: Mrs H A Middleton

School type:
Coeducational Day & Residential
Age range of pupils: 7–19
No. of pupils enrolled as at 01/01/2018: 150
Fees per annum as at 01/01/2018:
On request

Our vision is of a society where speech and language disabilities do not prevent a young person from achieving his or her learning and communication potential, building an independent life and contributing positively to society.

Moor House is a Non-Maintained Special School and College, a registered charity and a world class centre of excellence, consistently rated outstanding by Ofsted. It provides specialist education, therapy and residential care for children and young people with speech and language needs, increasingly referred to as Developmental Language Disorder (DLD).

We provide a nurturing environment where experienced teams care for the educational, emotional and developmental needs of each student, preparing them for a safe, happy and fulfilling life. Moor House provides integrated teaching, therapy and residential care services for students with DLD.

Each student is surrounded by a multi-disciplinary team, supporting their learning and emotional well- being with intensive speech and language therapy, specialist literacy intervention, occupational therapy, physiotherapy and psychotherapy. Students receive one-to-one and small group teaching and bespoke therapy, and have access to a range of activities to develop new skills and build friendships.

This enables students to reach their highest educational and communication potential, and also to develop much higher levels of independent living skills, self-expression, and self-esteem.

Learning
Students are taught in small groups by teachers with experience working with children with language difficulties. Adapted language and specialist teaching strategies are used so that students can understand and develop the language that they need for learning.

Speech and language therapists (SLTs) work closely with teachers to support each child's difficulties and strengths. Teachers plan and deliver lessons collaboratively with SLTs to help students develop curriculum language.

Curriculum and Progress (School)
An adapted National Curriculum is taught and tailored to the students' strengths while helping them with areas of difficulty, and there is a particular emphasis on English, literacy, life skills and social skills.

We deliver exceptional outcomes for DLD children, helping our students to make outstanding academic progress, narrowing the gap significantly between themselves and their mainstream peers. Students take qualifications that match with their skills and level of development. We offer GCSEs in English Language, English Literature, Mathematics, Science, ICT, History, Fine Art and Ceramics. We also offer Functional Skills qualifications in English and Maths, vocational qualifications such as Home Cooking Skills at Levels 1 and 2, the AQA Unit Award Scheme in Science, and Entry Level qualifications in subjects such as English, Maths, ICT, DT and Music.

College (Sixth Form) Curriculum
Our objective is to support students to gain vocational qualifications, make confident and appropriate life choices and to be prepared for the next stage of their adult life. Specialist staff support students to access local partner college courses in Art and Design, Child Care, Media Studies, Floristry, Construction, Catering, Sport, Performing Arts and Animal Management, from Foundation and Level 1 in Year 12 to Level 4 at the end of Year 14.

We provide specialist support to achieve additional qualifications in Maths and English and develop important skills for life and employment, through individual study programmes and after college support.

Speech and Language Therapy

SLTs work throughout the day with students, individually, in groups, as well as in the classroom where lessons such as English are jointly planned and delivered.

Each therapist has a small caseload of children and gets to know their abilities and personalities. The intensive therapy programme may focus on learning skills, developing strategies to communicate, and support the student to understand their own strengths and difficulties. We teach skills for talking in everyday situations, language for lessons, social skills, friendship skills and independence.

We have developed specialist evidence based methods such as Electropalatography (EPG), Shape Coding by Susan Ebbels® and signing with grammatical markers.

Occupational Therapy

Occupational Therapists (OTs) work on life skills to help students develop their independence in areas such as handwriting, touch typing, doing up a tie or shoe laces, travel or cooking skills. Strategies are provided to develop sensory processing in lessons to manage and improve attention control.

We have a dedicated Team of OTs and a fully equipped OT suite which includes sensory integration equipment. The therapists communicate regularly with parents about their child's progress.

Residential Care

Our residential community provides single room facilities within our beautiful Village; three newly built student houses, located around a communal square for relaxing after school.

The students frequently describe their house as a 'home from home' and their wellbeing is assured by their key workers, who look after students' emotional welfare and provide a range of therapeutic strategies after school in a happy, stimulating and caring environment.

Our Residential Care continues to be rated "Outstanding" by Ofsted who noted: 'Children and young people thrive in this residential setting … (they) blossom in their confidence and self-esteem. Those who have had very poor school experiences and, in some cases, have refused school, look forward to their return to the provision after the weekend. Children and young people who stay in the residential setting feel safe and secure. There is an excellent approach to supporting children and young people towards independence'.

Moor House Research and Training

Our pioneering institute for training and research into DLD informs our therapeutic practice and teaching methods. Our therapists engage in cutting edge research in all areas of speech and language, working with Universities and sharing knowledge with other professionals through journals and presentations. Moor House is deservedly highly regarded by academics and specialists in the field. For information on our research, please see www.moorhouse.surrey.sch.uk/research. For information on our training, please see www.moorhouse.surrey.sch.uk/courses-and-conferences.

Moor House also provides a range of outreach, information and training services in all aspects of speech and language disabilities for parents and the wider community.

More House School

(Founded 1939)

Moons Hill, Frensham, Farnham, Surrey
GU10 3AP
Tel: 01252 792303
Fax: 01252 797601
Email:
schooloffice@morehouseschool.co.uk
Website: www.morehouseschool.co.uk
Headmaster: Jonathan Hetherington
BA(Hons), MSc(ed), QTS

School type: Boys' Boarding & Day
Age range of boys: 8–18
No. of pupils enrolled as at 01/01/2018: 470
Fees per annum as at 01/01/2018:
Day: £13,113 – £18,378
Weekly Boarding: £23,322 – £26,409
Full Boarding: £25,515 – £28,605

Founded in 1939, More House School is an independent day and boarding school with more than 470 boys on roll, making it the largest specialist school of its type in the country. Many boys travel long distances to attend the school, which is currently used for placements by 30 local authorities.

We are dedicated to helping boys with a range of learning difficulties and styles, who require a small, supportive learning environment in which to flourish.

Our aim is to help each boy who joins us, achieve, in the widest possible sense, more than he, or his parents, ever expected. This is accomplished by knowing a great deal about each student – his strengths as well as his difficulties. For his strengths, he must first be helped to identify them

and, eventually, change them into a marketable form. His difficulties will not be static. We are mindful that we must be alert to changes caused by a student's own development, those of society and by the curriculum and make sure that each of our students is equipped to meet them.

The Learning Development Centre (LDC) is a purpose-built area, housed centrally in the school, where all therapy is delivered by fully qualified therapists and specialist tutors. Almost all boys in the school attend lessons weekly for between 2 and 8 half hour sessions, with support continuing through GCSE and A level year where necessary. Attendance in the LDC forms part of each boy's timetable, removing any need to miss lessons.

The work of the Learning Development Centre is fully integrated into school life, with many staff being form tutors and mentors. The pooling of shared expertise within the inclusive staff body of the school – highly qualified Speech and Language Therapists, Occupational Therapists, Literacy Therapists, Numeracy Therapists, Cognitive Behavioural Therapist, Adolescent Psychotherapeutic Counsellor, as well as classroom subject-specialist teachers experienced in supporting pupils with a broad range of learning difficulties.

More House School is a transformative experience for the students who attend and also their families, our students' journey's will vary hugely from that of their mainstream peer group, but the end result will be the same. Academic success and a platform with which to move on to the next stage of their lives.

St Catherine's School

St Catherine's School
For Speech, Language and Communication Needs

(Founded 1983)

Grove Road, Ventnor, Isle of Wight PO38 1TT

Tel: 01983 852722

Fax: 01983 857219

Email: general@stcatherines.org.uk

Website: www.stcatherines.org.uk

Principal: Mrs R Weldon

Appointed: September 2016

School type: Coeducational Boarding

Age range of pupils: 7–19+

No. of pupils enrolled as at 01/01/2018: 64

Boys: 49 **Girls:** 15 **Sixth Form:** 33

No. of boarders: 35

Fees per annum as at 01/01/2018:

On request

St Catherine's offers specialist education, therapy and residential care to students with speech, language, communication and occupational therapy needs, and associated conditions such as autism, dyspraxia and dyslexia. Our small school provides a nurturing and supportive environment for our students – a mixture of day, weekly and termly boarders – who come from across the UK.

What makes St Catherine's special?

- Our education, therapy and care departments provide a tailored package of individualised support for each student.
- Intensive speech, language and occupational therapy is integral to the education and residential care programme.
- We focus not only on academic success

but also on each student as a whole. Students take a wide range of qualifications including Entry Level exams, GCSEs and BTEC and we work to achieve success outside the classroom with a focus on life-relevant learning skills.

- Where required, we provide a Total Communication approach including the use of sign-supported English to aid understanding.
- We support each student with their social development, helping them with relationship management and developing social and emotional resilience.
- We provide a homely experience for our residential students, with each student having their own bedroom and access to personalised extra-curricular activities.
- Our seaside town-centre location

means that we are actively involved in the local community, which offers a range of activities and a 'real life' setting for practising essential life-skills such as shopping and independent travel.

- We have two dedicated nurses within St Catherine's, who work closely with the care, teaching and therapy teams.
- We offer a range of work-related experiences including accredited vocational courses, work experience and taster courses at the local College.
- On an individually-approved basis, we also offer provision to students aged 19+, where appropriate.

"The genuinely whole-school approach towards meeting the needs of young people is the main strength of the school."
Ofsted 2017

St Joseph's Specialist School & College

(Founded 1950)

Amlets Lane, Cranleigh, Surrey GU6 7DH
Tel: 01483 272449
Email: admissions@
st-josephscranleigh.surrey.sch.uk
Website:
www.st-josephscranleigh.surrey.sch.uk
Principal: Mrs Annie Sutton
Appointed: April 2016

School type: Coeducational Day &
Residential
Age range of pupils: 5–19
No. of pupils enrolled as at 01/01/2018: 65
Fees per annum as at 01/01/2018:
Day: From £57,905
Full Boarding: From £83,898

St Joseph's Specialist School & College is recognised by Ofsted as an "Outstanding" well established day school and Children's Home providing care over 52 weeks of the year for children and young people with special needs from ages 5 to 19 years.

Currently with 73% of students on the Autistic Spectrum we also specialise in a range of complex needs including Speech & Language difficulties, severe learning difficulties, social communication disorders and challenging behaviours. Autism Accredited by the National Autistic Society, St Joseph's is a proven solution for both families and Local Authorities seeking the next step for education, care and therapy.

With Specialisms in Communication Interaction and the Creative Arts, we offer tailor made teaching and learning styles, environment, therapies, and professional standards to meet all the needs of ASD students through personalised learning programmes based on an integrated curriculum, functional communication, visual structure and positive behaviour management. These programmes incorporate a number of methods recognised for working with ASD students: TEACHH, Intensive Interaction, PECS, Social Stories and MAKATON signing and symbols. By focusing on learning and behavioural needs, as well as personal preferences, enabling a truly bespoke and personalised approach is taken to ensure success. Information is carefully gathered from a wide range of sources including: the Education Health Care Plan; the diagnosis; developmental history; educational records and assessments; medical records; parents, care staff and observations.

The school is situated close to Cranleigh Village, which retains a great sense of 'community' with a range of amenities including a Leisure Centre, library, shops, cafes, Arts Centre, churches, sports and social clubs. With good transport links to both Horsham and Guildford where more leisure and social facilities including cinemas, theatre and indoor bowling can be found. The school is an active member of the local community and all students are encouraged to take an active part in community life, to maximise their potential and engage with local people.

Strong leadership, teaching, care and therapeutic intervention combine to deliver positive outcomes to meet high expectation and aspirations of both students and families. A calming environment takes into account a wide variety of complex sensory issues and uses

a variety of techniques – photographs, symbols and visual clues – children feel comfortable in their surroundings and cope easily with daily routines.

We specifically adapt the curriculum to meet each child's individual needs and focus on the development of personal social and communication along with independent living skills, especially for those aged 16+ years.

By maintaining routines within a structured environment and promoting functional communication we enable students to stay motivated, maximise their potential and work towards positive learning outcomes, whilst seeing a reduction in both anxiety and challenging behaviours.

Therapies

We have our own dedicated team of integrated therapists who work within both class and residential settings to enhance and complement the education and care of all students. Our Director of Therapies co-ordinates and leads a department which includes Speech and Language, Occupational Therapy, Music, Arts, Equine and Drama.

We believe communication underpins successful learning, self-esteem, positive behaviour and opportunities for life. All students are assessed and a therapy programme devised based on their individual needs. To ensure learning is transferred to real life situations, our therapists accompany our children and young people into the community on a regular basis to access local facilities and activities.

Residential Options

Registered as a Children's Home, we provide care, education and therapies for up to 52 weeks a year. We can offer a variety of Residential options to meet the needs of Local Authorities, Students and families, ranging from weekly boarding to 52 week placements.

We offer an environment where each student is supported and able to develop the skills needed to maximise personal independence. Each residential house is staffed on an individual basis and well equipped to provide a homely atmosphere. Our last Ofsted Inspection rated the Children's home as "Good". By maintaining a waking day curriculum we believe our students benefit greatly from a consistency of approach.

Fully integrated into our community we ensure all our students' skills are transferred and managed in realistic settings and reflects their levels of need. A Speech and Language therapist also regularly visits all the residential groups to ensure consistency across the waking day.

Supported Living

We also provide Supported Living for young people aged 19+. Springvale in Cranleigh and Long Barn in Beare Green offer accommodation for adults with learning difficulties where each young person has their own tenancy and is supported by a tailored individual support package reflecting their own lifestyle choices and activities.

St John's School & College

ST. JOHN'S

EMPOWERING VOICE. ENABLING CHOICE

Business Centre, 17 Walpole Road,
Brighton, East Sussex BN2 0AF
Tel: 01273 244000
Fax: 01273 602243

Email: admissions@st-johns.co.uk
Website: www.st-johns.co.uk
Principal & Chief Executive:
Mr Simon Charleton
Appointed: February 2017
School type:
Coeducational Boarding & Day

Age range of pupils: 7–25
No. of pupils enrolled as at 01/01/2018: 118
Boys: 96 **Girls:** 22
No. of boarders: 47
Fees per annum as at 01/01/2018:
Day: £50,000 approx
Full Boarding: £100,000 approx

St. John's is a non-maintained special school and independent specialist college, working with learners who have complex learning disabilities; including some learners who may have difficulties resulting from social, emotional and mental health needs, Autistic Spectrum Conditions, Asperger's Syndrome and Pathological Demand Avoidance Syndrome.

St. John's is a place where learning is shaped around your hopes and aspirations; where our courses are tailored to meet your goals and where you are supported by a highly skilled staff team who respect your choices and lifestyle.

St. John's innovative curriculum provides a full range of exciting, challenging and meaningful learning experiences (both accredited and non-accredited) that prepare each learner with relevant vocational and personal skills that will significantly impact on their future lives.

Our focus on vocational skills is carried out through real, work based learning, which allows our learners to work within and support the services and functions of our organisation, our own enterprises and community work experience placements.

Maths, English, Communications and ICT are embedded or are timetabled sessions along with PSHE, sport, termly options and community access.

Learners at St. John's have access to a variety of vibrant and age appropriate learning environments that reflect their needs. These include: our cafés providing real work experience, theatre for performing arts, fully equipped music and recording studio, construction workshop, community printing enterprise, IT and project hub and sensory areas.

Throughout their journey at St. John's learners are supported by our qualified and experienced Wellbeing team, who provide communication therapy, occupational therapy, behaviour support, nursing and counselling.

We also have a dedicated transitions team who support learners in visiting potential services for their future lives. The team works closely with the Wellbeing team in preparing learners for life beyond St. John's.

Foxes Academy

(Founded 1996)
Selbourne Place, Minehead, Somerset
TA24 5TY
Tel: 01643 708529
Email: admin@foxesacademy.ac.uk
Website: foxesacademy.ac.uk

Principal: Tracey Clare-Gray
School type: Coeducational Residential
Age range of pupils: 16–25
No. of pupils enrolled as at 01/01/2018: 80
Fees per annum as at 01/01/2018:
Available on request

About Foxes Academy

At Foxes Academy we strive for excellence within teaching and learning. Our courses are holistic, offering young adults with learning disabilities tuition in hospitality and catering skills in a working hotel – Foxes Hotel which is open to the general public. We believe in changing lives and giving our learners the skills, knowledge and confidence to achieve their potential.

Our curriculum promotes independent life skills and work-related experience that leads towards qualifications which are recognised by employers, along with outstanding outcomes.

Outstanding Outcomes

Our learners achieve nationally recognised qualifications in Hospitality and Catering. Young people develop their English, Maths and ICT skills in our Functional Skills courses leading to a range of ESB and City & Guilds qualifications. For the year 2016-17 learners achieved 100%

pass rates in all formal examinations and assessments.

In 2018 The Academy scooped two of the education sector's most prestigious national awards – Overall FE Provider and Specialist Provider 2018 at the TES FE Awards. The judging panel was unanimous in its decision. It said: 'The Academy aims to equip learners with the skills, knowledge and confidence to successfully shape their own futures.'

Independent Life Skills

Independent Living Skills are taught in structured sessions as well as embedded throughout the learners' Personal Development, Health & Welfare time. We also educate and track progress in the "soft skills" so valued in life and by employers such as confidence, teamwork and taking responsibility.

Accommodation

All of our residential accommodation is beautifully furnished and situated in

a prime location within the town. The students are carefully matched to each house depending on their ability and the progress that they make as they complete their course. Learners participate in house meetings and representatives form a Learner Voice committee. The Learner Voice reviews all aspects of the organisation and helps influence change and development.

Employment Outcomes

We actively source and develop work experience placements for our learners so they can transfer their learnt skills successfully into the workplace. To date we have worked with over 50 regional employers. We have a partnership with Hilton Hotels who offer paid employment to our graduates.

73 per cent of Foxes Academy's leavers from the past 3 years (2015 to 2017) have entered employment.

Overley Hall School

(Founded 1979)
Overley, Wellington, Telford,
West Midlands TF6 5HE
Tel: 01952 740262
Fax: 01952 740875

Email: info@overleyhall.com
Website: www.overleyhall.com
Headteacher: Mrs Beverley Doran
Appointed: September 2013
School type: Coeducational Residential

Age range of pupils: 8–19
No. of pupils enrolled as at 01/01/2018: 21
Boys: 20 **Girls:** 1
No. of boarders: 20

Overley Hall School is an independent, residential special school and Children's Home, providing education and care to children and young adults aged from eight to 19 years who have a wide range of complex needs including autism, epilepsy and severe learning disabilities. The school is committed to offering each child a wide range of good quality experiences; this occurs through partnerships with parents/carers, teachers and therapists in the delivery of a waking day curriculum by a dedicated team.

Our therapy team is comprised of language and communication and occupational therapists.

The school/residential home is set in a quiet, rural location which provides a calm and nurturing learning and living environment for young people in our care. Our school building, alongside the residential house, stands in 13 acres of lawn, walled kitchen garden and woodland.

Other facilities within the campus and grounds include a lifeskills room, indoor sensory hydropool, soft play space, art and craft workshops, sensory lodge, cinema room, farm shop, recreational and relaxation areas.

Our registered 'Forest School' operates within the woodland areas, and is led by qualified practitioners from Overley Hall School; this offers pupils opportunities for multi-sensory outdoor learning and recreation experiences throughout the seasons.

Fullerton House School

Autism | Learning Disabilities | Complex Needs

(Founded 1990)

Tickill Square, Denaby, Doncaster,
South Yorkshire DN12 4AR

Tel: 01709 861663
Fax: 01709 869635
Email: enquiries@hesleygroup.co.uk
Website: www.fullertonhouseschool.co.uk
General Manager: Heidi Dugdale-Dawkes
Appointed: 2017
Registered Manager: Ian Oliver

Head of Education: Michael Walsh
School type: Independent Specialist
Residential School
Age range of pupils: 8–19
Fees per annum as at 01/01/2018:
Available on request

A specialist residential school offering flexible education and care, principally as a 52-week service with limited capacity for day placements, for young people aged 8-19, all of whom have complex needs including behaviour that may challenge and a learning disability, often in association with autism.

Fullerton House School is situated in the heart of the village of Denaby Main, near Doncaster. Its central location provides easy access by road, rail or air. Our mission is to enhance the lives of the young people entrusted to us by focusing on their specific needs, capabilities and aspirations.

Education: Each person has a carefully designed Individual Learning Plan based on their EHCP as well as their specific needs in line with the National Curriculum, which supports their positive progress in a range of areas.

Extended learning: During evenings, weekends and school holidays a wide range of extra-curricular activities are on offer to ensure that people are fully engaged with stimulating and meaningful experiences both on and off-site.

Professional services: A dedicated on-site team including carers, teachers, tutors, communication, behaviour and occupational therapy , psychology and other specialists ensure that people have ready access to the services they require.

High-quality accommodation: Single person and small group occupancy of high-quality accommodation is provided at Fullerton House School. Each person has their own bedroom, the majority of which have en-suite bathrooms. We also have a range of on-site facilities to complement and enrich the lives of those who come to live and learn with us.

Keeping in contact: We understand that while we may offer a very positive option for the person, we may not be on your doorstep. Keeping in touch with loved ones is essential. Everyone has a plan to support optimum contact with family/carers and friends whether this be by phone, letter, email or Skype.

Specialist Colleges

Autism | Learning Disabilities | Complex Needs

(Founded 2013)

Fullerton House College

Tickhill Square, Denaby, Doncaster,

South Yorkshire DN12 4AR

Tel: 01709 861663

Fax: 01709 869635

Wilsic Hall College

Wadworth, Doncaster,

South Yorkshire, DN11 9AG

Tel: 01302 856382

Fax: 01709 853608

Email: enquiries@hesleygroup.co.uk

Website: www.hesleygroup.co.uk

General Manager: Heidi Dugdale-Dawkes

Appointed: 2017

School type: Independent Specialist Residential College

Age range of pupils: 18–25

Fullerton House College Capacity: 12

Wilsic Hall College Capacity: 8

Fees per annum as at 01/01/2018:

On request

Specialist residential colleges offering flexible education care and support for up to 52 weeks per year for young people aged 18-25, who have complex needs including behaviour that may challenge and a learning disability, often in association with autism.

At Wilsic Hall College, everyone lives within a beautiful rural setting with ready community access and at Fullerton House College in the heart of the community, in an urban setting with many local facilities including a sports centre, restaurants and shops.

Mission

We have 2 pathways available for the young people attending college.

Formal Education Pathway with a focus on gaining educational qualifications, skills and experience to move on to employment opportunity and further independence in their lives.

Next Steps Pathway for young people who have completed their formal educational route and are now wishing to build vocational and independence skills for life style experience and development- including social enterprise work.

Both pathways offer accreditation in the skills and qualifications the young people achieve, but the journeys are varied and personalised to the young persons needs and outcomes at this significant life stage.

Education: Everybody has a highly personalised programme of learning, equipping them with skills they will need for adult life.

Extended learning: During evenings, weekends and college holidays a wide range of extra-curricular activities are on offer to ensure people are fully engaged with stimulating experiences both on and off site providing further, meaningful learning opportunities.

Professional services: A dedicated multi-disciplinary therapeutic team including college tutors, college support workers, consultant clinical psychologist, consultant psychiatrist, applied behaviour analysts, speech and language therapists, occupational therapists, registered manager, care and support staff work together to support each individual's progress.

High quality accommodation: College accommodation includes individualised bedrooms, quality living spaces that promote independence and progressive skills development assisted by the appropriate use of specialist/adaptive technology. We also have a range of on-site and off-site facilities that offer progressive learning opportunities for young people with a range of needs and wishes.

Keeping in contact: We work to develop relationships between staff and families that are strong, positive and mutually respectful. People are supported to be in contact with their friends and family; we welcome visits to the colleges at any time. Everyone has a plan that will include the best means for them to maintain this contact whether by 'phone, letter, email or Skype.

Wilsic Hall School

Autism | Learning Disabilities | Complex Needs

(Founded 1996)
Wadworth, Doncaster,
South Yorkshire DN11 9AG

Tel: 01302 856382
Email: enquiries@hesleygroup.co.uk
Website: www.wilsichallschool.co.uk
Head: Geoff Turner
Appointed: 2008
School type:
Independent Specialist Residential School

Age range of pupils: 11–19
Capacity: 32
Fees per annum as at 01/01/2018:
Available on request

A specialist residential school offering flexible education and care, principally as a 52-week service with limited capacity for day placements, for young people aged 11-19, all of whom have complex needs including behaviour that may challenge and a learning disability, often in association with autism.

Wilsic Hall School is situated in its own 14-acre site approximately five miles south of Doncaster. Its central location provides easy access by road, rail or air. Our mission is to enhance the lives of the people entrusted to us by focusing on their specific needs, capabilities and aspirations.

Education: Each person has a carefully designed Individual Education Plan based on their specific needs in line with the National Curriculum, which supports their positive progress in a range of areas.

Extended learning: During evenings, weekends and school holidays a wide range of extra-curricular activities are on offer to ensure that people are fully engaged with stimulating and meaningful experiences both on and off-site.

Professional services: A dedicated team including carers, teachers, tutors, behaviour, communication and occupational therapy, psychology and other specialists ensure that each person has ready access to the services they require.

High-quality accommodation: Single person and small group occupancy of high-quality accommodation is provided at Wilsic Hall School. Each person has their own bedroom, the majority of which have en-suite bathrooms. We also have a range of on-site facilities to complement and enrich the lives of those who come to live and learn with us.

Keeping in contact: We understand that while we may offer a very positive option for the person, we may not be on your doorstep. Keeping in touch with loved ones is essential. Everyone has a plan to support optimum contact with family/carers and friends whether this be by phone, letter, email or Skype.

The New School

BUTTERSTONE

(Founded 1992)

Butterstone, Dunkeld, Perth & Kinross PH8 0HA

Tel: 01350 724216

Fax: 01350 724283

Email: info@thenewschool.co.uk

Website: www.thenewschool.co.uk

Head of School: Mr Bill Colley

Appointed: March 2018

School type: Coeducational Day & Boarding

Age range of pupils: 11–19

No. of pupils enrolled as at 01/01/2018: 25

Boys: 21 **Girls:** 4

Fees per annum as at 01/01/2018:

Available on request

Education should be enjoyable and meaningful – we believe all young people are able to develop and achieve their potential. Through a range of educational opportunities across the 24 hour curriculum we help to prepare for life beyond school.

We have clear expectations and the relaxed, flexible and supportive environment of The New School encourages our young people to feel comfortable with who they are, and to flourish as individuals.

We are a Theraputic Learning Community. Our provision is aimed at those young people who find mainstream education difficult to access. The New School specialises in education for fragile learners in general, for young people with Aspergers/Autistic Spectrum condition, ADHD, Tourette's syndrome and Foetal Alcohol syndrome. Skilled teaching and care staff support young people who have had interrupted learning, dissatisfying school experiences, or simply those who learn differently. We are a truly inclusive school.

The New School curriculum is broad, coherent and highly varied – meeting the different needs of each and every one of our young people. Our classes are small, with an average of five. Our students are encouraged to follow interests – making the learning motivating, relevant and meaningful for them, regardless of academic ability. We deliver a full menu of SQA accredited courses, from Curriculum for Excellence National 2 up to Higher level in most subjects. ASDAN accreditation system units and courses are offered to some students, helping them to develop independence, skills for work and skills for life. Speech and language therapy is offered to all students, if required. Our sector-leading 'Showcase' eprofile recording system ensures that the student population recognise and celebrate their own achievements – both academic and more broadly throughout their time here, evidence is gathered across the 24-hour curriculum. We are passionate about outdoor learning, and utilise the beautiful school situation to promote this in various ways. Our trained staff deliver full Duke of Edinburgh's Award up to Gold level.

Schools and colleges specialising in sensory or physical impairment

Mary Hare School

(Founded 1946)

Primary School: Mill Hall, Pigeons Farm Road, Thatcham, Newbury, RG19 8XA
Secondary School: Arlington Manor, Snelsmore Common, Newbury, West Berkshire RG14 3BQ
Tel: 01635 244200
Fax: 01635 248019

Email: enquiries@maryhare.org.uk
Website: www.maryhare.org.uk
Principal: Mr Peter Gale
School type: Coeducational Boarding & Day
Age range of pupils: 5–19
No. of pupils enrolled as at 01/01/2018: 245

Mary Hare is a school for deaf children taking children from Year 1 through to Year 13. We are the largest school for the deaf in the UK and take children from over 90 Local Authorities. We support pupils with a range of additional needs over and above their deafness. We offer boarding and day places.

We use the oral communication method so no use of BSL in the classroom. The use of English is really important and pupils thrive on learning to use their voice. Pupils will have the chance to sign in their social time if they wish.

We offer the full national curriculum with a focus on improving language skills which helps pupils to achieve better grades.

We offer small class sizes in acoustically treated classrooms. Teachers are subject specialists as well as trained Teachers of the Deaf. We have a full team of Speech and Language Therapists working with pupils on a one to one basis as well as in small groups. In addition, we have our own Audiology department on site.

For many pupils, joining Mary Hare means the opportunity to join a community with a large deaf peer group, lots of friends and the chance to feel 'the same' as everyone else. Confidence, self-esteem and having high aspirations are many of the things that we give our pupils.

To apply for a place, we offer every child an assessment of between three and five days depending on age. If we offer a place and you accept then you will need to approach your Local Authority for funding. Around 50% of places are funded from the start. Mary Hare will support you through the funding process.

To arrange a visit or assessment please book via our website, www.maryhare.org.uk/admissions.

Set your sights high

The Pace Centre

Specialist education and therapy
for children with motor disorders
(Founded 1990)

Philip Green House, Coventon Road,
Aylesbury, Buckinghamshire HP19 9JL
Tel: 01296 392739
Fax: 01296 334836
Email: info@thepacecentre.org
Website: www.thepacecentre.org

Head Teacher: Mrs Claire Smart
Appointed: September 2016
School type: Independent Special School
Age range of pupils: 1–16
Fees per annum as at 01/01/2018:
Available on request

A specialist school for children with motor disorders

Pace offers a nurturing, stimulating and rich environment to children and young people with a wide range of sensory motor disorders and related communication, educational and medical needs. Our aim is to unlock potential and empower children to live life as independently as possible.

Our highly skilled transdisciplinary team of experts work in close collaboration to deliver an individually tailored curriculum. Drawing on best practice from a range of clinical and educational disciplines, the curriculum is bespoke to each child's abilities and goals and delivers outstanding outcomes. Each class has a minimum ratio of one to one with a specialist leader for each session.

"Pupils make rapid progress against their individual targets. This is because teaching and continuous support from a wide range of professionals accurately meets pupils' needs." – Ofsted 2016

Our model

At the heart of our transdisciplinary approach lies the relationship between postural, movement, sensory and perceptual skills and how these impact on academic learning.

In December 2016, Ofsted rated Pace "Outstanding" for the fifth consecutive inspection.

What we offer

Education

Pre-school
Reception
Key stages 1-4
Dual placements
Community outreach
Commissioned services

Onsite therapy

Occupational therapy
Physiotherapy
Speech and language therapy
Hydrotherapy
Hippotherapy
Rebound therapy

Approaches we use

Conductive education
Sensory integration
Bobath

Communication

Alternative and augmentative communication
British Sign Language

Family support

Early intervention
Assessment and advice
Sleeping
Feeding

Moving and handling
Communication
Parent training and support
Parent partnership

Daily independence programmes

Group and individual programmes to develop sensory registration and processing skills
Specific programmes to develop movement skills, fine motor skills, hand skills, selfcare and independence skills
Wheelchair skills
Group and individual programmes to develop communication skills, including 'high tech' communication aides and ICT user groups
Engagement with the local community through regular citizenship activities.

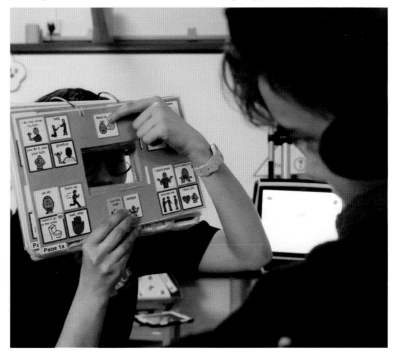

RNIB College Loughborough

RNIB College Loughborough

(Founded 1989)
Radmoor Road, Loughborough,
Leicestershire LE11 3BS
Tel: 01509 611077
Fax: 01509 232013
Email: enquiries@rnibcollege.ac.uk

Website: www.rnibcollege.ac.uk
Principal: June Murray
School type: Coeducational College and residence
Age range of pupils: 16–65
No. of pupils enrolled as at 01/01/2018: 100

We are a friendly residential college supporting young people and adults with vision impairment and additional disabilities to achieve their goals. Our programmes are designed to develop independence skills for involvement in community life.

Education and skills

Choose us for your Further Education and you'll learn practical skills and gain work experience within our enterprises – our Café, eBay business, Conference Centre, Arts Centre, Shop and Office. You could also choose a course at our partner mainstream college located next door.

If you are a young adult wanting to gain the skills and confidence to progress into independent or supported living, you may want to apply for our Bridge programme. It's a one-year residential programme which will help you to build your independence. You'll be encouraged and supported to do things you've previously had help for, making you ready to move into your own home.

Also on offer is Flexible Futures, our daytime activities programme. You could spend time in each of our different enterprises, providing a vital role in these real businesses and being part of college life. You could also go out and enjoy the local community.

Accommodation

Our Stan Bell Centre offers modern, purpose built, safe accommodation. Learners are encouraged to be as independent as possible; however we recognise that some people will always need a little more support. Our residence is staffed 24 hours a day.

Needs we support

- Vision impairment
- Learning difficulties and disabilities
- Autistic Spectrum Conditions
- Physical disabilities
- Communication difficulties
- Mild hearing problems
- Additional healthcare needs, such as epilepsy
- Additional emotional and behavioural difficulties

Wider services

RNIB offers a wide range of other services for children, young people, their families and the professionals who work with them. Find out more at www.rnib.org.uk/children

Visit us!

The best way to find out more about our college is to come and have a look round. Call us today to arrange your visit!

RNIB Sunshine House School

Sunshine House School

33 Dene Road, Northwood, Middlesex
HA6 2DD
Tel: 01923 822538
Fax: 01923 826227
Email: sunshinehouse@rnib.org.uk

Website: www.rnib.org.uk/sunshinehouse
Head: Jackie Seaman and Mark Fuel
School type: Coeducational
Age range of pupils: 2–14

At RNIB Sunshine House School we offer specialist support to blind and partially sighted children with significant learning difficulties and disabilities and their families.

With a range of specialist indoor and outdoor facilities, we provide a safe and supportive environment for children to meet their full potential.

We're part of a family of five local special schools with The Eden Academy, working together to offer your child access to an enhanced range of expertise, activities and resources.

Education and Curriculum

Everyone at Sunshine House is treated as an individual with their own specific needs and learning goals. Working together with parents and specialists we ensure that achievements go beyond the classroom into everyday life.

Our specialist school educates children and young people from two to 14 years who have a range of physical, learning and sensory needs. Children follow an individually tailored curriculum supporting their special education needs. Most children are working between P levels 1 and 8. Each class has no more than eight children with a minimum support ratio of two adults for every three children.

Therapies and Healthcare

Our team of in-house therapists combine their work with a child's learning, making therapies a part of everyday school life. We also have a paediatric community nurse who ensures that all health needs are met.

Family services

You can get to know other parents and children and have fun through our thriving family services. Activities include after-school and holiday clubs, family events, sibling support groups, networking and advice for parents.

Needs we support

- Vision impairment
- Multi-sensory impairment and deaf-blindness
- Significant learning difficulties and disabilities
- Physical disabilities
- Communication difficulties
- Additional medical and health needs, including long-term ventilation or life-threatening or life-limiting conditions

Wider services

RNIB offers a wide range of other services for children, young people, their families and the professionals who work with them. Find out more at www.rnib.org.uk/children

Visit us!

The best way to find out more about our school is to come and have a look round. Call us today to arrange your visit!

Chailey Heritage School

(Founded 1903)

Haywards Heath Road, North Chailey,
Lewes, East Sussex BN8 4EF
Tel: 01825 724444
Fax: 01825 723773
Email: office@chf.org.uk
Website: www.chf.org.uk
Charity Chief Executive: Helen Hewitt
Headteacher: Simon Yates

Director of Social Care: Denise Banks
School type: Coeducational Boarding & Day
Age range of pupils: 3–19
No. of pupils enrolled as at 01/01/2018: 95
Fees per annum as at 01/01/2018:
Please contact the school for details

Chailey Heritage School, part of Chailey Heritage Foundation, is a non-maintained special school for children and young people aged 3-19 with complex physical disabilities and health needs. Chailey Heritage School was judged to be 'Outstanding' by Ofsted in October 2014 for a third consecutive time. Chailey Heritage Residential is a registered children's home and offers flexible care packages from short breaks to 52 weeks of the year.

Meeting Children's Health and Therapy Needs

Chailey Heritage School has a unique on-site partnership with Chailey Clinical, part of Sussex Community NHS Foundation Trust. The pupils' health and therapy needs are met by a highly skilled team that includes Paediatric Medical Consultants and Doctors, Therapists, residential Nursing team and Rehabilitation Engineers, as well as our expert teachers.

Purposeful Learning

Chailey Heritage School has developed its own curriculum driven by the individual learner's needs, skills and desired outcomes. It is meaningful to each child and their family as it covers all aspects of their development and it weighs up the input that is needed specifically for them.

Support for Parents and Families at Every Step

We work with parents and families at each point of their Chailey Heritage journey by providing support at difficult times whilst also celebrating achievements together.

Chailey Heritage Residential

Chailey Heritage Residential is a nationally recognised, registered children's home for 3 to 19 year olds with complex physical disabilities and health needs. We offer flexible residential provision ranging from short breaks to 52 weeks a year.

Find Out More

We would be delighted to show you around our site. Please get in touch to arrange a visit.

Chailey Heritage School and Chailey Heritage Residential are part of Chailey Heritage Foundation, registered charity number 1075837, registered in England as a charitable company limited by guarantee No. 3769775

St Mary's School & 6th Form College

(Founded 1922)
Wrestwood Road, Bexhill-on-Sea, East Sussex TN40 2LU
Tel: 01424 730740
Fax: 01424 733575
Email: admin@stmarysbexhill.org

Website: www.stmarysbexhill.org
Headteacher: Mark Bryant
School type: Coeducational Boarding & Day
Age range of pupils: 7–19
No. of pupils enrolled as at 01/01/2018: 63

St Mary's is a residential School and College for young people aged 7-19 with speech, language and communication difficulties and associated complex needs. We are committed to providing the best learning opportunities through the delivery of integrated education, therapy and care tailored to each young person's individual abilities and aspirations. The pupils are taught in small groups and follow individual pathways through an exciting broad and balanced curriculum, delivered by highly qualified teachers and support staff with the integrated support of therapists. Depending on their needs, pupils access individual therapy programmes which may include specialist support from Speech and Language Therapists, Physiotherapists, Occupational Therapists, and Health and Wellbeing Team including and an Educational Psychologist, Clinical Psychologist, Nurse and Health Care Assistant. Other specialist professionals include a team of Sign Language Tutors and a Child and Family Support Worker. Here at St Mary's, we do all we can to support each pupil to develop and maximise their communication skills. Parent signing classes are offered on site or via Skype to ensure families can communicate with their child as effectively as possible. At St Mary's, our residences are warm and caring places, creating a 'home from home' feel. In nurturing and stimulating environments we work with our pupils to develop life skills and encourage everyone to learn and live with each other. Opportunities to take part in a wide range of activities are available every day, with children and young people accessing the local community on a regular basis.

Our facilities include:
- Aspire Vocational Centre with café, car wash, printers, hairdressers and shop

- Sensory Room
- Physiotherapy Room
- Adventure Playground
- Swimming and Hydrotherapy pool
- Sensory Integration Room
- Traversing Wall
- Nature Trail

- Music & Drumming Room
- Outdoor Tennis Courts
- Science Lab
- ICT Suite
- Horticultural area & Polytunnel

The Children's Trust School
Non-Maintained Special School

The Children's Trust School

(Founded 1985)

Tadworth Court, Tadworth,
Surrey KT20 5RU
Tel: 01737 365810
Fax: 01737 365819
Email: school@thechildrenstrust.org.uk
Website:
www.thechildrenstrustschool.org.uk

Head Teacher: Samantha Newton
School type:
Day and Residential to 52 weeks
Age range of pupils: 2–19
No. of pupils enrolled as at 01/01/2018: 44
Fees per annum as at 01/01/2018:
On application

At The Children's Trust School our aim is to provide high quality education and expertise to meet each pupil's individual special educational needs and to celebrate all achievements in a happy, secure environment.

As a non-maintained special school for 2-19 year olds, we pride ourselves on seeing the 'whole' child and delivering education, health and care for children and young people with complex needs in an integrated and holistic approach.

Through day and residential placements (of up to 52 weeks) we focus on personalised planning supporting pupils to improve and develop understanding of the world around them and their functional skills.

We have a skilled team of teachers, classroom and care support staff and nursing and medical staff. We also have an extensive team of therapists, ranging from occupational, physio and speech and language to play, leisure and music therapists. We also offer education, care and therapy to children from the age of three. Our early years pupils are offered age-appropriate education and activities based on our specially-developed curriculum. Taddies is a weekly run parent and child group for children aged 0-5 years old who have additional needs.

Our curriculum focuses on communication, language and literacy, fine and gross motor physical skills, environmental control technology, social, emotional and personal wellbeing and cognitive development.

We provide stimulating educational opportunities, supported by unparalleled expertise delivering significant outcomes for our pupils.

Treloar School

(Founded 1908)

Holybourne, Alton, Hampshire GU34 4GL
Tel: 01420 547400
Email: admissions@treloar.org.uk
Website: www.treloar.org.uk
Principal: Martin Ingram
School type:
Coeducational Boarding & Day

Religious Denomination: Non-denominational
Age range of pupils: 2–19
No. of pupils enrolled as at 01/01/2018: 80
Boys: 40 **Girls:** 40 **Sixth Form:** 20
No. of boarders: 38
Fees per annum as at 01/01/2018:
As per assessment

Treloar Nursery and School provide outstanding education, care, therapy and independence training to children and young people from 2 to 19 years of age with complex physical disabilities. Provision is both day and residential and students come from across the UK and overseas. Both our educational and residential School provision were rated Outstanding by Ofsted in 2018. Our College, based on the same site, offers continued education and care up to the age of 25 and was similarly rated Outstanding by Ofsted in 2017. At Treloar's we prepare students for life after they leave and equip them with the confidence, the independence skills and, where applicable, qualifications they require.

Students have access to an on-site health centre, occupational as well as speech and language and physio therapists. There are also educational psychologists, visual impairment and assistive technology specialists plus dieticians and counsellors on-site. Therapy is integrated into the school day to maximise opportunities for learning. Our transition team work with each student from assessment through to their expected destination to help them reach their goals and aspirations.

Entry Requirement

Admission is considered on the basis of each student's needs following discussion and assessment with education, medical, therapy and care staff. Each student's

programme is constructed to ensure we meet their individual needs. Part-time placements, limited time placements and respite for day students are all available.

Life on Campus

Treloar's is situated in beautiful East Hampshire on the edge of Alton with a good road and rail network. We ensure a varied range of extra-curricular activities including sports, art, drama, clubs and visits off-site utilising our own specialist fleet of vehicles. On-site facilities include a swimming pool, all weather sports facilities, a hydrotherapy pool, a Rebound Therapy room and a social club.

Treloar Trust is a registered charity which supports Treloar School and College (Charity No 1092857).

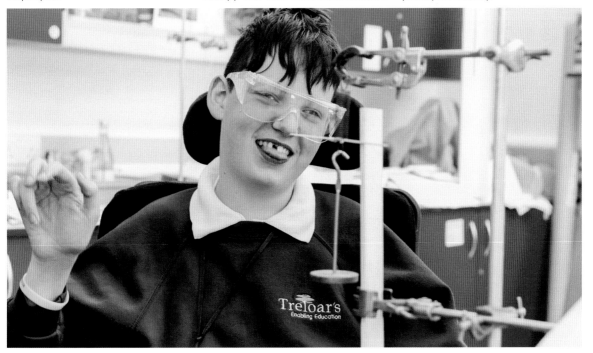

RNIB Pears Centre for Specialist Learning

(Founded 1957)
Wheelwright Lane, Ash Green, Coventry,
West Midlands CV7 9RA
Tel: 024 7636 9500
Fax: 024 7636 9501
Email: pearscentre@rnib.org.uk

Website: www.rnib.org.uk/pearscentre
Principal: Robert Jones
School type: Coeducational day school and Children's Home
Age range of pupils: 4–19
No. of pupils enrolled as at 01/01/2018: 31

At RNIB Pears Centre, we provide a stimulating, creative and purpose-built setting for children and young people with complex needs and vision impairment to live, learn and grow.

We support children to make progress, to develop their independence, and to make their own choices.

Our co-located school and children's home offer flexible packages of support to children and families, depending on what you need:

- Education with up to 52-week residential care
- Education only (if your child lives at home, for example)
- 24-hour residential and/or nursing care only.

This includes therapies and health support, depending on what your child needs.

Education
If you're looking for a specialist school, our education celebrates a child's abilities and stimulates all of their senses. Our broad, balanced and relevant curriculum is fully personalised to meet individual learning needs.

Therapies
Our in-house therapy and school team offers specialist expertise in vision impairment, multi-sensory impairment, complex needs and learning disabilities, physiotherapy, speech and language therapy, behaviour management and mobility/habilitation. Hydrotherapy, music therapy, rebound therapy, clinical psychology, occupational therapy and medical led support of health and wellbeing are also part of our provision. Our new hydrotherapy pool is also improving the quality of life and learning experiences for children and young people.

Specialist care and leisure
Sometimes, the chance to share the care of a child can help to relieve pressure on families. Our children's home offers 24-hour care all year round, with waking night staff in spacious bungalows.

Each young person living with us has their own bedroom, which is made safe and personal to them. We support children to access a range of activities and community events, like pop concerts and swimming.

If your child has high health and medical needs, our nursing care offers rehabilitation and a real alternative to long stays in hospital.

Needs we support
- Vision impairment
- Multi-sensory impairment and deaf-blindness
- Significant learning difficulties and disabilities
- Autistic Spectrum Conditions
- Physical disabilities
- Communication difficulties
- Additional medical and health needs, including long-term ventilation or life-threatening or life-limiting conditions
- Additional emotional and behavioural difficulties

Our board of trustees allows us to accommodate a number of children who do not have vision impairment as their primary need.

Wider services
RNIB offers a wide range of other services for children, young people, their families and the professionals who work with them. Find out more at www.rnib.org.uk/children

Visit us!
The best way to find out more about what we offer is to come and have a look round. Call us today to arrange your visit!

Doncaster School for the Deaf

Doncaster School for the Deaf

(Founded 1829)

Leger Way, Doncaster, South Yorkshire
DN2 6AY
Tel: 01302 386733
Fax: 01302 361808
Email: jgoodman@ddt-deaf.org.uk
Website: www.deaf.school.org.uk

Executive Principal: Mr Alan W Robinson
School type: Non-maintained (Special)
Coeducational Boarding and Day
Age range of pupils: 4–19
No. of pupils enrolled as at 01/01/2017: 32
Boys: 20 **Girls:** 12
Fees per annum as at 01/01/2017:
On request

We offer a broad and balanced curriculum which is accessible to all our pupils, providing smooth progression and continuity through all Key Stages.

The language and communication policy at Doncaster School for the Deaf is a pupil-centred approach, based on their method of preferred communication. We aim to meet the needs of pupils who communicate through British Sign Language (BSL) or English.

The School has a full-time Audiologist, Speech and Language Therapists and a team of Teaching Assistants as well as an on-site fully qualified Nurse. Most teachers are experienced and qualified teachers of the deaf.

Provision for resident pupils is in a modern comfortable house sympathetically converted to provide high standards of living accommodation.

Qualifications include A Levels, AS Levels, GCSE, Entry Level Certificate of Achievement, ASDAN unit Awards and Signature (BSL). The school believes that the school curriculum should be broad, balanced and personalised in order to reflect the needs of each pupil and to nurture a lifelong desire to learn. In addition to curriculum subjects pupils access speech therapy, BSL lessons and Deaf Studies. Some KS4 and KS5 pupils are able to access vocational courses as part of the 14-19 curriculum.

The School works in partnership with Little Learners Day Nursery and Communication Specialist College Doncaster (formerly Doncaster College for the Deaf) which share the same campus.

We have close links with parents, and other professionals.

The school occupies a large, pleasant site. A superb sports hall, heated indoor swimming pool and extensive playing fields. The school welcomes visitors.

St John's Catholic School for the Deaf

St John's
Catholic School for the Deaf
Boston Spa, Yorkshire

(Founded 1870)
Church Street, Boston Spa, Wetherby,
West Yorkshire LS23 6DF

Tel: 01937 842144
Fax: 01937 541471
Email: info@stjohns.org.uk
Website: www.stjohns.org.uk
Headteacher: Mrs A Bradbury BA(Hons),
MSc, NPQH

School type: Coeducational Boarding
& Day
Age range of pupils: 4–19
No. of pupils enrolled as at 01/01/2018: 62
Fees per annum as at 01/01/2018:
On application

Special needs catered for

St John's Catholic School is a centre of excellence for sensory and communication needs for pupils aged 4-19. It is a school where spoken language is used, and where every young person communicates equally and successfully with others. We encourage and nurture ambition, self-esteem and confidence in all pupils.

The school offers a broad and balanced curriculum offering the opportunity to take GCSEs, entry level qualifications and a wide range of vocational courses. There is specialist unit for pupils with very complex needs, including multi-sensory impairment

and autism. Older pupils attend the well-established sixth form, where courses are hosted in local FE colleges and pupils are supported by qualified and experienced learning mentors. We accept day and weekly boarding pupils, and welcome pupils of all faiths and denominations.

Specialist facilities

All pupils are taught by teachers with additional qualifications in deafness or multi-sensory impairments. The school classrooms are acoustically treated and benefit from Soundfield technology. There is a resident audiologist and health and medical needs are coordinated by the school nurse and supported by a

programme of personal, social and health education. There are strong links with the local child and adolescent mental health team who specialise in working with deaf young people.

We have a team of highly specialised speech and language therapists who deliver both individual and group therapy sessions to all pupils. The therapists work with staff across the whole school and maintain close contact with parents, so everyone is clear how to maximise pupils' progress.

Primary

Teaching is tailored to pupils' individual needs by specialist teachers and a broad and imaginative curriculum inspires creative and enthusiastic learners. Indoor and outdoor zones provide a vibrant learning environment, and there are sensory and soft play rooms for sensory integration. Primary pupils enjoy regular integration and social opportunities at neighbouring schools and take part in an extensive programme of enrichment activities.

Secondary

There is a high level of personalisation in the curriculum for secondary pupils – more than sixteen subjects can be studied at different levels, from entry level to GCSEs and their equivalent. The development of literacy and numeracy is a key priority, and this is achieved through intensive specialist teaching in small classes. As well as traditional academic subjects, our curriculum provides a strong focus on creative and practical subjects that develop social communication and other essential skills for future adult life.

Sixth form

The sixth form offers our students the opportunity to study a wide range of academic and vocational courses

linked to two local colleges. Students have full time support from learning mentors who are all trained to support the communication needs of deaf people. Linking with mainstream colleges helps students build wider friendship groups and offers new social opportunities.

The sixth form residential setting provides a full life-skills programme which is accessible for young people with a range of additional needs such as visual impairments. By the end of their time at St John's, students have well-developed independence skills for adult life.

Multi-sensory impairment

There is a small specialist unit for pupils who have more complex needs, including multi-sensory impairment (MSI) and autism. These young people are supported by expert staff, and learning concentrates on presenting meaningful experiences that avoid sensory overload. Communication systems are built around the child's preferences, including PECs (Picture Exchange Communication system), Makaton, hand over hand signing and computer aided systems.

Boarding facilities

The residential areas are homely and welcoming. Young people who board live in small family units and are looked after by an experienced and knowledgeable staff team, who help them to form positive relationships and develop negotiation and co-operation skills. There is a full programme of leisure activities, and children have the opportunity to participate in local clubs and sports societies. The school offers weekly or flexi-boarding, and all students go home every weekend.

Home school links

Very close links with families are maintained, with regular updates on progress and achievements. Parents are welcome to visit the school, and are kept up to date with activities by the half termly newsletter.

General environment

The school is within walking distance of the elegant and vibrant Georgian village of Boston Spa, where there are shops, cafés and parks. The extensive buildings are well-equipped and include a gym with specialist fitness equipment, a purpose built theatre and sound recording room, a fully stocked library, an IT suite and a number of sensory rooms. The grounds are perfect for sports and leisure activities, with marked pitches and a newly-developed sensory garden.

The Royal Blind School

THE ROYAL BLIND SCHOOL
(Founded 1835)
43 Canaan Lane, Edinburgh, EH10 4SG

Tel: 0131 446 3120
Fax: 0131 447 9266
Email: office@royalblindschool.org.uk
Website: www.royalblind.org/education
Head Teacher: Elaine Brackenridge (BEd)

School type: Coeducational, National Grant Aided Special School
Age range of pupils: 5–19
Fees per annum as at 01/01/2018:
Available on request

The Royal Blind School was founded in 1835. It is run by Scotland's largest vision impairment charity, Royal Blind, and is regulated by Education Scotland and the Care Inspectorate. We are a grant-aided special school supported by the Scottish Government.

The school, situated in Morningside, Edinburgh, is Scotland's only residential school specialising in the care and education of visually impaired young people, including those with complex needs.

Places are paid for through fees from local authorities or privately. We offer 52-week residential or term-time boarding, as well as nightly and weekly boarding. Our residential houses are fully accessible and designed to be a home from home.

We enrol pupils from P1 to S6 and in addition there is a free pre-school playgroup held on Friday mornings during term-time.

The Royal Blind School has a high ratio of staff to pupils and we offer a full curriculum of subjects. Each child follows an individualised education programme underpinned by the Curriculum for Excellence and Getting it Right for Every Child (GIRFEC). We deliver a broad general education and offer qualifications and accreditation by the Scottish Qualifications Authority (SQA), Junior Awards Scheme Scotland, Personal Achievement Awards and ASDAN in the senior phase.

Our approach is inclusive and pupil-centred, providing many opportunities for experience and achievement. We strive to make learning fun, challenging and self-affirming. We deliver independent living skills, building self-confidence and self-esteem by providing a greater awareness of the wider environment through mobility and orientation to ensure that all pupils become as independent as possible.

Pupils in fourth, fifth and sixth year have the opportunity to take part in work experience. Some pupils are involved in a Coffee Shop Enterprise Project. This activity gives young people the opportunity to develop a valuable range of life skills such as social interaction, handling money, planning, shopping and baking.

Outreach Support

We also provide an education outreach service offering support, training, resources and advice to staff in mainstream schools who are working with visually impaired pupils through our Learning Hub, www.royalblind.org/learninghub.

For more information please visit our website www.royalblind.org/education or telephone 0131 446 3120, or email office@royalblindschool.org.uk.

Scottish Charity No. SC 017167.

Directory

Schools and colleges specialising in social interaction difficulties (Autism, ASC & ASP)

Abbreviations

ACLD	Autism, Communication and Associated Learning Difficulties
ADD	Attention Deficit Disorder
ADHD	Attention Deficit and Hyperactive Disorder (Hyperkinetic Disorder)
ASC	Autistic Spectrum Conditions
ASP	Asperger Syndrome
AUT	Autism
BESD	Behavioural, Emotional and Social Difficulties
CCD	Complex Communication Difficulties
CLD	Complex Learning Difficulties
CP	Cerebral Palsy
D	Deaf
DEL	Delicate
DYS	Dyslexia
DYSP	Dyspraxia
EBD	Emotional and Behavioural Difficulties
EBSD	Emotional, Behavioural and/ or Social Difficulties
EPI	Epilepsy
GLD	General Learning Difficulties
HA	High Ability
HI	Hearing Impairment
HS	Hospital School
LD	Learning Difficulties
MLD	Moderate Learning Difficulties
MSI	Multi-sensory Impairment
OCD	Obsessive Compulsive Disorder
PD	Physical Difficulties
PH	Physical Impairment
Phe	Partially Hearing
PMLD	Profound and Multiple Learning Difficulties
PNI	Physical Neurological Impairment
PRU	Pupil Referral Unit
SCD	Social and Communication Difficulties
SCLD	Severe and Complex Learning Difficulties
SEBD	Severe Emotional and Behavioural Disorders
SEBN	Social, Emotional and Behavioural Needs
SLD	Severe Learning Difficulties
SLI	Specific Language Impairment
SPLD	Specific Learning Difficulties
SP&LD	Speech and Language Difficulties
SLCN	Speech Language & Communication Needs
VIS	Visually Impaired

Key to Symbols

Type of school:

Boys' school

Girls' school

International school

School offers:

A levels

Residential

Entrance at 16+

Vocational qualifications

Learning support

This is a DfE approved independent or non-maintained school under section 41 of the Children and Families Act 2014 or section 342 of the 1996 Education Act

Please note: Unless otherwise indicated, all schools are coeducational day schools. Single-sex and boarding schools will be indicated by the relevant icon.

Central & West

Bath & North-East Somerset

Rookery Radstock
Wells Road, Radstock, Bath, Bath & North-East Somerset BA3 3RS
Tel: 01761 438611
Age range: 18–25
No. of pupils: 27
Special needs catered for: ASC, ASP
🔞 🏛

Bristol

Aurora Hedgeway School
Rookery Lane, Pilning, Bristol BS35 4JN
Tel: 01454 632532
Age range: 7–19
Special needs catered for: ASC, ASP, AUT, LD, SCD
🔞

Buckinghamshire

Cambian Bletchley Park School
Whaddon Way, Bletchley, Milton Keynes, Buckinghamshire MK3 7EB
Tel: 01908 048380
Age range: 7–19
No. of pupils: 60
Special needs catered for: ASC, ASP, AUT, BESD, EBD, SCD
🔞

Oxfordshire

LVS OXFORD
For further details see p. 68
Spring Hill Road, Begbroke, Oxfordshire OX5 1RX
Tel: 01865 595170
Email: enquiries@lvs-oxford.org.uk
Website: www.lvs-oxford.org.uk
Head Teacher: Mrs Louisa Allison-Bergin
Age range: 11–19
No. of pupils: 58
Special needs catered for: ASC, ASP, AUT
🔞

Swalcliffe Park School Trust
Swalcliffe, Banbury, Oxfordshire OX15 5EP
Tel: 01295 780302
Age range: B11–19
No. of pupils: 45
Special needs catered for: ADHD, ASC, BESD, DYS, DYSP, MLD, SP&LD
🧍 🏛 🔞 ✔

West Berkshire

PRIOR'S COURT SCHOOL
For further details see p. 66
Hermitage, Thatcham, West Berkshire RG18 9NU
Tel: 01635 247202/245914
Email: mail@priorscourt.org.uk
Website: www.priorscourt.org.uk
Director of Education and Learning: Sue Piper
Age range: 5–19
No. of pupils: 65 VIth23
Special needs catered for: ASC, AUT, CLD, EPI, MLD, SCLD
🏛 ✔

Wiltshire

Farleigh Further Education College Swindon
Fairview House, 43 Bath Road, Old Town, Swindon, Wiltshire SN1 4AS
Tel: 01793 719500
Age range: 16–25
No. of pupils: 63
Special needs catered for: ASP, LD
🔞 🏛

Stratford Lodge
4 Park Lane, Castle Road, Salisbury, Wiltshire SP1 3NP
Tel: 0800 138 1184
Age range: 16–19
Special needs catered for: ADHD, ASC, ASP
🏛 🔞

East

Cambridgeshire

Gretton School
Manor Farm Road, Girton, Cambridge, Cambridgeshire CB3 0RX
Tel: 01223 277438
Age range: 5–19
No. of pupils: 100 VIth12
Special needs catered for: ASC, ASP, AUT
Ⓐ 🏛 🔞 ✔

On Track Training Centre
Enterprise House, Old Field Lane, Wisbech, Cambridgeshire PE13 2RJ
Tel: 01945 580898
Age range: 11–18
Special needs catered for: ADHD, ASP, EBD
🔞 ✔

Park House
Wisbech Road, Thorney, Peterborough, Cambridgeshire PE6 0SA
Tel: 01733 271187
Age range: 4–16
Special needs catered for: AUT
✔

The Beeches Independent School
218 Dogsthorpe Road, Peterborough, Cambridgeshire PE1 3PB
Tel: 01733 344448
Age range: G10–18
Special needs catered for: AUT
🔞

Essex

NAS ANDERSON SCHOOL
For further details see p. 69
Luxborough Lane, Chigwell, Essex IG7 5AB
Email: theandersonschool@nas.org.uk
Website: www.andersonschool.org.uk
Principal: Gary Simm
Age range: 11–19
No. of pupils: 78
Special needs catered for: ASC, ASP, AUT
🏛 🔞

The Yellow House School
1 Alderford Street, Sible Hedingham, Halstead, Essex CO9 3HX
Tel: 01787 462504
Age range: 13–17
No. of pupils: 11
Special needs catered for: ADHD, ASP, EBD
✔

Hertfordshire

NAS RADLETT LODGE SCHOOL
For further details see p. 70
Harper Lane, Radlett, Hertfordshire WD7 9HW
Tel: 01923 854922
Email: radlett.lodge@nas.org.uk
Website: www.radlettlodgeschool.org.uk
Principal: Jeremy Keeble
Age range: 4–19
No. of pupils: 55
Special needs catered for: ASC, ASP, AUT
🏛 🔞 ✔

Norfolk

Acorn Park
Mill Road, Banham, Norwich, Norfolk NR16 2HU
Tel: 01953 888656
Age range: 6–19
Special needs catered for: ASC, AUT, CLD, EPI, LD, MLD, SCD, SCLD, SLD, SPLD
🏛 🔞

Aurora Eccles School
Quidenham, Quidenham, Norfolk NR16 2NZ
Tel: 01953 887217
Age range: 5–19
No. of pupils: 150
Fees: Day £6,945–£11,370
FB £16,740–£19,785
Special needs catered for: ASC, ASP, AUT, DYS, LD, MLD, SCD
🧍 🏛 £ ✎ 🔞 ✔

East Midlands

Derbyshire

High Grange School
Hospital Lane, Mickleover,
Derby, Derbyshire DE3 0DR
Tel: 01332 412777
Age range: 8–19
Special needs catered for:
ADHD, ASC, ASP, AUT
(A) (16+) (✓)

Leicestershire

Sketchley School
and Forest House
Manor Way, Sketchley, Burbage,
Leicestershire LE10 3HT
Tel: 01455 890 023
Age range: 8–19
No. of pupils: 30
Special needs catered for:
ASC, ASP, AUT
(16+) (✓)

Lincolnshire

Doulton House School
Main Street, Anwick, Sleaford,
Lincolnshire NG34 9SJ
Tel: 01526 831055
Age range: 11–18
No. of pupils: 8
Fees: Day £60,000
Special needs catered for: BESD
(16+)

Northamptonshire

Cambian Potterspury
Lodge School
Towcester, Northamptonshire
NN12 7LL
Tel: 0800 138 1184
Age range: B8–18
No. of pupils: 70
Special needs catered for:
ADD, ADHD, ASC, ASP, AUT, DYS,
DYSP, EBD, SCD, SEMH, SP&LD
(†) (♿) (16+) (✓)

Hill Farm College
c/o The Manor House,
Squires Hill, Rothwell,
Northamptonshire NN14 6BQ
Tel: 01536 711111
Age range: 14–19
No. of pupils: 12
Special needs catered for:
ADHD, ASC, ASP
(♿) (16+)

Rutland

Wilds Lodge School
Stamford Road, Empingham,
Rutland LE15 8QQ
Tel: 01780 767254
Age range: 5–18
Special needs catered for:
ASC, MLD, SEMH
(16+)

Greater London

Kent

BASTON HOUSE SCHOOL
For further details see p. 71
Baston Road, Hayes,
Bromley, Kent BR2 7AB
Tel: 020 8462 1010
Email: info@
bastonhouseschool.org.uk
Website:
www.bastonhouseschool.org.uk
Headteacher: Mr Greg Sorrell
Age range: 5–19 years
Special needs catered for:
ASC, AUT, LD, MLD
(16+)

Middlesex

HILLINGDON
MANOR SCHOOL
For further details see p. 72
The Manor, Harlington Road,
Hillingdon, Middlesex UB8 3HD
Tel: 01895 813679
Email: enquiries@
hmschool.org.uk
Website: www.hillingdon
manorschool.org.uk
Secondary Headteacher: Mr
Richard McCabe
Age range: 3–19 years
Special needs catered for:
ASC, AUT, LD, MLD
(16+)

NAS SYBIL ELGAR
SCHOOL
For further details see p. 73
Havelock Road, Southall,
Middlesex UB2 4NY
Tel: 020 8813 9168
Email: sybil.elgar@nas.org.uk
Website:
www.sybilelgarschool.org.uk
Principal: Chloe Phillips
Age range: 4–22
No. of pupils: 90
Special needs catered for:
ASC, ASP, AUT
(♿) (16+) (✓)

Options West London
Community College
The Courtyard Campus, Church
Rd, Hayes, Middlesex UB3 2UH
Tel: 0208 573 7419
Age range: 16+
Special needs catered for:
ASC, ASP, AUT
(16+)

Surrey

Link Secondary
Day School
82-86 Croydon Road, Beddington,
Croydon, Surrey CR0 4PD
Tel: 020 8688 7691
Age range: 11–19
No. of pupils: 48 VIth9
Special needs catered for:
ASC, ASP, SP&LD, SLI
(✓)

London

North London

Kestrel House School
104 Crouch Hill, London N8 9EA
Tel: 020 8348 8500
Age range: 5–16
Special needs catered for:
ASC, ASP, AUT
(✓)

The Holmewood School
88 Woodside Park Road,
London N12 8SH
Tel: 020 8920 0660
Age range: 7–19
Special needs catered for:
ASC, ASP, AUT, SP&LD
(IB) (16+) (✓)

TreeHouse School
Woodside Avenue, London N10 3JA
Tel: 020 8815 5424
Age range: 3–19
No. of pupils: 67
Special needs catered for:
ASC, AUT
(16+) (✓)

South-East London

Riverston School
63-69 Eltham Road, Lee
Green, London SE12 8UF
Tel: 020 8318 4327
Age range: 9 months–19 years
No. of pupils: 215
Special needs catered for:
ASC, ASP, AUT, LD
(♿) (£) (✎)

South-West London

Park House School
48 North Side, Wandsworth
Common, London SW18 2SL
Tel: 020 3031 9700
Age range: 4–13
Special needs catered for:
ASC, ASP, AUT, SCD
(✓)

Priory Lodge School
Priory Lane, London SW15 5JJ
Tel: 020 8392 4410
Age range: 5–19
No. of pupils: 40
Special needs catered for:
ADHD, ASC, ASP, AUT, LD
(16) (✓)

The Chelsea Group of Children
The Hall, Waynflete Street,
London SW18 3QG
Tel: 020 8946 8330
Age range: 4–8
Special needs catered for: ADHD, ASP, AUT, LD, MLD, SP&LD, SPLD
(✓)

Tram House School
520 Garratt Lane, London SW17 0NY
Tel: +44 (0)20 3031 9707
Age range: 14–19
Special needs catered for:
ASC, ASP, AUT

North-East

Durham

Hurworth House School
Westfield Drive, Hurworth,
Darlington, Durham DL2 2AD
Tel: 01325 729 080
Age range: 7–19
No. of pupils: 30
Special needs catered for:
AUT, BESD, EBD
(16)

Tyne & Wear

Ashbrooke School
Ashbrooke Road, Sunderland,
Tyne & Wear SR2 7JA
Tel: 0191 6075610
Age range: 5–18
Special needs catered for:
ADHD, ASC, ASP, AUT, SEMH

ESPA College
6-7 The Cloisters, Ashbrooke,
Sunderland, Tyne & Wear SR2 7BD
Tel: 0191 510 2600
Age range: 16–25
No. of pupils: 100
Special needs catered for:
ASC, ASP, AUT
(🏛)

Thornhill Park School
21 Thornhill Park, Sunderland,
Tyne & Wear SR2 7LA
Tel: 0191 514 0659
Age range: 4–19
No. of pupils: 74
Fees: Day £33,752–£45,806
FB £117,433–£204,986
Special needs catered for:
ASC, ASP, AUT
(🏛) (16) (✓)

North-West

Cheshire

Inscape House School
Together Trust Campus,
Schools Hill, Cheadle,
Stockport, Cheshire SK8 1JE
Tel: 0161 283 4750
Age range: 5–19
No. of pupils: 100
Special needs catered for:
ASC, ASP, AUT, CLD
(16) (✓)

Royal College Manchester
Seashell Trust, Stanley Road,
Cheadle, Cheshire SK8 6RQ
Tel: 01616 100100
Age range: 19–25
No. of pupils: 70
Special needs catered for:
ASC, D, MSI, PD, PMLD, VIS
(🏛)

Royal School Manchester
Seashell Trust, Stanley Road,
Cheadle, Cheshire SK8 6RQ
Tel: 01616 100100
Age range: 2–19
No. of pupils: 45
Special needs catered for:
ASC, D, HI, MSI, PMLD
(16)

Cumbria

Lindeth College
Wigton Road, Carlisle,
Cumbria CA2 6LB
Tel: 01228 822649
Age range: 16–25
No. of pupils: 30
Special needs catered for:
MLD, SLD
(16) (🏛)

Greater Manchester

Fairfield House School
59 Warburton Lane, Partington,
Manchester, Greater
Manchester M31 4NL
Tel: 0161 7762827
Age range: 8–19
Special needs catered for: ASC
(16) (✓)

Great Howarth
Rochdale, Greater
Manchester OL12 9HJ
Tel: 01706 631 804
Age range: 7–18
Special needs catered for: ASC,
ASP, AUT, BESD, EBD, SEMH

Lancashire

Aurora Brambles East School
Woodlands, Holly Tree Close,
Darwen, Lancashire BB3 2NG
Tel: 01254 706 600
Age range: B10–16
Special needs catered for: ADHD,
ASC, ASP, AUT, DYS, MLD, SEMH
(♿)

Bracken School
1 Harbour Lane, Warton,
Preston, Lancashire PR4 1YA
Tel: 01772 631531
Age range: G11–16
No. of pupils: 5
Special needs catered for:
ADHD, DYS, MLD
(♿)

Oliver House School
Hallgate, Astley Village,
Chorley, Lancashire PR7 1XA
Tel: 01257 220 011
Age range: 6–19
No. of pupils: 28
Special needs catered for:
ASC, ASP, AUT, LD
(🏛) (16) (✓)

Red Rose School
28-30 North Promenade,
St Annes on Sea, Lytham St
Annes, Lancashire FY8 2NQ
Tel: 01253 720570
Age range: 5–16
Special needs catered for:
ASC, DEL, SPLD
(✓)

Rossendale School
Bamford Road, Ramsbottom,
Bury, Lancashire BL0 0RT
Tel: 01706 822779
Age range: 8–18
Special needs catered for:
ADD, ADHD, ASC, ASP, AUT,
BESD, CLD, DYS, DYSP, EBD, EPI,
HA, SCD, SEMH, SLD, SPLD
(A) (🏛) (✓)

Trax Academy
1 Stuart Road, Bredbury,
Stockport, Lancashire SK6 2SR
Tel: 0161 483 1505
Age range: 11–18
No. of pupils: 30
Special needs catered for:
ADHD, EBD
(16) (✓)

Westmorland School
Weldbank Lane, Chorley,
Lancashire PR7 3NQ
Tel: 01257 278899
Age range: 5–11
Special needs catered for:
ADHD, ASC, ASP, AUT, BESD,
MLD, SEMH, SP&LD, SPLD
(✓)

Merseyside

Arden College
40 Derby Road, Southport,
Merseyside PR9 0TZ
Tel: 01704 534 433
Age range: 16–25
No. of pupils: 53
Special needs catered for: ASC, LD
(16) (🏛)

Lakeside School
Naylors Road, Huyton, Liverpool, Merseyside L27 2YA
Tel: 0151 4877211
Age range: 5–13
Special needs catered for: ADD, ADHD, ASC, ASP, AUT, BESD, CLD, DEL, DYS, DYSP, EPI, HA, HI, LD, MLD, PH, SCD, SEMH, SP&LD, SPLD, SLI, VIS
(✓)

Peterhouse School for Pupils with Autism & Asperger's Syndrome
Preston New Road, Southport, Merseyside PR9 8PA
Tel: 01704 506682
Age range: 5–19
No. of pupils: 47 VIth23
Fees: Day £38,190
WB £90,896 FB £120,045
Special needs catered for: ASC, ASP, AUT
(☎) (16+) (✓)

WEST KIRBY SCHOOL AND COLLEGE
For further details see p. 74
Meols Drive, West Kirby, Wirral, Merseyside CH48 5DH
Tel: 0151 632 3201
Website: www.wkrs.co.uk
Principal: Mr Iain Sim
Age range: 5–19
No. of pupils: 87
Special needs catered for: ADHD, ASC, ASP, AUT, BESD, SCD, SEMH, SLI
(☎) (✓)

South-East

Berkshire

Heathermount, The Learning Centre
Devenish Road, Ascot, Berkshire SL5 9PG
Tel: 01344 875101
Age range: 5–19
No. of pupils: 25
Special needs catered for: ASC, ASP, AUT
(16+) (✓)

NAS THAMES VALLEY SCHOOL
For further details see p. 77
Conwy Close, Tilehurst, Reading, Berkshire RG30 4BZ
Tel: 0118 9424 750
Email: thames.valley@nas.org.uk
Website: www.thames valleyschool.org.uk
Principal: David Stewart
Age range: 5–16
No. of pupils: 50
Special needs catered for: ASC, ASP, AUT

East Sussex

Rookery Hove
22-24 Sackville Gardens, Hove, East Sussex BN3 4GH
Tel: 01273 202 520
Age range: 18–35
No. of pupils: 13
Special needs catered for: ASC, ASP
(16+) (☎)

Step by Step School for Autistic Children
Neylands Farm, Grinstead Lane, Sharpethorne, East Sussex RH19 4HP
Tel: 01342 811852
Age range: 4–11
No. of pupils: 12
Special needs catered for: AUT
(✓)

Sussex Dyslexia College
Basement, Brighthelm Centre, North Rd, Brighton BN1 1YD
Tel: 01273 569109
Special needs catered for: DYS

Hampshire

Grateley House School
Pond Lane, Grateley, Andover, Hampshire SP11 8TA
Tel: 0800 138 1184
Age range: 9–19
Special needs catered for: ASC, ASP
(☎) (16+) (✓)

Hill House School
Rope Hill, Boldre, Lymington, Hampshire SO41 8NE
Tel: 0800 138 1184
Age range: 11–19
Special needs catered for: ASC, AUT, SCD, SCLD, SLD
(☎) (16+) (✓)

Southlands School
Vicars Hill, Boldre, Lymington, Hampshire SO41 5QB
Tel: 0800 138 1184
Age range: B7–19
Special needs catered for: ASC, ASP
(🚹) (☎) (16+) (✓)

Tadley Court School
Tadley Common Road, Tadley, Basingstoke, Hampshire RG26 3TB
Tel: 0118 981 7720
Age range: 5–19
No. of pupils: 67
Special needs catered for: ASC, ASP, AUT
(☎) (16+) (✓)

Kent

Blue Skies School
126 Maidstone Road, Chatham, Kent ME4 6DQ
Tel: 01634 357770
Age range: 11–19
No. of pupils: 17
Special needs catered for: ASC, ASP, AUT
(16+) (✓)

NAS HELEN ALLISON SCHOOL
For further details see p. 76
Longfield Road, Meopham, Kent DA13 0EW
Tel: 01474 814878
Email: helen.allison@nas.org.uk
Website: www.helenallisonschool.org.uk
Principal: Kim McConnell
Age range: 5–19
No. of pupils: 77
Special needs catered for: ASC, ASP, AUT
(☎) (16+) (✓)

The Quest School
The Hop Farm, Maidstone Road, Paddock Wood, Tonbridge, Kent TN12 6PY
Tel: 01732 522700
Age range: 4–14
No. of pupils: 8
Special needs catered for: AUT, EBD
(✓)

Surrey

Aurora Redehall School
Redehall Rd, Smallfield, Horley, Surrey RH6 9QA
Tel: 01342 778650
Age range: 6–16
Special needs catered for: ASC, ASP, AUT, SCD

Eagle House School (Mitcham)
224 London Road, Mitcham, Surrey CR4 3HD
Tel: 020 8687 7050
Age range: 4–11
Special needs catered for: ASC, ASP, AUT, MLD, SCD, SLD
(✓)

Eagle House School (Sutton)
95 Brighton Road, Sutton, Surrey SM2 5SJ
Tel: 020 8661 1419
Age range: 11–19
Special needs catered for: AUT
(16+) (✓)

Jigsaw CABAS® School
Building 20, Dunsfold Park, Stovolds Hill, Cranleigh, Surrey GU6 8TB
Tel: 01483 273874
Age range: 4–19
No. of pupils: VIth17
Fees: Day £49,900–£52,732
Special needs catered for: ASC, AUT
(16+) (✓)

Papillon House School
Pebble Close, Tadworth, Surrey KT20 7PA
Tel: 01372 363663
Age range: 4–16
Fees: Day £45,000
Special needs catered for: ASC, AUT
(✓)

Unsted Park School and Sixth Form
Munstead Heath Road, Godalming, Surrey GU7 1UW
Tel: 01483 892 061
Age range: 7–19
No. of pupils: 55
Special needs catered for: ASC, ASP, AUT
(☎) (16+) (✓)

West Sussex

LVS HASSOCKS
For further details see p. 75
London Road, Sayers Common, Hassocks, West Sussex BN6 9HT
Tel: 01273 832901
Email: office@lvs-hassocks.org.uk
Website: www.lvs-hassocks.org.uk
Head Teacher: Ms Terry Kelly
Age range: 11–19
No. of pupils: 55
Special needs catered for: ASC, ASP, AUT
(16+)

Slindon College
Slindon House, Slindon, Arundel,
West Sussex BN18 0RH
Tel: 01243 814320
Age range: B8–18 years
No. of pupils: 80 VIth17
Fees: Day £7,053
WB £10,445 FB £10,445
Special needs catered for:
ADHD, ASC, AUT, DYS, DYSP

South-West

Cornwall

**Three Bridges
Education Centre**
East Hill, Blackwater, Truro,
Cornwall TR4 8EG
Tel: 01872 561010
Age range: 11–19
No. of pupils: 8
Special needs catered for:
ASC, ASP, AUT

Devon

Acorn School
Little Oak, Knowstone, South
Molton, Devon EX36 4SA
Tel: 01271 859720
Age range: 11–16
Special needs catered for:
BESD, EBD, SEMH

**Devon Education and
Children's Services**
Bere Alston, Yelverton,
Devon PL20 7EX
Tel: 01822 840379
Age range: 7–19
No. of pupils: 63
Special needs catered for:
ADHD, ASC, ASP, AUT, BESD, CLD,
EBD, GLD, MLD, SCD, SCLD

Dorset

Cambian Wing College
126 Richmond Park Road,
Bournemouth, Dorset BH8 8TH
Tel: 0800 138 1184
Age range: B16–25
No. of pupils: 46
Special needs catered for:
ASC, ASP

Portfield School
Parley Lane, Christchurch,
Dorset BH23 6BP
Tel: 01202 573808
Age range: 3–19
No. of pupils: 59
Special needs catered for:
ASC, AUT

Purbeck View School
Northbrook Road, Swanage,
Dorset BH19 1PR
Tel: 0800 138 1184
Age range: 7–19
Special needs catered for:
ASC, AUT

The Forum School
Shillingstone, Blandford
Forum, Dorset DT11 0QS
Tel: 0800 138 1184
Age range: 7–19
Special needs catered for:
ASC, AUT

Somerset

3 Dimensions
Chardleigh House, Chardleigh
Green, Wadeford, Chard,
Somerset TA20 3AJ
Tel: 01460 68055
Age range: 7–25
No. of pupils: 16
Special needs catered for:
ADHD, AUT, LD, SEMH

Farleigh College Mells
Newbury, Nr Mells, Frome,
Somerset BA11 3RG
Tel: 01373 814980
Age range: 11–19
No. of pupils: 52
Special needs catered for: ADD,
ADHD, ASC, ASP, AUT, DYS, DYSP

**Farleigh Further Education
College Frome**
North Parade, Frome,
Somerset BA11 2AB
Tel: 01373 475470
Age range: 16–19
No. of pupils: 87
Special needs catered for: ASP, LD

North Hill House School
Fromefield, Frome,
Somerset BA11 2HB
Tel: 01373 466 222
Age range: B6–19
No. of pupils: 62
Special needs catered for:
ADD, ADHD, ASC, ASP, AUT

West Midlands

Shropshire

CRUCKTON HALL
For further details see p. 78
Cruckton, Shrewsbury,
Shropshire SY5 8PR
Tel: 01743 860206
Email: robert.arrowsmith@
cruckton.com
Website: www.cruckton.com
Head Teacher: Robert
Arrowsmith
Age range: B8–19
No. of pupils: 80
Special needs catered for:
ADD, ADHD, ASP, AUT, BESD,
DYS, EBD, PMLD, SEMH, SPLD,

OPTIONS HIGFORD
For further details see p. 81
Higford Hall, Higford, Shifnal,
Shropshire TF11 9ET
Tel: 01952 630600
Email: info@optionsautism.co.uk
Website:
www.optionsautism.co.uk
Headteacher: Ms Anne Adams
Age range: 8–19 years
Special needs catered for: ASC,
AUT, CLD, LD, MLD, SCLD,

Staffordshire

Aurora Hanley School
Cambrian Way, off Eaves Lane,
Bucknall, Staffordshire ST2 8PQ
Tel: 01782 973737
Age range: 6–19
Special needs catered for:
ASC, ASP, AUT, LD, SCD

**NAS CHURCH
LAWTON SCHOOL**
For further details see p. 80
Cherry Tree Avenue, Church
Lawton, Stoke-on-Trent,
Staffordshire ST7 3EL
Tel: 01270 877601
Email: church.lawton@
nas.org.uk
Website: www.church
lawtonschool.org.uk
Principal: Paul Scales
Age range: 4–19
No. of pupils: 60
Special needs catered for:
ASC, AUT,

Social interaction difficulties (Autism, ASC & ASP)

OPTIONS TRENT ACRES
For further details see p. 82
Alrewas Road, Kings Bromley,
Staffordshire DE13 7HR
Tel: 01543 473772
Email: info@optionsautism.co.uk
Website:
www.optionsautism.co.uk
Headteacher: Ms Melanie
Callaghan-Lewis
Age range: 8–18 years
Special needs catered for: ASC,
ASP, AUT, CLD, LD, MLD, SCLD,
16+

Priory Highfields
9 & 11 Highfields Road, Chasetown,
Burntwood, Staffordshire WS7 4QR
Tel: 01543 672 173
Age range: 18–25
No. of pupils: 10
Special needs catered for: ASC
16+

Rugeley School
Blithbury Road, Blithbury, Rugeley,
Staffordshire WS15 3JQ
Tel: 01889 504 400
Age range: 5–19
No. of pupils: 48
Special needs catered for:
ASC, ASP, AUT, MLD, SLD
16+ ✓

Strathmore College
Unit 7 Imex Centre, Technology
Park, Stoke-on-Trent,
Staffordshire ST4 8LJ
Tel: 01782 647380
Age range: 16–25
No. of pupils: 37
Special needs catered for: ASC,
ASP, BESD, CLD, GLD, LD, MLD, SLD
16+

Warwickshire

Avon Park School
St John's Avenue, Rugby,
Warwickshire CV22 5HR
Tel: 01788 524448
Age range: 5–16
Special needs catered for: ADD,
ADHD, ASC, ASP, AUT, BESD, CLD,
DYSP, LD, SCD, SEMH, SP&LD

West Midlands

**QUEEN ALEXANDRA
COLLEGE (QAC)**
For further details see p. 83
Court Oak Road,
Harborne, Birmingham,
West Midlands B17 9TG
Tel: 0121 428 5050
Email: info@qac.ac.uk
Website: www.qac.ac.uk
Principal: Hugh J Williams
Age range: 16+
No. of pupils: 250
Special needs catered for:
ADD, ADHD, ASC, ASP, AUT,
BESD, CLD, CP, D, DYS, DYSP,
EBD, EPI, GLD, HA, HI, LD, MLD,
MSI, PD, Phe, PH, PNI, SCD,
SCLD, SLD, SP&LD, SPLD, SLI, VIS,
£

The Island Project School
Diddington Hall, Diddington Lane,
Meriden, West Midlands CV7 7HQ
Tel: 01675 442588
Age range: 6–19
Special needs catered for:
ASC, AUT
✓

Yorkshire & Humberside

Lincolnshire

OPTIONS BARTON
For further details see p. 87
Barrow Road, Barton-upon-
Humber, Lincolnshire DN18 6DA
Tel: 01652 631280
Email: info@optionsautism.co.uk
Website:
www.optionsautism.co.uk
Headteacher: Mr Ed Watkins
Age range: 8–19 years
Special needs catered for:
ASC, AUT, LD, MLD
16+

North Lincolnshire

Demeter House School
Bigby Street, Brigg, North
Lincolnshire DN20 8EF
Tel: 01652 654251
Age range: B5–14
No. of pupils: 5
Special needs catered for:
ADD, EBD
✓

South Yorkshire

**FULLERTON HOUSE
COLLEGE**
For further details see p. 85
Tickhill Square, Denaby,
Doncaster, South
Yorkshire DN12 4AR
Tel: 01709 861663
Email: enquiries@
hesleygroup.co.uk
Website:
www.hesleygroup.co.uk
General Manager: Heidi
Dugdale-Dawkes
Age range: 18–25
No. of pupils: 12
Special needs catered for:
ASC, ASP, AUT, CLD, DYS, DYSP,
GLD, LD, MLD, SCLD, SLD, SPLD

**FULLERTON HOUSE
SCHOOL**
For further details see p. 84
Tickill Square, Denaby,
Doncaster, South
Yorkshire DN12 4AR
Tel: 01709 861663
Email: enquiries@
hesleygroup.co.uk
Website: www.fullerton
houseschool.co.uk
General Manager: Heidi
Dugdale-Dawkes
Age range: 8–19
Special needs catered for:
ASC, ASP, AUT, CLD, DYS, DYSP,
GLD, LD, MLD, SCLD, SLD, SPLD
16+ ✓

**NAS ROBERT
OGDEN SCHOOL**
For further details see p. 86
Clayton Lane, Thurnscoe,
Rotherham, South
Yorkshire S63 0BG
Tel: 01709 874443
Email: robert.ogden@nas.org.uk
Website:
www.robertogdenschool.org.uk
Principal: Lorraine Dormand
Age range: 5–19
No. of pupils: 127
Special needs catered for:
ASC, ASP, AUT
16+ ✓

WILSIC HALL COLLEGE
For further details see p. 85
Wadworth, Doncaster,
South Yorkshire DN11 9AG
Tel: 01302 856382
Email: enquiries@
hesleygroup.co.uk
Website:
www.hesleygroup.co.uk
General Manager: Heidi
Dugdale-Dawkes
Age range: 18–25
No. of pupils: 8
Special needs catered for:
ASC, ASP, AUT, CLD, DYS, DYSP,
GLD, LD, MLD, SCLD, SLD, SPLD

WILSIC HALL SCHOOL
For further details see p. 88
Wadworth, Doncaster,
South Yorkshire DN11 9AG
Tel: 01302 856382
Email: enquiries@
hesleygroup.co.uk
Website:
www.wilsichallschool.co.uk
Head: Geoff Turner
Age range: 11–19
No. of pupils: 32
Special needs catered for:
ASC, ASP, AUT, CLD, DYS, DYSP,
GLD, LD, MLD, SCLD, SLD, SPLD
16+ ✓

Scotland

Aberdeenshire

Troup House School
Gamrie, Banff, Aberdeenshire
AB45 3JN
Tel: 01261 851 584
Age range: 8–16+
No. of pupils: 12
Special needs catered for:
AUT, BESD

East Ayrshire

**NAS DALDORCH
HOUSE SCHOOL**
For further details see p. 89
Sorn Road, Catrine, East
Ayrshire KA5 6NA
Tel: 01290 551666
Email: daldorch@nas.org.uk
Website: www.daldorch
houseschool.org.uk
Principal: Bernadette Casey
Age range: 8–21
Special needs catered for:
ASC, ASP, AUT

South Lanarkshire

**NAS Daldorch
Satellite School**
St Leonards, East Kilbride,
South Lanarkshire G74
Tel: 01355 246242
Age range: 5–19
No. of pupils: 5
Special needs catered for:
ASC, ASP, AUT

Wales

Carmarthenshire

Coleg Elidyr
Rhandirmwyn, Llandovery,
Carmarthenshire SA20 0NL
Tel: 01550 760400
Age range: 18–25
No. of pupils: 43
Special needs catered for:
ADD, ADHD, ASC, ASP, AUT,
BESD, CLD, DEL, DYSP, EBD, EPI,
GLD, LD, MLD, Phe, SCD, SLD

Flintshire

OPTIONS KINSALE
For further details see p. 90
Kinsale Hall, Llanerch-y-Mor,
Holywell, Flintshire CH8 9DX
Tel: 01745 562500
Email: info@optionsautism.co.uk
Website:
www.optionsautism.co.uk
Headteacher: Mr Ian Roberts
Age range: 8–19 years
Special needs catered for:
ASC, AUT, CLD, LD, MLD, SCLD

Torfaen

Priory College South Wales
Coleg Gwent, Pontypool
Campus, Blaendare Road,
Pontypool, Torfaen NP4 5YE
Tel: 01495 762 609
Age range: 16–25
No. of pupils: 11
Special needs catered for:
ASC, ASP, LD

Vale of Glamorgan

Beechwood College
Hayes Road, Penarth, Vale
of Glamorgan CF64 5SE
Tel: 029 2053 2210
Age range: 16+
No. of pupils: 66
Special needs catered for:
ASC, ASP, SLD

Wrexham

Priory College North Wales
Ty Dewi Sant, Rhosddu
Road, Wrexham LL11 0ZX
Tel: 01978 340580
Age range: 16–25
No. of pupils: 5
Special needs catered for:
ASC, ASP, LD

Schools and colleges specialising in emotional, behavioural and/or social difficulties (EBSD)

Abbreviations

ACLD	Autism, Communication and Associated Learning Difficulties
ADD	Attention Deficit Disorder
ADHD	Attention Deficit and Hyperactive Disorder (Hyperkinetic Disorder)
ASC	Autistic Spectrum Conditions
ASP	Asperger Syndrome
AUT	Autism
BESD	Behavioural, Emotional and Social Difficulties
CCD	Complex Communication Difficulties
CLD	Complex Learning Difficulties
CP	Cerebral Palsy
D	Deaf
DEL	Delicate
DYS	Dyslexia
DYSP	Dyspraxia
EBD	Emotional and Behavioural Difficulties
EBSD	Emotional, Behavioural and/ or Social Difficulties
EPI	Epilepsy
GLD	General Learning Difficulties
HA	High Ability
HI	Hearing Impairment
HS	Hospital School
LD	Learning Difficulties
MLD	Moderate Learning Difficulties
MSI	Multi-sensory Impairment
OCD	Obsessive Compulsive Disorder
PD	Physical Difficulties
PH	Physical Impairment
Phe	Partially Hearing
PMLD	Profound and Multiple Learning Difficulties
PNI	Physical Neurological Impairment
PRU	Pupil Referral Unit
SCD	Social and Communication Difficulties
SCLD	Severe and Complex Learning Difficulties
SEBD	Severe Emotional and Behavioural Disorders
SEBN	Social, Emotional and Behavioural Needs
SLD	Severe Learning Difficulties
SLI	Specific Language Impairment
SPLD	Specific Learning Difficulties
SP&LD	Speech and Language Difficulties
SLCN	Speech Language & Communication Needs
VIS	Visually Impaired

Key to Symbols

Type of school:

(symbol)	Boys' school
(symbol)	Girls' school
(symbol)	International school

School offers:

(A)	A levels
(symbol)	Residential
(16+)	Entrance at 16+
(symbol)	Vocational qualifications
(symbol)	Learning support
(✓)	This is a DfE approved independent or non-maintained school under section 41 of the Children and Families Act 2014 or section 342 of the 1996 Education Act

Please note: Unless otherwise indicated, all schools are coeducational day schools. Single-sex and boarding schools will be indicated by the relevant icon.

Central & West

Buckinghamshire

Benjamin College
4 Wren Path, Fairford Leys,
Aylesbury, Buckinghamshire
HP19 7AR
Tel: 01296 483584
Special needs catered for: BESD

Gloucestershire

Cotswold Chine School
Box, Stroud, Gloucestershire
GL6 9AG
Tel: 01453 837550
Age range: 9–19
No. of pupils: 48
Special needs catered for:
ADD, ADHD, ASP, AUT, DYS,
DYSP, EBD, EPI, MLD, SP&LD

Oxfordshire

Action for Children Parklands Campus
Chardleigh House, Near Appleton,
Abingdon, Oxfordshire OX13 5QB
Tel: 01865 390436
Age range: 11–19
No. of pupils: 7 VIth2
Fees: Day £50,000 FB £192,000
Special needs catered for: ADD,
ADHD, ASC, ASP, AUT, BESD,
EBD, LD, MLD, SEMH, SPLD

Chilworth House School
Thame Road, Wheatley, Oxford,
Oxfordshire OX33 1JP
Tel: 01844 339077
Age range: 4–11
No. of pupils: 29
Special needs catered for:
ADHD, ASC, ASP, AUT, BESD,
EBD, MLD, SCD, SEMH, SLD

Chilworth House Upper School
Grooms Farm, Thame Road,
Wheatley, Oxfordshire OX33 1JP
Tel: 01844 337720
Age range: 11–18
Special needs catered for: ADD,
ADHD, ASC, ASP, AUT, BESD,
DEL, GLD, HI, LD, MLD, Phe, SCD,
SCLD, SEMH, SP&LD, SPLD

HILLCREST PARK SCHOOL
For further details see p. 93
Southcombe, Chipping Norton,
Oxford, Oxfordshire OX7 5QH
Tel: 01608 644621
Email: info@hillcrestcs.co.uk
Website: www.hillcrest
childrensservices.co.uk
Headteacher: Mr
David Davidson
Age range: 7–18 years
No. of pupils: 28
Special needs catered for:
ADD, ADHD, ASC, AUT,
BESD, EBD, SCD, SEMH

Mulberry Bush School
Standlake, Witney,
Oxfordshire OX29 7RW
Tel: 01865 300202
Age range: 5–12
No. of pupils: 36
Special needs catered for: EBD

West Berkshire

HILLCREST NEW BARN SCHOOL
For further details see p. 92
The Long Barn, Welford,
Newbury, West
Berkshire RG20 8HZ
Tel: 01488 505145
Email: info@hillcrestcs.co.uk
Website: www.hillcrest
childrensservices.co.uk
Headteacher: Ms Alice Anstee
Age range: 6–16 years
No. of pupils: 20
Special needs catered for: ADD,
ADHD, BESD, EBD, SCD, SEMH

East

Bedfordshire

Walnut Tree Lodge School
Wilden Road, Bedford,
Bedfordshire MK44 2PY
Tel: 01234 772081
Age range: 11–16
Special needs catered for: EBD

Cambridgeshire

Cambian Home Tree School
172 March Road, Friday Bridge,
Wisbech, Cambridgeshire PE14 0LP
Tel: 01945 660988
Age range: 12–18
No. of pupils: 20
Special needs catered for:
EBD, SEMH

Cambian Wisbech School
The Old Sessions House, 32
Somers Road, Wisbech,
Cambridgeshire PE13 1JF
Tel: 0800 138 1184
Age range: 7–17
No. of pupils: 40
Special needs catered for:
EBD, SEMH

Chartwell House School
Goodens Lane, Newton, Wisbech,
Cambridgeshire PE13 5HQ
Tel: 01945 870793
No. of pupils: 8
Fees: FB £67,600
Special needs catered for: DYS, EBD

The Old School House
March Road, Friday Bridge,
Wisbech, Cambridgeshire PE14 0HA
Tel: 01945 861114
Age range: B7–13
Special needs catered for: EBD

Essex

Cambian Essex School
Unit 13, Flitch Industrial Estate,
Chelmsford Road, Great
Dunmow, Essex CM6 1XJ
Tel: 0800 138 1184
Age range: 11–19
Special needs catered for: BESD

ESSEX FRESH START INDEPENDENT SCHOOL (EFS)
For further details see p. 94
Church Street, Witham,
Essex CM8 2JL
Tel: 01376 780088
Email: referrals@tces.org.uk
Website: www.tces.org.uk
Head Teacher: Cheryl Rutter
Age range: 7–19 years
Special needs catered for: ASC,
AUT, BESD, EBD, SEMH, SP&LD

Hopewell School
Harmony House, Baden Powell
Close, Dagenham, Essex RM9 6XN
Tel: 020 8593 6610
Age range: 5–18
Special needs catered for:
EBD, MLD, SEMH

Jacques Hall
Harwich Road, Bradfield,
Manningtree, Essex CO11 2XW
Tel: 01255 870311
Age range: 11–18
No. of pupils: 21
Special needs catered for:
ADHD, BESD, EBD, MLD, SEMH

The Ryes College & Community
New Road, Aldham,
Colchester, Essex CO6 3PN
Tel: 01787 372 611
Age range: 7–24
Special needs catered for:
ADD, ADHD, ASC, ASP, AUT,
BESD, EBD, SCD, SEMH

Norfolk

Avocet House
The Old Vicarage, School Lane,
Heckingham, Norfolk NR14 6QP
Tel: 01508 549320
Age range: B8–16
No. of pupils: 8
Special needs catered for:
EBD, SEMH, SPLD

Future Education
168b Motum Road, Norwich,
Norfolk NR5 8EG
Tel: 01603 250505
Age range: 14–16
Special needs catered for: BESD

Sheridan School
Thetford Road, Northwold,
Thetford, Norfolk IP26 5LQ
Tel: 01366 726 040
Age range: 8–17
No. of pupils: 40
Special needs catered for:
ASC, ASP, BESD, SPLD

Suffolk

Bramfield House School
Walpole Road, Bramfield,
Halesworth, Suffolk IP19 9AB
Tel: 01986 784235
Age range: B7–16
No. of pupils: 51
Special needs catered for:
ADD, ADHD, BESD, DEL, EBD
(†) (🏫) (✔)

On Track Education Centre (Mildenhall)
82E & F Fred Dannatt Road,
Mildenhall, Suffolk IP28 7RD
Tel: 01638 715555
Age range: 11–18
Special needs catered for: EBD
(16+) (✔)

East Midlands

Derbyshire

Eastwood Grange School
Milken Lane, Ashover, Chesterfield,
Derbyshire S45 0BA
Tel: 01246 590255
Age range: B9–16+
No. of pupils: 34
Special needs catered for: BESD
(†) (🏫) (✔)

Longdon Park School
Park Hill, Hilton Road, Egginton,
Derbyshire DE65 6GU
Tel: 01283 733 195
Age range: 7–18
Special needs catered for:
ASC, AUT, BESD, EBD, SEMH

The Linnet Independent Learning Centre
107 Mount Pleasant Road,
Castle Gresley, Swadlincote,
Derbyshire DE11 9JE
Tel: 01283 213989
Age range: 5–16
No. of pupils: 13
Fees: Day £74,250
Special needs catered for: ADD,
ADHD, ASC, ASP, BESD, CLD,
DEL, DYS, DYSP, EBD, GLD, LD,
MLD, SCD, SEMH, SP&LD, SPLD
(✔)

The Meadows
Beech Lane, Dove Holes,
Derbyshire SK17 8DJ
Tel: 01298 814000
Age range: 11–16
Special needs catered for: EBD
(✔)

Leicestershire

Gryphon School
Quorn Hall, Meynell Road,
Quorn, Leicestershire LE12 8BQ
Tel: 01509 414 338
Age range: 11–17
Special needs catered for: EBD
(✔)

Lewis Charlton Learning Centre
North Street, Ashby-De-La-
Zouch, Leicestershire LE65 1HU
Tel: 01530 560775
Age range: 11–16
No. of pupils: 20
Special needs catered for: EBD
(🏫) (✔)

Meadow View Farm School
c/o Brookland Farm House, Kirby
Road, Barwell, Leicestershire LE9 8FT
Tel: 01455 840 825
Age range: 6–11
Special needs catered for:
ASC, BESD, SCD
(✔)

Oakwood School
20 Main Street, Glenfield,
Leicester, Leicestershire LE3 8DG
Tel: 0116 2876218
Age range: 8–18
No. of pupils: 18
Special needs catered for: EBD
(✔)

Trinity College
Moor Lane, Loughborough,
Leicestershire LE11 1BA
Tel: 01509 218906
Age range: 9–16
No. of pupils: 36
Fees: Day £36,075
Special needs catered for:
EBD, MLD, SEMH
(✔)

Lincolnshire

Broughton House
Brant Broughton,
Lincolnshire LN5 0SL
Tel: 0800 138 1184
Age range: 16–25
Special needs catered for: AUT,
BESD, LD, SCD, SCLD, SEMH, SLD
(16+) (🏫)

Northamptonshire

Ashmeads School
Buccleuch Farm, Haigham
Hill, Burton Latimer, Kettering,
Northamptonshire NN15 5PH
Tel: 01536 725998
Age range: 11–16
No. of pupils: 12
Special needs catered for: EBD
(✔)

Belview Lodge
124b Midland Road,
Wellingborough,
Northamptonshire NN8 1NF
Tel: 01933 441877
Age range: 11–17
No. of pupils: 4
Special needs catered for: BESD
(✔)

Cambian Northampton School
67a Queens Park Parade,
Kingsthorpe, Northampton,
Northamptonshire NN2 6LR
Tel: 0800 138 1184
Age range: 11–18
No. of pupils: 24
Special needs catered for:
BESD, EBD, MLD, SEMH
(16+) (✔)

Thornby Hall School
Thornby Hall, Thornby,
Northampton,
Northamptonshire NN6 8SW
Tel: 01604 740001
Age range: 12–18
No. of pupils: 20
Fees: FB £106,177
Special needs catered for: EBD
(🏫) (16+) (✔)

Nottinghamshire

Freyburg School
The Poppies, Greenmile
Lane, Babworth,
Nottinghamshire DN22 8JW
Tel: 01777 709061
Age range: B11–16
Special needs catered for: BESD
(†) (✔)

Hope House School
Barnby Road, Newark,
Nottinghamshire NG24 3NE
Tel: 01636 700 380
Age range: 4–19
No. of pupils: 3
Fees: Day £135,000–£155,000
FB £160,000–£180,000
Special needs catered for:
ADD, ADHD, ASC, ASP, AUT,
BESD, DEL, EBD, SCD, SEMH
(16+) (✔)

Wings School, Nottinghamshire
Kirklington Hall, Kirklington, Newark,
Nottinghamshire NG22 8NB
Tel: 01636 817430
Age range: 9–17
Special needs catered for:
ADD, ADHD, ASP, BESD, EBD
(🏫) (✔)

Rutland

The Grange Therapeutic School
Knossington, Oakham,
Rutland LE15 8LY
Tel: 01664 454264
Age range: 8–17
No. of pupils: 75
Special needs catered for:
BESD, EBD, SEMH
(†) (🏫) (16+) (✔)

Greater London

Essex

Barnardos
Tanners Lane, Barkingside,
Ilford, Essex IG6 1QG
Tel: 020 8550 8822
Special needs catered for: AUT,
EBD, MLD, PMLD, SLD, SP&LD, SPLD

Middlesex

Unity School
62 The Ride, Hounslow,
Middlesex TW8 9LA
Age range: 11–16
No. of pupils: 4
Special needs catered for: EBD

Surrey

Cressey College
Croydon, Surrey CR0 6XJ
Tel: 0208 655 2798
Age range: 11–17
Special needs catered for:
BESD, EBD, SCD

Kingsdown Secondary School
112 Orchard Road, Sanderstead,
Croydon, Surrey CR2 9LQ
Tel: 020 8657 1200
Age range: 11–16
No. of pupils: 12
Special needs catered for:
ASC, ASP, EBD, SPLD

London

East London

EAST LONDON INDEPENDENT SCHOOL (ELIS)
For further details see p. 95
Stratford Marsh, Welfare
Road, London E15 4HT
Tel: 020 8555 6737
Email: referrals@tces.org.uk
Website: www.tces.org.uk
Head Teacher: Sandra Harrison
Age range: 7–19 years
Special needs catered for:
ASC, AUT, BESD, EBD, SEMH

Leaways School London
Theydon Road, Clapton,
London E5 9NZ
Tel: 020 8815 4030
Age range: 10–17
Special needs catered for: SEMH

North-West London

Gloucester House
The Tavistock Children's Day
Unit, 33 Daleham Gardens,
London NW3 5BU
Tel: 0207 794 3353
Age range: B5–12
Special needs catered for: BESD

South-East London

Cavendish School
58 Hawkstone Road, Southwark
Park, London SE16 2PA
Tel: 020 7394 0088
Age range: 11–16
No. of pupils: 42
Special needs catered for: EBD

Octavia House School, Vauxhall
Vauxhall Primary School, Vauxhall
Street, London SE11 5LG
Tel: 02036 514396 (Option:1)
Age range: 5–14
No. of pupils: 65
Special needs catered for: ADD,
ADHD, BESD, EBD, SCD, SEMH

Octavia House School, Walworth
Larcom House, Larcom
Street, London SE17 1RT
Tel: 02036 514396 (Option:2)
Special needs catered for: ADD,
ADHD, BESD, EBD, SCD, SEMH

West London

Insights School & Skills Academy
3-5 Alexandria Road,
Ealing, London W13 0NP
Tel: 020 8840 9099
Age range: 7–18
No. of pupils: 62
Special needs catered for: ADD,
ADHD, ASC, ASP, BESD, DYS,
EBD, GLD, MLD, SCD, SPLD

NORTH WEST LONDON INDEPENDENT SCHOOL (NWLIS)
For further details see p. 96
85 Old Oak Common Lane,
Acton, London W3 7DD
Tel: 020 8749 5403
Email: referrals@tces.org.uk
Website: www.tces.org.uk
Head Teacher: Katrina Medley
Age range: 7–19 years
No. of pupils: 69
Special needs catered for: ASC,
AUT, BESD, EBD, SEMH, SP&LD

North-East

Durham

Highcroft School
The Green, Cockfield, Bishop
Auckland, Durham DL13 5AG
Tel: 077 02916189
Age range: 11–16
No. of pupils: 3
Special needs catered for: BESD

Priory Pines House
Middleton St George,
Darlington, Durham DL2 1TS
Tel: 01325 331177
Age range: 7–16
No. of pupils: 16
Special needs catered for: EBD

East Riding of Yorkshire

Cambian Beverley School
Units 19 & 20, Priory Road
Industrial Estate, Beverley, East
Riding of Yorkshire HU17 0EW
Tel: 0800 138 1184
Age range: 10–18
Special needs catered for:
EBD, LD, SEMH

Hartlepool

Cambian Hartlepool School
Unit E, Sovereign Park, Brenda
Road, Hartlepool TS25 1NN
Tel: 0800 138 1184
Age range: 11–17
No. of pupils: 18
Special needs catered for: EBD

Northumberland

Cambois House School
Cambois, Blyth,
Northumberland NE24 1SF
Tel: 01670 857689
Age range: 11–16
No. of pupils: 8
Special needs catered for:
BESD, EBD

Tyne & Wear

Talbot House School
Hexham Road, Walbottle,
Newcastle upon Tyne,
Tyne & Wear NE15 8HW
Tel: 0191 229 0111
Age range: 7–18
No. of pupils: 40
Special needs catered for: ADD,
ADHD, ASC, BESD, EBD, MLD

Thornbeck College
14 Thornhill Park, Sunderland,
Tyne & Wear SR2 7LA
Tel: 0191 5102038
Special needs catered for: ASP, AUT

West Yorkshire

Broadwood School
252 Moor End Road, Halifax,
West Yorkshire HX2 0RU
Tel: 01422 355925
Age range: 11–18
No. of pupils: 38
Special needs catered for: EBD
✓

Meadowcroft School
24 Bar Lane, Wakefield,
West Yorkshire WF1 4AD
Tel: 01924 366242
Age range: 5–19
Special needs catered for:
ASC, AUT, BESD, EBD, SEMH
(16) ✓

North-West

Cheshire

Halton School
33 Main Street, Halton Village,
Runcorn, Cheshire WA7 2AN
Tel: 01928 589810
Age range: 7–14
No. of pupils: 14
Special needs catered for: EBD
✓

High Peak School
Mudhurst Lane, Higher Disley,
Stockport, Cheshire SK12 2AP
Tel: 01663 721 731
Age range: 9–19
Special needs catered for: SEMH
(🏛)

Hope Corner Academy
70 Clifton Road, Runcorn,
Cheshire WA7 4TD
Tel: 01928 580860
Age range: 14–16
Special needs catered for:
ASC, BESD, MLD

Cumbria

APPLETREE SCHOOL
For further details see p. 97
Natland, Kendal,
Cumbria LA9 7QS
Tel: 01539 560253
Email: clair.davies@
appletreeschool.co.uk
Website: www.appletree
treatmentcentre.co.uk
Head of Education: Mr R
Davies BEd, MSpEd
Age range: 6–12
Special needs catered for: ADD,
ADHD, BESD, DEL, DYS, DYSP, EBD,
GLD, HA, LD, MLD, SCD, SEMH
(🏛) ✓

Cambian Whinfell School
110 Windermere Road,
Kendal, Cumbria LA9 5EZ
Tel: 0800 138 1184
Age range: B11–19
No. of pupils: 14
Special needs catered for:
ASC, AUT, BESD, EBD, SEMH
(🧍)(🏛)(16) ✓

Eden Grove School
Bolton, Appleby, Cumbria CA16 6AJ
Tel: 01768 361346
Age range: 8–19
No. of pupils: 65
Special needs catered for:
ADHD, ASP, AUT, BESD, CP, DYS,
EBD, EPI, MLD, PH, SP&LD
(🏛)(16) ✓

Eden Park Academy
119 Warwick Road, Carlisle,
Cumbria CA1 1JZ
Tel: 01228 537 609
Age range: 11–16
No. of pupils: 6
Special needs catered for: EBD

Fell House School
Grange Fell Road, Grange-
Over-Sands, Cumbria LA11 6AS
Tel: 01539 535926
Age range: 7–12
No. of pupils: 8
Special needs catered for: EBD
(🏛) ✓

KIRBY MOOR SCHOOL
For further details see p. 98
Longtown Road, Brampton,
Cumbria CA8 2AB
Tel: 016977 42598
Email: info@nlcs.uk.com
Website:
www.nlcs.uk.com/our-school/
Headteacher: Mrs
Catherine Garton
Age range: B7–18
Special needs catered for:
ADHD, ASC, AUT,
BESD, EBD, SEMH
(🧍)(🏛)(16) ✓

Oversands School
Witherslack, Grange-Over-
Sands, Cumbria LA11 6SD
Tel: 01539 552397
Age range: 8–19
Special needs catered for:
ADHD, ASC, ASP, AUT, BESD,
EBD, MLD, SEMH, SPLD
(🧍)(🏛) ✓

Underley Garden
Kirkby Lonsdale, Carnforth,
Cumbria LA6 2DZ
Tel: 01524 271569
Age range: 9–19
No. of pupils: 43
Special needs catered for:
ADD, ADHD, ASP, SLD, SP&LD
(🏛) ✓

Wings School, Cumbria
Whassett, Milnthorpe,
Cumbria LA7 7DN
Tel: 01539 562006
Age range: 11–17
Special needs catered for:
ADD, ADHD, ASP, BESD, EBD
(🏛) ✓

Greater Manchester

Acorns School
19b Hilbert Lane, Marple, Stockport,
Greater Manchester SK6 7NN
Tel: 0161 449 5820
Age range: 5–17
No. of pupils: 40
Special needs catered for: EBD
✓

Ashcroft School
Together Trust Campus,
Schools Hill, Cheadle, Greater
Manchester SK8 1JE
Tel: 0161 283 4832
Age range: 8–18
No. of pupils: 81
Special needs catered for:
BESD, EBD, SEMH
✓

Cambian Birch House School
98-100 Birch Lane, Longsight,
Manchester, Greater
Manchester M13 0WN
Tel: 0800 138 1184
Age range: 11–19
No. of pupils: 22
Special needs catered for:
BESD, EBD, SEMH
(16) ✓

Cambian Chesham House School
Chesham House, Thrush Drive,
Bury, Greater Manchester BL9 6JD
Tel: 0800 138 1184
Age range: 10–18
No. of pupils: 20
Special needs catered for:
BESD, EBD, SEMH
✓

Cambian Tyldesley School
Shuttle Street, Tyldesley, Leigh,
Greater Manchester M29 8BS
Tel: 01942 877660
Age range: 11–19
No. of pupils: 34
Special needs catered for: EBD,
GLD, LD, SCLD, SEMH, SLD
✓

Lime Meadows
73 Taunton Road, Ashton-Under-
Lyne, Greater Manchester OL7 9DU
Tel: 0161 3399412
Age range: B14–19
No. of pupils: 5
Special needs catered for: EBD
(🧍)(🏛)(16) ✓

Nugent House School
Carr Mill Road, Billinge, Wigan,
Greater Manchester WN5 7TT
Tel: 01744 892551
Age range: B7–19
No. of pupils: 65
Fees: Day £63,036–£84,048
Special needs catered for: EBD
(🧍)(🏛)(16) ✓

Reddish Hall School
Denstone Road, Reddish,
Stockport, Greater
Manchester SK5 6UY
Tel: 0161 442 1197
Special needs catered for:
BESD, EBD, SEMH

St. John Vianney School
Rye Bank Road, Firswood, Stretford,
Greater Manchester M16 0EX
Tel: 0161 881 7843
Age range: 4–19
No. of pupils: 80
Fees: Day £7,155
Special needs catered for: MLD
(16) ✓

Lancashire

Aurora Brambles School
159 Longmeanygate, Midge Hill,
Leyland, Lancashire PR26 7TB
Tel: 01772 454 826
Age range: B9–16
Special needs catered for: ASC,
ASP, AUT, DYS, EBD, MLD, SEMH
(🧍) ✓

Aurora Keyes Barn School
Station Road, Salwick, Preston,
Lancashire PR4 0YH
Tel: 01772 673 672
Age range: 5–12
Special needs catered for: EBD
✦

Belmont School
Haslingden Road, Rawtenstall,
Rossendale, Lancashire BB4 6RX
Tel: 01706 221043
Age range: B5–16
No. of pupils: 70
Special needs catered for:
ADD, ADHD, ASC, ASP, AUT,
BESD, DEL, EBD, SCD, SEMH
✦ ✓

Cambian Red Rose School
Meadow Lane, Bamber Bridge,
Preston, Lancashire PR5 8LN
Tel: 01772 281140
Age range: 5–18
No. of pupils: 30
Special needs catered for:
ADHD, BESD, EBD, SEMH
✓

Cedar House School
Bentham, Lancaster,
Lancashire LA2 7DD
Tel: 015242 61149
Age range: 7–18
No. of pupils: 63
Special needs catered for:
ADD, ADHD, ASC, ASP, BESD,
DYSP, EBD, EPI, GLD, LD, MLD,
SCD, SEMH, SP&LD, SPLD
✦ ✓

Crookhey Hall School
Crookhey Hall, Garstang
Road, Cockerham, Lancaster,
Lancashire LA2 0HA
Tel: 01524 792618
Age range: B10–17
No. of pupils: 64
Special needs catered for: ADD,
ADHD, BESD, DEL, EBD, SCD, SEMH
✦ ✓

Cumberland School
Church Road, Bamber Bridge,
Preston, Lancashire PR5 6EP
Tel: 01772 284435
Age range: 11–18
Special needs catered for: ADHD,
ASC, ASP, BESD, MLD, SEMH, SP&LD
✓

Elland House School
Unit 7, Roman Road, Royton,
Lancashire OL2 5PJ
Tel: 0161 6283600
Age range: 11–16
Special needs catered for: BESD
✓

Learn 4 Life
Quarry Bank Community Centre,
364 Ormskirk Road, Tanhouse,
Skelmersdale, Lancashire WN8 9AL
Tel: 01695 768960
Age range: 11–16
No. of pupils: 4
Special needs catered for:
ADD, ADHD, ASC, ASP, AUT,
BESD, DYS, EBD, GLD, SCD
✓

Moorland View
Manchester Road, Dunnockshaw,
Burnley, Lancashire BB11 5PQ
Tel: 01282 431144
Age range: 11–16
No. of pupils: 12
Special needs catered for: EBD
✓

Oakfield House School
Station Road, Salwick, Preston,
Lancashire PR4 0YH
Tel: 01772 672630
Age range: 5–12
No. of pupils: 23
Special needs catered for: ASC,
AUT, BESD, EBD, SEMH, SLD

Roselyn House School
Moss Lane, Off Wigan Road,
Leyland, Lancashire PR25 4SE
Tel: 01772 435948
Age range: 11–16
No. of pupils: 21
Special needs catered for: AUT, EBD
✓

Waterloo Lodge School
Preston Road, Chorley,
Lancashire PR6 7AX
Tel: 01257 230894
Age range: 11–18
No. of pupils: 45
Fees: Day £29,649
Special needs catered for: ADD,
ADHD, BESD, DEL, EBD, SCD, SEMH
✦ ✓

Merseyside

Clarence High School
West Lane, Freshfield,
Merseyside L37 7AS
Tel: 01704 872151
Age range: 7–17
Special needs catered for: EBD
✦ ✓

Olsen House School
85-87 Liverpool Rd, GT. Crosby,
Liverpool, Merseyside L23 5TD
Tel: 0151 924 0234
Age range: 9–16
Special needs catered for: SEMH

Warrington

Chaigeley
Thelwall, Warrington WA4 2TE
Tel: 01925 752357
Age range: B8–16
No. of pupils: 75
Special needs catered for:
ADD, ADHD, ASC, ASP, AUT,
BESD, DYS, EBD, GLD, HA, LD,
MLD, SCD, SEMH, SLD, SP&LD
✦ ✦ ✓

Cornerstones
2 Victoria Road, Grappenhall,
Warrington WA4 2EN
Tel: 01925 211056
Age range: B7–18
No. of pupils: 11
Special needs catered for: AUT, EBD
✦ ✦ 16 ✓

South-East

Berkshire

Beech Lodge School
13 Home Farm, Honey Lane,
Hurley, Berkshire SL6 6TG
Tel: 01628 879384
Special needs catered for:
ADHD, BESD, DYS, SEMH

Cressex Lodge (SWAAY)
Terrace Road South, Binfield,
Bracknell, Berkshire RG42 4DE
Tel: 01344 862221
Age range: B11–16
No. of pupils: 9
Special needs catered for: BESD
✦ ✓

High Close School
Wiltshire Road, Wokingham,
Berkshire RG40 1TT
Tel: 0118 9785767
Age range: 7–18
Special needs catered for: ADHD,
ASC, ASP, BESD, EBD, MLD
✦ 16 ✓

Buckinghamshire

Unity College
150 West Wycombe
Road, High Wycombe,
Buckinghamshire HP12 3AE
Tel: 077 02916189
Age range: 11–16
No. of pupils: 12
Special needs catered for:
BESD, MLD, SEMH
✓

East Sussex

Headstart School
Crouch Lane, Ninfield, Battle,
East Sussex TN33 9EG
Tel: 01424 893803
Age range: 7–18
Special needs catered for: BESD
16 ✓

Springboard Education Junior
39 Whippingham Road, St
Wilfred\'s Upper Hall, Brighton,
East Sussex BN2 3PS
Tel: 01273 885109
Age range: 7–13
Special needs catered for:
ADHD, BESD

The Lioncare School
87 Payne Avenue, Hove,
East Sussex BN3 5HD
Tel: 01273 734164
Age range: 7–16
No. of pupils: 15
Special needs catered for: ADHD,
ASC, BESD, EBD, MLD, SLD
✓

The Mount Camphill Community
Faircrouch Lane, Wadhurst,
East Sussex TN5 6PT
Tel: 01892 782025
Age range: 16–24
No. of pupils: 35
Special needs catered for: ADD,
ADHD, ASC, ASP, AUT, BESD, CLD,
CP, DEL, DYS, DYSP, EBD, EPI, GLD,
HI, LD, MLD, MSI, PD, Phe, PH,
PNI, SCD, SLD, SP&LD, SPLD, SLI
✦

Hampshire

Coxlease Abbeymead
Palace Lane, Beaulieu,
Hampshire SO42 7YG
Tel: 02380 283 633
Age range: 9–16
No. of pupils: 5
Special needs catered for: EBD
✦

Coxlease School
Clay Hill, Lyndhurst,
Hampshire SO43 7DE
Tel: 023 8028 3633
Age range: 9–18
No. of pupils: 55
Special needs catered for: BESD, LD
✦ 16 ✓

HILLCREST JUBILEE SCHOOL
For further details see p. 99
84-86 Jubilee Road,
Waterlooville,
Hampshire PO7 7RE
Tel: 02392 250963
Email: info@hillcrestcs.co.uk
Website: www.hillcrest
childrensservices.co.uk
Headteacher: Mr Tim Rogers
Age range: 8–16 years
No. of pupils: 22
Special needs catered for: ADD,
ADHD, BESD, EBD, SCD, SEMH

St Edward's School
Melchet Court, Sherfield English,
Romsey, Hampshire SO51 6ZR
Tel: 01794 885252
Age range: B9–18
No. of pupils: 38
Special needs catered for: ADD,
ADHD, ASC, ASP, AUT, BESD, DYS,
EBD, MLD, SCD, SEMH, SPLD

The Serendipity School
399 Hinkler Road, Southampton,
Hampshire SO19 6DS
Tel: 023 8042 2255
Age range: G9–19
No. of pupils: 15
Special needs catered for:
BESD, EBD, SEMH

Kent

Brewood School
86 London Road, Deal,
Kent CT14 9TR
Tel: 01304 363000
Age range: 11–18
No. of pupils: 12
Fees: Day £23,863
Special needs catered for: ADD,
ADHD, ASC, ASP, AUT, BESD, CLD,
DEL, EBD, EPI, GLD, HA, HI, LD,
MLD, PH, SCD, SLD, SP&LD, SLI

Browns School
Cannock House, Hawstead Lane,
Chelsfield, Orpington, Kent BR6 7PH
Tel: 01689 876816
Age range: 7–12
No. of pupils: 32
Special needs catered for:
EBD, SPLD

Caldecott Foundation School
Hythe Road, Smeeth,
Ashford, Kent TN25 6PW
Tel: 01303 815678
Age range: 5–18
No. of pupils: 56
Special needs catered for: EBD

Esland School
Units 12-13, Oare Gunpowder
Works, Off Bysingwood Road,
Faversham, Kent ME13 7UD
Tel: 01795 531730
Age range: 12–17
No. of pupils: 9
Special needs catered for: BESD

Greenfields School
Tenterden Road, Biddenden,
Kent TN27 8BS
Tel: 01580 292523
Age range: 5–11
No. of pupils: 13
Fees: Day £29,004
Special needs catered for: EBD

Heath Farm School
Egerton Road, Charing Heath,
Ashford, Kent TN27 0AX
Tel: 01233 712030
Age range: 5–18
No. of pupils: 70
Special needs catered for:
ASC, EBD, SEMH

Hope View School
Station Approach, Chilham,
Canterbury, Kent CT4 8EG
Tel: 01227 738000
Age range: 11–17
No. of pupils: 16
Special needs catered for:
ADD, ADHD, ASC, ASP, BESD

ISP Sittingbourne School
Church Street, Sittingbourne,
Kent ME10 3EG
Tel: 01795 422 044
Age range: 11–16
Special needs catered for:
BESD, SCD, SEMH

Learning Opportunities Centre
Ringwould Road, Ringwould,
Deal, Kent CT14 8DN
Tel: 01304 381906
Age range: 11–16
No. of pupils: 40
Special needs catered for: EBD

Little Acorns School
London Beach Farm,
Ashford Road, St Michael's,
Tenterden, Kent TN30 6SR
Tel: 01233 850422
Age range: 4–14
No. of pupils: 7
Special needs catered for: EBD

Meadows School and Meadows 16+
London Road, Southborough,
Kent TN4 0RJ
Tel: 01892 529144
Age range: 11–19
No. of pupils: 45
Special needs catered for: ADHD,
ASP, AUT, DYS, DYSP, EBD, MLD, SEMH

Ripplevale School
Chapel Lane, Ripple,
Deal, Kent CT14 8JG
Tel: 01304 373866
Age range: B9–16
No. of pupils: 30
Special needs catered for: ADD,
ADHD, ASC, ASP, AUT, BESD, CLD,
DYS, DYSP, EBD, GLD, HA, LD, MLD,
PMLD, SCD, SCLD, SP&LD, SPLD

Small Haven School
146 Newington Road,
Ramsgate, Kent CT12 6PT
Tel: 01843 597088
Age range: 5–13
No. of pupils: 8
Fees: Day £23,863
Special needs catered for: ADD,
ADHD, ASC, ASP, AUT, BESD, CLD,
DEL, EBD, EPI, GLD, HA, HI, LD,
MLD, PH, SCD, SLD, SP&LD, SLI

The Davenport School
Foxborough Hill, Eastry,
Sandwich, Kent CT13 0NY
Tel: 01843 589018
Age range: B7–11
Special needs catered for: EBD

The Lighthouse School
24 Clarendon Road,
Margate, Kent CT9 2QL
Tel: 01843 482043
Age range: 5–18
No. of pupils: 5
Special needs catered for:
BESD, SEMH

The Old Priory School
Priory Road, Ramsgate,
Kent CT11 9PG
Tel: 01843 599322
Age range: B10–15
Special needs catered for: EBD

WEST HEATH SCHOOL
For further details see p. 102
Ashgrove Road, Sevenoaks,
Kent TN13 1SR
Tel: 01732 460553
Email: admissions@
westheathschool.com
Website:
www.westheathschool.com
Principal: Mr James Nunns
Age range: 10–20
No. of pupils: 135
Fees: Day £52,500
Special needs catered for: ADD,
ADHD, ASC, ASP, BESD, DEL,
EBD, SCD, SEMH, SP&LD, SPLD

Surrey

Cornfield School
53 Hanworth Road, Redhill,
Surrey RH1 5HS
Tel: 01737 779578
Age range: G11–18
No. of pupils: 25
Special needs catered for: EBD

Grafham Grange School
Nr Bramley, Guildford,
Surrey GU5 0LH
Tel: 01483 892214
Age range: B10–19
Special needs catered for:
ADHD, ASC, BESD, EBD, SP&LD

West Sussex

Brantridge School
Staplefield Place, Staplefield,
Haywards Heath, West
Sussex RH17 6EQ
Tel: 01444 400228
Age range: B6–13
No. of pupils: 27
Special needs catered for:
ADHD, ASC, ASP, BESD, EBD, LD

Farney Close School
Bolney Court, Bolney,
West Sussex RH17 5RD
Tel: 01444 881811
Age range: 11–16
No. of pupils: 78
Fees: Day £55,222.10
Special needs catered for: ADHD,
ASP, DYS, EBD, MLD, SP&LD

HILLCREST SLINFOLD SCHOOL
For further details see p. 100
Stane Street, Slinfold, Horsham,
West Sussex RH13 0QX
Tel: 01403 790939
Email: info@hillcrestcs.co.uk
Website: www.hillcrest
childrensservices.co.uk/
hillcrest-slinfold-school
Headteacher: Mr John Stacey
Age range: B11–16 years
No. of pupils: 20
Special needs catered for:
ADD, ADHD, ASC, AUT,
BESD, EBD, SCD, SEMH

Muntham House School Ltd
Barns Green, Muntham Drive,
Horsham, West Sussex RH13 0NJ
Tel: 01403 730302
Age range: B8–18
No. of pupils: 51 VIth12
Special needs catered for:
ADD, ADHD, ASC, BESD, DYS,
EBD, MLD, SP&LD, SPLD

PHILPOTS MANOR SCHOOL
For further details see p. 101
West Hoathly, East Grinstead,
West Sussex RH19 4PR
Tel: 01342 810268
Email: info@
philpotsmanorschool.co.uk
Website: www.philpots
manorschool.co.uk
Education Co-ordinator: Mr
Darin Nobes BA (Hons),
PGCE, NPQH
Age range: 7–19
No. of pupils: 43
Fees: Day £65,000 WB £65,000
Special needs catered for:
ADD, ADHD, ASC, ASP, AUT,
BESD, DEL, DYS, EBD, EPI, GLD,
LD, MLD, SCD, SEMH, SP&LD

Springboard Education Senior
55 South Street, Lancing,
West Sussex BN15 8HA
Tel: 01903 605980
Age range: 11–18
No. of pupils: 10
Special needs catered for: ADD,
ADHD, ASC, ASP, AUT, BESD, EBD

South-West

Cornwall

Oak Tree School
Truro Business Park, Threemilestone,
Truro, Cornwall TR4 9NH
Tel: 01872 264 221
Age range: 8–16
Special needs catered for:
ASC, AUT, BESD, EBD, SEMH

Devon

Cambian Devon School
Intek House, 52 Borough Road,
Paignton, Devon TQ4 7DQ
Tel: 0800 138 1184
Age range: 10–18
No. of pupils: 30
Special needs catered for:
ASP, AUT, BESD, EBD, SEMH

Oakwood Court College
7/9 Oak Park Villas, Dawlish,
Devon EX7 0DE
Tel: 01626 864066
Age range: 16–25
Special needs catered for: ADHD,
ASP, DYS, DYSP, EBD, EPI, MLD, SLD

The Libra School
Edgemoor Court, South Radworthy,
South Molton, Devon EX36 3LN
Tel: 01598 740044
Age range: 8–18
Special needs catered for: EBD

Gloucestershire

Marlowe Education Unit
Hartpury Old School,
Gloucester Road, Hartpury,
Gloucestershire GL19 3BG
Tel: 01452 700855
Age range: 8–16
No. of pupils: 8
Special needs catered for:
EBD, MLD

Somerset

Cambian Somerset School
Creech Court Lane, Creech St.
Michael, Taunton, Somerset TA3 5PX
Tel: 0800 138 1184
Age range: 10–18
No. of pupils: 40
Special needs catered for:
EBD, SEMH

Inaura School
Moorview House, Burrowbridge,
Bridgwater, Somerset TA7 0RB
Tel: 01823 690211
Age range: 8–18
No. of pupils: 26
Fees: Day £53,990
Special needs catered for: ADHD,
ASC, BESD, CLD, EBD, LD, SCD

Newbury Manor School
Newbury, Mells, Nr. Frome,
Somerset BA11 3RG
Tel: 01373 814 980
Age range: 7–19
Special needs catered for:
ASC, ASP, AUT, SPLD

Phoenix Academy
Newton Road, North Petherton,
Somerset TA6 6NA
Tel: 01271 318 110
Age range: 11–16
Special needs catered for: EBD

Somerset Progressive School
Bath House Farm, West Hatch,
Taunton, Somerset TA3 5RH
Tel: 01823 481902
Age range: 9–19
No. of pupils: 20
Special needs catered for: EBD

The Marchant-Holliday School
North Cheriton, Templecombe,
Somerset BA8 0AH
Tel: 01963 33234
Age range: B5–13
No. of pupils: 38
Special needs catered for:
ADD, ADHD, ASC, ASP, BESD,
DYS, DYSP, EBD, SCD

Wiltshire

The Faringdon Centre
School Lane, Salisbury,
Wiltshire SP1 3YA
Tel: 01722 820 970
Age range: 11–16
No. of pupils: 8
Special needs catered for:
EBD, MLD

Wessex College
Wessex Lodge, Nunney Road,
Frome, Wiltshire BA11 4LA
Tel: 01373 453414
Age range: 11–16
No. of pupils: 6
Special needs catered for: EBD

West Midlands

Cheshire

Aidenswood
48 Parson Street, Congleton,
Cheshire CW12 4ED
Tel: 01260 281 353
Age range: B11–17
No. of pupils: 6
Special needs catered for:
EBD, MLD
(†) (‡) (✓)

Herefordshire

Cambian Hereford School
Coningsby Road, Leominster,
Herefordshire HR6 8LL
Tel: 0800 1381184
Age range: 11–19
No. of pupils: 20
Special needs catered for:
BESD, EBD, SEMH
(16) (✓)

Queenswood School
Callows Hills Farm, Hereford Road,
Ledbury, Herefordshire HR8 2PZ
Tel: 01531 670 632
Age range: 11–18
No. of pupils: 15
Special needs catered for: ADD,
ADHD, ASC, BESD, DYS, DYSP,
MLD, SEMH, SP&LD, SPLD
(‡) (16) (✓)

Shropshire

Care UK Children's Services
46 High Street, Church
Stretton, Shropshire SY6 6BX
Tel: 01694 724488
Age range: 10–18
No. of pupils: 24
Special needs catered for: EBD
(16)

HILLCREST SHIFNAL SCHOOL
For further details see p. 104
Lamledge Lane, Shifnal,
Shropshire TF11 8SD
Tel: 01952 468220
Email: info@hillcrestcs.co.uk
Website: www.hillcrest
childrensservices.co.uk
Headteacher: Mr David Coles
Age range: 7–19 years
No. of pupils: 55
Special needs catered for:
ADD, ADHD, BESD, EBD, SEMH,
(‡) (16)

Smallbrook School
Smallbrook Lodge,
Smallbrook Road, Whitchurch,
Shropshire SY13 1BX
Tel: 01948 661110
Age range: 11–19
No. of pupils: 15
Special needs catered for:
BESD, EBD, SEMH
(16) (✓)

Staffordshire

Bloomfield College
Bloomfield Road, Tipton,
Staffordshire DY4 9AH
Tel: 0121 5209408
Age range: 11–16
Special needs catered for: EBD
(✓)

Draycott Moor College
Draycott Old Road, Draycott-
in-the-Moors, Stoke-on-Trent,
Staffordshire ST11 9AH
Tel: 01782 399849
Age range: 11–16
Special needs catered for:
EBD, SCLD
(✓)

HILLCREST GLEBEDALE SCHOOL
For further details see p. 103
Grove Road, Heron Cross, Stoke-
on-Trent, Staffordshire ST4 3AY
Tel: 01782 320773
Email: info@hillcrestcs.co.uk
Website: www.hillcrest
childrensservices.co.uk
Headteacher: Ms Karen Caswell
Age range: 7–19 years
No. of pupils: 30
Special needs catered for: ADD,
ADHD, BESD, EBD, SCD, SEMH,
(‡) (16)

Longdon Hall School
Longdon Hall, Rugeley,
Staffordshire WS15 4PT
Tel: 01543 491051
Age range: 7–18
Special needs catered for:
BESD, EBD, SEMH
(16) (✓)

THE ROACHES INDEPENDENT SCHOOL
For further details see p. 105
Tunstall Road, Knypersley, Stoke-
on-Trent, Staffordshire ST8 7AB
Tel: 01782 523479
Website: www.caretoday.co.uk
Age range: 7–16
Special needs catered for:
BESD, EBD, SEMH,
(‡) (✓)

Warwickshire

Arc School Ansley
Ansley Lane, Ansley, Nuneaton,
Warwickshire CV10 9ND
Tel: 01676 543 810
Age range: 7–16
Special needs catered for:
ADHD, ASC, SEMH

Arc School Napton
Vicarage Road, Napton-on-the-
Hill, Warwickshire CV47 8NA
Tel: 01926 817 547
Age range: 7–16
Special needs catered for:
ADHD, ASC

Arc School Old Arley
Old Arley, Ansley, Nuneaton,
Warwickshire CV7 8NU
Tel: 01676 543200
Age range: 7–11
No. of pupils: 30
Special needs catered for: BESD
(‡) (✓)

Wathen Grange School
Church Walk, Mancetter,
Atherstone, Warwickshire CV9 1PZ
Tel: 01827 714454
Age range: 11–16
No. of pupils: 15
Special needs catered for: EBD
(✓)

West Midlands

Blue River Academy
Sara Park, 160 Herbert Road,
Small Heath, Birmingham,
West Midlands B10 0PR
Tel: 0121 753 1933
Age range: B14–16
Special needs catered for: BESD
(†) (✓)

Values Academy Birmingham
15 Key Hill, Hockley Hill,
Hockley, Birmingham, West
Midlands B18 5AQ
Tel: 0121 5230222
Age range: 11–17
No. of pupils: 25
Special needs catered for:
BESD, EBD, SEMH
(✓)

Yorkshire & Humberside

East Riding of Yorkshire

Horton House School
Hilltop Farm, Sutton Road,
Wawne, Kingston upon Hull, East
Riding of Yorkshire HU7 5YY
Tel: 01482 875191
Age range: 8–23
Fees: Day £25,000–£50,000
WB £75,000–£150,000 FB £180,000
Special needs catered for: ADD,
ADHD, ASC, ASP, AUT, BESD, CLD,
DYS, DYSP, EBD, EPI, GLD, LD, MLD,
SCD, SCLD, SEMH, SLD, SPLD
(‡) (✓)

North Yorkshire

Breckenbrough School
Sandhutton, Thirsk, North
Yorkshire YO7 4EN
Tel: 01845 587238
Age range: B9–19
No. of pupils: 49
Special needs catered for: ADD,
ADHD, ASP, BESD, DEL, DYS, EBD, HA
(†) (‡) (16) (✓)

Cambian Scarborough School
Unit 11, Plaxton Park
Industrial Estate, Cayton
Low Road, Scarborough,
North Yorkshire YO11 3BQ
Tel: 0800 138 1184
Age range: 8–18
No. of pupils: 18
Special needs catered for:
BESD, EBD, SEMH
(16) (✓)

Cambian Spring Hill School
Palace Road, Ripon, North
Yorkshire HG4 3HN
Tel: 0800 138 1184
Age range: 8–19
No. of pupils: 23
Special needs catered for:
ADHD, ASP, AUT, CP, DEL, DYS,
DYSP, EBD, EPI, MLD, SLD, SP&LD
(‡) (16) (✓)

Clervaux
Clow Beck Centre, Jolby
Lane, Croft-on-Tees, North
Yorkshire DL2 2TF
Tel: 01325 729860
Age range: 16–25+
Special needs catered for:
ASC, ASP, AUT, BESD, CLD

South Yorkshire

Brantwood Specialist School
1 Kenwood Bank, Nether Edge, Sheffield, South Yorkshire S7 1NU
Tel: 0114 258 9062
Age range: 7–19
Special needs catered for: ADD, ADHD, ASC, ASP, BESD, CLD, EBD, GLD, LD, MLD, PMLD, SCD, SCLD, SEMH, SPLD
16+ ✔

West Yorkshire

Denby Grange School
Stocksmoor Road, Midgley, Wakefield, West Yorkshire WF4 4JQ
Tel: 01924 830096
Age range: 11–17
No. of pupils: 36
Special needs catered for: EBD, SCD
✔

New Gables School
2 New Close Road, Shipley, West Yorkshire BD18 4AB
Tel: 01274 584705
Age range: 11–16
Special needs catered for: SEMH

The Grange School
2 Milner Way, Ossett, Wakefield, West Yorkshire WF5 9JE
Tel: 01924 378957
Age range: 7–14
No. of pupils: 12
Special needs catered for: BESD
✔

William Henry Smith School
Boothroyd, Brighouse, West Yorkshire HD6 3JW
Tel: 01484 710123
Age range: B8–19
No. of pupils: 64
Fees: Day £57,810 FB £70,435
Special needs catered for: ADD, ADHD, ASC, BESD, CLD, GLD, SCD, SEMH, SPLD
🚹 🏢 ✎ 16+ ✔

Northern Ireland

County Down

Camphill Community Glencraig
Craigavad, Holywood, County Down BT18 0DB
Tel: 028 9042 3396
Age range: 7–19
No. of pupils: 32
Fees: FB £66,500
Special needs catered for: ADHD, ASP, AUT, CP, DYSP, EBD, EPI, HI, MLD, PH, PMLD, SLD, SP&LD, SPLD, VIS
16+ 🏢 16+

Scotland

Edinburgh

Harmeny Education Trust Ltd
Harmeny School, Balerno, Edinburgh EH14 7JY
Tel: 0131 449 3938
Age range: 6–13
No. of pupils: 36
Special needs catered for: ADD, ADHD, ASP, DYS, EBD, SPLD
🏢

Fife

Falkland House School
Falkland Estate, Cupar, Fife KY15 7AE
Tel: 01337 857268
Age range: B5–18
No. of pupils: 30
Fees: FB £70,000
Special needs catered for: ADD, ADHD, ASP, BESD, DYS, EBD, EPI, SCD, SPLD
🚹 🏢 ✎ 16+

Hillside School
Hillside, Aberdour, Fife KY3 0RH
Tel: 01383 860731
Age range: B10–16
No. of pupils: 39
Fees: Day £10,830 FB £26,594–£58,959
Special needs catered for: DYS, EBD, SPLD
🚹 🏢

Starley Hall School
Aberdour Road, Burntisland, Fife KY3 0AG
Tel: 01383 860314
Age range: 10–16
No. of pupils: 48
Special needs catered for: EBD, MLD
🏢

North Lanarkshire

St Philip's School
10 Main Street, Plains, Airdrie, North Lanarkshire ML6 7SF
Tel: 01236 765407
Age range: B12–16
No. of pupils: 61
Special needs catered for: EBD
🚹 🏢

Perth & Kinross

Balnacraig School
Fairmount Terrace, Perth, Perth & Kinross PH2 7AR
Tel: 01738 636456
Age range: 12–16
No. of pupils: 24
Special needs catered for: BESD, EBD

Seamab School
Rumbling Bridge, Kinross, Perth & Kinross KY13 0PT
Tel: 01577 840307
Age range: 5–12
No. of pupils: 15
Special needs catered for: EBD
🏢

Renfrewshire

Kibble Education and Care Centre
Goudie Street, Paisley, Renfrewshire PA3 2LG
Tel: 0141 889 0044
Age range: 12–16
No. of pupils: 93
Special needs catered for: EBD, MLD, SCD, SLD, SPLD
🏢

Spark of Genius
Trojan House, Phoenix Business Park, Paisley, Renfrewshire PA1 2BH
Tel: 0141 587 2710
Age range: 5–18
No. of pupils: 120
Special needs catered for: ADHD, ASC, DYS, DYSP, EBD, SEMH
🏢

The Good Shepherd Secure/Close Support Unit
Greenock Road, Bishopton, Renfrewshire PA7 5PW
Tel: 01505 864500
Age range: G12–17
Special needs catered for: EBD, MLD
🚹 🏢

Stirling

Ballikinrain Residential School
Fintry Road, Balfron, Stirling G63 0LL
Tel: 01360 440244
Age range: B8–14
No. of pupils: 40
Special needs catered for: BESD
🚹 🏢

Snowdon School
31 Spittal Street, Stirling FK8 1DU
Tel: 01786 464746
Age range: G13–17
Special needs catered for: BESD
🚹 🏢

West Lothian

Moore House School
21 Edinburgh Road, Bathgate, West Lothian EH48 1EX
Tel: 01506 652312
Age range: 8–16
No. of pupils: 37
Special needs catered for: ADHD, EBD
🏢

Wales

Denbighshire

The Branas School
Branas Isaf, Llandrillo, Corwen, Denbighshire LL21 0TA
Tel: 01490 440545
Age range: B12–17
No. of pupils: 12
Special needs catered for: EBD
(符)

Monmouthshire

Talocher School
Talocher Farm, Wonastow Road, Monmouth, Monmouthshire NP25 4DN
Tel: 01600 740 777
Age range: 9–19
No. of pupils: 25
Special needs catered for: ADD, ADHD, BESD, DYS, DYSP, MLD, SEMH, SPLD
(符)(16)

Pembrokeshire

Marlowe St David's Education Unit
Pembroke House, Brawdy Business Park, Haverfordwest, Pembrokeshire SA62 6NP
Tel: 01437 721234
Age range: 8–17
No. of pupils: 7
Special needs catered for: EBD

Wrexham

Woodlands
27 Pentrefelyn Road, Wrexham LL13 7NB
Tel: 01978 262777
Age range: B11–18
No. of pupils: 14
Special needs catered for: ADD, ADHD, ASC, ASP, AUT, BESD, DYS, DYSP, EBD, GLD, HA, HI, LD, MLD, SCD, SLD
(符)

Schools and colleges specialising in learning difficulties (including dyslexia/SPLD)

Abbreviations

ACLD	Autism, Communication and Associated Learning Difficulties
ADD	Attention Deficit Disorder
ADHD	Attention Deficit and Hyperactive Disorder (Hyperkinetic Disorder)
ASC	Autistic Spectrum Conditions
ASP	Asperger Syndrome
AUT	Autism
BESD	Behavioural, Emotional and Social Difficulties
CCD	Complex Communication Difficulties
CLD	Complex Learning Difficulties
CP	Cerebral Palsy
D	Deaf
DEL	Delicate
DYS	Dyslexia
DYSP	Dyspraxia
EBD	Emotional and Behavioural Difficulties
EBSD	Emotional, Behavioural and/or Social Difficulties
EPI	Epilepsy
GLD	General Learning Difficulties
HA	High Ability
HI	Hearing Impairment
HS	Hospital School
LD	Learning Difficulties
MLD	Moderate Learning Difficulties
MSI	Multi-sensory Impairment
OCD	Obsessive Compulsive Disorder
PD	Physical Difficulties
PH	Physical Impairment
Phe	Partially Hearing
PMLD	Profound and Multiple Learning Difficulties
PNI	Physical Neurological Impairment
PRU	Pupil Referral Unit
SCD	Social and Communication Difficulties
SCLD	Severe and Complex Learning Difficulties
SEBD	Severe Emotional and Behavioural Disorders
SEBN	Social, Emotional and Behavioural Needs
SLD	Severe Learning Difficulties
SLI	Specific Language Impairment
SPLD	Specific Learning Difficulties
SP&LD	Speech and Language Difficulties
SLCN	Speech Language & Communication Needs
VIS	Visually Impaired

Key to Symbols

Type of school:

(symbol)	Boys' school
(symbol)	Girls' school
(symbol)	International school

School offers:

(A)	A levels
(symbol)	Residential
(16+)	Entrance at 16+
(symbol)	Vocational qualifications
(symbol)	Learning support
(✓)	This is a DfE approved independent or non-maintained school under section 41 of the Children and Families Act 2014 or section 342 of the 1996 Education Act

Please note: Unless otherwise indicated, all schools are coeducational day schools. Single-sex and boarding schools will be indicated by the relevant icon.

Central & West

Bristol

Aurora St Christopher's School
Westbury Park, Bristol BS6 7JE
Tel: 0117 973 6875
Age range: 5–19
Special needs catered for:
ASC, AUT, CLD, CP, EPI, PD, Phe,
PMLD, SCLD, SLD, SP&LD

Belgrave School
10 Upper Belgrave Road,
Clifton, Bristol BS8 2XH
Tel: 0117 974 3133
Age range: 5–13
Fees: Day £6,000
Special needs catered for: ADD,
DEL, DYS, DYSP, SP&LD, SLI

Bristol Dyslexia Centre
10 Upper Belgrave Road,
Clifton, Bristol BS8 2XH
Tel: 0117 973 9405
Special needs catered for:
DYS, DYSP, SLD

Sheiling School, Thornbury
Thornbury Park, Thornbury,
Bristol BS35 1HP
Tel: 01454 412194
Age range: 6–19
No. of pupils: 22
Fees: Day £66,419–£83,428
WB £125,931–£172,096
FB £140,578–£197,157
Special needs catered for: ADD,
ADHD, ASC, ASP, AUT, BESD, CLD,
CP, DEL, DYS, DYSP, EBD, EPI, GLD,
HA, HI, LD, MLD, MSI, PD, Phe, SCD,
SCLD, SEMH, SLD, SP&LD, SPLD, SLI

Buckinghamshire

MacIntyre Wingrave School
Leighton Road, Wingrave,
Buckinghamshire HP22 4PA
Tel: 01296 681274
Age range: 10–19
No. of pupils: 38
Fees: FB £182,000
Special needs catered for:
ASC, SCD, SLD

Gloucestershire

Bredon School
Pull Court, Bushley, Tewkesbury,
Gloucestershire GL20 6AH
Tel: 01684 293156
Age range: 7–18
Special needs catered for:
DYS, DYSP, SPLD

Cambian Southwick Park School
Gloucester Road, Tewkesbury,
Gloucestershire GL20 7DG
Tel: 0800 138 1184
Age range: 7–19
No. of pupils: 40
Special needs catered for: ASC,
AUT, CLD, DYSP, GLD, LD, MLD,
SCD, SCLD, SEMH, SLD, SP&LD, SLI

Ruskin Mill College
The Fisheries, Horsley,
Gloucestershire GL6 0PL
Tel: 01453 837502
Age range: 16–25
Special needs catered for: ADHD,
ASC, ASP, BESD, CLD, EBD, GLD, LD,
MLD, PMLD, SCD, SCLD, SEMH, SPLD

William Morris College
Eastington, Stonehouse,
Gloucestershire GL10 3SH
Tel: 01453 824025
Age range: 16–25
No. of pupils: 30
Special needs catered for:
ASP, AUT, DYSP, EBD, EPI, MLD

Oxfordshire

Bruern Abbey School
Chesterton, Bicester,
Oxfordshire OX26 1UY
Tel: 01869 242448
Age range: B7–13
No. of pupils: 44
Fees: Day £5,703 WB £7,791
Special needs catered for:
DYS, DYSP

The Unicorn School
20 Marcham Road, Abingdon,
Oxfordshire OX14 1AA
Tel: 01235 530222
Age range: 6–16 years
No. of pupils: 74
Fees: Day £19,500
Special needs catered for:
DYS, DYSP

Wiltshire

Calder House School
Thickwood Lane, Colerne,
Wiltshire SN14 8BN
Tel: 01225 743566
Age range: 6–13
No. of pupils: 48
Fees: Day £16,200
Special needs catered for: DEL,
DYS, DYSP, SP&LD, SPLD, SLI

Fairfield Farm College
Dilton Marsh, Westbury,
Wiltshire BA13 4DL
Tel: 01373 866066
Age range: 16–25
Special needs catered for: MLD

Tumblewood Project School
The Laurels, 4 Hawkeridge
Road, Heywood, Westbury,
Wiltshire BA13 4LF
Tel: 01373 824 466
Age range: G11–18
No. of pupils: 12
Special needs catered for:
ADHD, DYS, DYSP, LD

East

Cambridgeshire

Holme Court School
Abington Woods, Church
Lane, Little Abington,
Cambridgeshire CB21 6BQ
Tel: 01223 778030
Age range: 5–16
No. of pupils: 27
Special needs catered for: ADD,
ADHD, ASP, CLD, DYS, DYSP, GLD,
HA, LD, MLD, SCD, SP&LD, SPLD, VIS

Essex

Doucecroft School
Abbots Lane, Eight Ash Green,
Colchester, Essex CO6 3QL
Tel: 01206 771234
Age range: 3–19
No. of pupils: 46
Fees: Day £52,779–£54,291
WB £86,211–£88,211
Special needs catered for:
ASC, ASP, AUT

Woodcroft School
Whitakers Way, Loughton,
Essex IG10 1SQ
Tel: 020 8508 1369
Age range: 2–11
No. of pupils: 36
Special needs catered for:
ADD, ADHD, ASC, ASP, AUT,
CLD, CP, DEL, DYSP, EBD, EPI,
LD, MLD, MSI, PH, PMLD, SCLD,
SLD, SP&LD, SPLD, SLI, VIS

Hertfordshire

Egerton Rothesay School
Durrants Lane, Berkhamsted,
Hertfordshire HP4 3UJ
Tel: 01442 865275
Age range: 6–19
No. of pupils: 179
Fees: Day £15,555–£22,140
Special needs catered for:
ASC, AUT, DYS, DYSP, SP&LD

Lincolnshire

Kisimul Upper School
Acacia Hall, Shortwood
Lane, Friesthorpe, Lincoln,
Lincolnshire LN3 5AL
Tel: 01673 880022
Age range: 8–19
Special needs catered for: ASC, SLD

Norfolk

Copperfield School
22 Euston Road, Great
Yarmouth, Norfolk NR30 1DX
Tel: 01493 849 499
Age range: 11–16
No. of pupils: 12
Special needs catered for:
ADD, ADHD, ASP, BESD, CLD,
DYS, DYSP, EBD, GLD, LD, MLD,
SCD, SCLD, SEMH, SPLD

Suffolk

Centre Academy East Anglia
Church Road, Brettenham,
Ipswich, Suffolk IP7 7QR
Tel: 01449 736404
Age range: 4–19
Fees: Day £18,000–£25,875
WB £24,999–£36,225
Special needs catered for:
ADHD, ASP, CLD, DYS, DYSP,
GLD, HA, LD, SP&LD, SPLD
🏫 £ ✔

Riverwalk School
Chevington Close, Bury St
Edmunds, Suffolk IP33 3JZ
Tel: 01284 764280
Age range: 3–19
Special needs catered for: SCLD
16+

East Midlands

Derbyshire

Alderwasley Hall School & Sixth Form Centre
Alderwasley, Belper,
Derbyshire DE56 2SR
Tel: 01629 822586
Age range: 5–19
Fees: Day £62,900
WB £91,500 FB £179,500
Special needs catered for:
ADHD, ASC, ASP, AUT, DYSP, GLD,
HA, LD, SCD, SP&LD, SPLD, SLI
A 🏫 16+

Pegasus School
Caldwell Hall, Main Street,
Caldwell, Derbyshire DE12 6RS
Tel: 01283 761352
Age range: 8–19
Fees: Day £102,200
WB £230,100 FB £299,400
Special needs catered for: ADHD,
ASC, AUT, CLD, EPI, HI, LD, PMLD,
SCLD, SLD, SP&LD, SPLD, SLI, VIS
🏫 16+ ✔

Lincolnshire

KISIMUL SCHOOL
For further details see p. 108
The Old Vicarage, 61 High
Street, Swinderby, Lincoln,
Lincolnshire LN6 9LU
Tel: 01522 868279
Email: admissions@kisimul.co.uk
Website: www.kisimul.co.uk
Director of Education: Mr Danny
Carter BA(Hons), MA, MEd
Age range: 8–19
No. of pupils: 60
Special needs catered for:
ASC, AUT, CLD, EBD, EPI,
LD, MSI, PMLD, SCLD,
SEMH, SLD, SP&LD, SPLD
🏫 16+ ✔

Linkage College – Toynton Campus
Toynton All Saints, Spilsby,
Lincolnshire PE23 5AE
Tel: 01790 752499
Age range: 16–25
Special needs catered for: ADD,
ADHD, ASC, ASP, AUT, CLD, CP,
D, DEL, DYS, DYSP, EPI, GLD,
HI, LD, MLD, PD, Phe, PH, SCD,
SCLD, SLD, SP&LD, SPLD, VIS
16+ 🏫

Nottinghamshire

I CAN'S DAWN HOUSE SCHOOL
For further details see p. 110
Helmsley Road, Rainworth,
Mansfield, Nottinghamshire
NG21 0DQ
Tel: 01623 795361
Email: dawnhouse@
ican.notts.sch.uk
Website:
www.dawnhouseschool.org.uk
Principal: Jenny McConnell
Age range: 5–19
No. of pupils: 79
Special needs catered for:
ASP, CLD, DYS, DYSP, SCD,
SLD, SP&LD, SPLD
🏫 16+ ✔

Sutherland House - Continuing Education Centre
8 Clinton Avenue, Nottingham,
Nottinghamshire NG5 1AW
Tel: 0115 9693373
Age range: 11–19
Special needs catered for:
ASC, AUT
16+

Sutherland House School
Bath Street, Sneinton, Nottingham,
Nottinghamshire NG1 1DA
Tel: 0115 960 9263
Age range: 3–19
No. of pupils: 84
Fees: Day £41,525–£45,473
Special needs catered for:
ASC, ASP, AUT
16+ ✔

Greater London

Essex

St John's RC Special School
Turpins Lane, Woodford
Bridge, Essex IG8 8AX
Tel: 020 8504 1818
Age range: 5–19
No. of pupils: 100
Special needs catered for:
AUT, MLD, SLD, SP&LD
✔

Middlesex

Pield Heath House School
Pield Heath Road, Uxbridge,
Middlesex UB8 3NW
Tel: 01895 258507
Age range: 7–19
No. of pupils: 96
Special needs catered for:
MLD, SLD, SP&LD
🏫 16+ ✔

Surrey

Rutherford School
1A Melville Avenue, South
Croydon, Surrey CR2 7HZ
Tel: 020 8688 7560
Age range: 3–19
No. of pupils: 26
Fees: Day £50,400
Special needs catered for:
CP, D, EPI, HI, MSI, PD, Phe, PH,
PMLD, PNI, SLD, SP&LD, VIS
16+ ✔

THE LINK PRIMARY SCHOOL
For further details see p. 111
138 Croydon Road, Beddington,
Croydon, Surrey CR0 4PG
Tel: 020 8688 5239
Email: office@linkprim.co.uk
Website: www.linkprim.co.uk
Head Teacher: Mrs Sandy Turner
Age range: 4–11
No. of pupils: 50
Special needs catered for:
ASC, ASP, DYSP, GLD, LD,
MLD, SCD, SP&LD, SLI
✔

Blossom Lower School and Upper House (Motspur Park)
Station Road, Motspur Park,
New Malden, London KT3 6JJ
Tel: 020 8946 7348
Age range: 3–19
No. of pupils: 214
Special needs catered for:
ADD, ADHD, ASP, DYS,
DYSP, SCD, SP&LD, SPLD
(16+) (✓)

London

East London

Side by Side Kids School
9 Big Hill, London E5 9HH
Tel: 020 8880 8300
Age range: 2–16
No. of pupils: 60
Special needs catered for:
MLD, SLD, SP&LD
(✓)

North London

Limespring School
Park House, 16 High Road, East
Finchley, London N2 9PJ
Tel: 020 8444 1387
Age range: 7–11
Special needs catered for:
DYS, DYSP
(✓)

North-West London

Abingdon House School
Broadley Terrace, London NW1 6LG
Tel: 020 3750 5526
Age range: 5–16
Special needs catered for: ADD,
ADHD, ASP, DYS, DYSP, SP&LD, SPLD
(globe)(pencil)(✓)

BLOSSOM LOWER SCHOOL AND UPPER HOUSE
For further details see p. 112
1-5 Christopher Place, Chalton
Street, London NW1 1JF
Tel: 020 7383 3834
Email: admincp@
blossomhouseschool.co.uk
Website: www.blossom
houseschool.co.uk
Principal: Joanna Burgess OBE
Age range: 3–11
No. of pupils: 17
Special needs catered for:
ADD, ADHD, ASP, DYS,
DYSP, SCD, SP&LD, SPLD
(✓)

Kisharon School
1011 Finchley Road,
London NW11 7HB
Tel: 020 8455 7483
Age range: 4–19
No. of pupils: 35
Fees: Day £27,000–£42,000
Special needs catered for: ADD,
ADHD, ASC, ASP, AUT, BESD, CLD,
CP, D, DEL, DYS, DYSP, EBD, EPI,
GLD, HA, HI, LD, MLD, MSI, PD,
Phe, PH, PMLD, PNI, SCD, SCLD,
SEMH, SLD, SP&LD, SPLD, SLI, VIS
(✓)

South-East London

Octavia House School, Kennington
214b Kennington Road,
London SE11 6AU
Tel: 020 3651 4396 (Option:3)
Special needs catered for: ADD,
ADHD, BESD, EBD, SCD, SEMH

South-West London

Centre Academy London
92 St John's Hill, Battersea,
London SW11 1SH
Tel: 020 7738 2344
Age range: 9–19
Fees: Day £27,600–£40,100
Special needs catered for:
ADD, ADHD, ASC, ASP, AUT,
CLD, DYS, DYSP, HA, SP&LD
(£)(pencil)(16+)(✓)

Fairley House School
30 Causton Street,
London SW1P 4AU
Tel: 020 7976 5456
Age range: 5–16
No. of pupils: 203
Fees: Day £30,300
Special needs catered for:
DYS, DYSP, SPLD
(globe)(✓)

Frederick Hugh House
48 Old Church Street,
London SW3 5BY
Tel: 0207 349 8833
Age range: 10–16
Special needs catered for:
ADHD, ASC, AUT, CLD, CP,
DEL, DYSP, EPI, GLD, LD, MLD,
MSI, PD, SCD, SP&LD, SPLD
(✓)

Parayhouse School
Hammersmith and Fulham College,
Gliddon Road, London W14 9BL
Tel: 020 8741 1400
Age range: 7–16
No. of pupils: 46
Fees: Day £27,540
Special needs catered for: ADD,
BESD, CLD, CP, DEL, EBD, EPI, MLD,
Phe, SCD, SCLD, SLD, SP&LD
(✓)

The Dominie
55 Warriner Gardens,
Battersea, London SW11 4DX
Tel: 020 7720 8783
Age range: 6–13
No. of pupils: 30
Special needs catered for:
DYS, DYSP, SP&LD
(✓)

The Moat School
Bishops Avenue, Fulham,
London SW6 6EG
Tel: 020 7610 9018
Age range: 9–16
Fees: Day £28,800
Special needs catered for:
DYS, DYSP, SPLD
(globe)(pencil)(✓)

North-East

Northumberland

Cambian Dilston College
Dilston Hall, Corbridge,
Northumberland NE45 5RJ
Tel: 0800 138 1184
Age range: 16–25
No. of pupils: 60
Special needs catered for: ADD,
ADHD, ASC, ASP, AUT, BESD, CP,
DEL, EBD, EPI, GLD, LD, MLD, SCD,
SCLD, SEMH, SLD, SP&LD, SPLD
(bed)(16+)

Nunnykirk Centre for Dyslexia
Netherwitton, Morpeth,
Northumberland NE61 4PB
Tel: 01670 772685
Age range: 9–18
Special needs catered for:
ASC, DYS, SEMH, SPLD
(A)(bed)(pencil)(16+)(✓)

North-West

Cheshire

The David Lewis School
Mill Lane, Warford, Alderley
Edge, Cheshire SK9 7UD
Tel: 01565 640066
Age range: 14–19
No. of pupils: 20
Special needs catered for:
AUT, CP, EPI, HI, PD, PMLD,
SCD, SLD, SP&LD, SPLD, VIS
🏫 16+ ✓

Greater Manchester

Birtenshaw School (Bolton)
Darwen Road, Bolton, Greater
Manchester BL7 9AB
Tel: 01204 306043
Age range: 3–19
No. of pupils: 35 VIth25
Fees: Day £49,757–£71,084
Special needs catered for: ADD,
ADHD, ASC, ASP, AUT, CLD, CP,
DEL, EPI, GLD, HI, LD, MLD, MSI,
PD, Phe, PH, PMLD, PNI, SCD,
SCLD, SLD, SP&LD, SLI, VIS
🏫 16+ ✓

Bridge College
Openshaw Campus, Whitworth
Street, Manchester, Greater
Manchester M11 2GR
Tel: 0161 487 4293
Age range: 16–25
No. of pupils: 90
Special needs catered for: ASC,
AUT, CLD, PH, PMLD, SCD

Langdon College
9 Leicester Avenue, Salford,
Greater Manchester M7 4HA
Tel: 0161 740 5900
Age range: 16–25
Special needs catered for:
ASC, ASP, AUT, BESD, DYS, DYSP,
EBD, GLD, HI, LD, MLD, Phe, PH,
SCD, SP&LD, SPLD, SLI, VIS

Lancashire

Pontville
Black Moss Lane, Ormskirk,
Lancashire L39 4TW
Tel: 01695 578734
Age range: 5–19
Special needs catered for:
ADHD, ASC, ASP, CLD, MLD,
SCD, SEMH, SP&LD, SPLD, SLI
🏫 16+ ✓

Progress School
Gough Lane, Bamber Bridge,
Preston, Lancashire PR26 7TZ
Tel: 01772 334832
Age range: 7–19
No. of pupils: 17
Fees: WB £3,269 FB £170,000
Special needs catered for:
AUT, PMLD, SCLD, SLD
🏫 16+ ✓

Merseyside

Birtenshaw School (Merseyside)
82 Higher Lane, Liverpool L9 7AB
Tel: 0151 317 8277
Age range: 3–19
Special needs catered for:
ASC, MSI, PD, SCD
16+

Liverpool Progressive School
Rice Lane, Liverpool,
Merseyside L9 1NR
Tel: 0151 525 4004
Age range: 8–19
No. of pupils: 20
Special needs catered for: AUT, SLD
16+ ✓

Wargrave House School
449 Wargrave Road, Newton-le-
Willows, Merseyside WA12 8RS
Tel: 01925 224899
Age range: 5–19
No. of pupils: 70
Special needs catered for: ASP, AUT
🏫 16+ ✓

South-East

East Sussex

Frewen College
Brickwall, Rye Road, Northiam,
Rye, East Sussex TN31 6NL
Tel: 01797 252 494
Age range: 7–19
No. of pupils: 103
Fees: Day £13,686–£21,801
WB £21,078–£30,264
FB £21,078–£30,264
Special needs catered for:
DYS, DYSP, SP&LD, SPLD
🎨 🏫 £ ✎ ✓

Northease Manor School
Rodmell, Lewes, East Sussex BN7 3EY
Tel: 01273 472915
Age range: 10–17
No. of pupils: 95
Special needs catered for:
ADD, ADHD, ASC, ASP, DYS,
DYSP, SCD, SP&LD, SPLD
🎨 🏫 ✓

Owlswick School
Newhaven Road, Kingston,
Lewes, East Sussex BN7 3NF
Tel: 01273 473078
Age range: 10–17
Special needs catered for: ADD,
ADHD, ASC, ASP, BESD, DYS,
DYSP, EBD, GLD, LD, MLD, SCD
🏫 16+ ✓

ST JOHN'S SCHOOL & COLLEGE
For further details see p. 122
Business Centre, 17
Walpole Road, Brighton,
East Sussex BN2 0AF
Tel: 01273 244000
Email: admissions@st-johns.co.uk
Website: www.st-johns.co.uk
Principal & Chief Executive: Mr
Simon Charleton
Age range: 7–25
No. of pupils: 118
Fees: Day £50,000 FB £100,000
Special needs catered for:
ADD, ADHD, ASC, ASP, AUT,
BESD, CLD, CP, D, DEL, DYS,
DYSP, EBD, EPI, GLD, HA, LD,
MLD, PD, PNI, SCD, SCLD,
SEMH, SLD, SP&LD, SPLD, SLI
🏫 16+

Hampshire

Chiltern Tutorial School
Otterbourne New Hall,
Cranbourne Drive, Otterbourne,
Winchester, Hampshire SO21 2ET
Tel: 01962 717696
Age range: 7–12
No. of pupils: 20
Fees: Day £8,850
Special needs catered for:
DYS, DYSP
✓

Clay Hill School
Clay Hill, Lyndhurst,
Hampshire SO43 7DE
Tel: 023 8028 3633
Age range: 5–19
Special needs catered for: ASC, LD

Minstead Training Project
Minstead Lodge, Minstead,
Lyndhurst, Hampshire SO43 7FT
Tel: 023 80812254
Age range: 18+
No. of pupils: 14
Special needs catered for:
GLD, LD, MLD
16+

Sheiling College
Horton Road, Ashley, Ringwood,
Hampshire BH24 2EB
Tel: 01425 477488
Age range: 19–25
No. of pupils: 32
Special needs catered for: ASC,
AUT, CLD, EPI, GLD, LD, MLD,
SCD, SCLD, SLD, SP&LD, SPLD
🏫

Sheiling School
Horton Road, Ashley, Ringwood,
Hampshire BH24 2EB
Tel: 01425 477488
Age range: 6–19
No. of pupils: 31
Fees: Day £39,070
WB £88,260 FB £106,008
Special needs catered for: ASC,
AUT, CLD, EBD, EPI, GLD, LD, MLD,
SCD, SCLD, SLD, SP&LD, SPLD
16+ 🏫 16+ ✓

The Loddon School
Wildmoor Lane, Sherfield-
on-Loddon, Hook,
Hampshire RG27 0JD
Tel: 01256 884600
Age range: 8–19
No. of pupils: 26
Fees: FB £229,000
Special needs catered for:
ADD, ADHD, ASC, AUT, CLD,
EPI, SCLD, SLD, SP&LD
🏫 16+ ✓

Isle of Wight

ST CATHERINE'S SCHOOL
For further details see p. 119
Grove Road, Ventnor,
Isle of Wight PO38 1TT
Tel: 01983 852722
Email: general@
stcatherines.org.uk
Website:
www.stcatherines.org.uk
Principal: Mrs R Weldon
Age range: 7–19+
No. of pupils: 64 VIth33
Special needs catered for:
ADD, ADHD, ASC, ASP, AUT,
DYS, DYSP, SCD, SLD, SP&LD, SLI
🏫 16+ ✓

Kent

Great Oaks Small School
Ebbsfleet Farmhouse,
Ebbsfleet Lane, Minster,
Ramsgate, Kent CT12 5DL
Tel: 01843 822 022
Age range: 10–18
No. of pupils: 18 VIth3
Special needs catered for: SPLD
(A) (✓)

West London

Trinity School & College
10-13 New Road, Rochester,
Kent ME1 1BG
Tel: 01634 812233
Age range: 6–25
Special needs catered for:
ASC, ASP, AUT, DYS, DYSP
(✓) (16)

Surrey

KISIMUL SCHOOL –
WOODSTOCK HOUSE
For further details see p. 114
Woodstock Lane North, Long
Ditton, Surbiton, Surrey KT6 5HN
Tel: 020 8335 2570
Email: admissions@kisimul.co.uk
Website: www.kisimul.co.uk
Director of Education: Mr Danny
Carter BA(Hons), MA, MEd
Age range: 8–19
No. of pupils: 40
Special needs catered for:
ASC, AUT, BESD, CLD, EBD,
EPI, LD, MSI, PMLD, SCLD,
SEMH, SLD, SP&LD, SPLD
(♿) (16) (✓)

Moon Hall College
Burys Court, Flanchford Road,
Leigh, Reigate, Surrey RH2 8RE
Tel: 01306 611372
Age range: 3–16
Fees: Day £6,630–£17,220
Special needs catered for:
DYS, LD, SPLD

Moon Hall School
Pasturewood Road, Holmbury St
Mary, Dorking, Surrey RH5 6LQ
Tel: 01306 731464
Age range: 7–13
Fees: Day £14,400–£16,470
WB £16,015–£18,085
Special needs catered for:
DYS, SPLD
(♿) (♿) (✓)

MOOR HOUSE
SCHOOL & COLLEGE
For further details see p. 116
Mill Lane, Hurst Green,
Oxted, Surrey RH8 9AQ
Tel: 01883 712271
Email: information@
moorhouseschool.co.uk
Website:
www.moorhouseschool.co.uk
Principal: Mrs H A Middleton
Age range: 7–19
No. of pupils: 150
Special needs catered for: ASP,
DYS, DYSP, SCD, SLD, SP&LD, SLI
(A) (♿) (✓)

I CAN'S MEATH SCHOOL
For further details see p. 113
Brox Road, Ottershaw,
Surrey KT16 0LF
Tel: 01932 872302
Email: meath@meath-
ican.org.uk
Website:
www.meathschool.org.uk
Headteacher: Janet Dunn
OBE, MA, AdvDipSpecEduc
No. of pupils: 60
Special needs catered for:
ASC, ASP, AUT, SCD, SP&LD
(♿) (✓)

MORE HOUSE SCHOOL
For further details see p. 118
Moons Hill, Frensham,
Farnham, Surrey GU10 3AP
Tel: 01252 792303
Email: schooloffice@
morehouseschool.co.uk
Website:
www.morehouseschool.co.uk
Headmaster: Jonathan
Hetherington BA(Hons),
MSc(ed), QTS
Age range: B8–18
No. of pupils: 470
Fees: Day £13,113–£18,378
WB £23,322–£26,409
FB £25,515–£28,605
Special needs catered for:
LD, MLD, SCD, SPLD
(♂) (♿) (♿) (16) (✓)

Orchard Hill College
and Academy Trust
BedZED, 20 Sandmartin Way,
Hackbridge, Surrey SM6 7DF
Tel: 0345 402 0453
Age range: 16+
Special needs catered for: ADD,
ADHD, ASC, ASP, AUT, BESD, CLD,
CP, DEL, DYS, DYSP, EBD, EPI,
GLD, HA, HI, LD, MLD, MSI, PD,
Phe, PH, PMLD, PNI, SCD, SCLD,
SEMH, SLD, SP&LD, SPLD, SLI, VIS

St Dominic's School
Hambledon, Godalming,
Surrey GU8 4DX
Tel: 01428 684693/682741
Age range: 7–19
No. of pupils: 77 VIth19
Special needs catered for: ADD,
ADHD, ASC, ASP, BESD, CLD, DEL,
DYS, DYSP, EPI, HA, SCD, SP&LD, SPLD
(♿) (✏) (✓)

ST JOSEPH'S SPECIALIST
SCHOOL & COLLEGE
For further details see p. 120
Amlets Lane, Cranleigh,
Surrey GU6 7DH
Tel: 01483 272449
Email: admissions@st-
josephscranleigh.surrey.sch.uk
Website: www.st-josephs
cranleigh.surrey.sch.uk
Principal: Mrs Annie Sutton
Age range: 5–19
No. of pupils: 65
Fees: Day £57,905 FB £83,898
Special needs catered for:
ADHD, ASC, ASP, AUT,
CLD, DYS, DYSP, EPI, MLD,
SCLD, SEMH, SLD, SP&LD
(♿) (✏) (16) (✓)

The Knowl Hill School
School Lane, Pirbright,
Woking, Surrey GU24 0JN
Tel: 01483 797032
Age range: 7–16
No. of pupils: 57
Fees: Day £15,606
Special needs catered for:
DYS, DYSP, SPLD
(£) (✏) (✓)

Wiltshire

Appleford School
Shrewton, Salisbury,
Wiltshire SP3 4HL
Tel: 01980 621020
Age range: 7–18
No. of pupils: 126
Fees: Day £16,608 FB £25,491
Special needs catered for:
ADD, ADHD, ASP, DYS, DYSP,
HA, MLD, SP&LD, SPLD
(♿) (♿) (16) (✓)

South-West

Devon

Highgate Hill House School
Whitstone, Holsworthy,
Devon EX22 6TJ
Tel: 01288 341998
Age range: 5–16
Special needs catered for: ASC,
ASP, AUT, BESD, LD, MSI, PD, PH

Kingsley School
Northdown Road, Bideford,
Devon EX39 3LY
Tel: 01237 426200
Age range: 0–18
No. of pupils: 395
Fees: Day £1,950
WB £5,495 FB £7,095
Special needs catered for:
DYS, DYSP
(♿) (A) (♿) (£) (✏) (16)

Somerset

Cambian Lufton College
Lufton, Yeovil, Somerset BA22 8ST
Tel: 0800 138 1184
Age range: 16–25
No. of pupils: 120
Special needs catered for: HI,
LD, MLD, PH, PMLD, SCLD, SLD
(♿)

FOXES ACADEMY
For further details see p. 123
Selbourne Place, Minehead,
Somerset TA24 5TY
Tel: 01643 708529
Email: admin@
foxesacademy.ac.uk
Website: foxesacademy.ac.uk
Principal: Tracey Clare-Gray
Age range: 16–25
No. of pupils: 80
Special needs catered for:
ADD, ADHD, ASC, ASP, AUT,
CLD, CP, DYS, DYSP, EPI, GLD,
HI, LD, MLD, Phe, PMLD,
SCD, SLD, SP&LD, SPLD
(♿) (16)

Mark College
Highbridge, Somerset TA9 4NP
Tel: 01278 641 632
Age range: 10–19
Special needs catered for:
DYS, DYSP, LD, SP&LD, SPLD
🌍 🏫 16+

Shapwick School
Shapwick Manor, Station Road,
Shapwick, Somerset TA7 9NJ
Tel: 01458 210384
Age range: 8–19
No. of pupils: 84
Fees: Day £18,519–£19,386
WB £24,258 FB £25,560–£27,858
Special needs catered for:
DYS, DYSP
🌍 🏫 ✓

West Midlands

Herefordshire

Rowden House School
Rowden, Bromyard,
Herefordshire HR7 4LS
Tel: 01885 488096
Age range: 8–19
Fees: Day £102,200
WB £230,100 FB £299,400
Special needs catered for: ADHD,
ASC, AUT, CLD, EPI, HI, LD, PMLD,
SCLD, SLD, SP&LD, SPLD, SLI, VIS
🏫 16+ ✓

Shropshire

Access School
Holbrook Villa Farm, Harmer
Hill, Broughton, Shrewsbury,
Shropshire SY4 3EW
Tel: 01939 220797
Age range: 5–16
No. of pupils: 10
Special needs catered for:
EBD, GLD, MLD
✓

Queensway HLC
Hadley, Telford, Shropshire TF1 6AJ
Tel: 01952 388555
Age range: 11–16
Special needs catered for:
EBD, SPLD
✓

Staffordshire

Bladon House School
Newton Solney, Burton upon
Trent, Staffordshire DE15 0TA
Tel: 01283 563787
Age range: 5–19
Fees: Day £77,000
WB £190,100 FB £229,200
Special needs catered for: ADD,
ADHD, ASC, AUT, CLD, EPI, HI,
LD, MLD, SP&LD, SPLD, SLI, VIS
🏫 16+ ✓

**Maple Hayes
Dyslexia School**
Abnalls Lane, Lichfield,
Staffordshire WS13 8BL
Tel: 01543 264387
Age range: 7–17
No. of pupils: 118
Fees: Day £14,760–£19,725
Special needs catered for:
DYS, DYSP, SPLD
🌍 £ ✓

Regent College
77 Shelton New Road, Shelton,
Stoke-on-Trent, Staffordshire ST4 7AA
Tel: 01782 263326
Age range: 16–25
No. of pupils: 30
Special needs catered for:
CLD, EPI, PD, SLD, SP&LD

West Midlands

Argent College
New Standard Works, 43-47
Vittoria Street, Birmingham,
West Midlands B1 3PE
Tel: 01453 837502
Age range: 16–25
Special needs catered for:
ASC, ASP, AUT, BESD, CLD,
EBD, LD, SCLD, SEMH
16+

Glasshouse College
Wollaston Road, Amblecote,
Stourbridge, West Midlands DY8 4HF
Tel: 01453 837502
Age range: 16–25
Special needs catered for: ADHD,
ASC, ASP, BESD, CLD, EBD, GLD, LD,
PMLD, SCD, SCLD, SEMH, SLD, SPLD
16+ 🏫

OVERLEY HALL SCHOOL
For further details see p. 124
Overley, Wellington, Telford,
West Midlands TF6 5HE
Tel: 01952 740262
Email: info@overleyhall.com
Website: www.overleyhall.com
Headteacher: Mrs
Beverley Doran
Age range: 8–19
No. of pupils: 21
Special needs catered for:
ADD, ADHD, ASC, ASP, AUT,
CLD, DYSP, EPI, GLD, LD, PMLD,
SCD, SCLD, SLD, SP&LD,
🏫 16+ ✓

Sunfield School
Clent Grove, Woodman Lane,
Stourbridge, West Midlands DY9 9PB
Tel: 01562 882253
Age range: 6–19
Special needs catered for: ADD,
ADHD, ASC, AUT, BESD, CLD, DYS,
EPI, GLD, LD, MLD, MSI, PMLD,
SCD, SCLD, SEMH, SLD, SP&LD, SLI
🏫 16+ ✓

Worcestershire

Our Place School
The Orchard, Bransford,
Worcestershire WR6 5JE
Tel: 01886 833378
Special needs catered for:
ASC, MLD, PMLD, SLD

Yorkshire & Humberside

North-East Lincolnshire

**Linkage College –
Weelsby Campus**
Weelsby Road, Grimsby, North-
East Lincolnshire DN32 9RU
Tel: 01472 241044
Age range: 16–25
No. of pupils: 220
Special needs catered for:
ADD, ADHD, ASC, ASP, AUT,
CLD, CP, D, DEL, DYS, DYSP, EPI,
GLD, HI, LD, MLD, Phe, PH, SCD,
SCLD, SLD, SP&LD, SPLD, VIS
16+ 🏫

South Yorkshire

Freeman College
Sterling Works, 88 Arundel Street,
Sheffield, South Yorkshire S1 2NG
Tel: 01453 837502
Age range: 16–25
Special needs catered for: ADHD,
ASC, ASP, BESD, CLD, EBD, GLD, LD,
MLD, PMLD, SCD, SCLD, SEMH, SLD
16+ 🏫 ✓

**FULLERTON HOUSE
COLLEGE**
For further details see p. 126
Tickhill Square, Denaby,
Doncaster, South
Yorkshire DN12 4AR
Tel: 01709 861663
Email: enquiries@
hesleygroup.co.uk
Website:
www.hesleygroup.co.uk
General Manager: Heidi
Dugdale-Dawkes
Age range: 18–25
No. of pupils: 12
Special needs catered for:
ASC, ASP, AUT, CLD, DYS, DYSP,
GLD, LD, MLD, SCLD, SLD, SPLD
🏫

**FULLERTON HOUSE
SCHOOL**
For further details see p. 125
Tickill Square, Denaby,
Doncaster, South
Yorkshire DN12 4AR
Tel: 01709 861663
Email: enquiries@
hesleygroup.co.uk
Website: www.fullerton
houseschool.co.uk
General Manager: Heidi
Dugdale-Dawkes
Age range: 8–19
Special needs catered for:
ASC, ASP, AUT, CLD, DYS, DYSP,
GLD, LD, MLD, SCLD, SLD, SPLD
🏫 16+ ✓

WILSIC HALL COLLEGE
For further details see p. 126
Wadworth, Doncaster,
South Yorkshire DN11 9AG
Tel: 01302 856382
Email: enquiries@
hesleygroup.co.uk
Website:
www.hesleygroup.co.uk
General Manager: Heidi
Dugdale-Dawkes
Age range: 18–25
No. of pupils: 8
Special needs catered for:
ASC, ASP, AUT, CLD, DYS, DYSP,
GLD, LD, MLD, SCLD, SLD, SPLD

WILSIC HALL SCHOOL
For further details see p. 127
Wadworth, Doncaster,
South Yorkshire DN11 9AG
Tel: 01302 856382
Email: enquiries@
hesleygroup.co.uk
Website:
www.wilsichallschool.co.uk
Head: Geoff Turner
Age range: 11–19
No. of pupils: 32
Special needs catered for:
ASC, ASP, AUT, CLD, DYS, DYSP,
GLD, LD, MLD, SCLD, SLD, SPLD

West Yorkshire

Hall Cliffe School
Dovecote Lane, Horbury,
Wakefield, West Yorkshire WF4 6BB
Tel: 01924 663 420
Age range: 8–16
Special needs catered for:
ADHD, ASC, ASP, AUT, BESD,
MLD, SCD, SLD, SPLD

Pennine Camphill Community
Wood Lane, Chapelthorpe,
Wakefield, West Yorkshire WF4 3JL
Tel: 01924 255281
Age range: 16–25
No. of pupils: 56
Fees: Day £14,000–£45,000
FB £26,000–£69,000
Special needs catered for: ADHD,
ASC, ASP, AUT, CLD, DYSP, EBD,
EPI, LD, MLD, SCLD, SLD, SPLD

Northern Ireland

County Tyrone

Parkanaur College
57 Parkanaur Road, Dungannon,
County Tyrone BT70 3AA
Tel: 028 87761272
Age range: 18–65
Special needs catered for: ADD,
ADHD, ASP, AUT, BESD, CLD, CP,
DYS, DYSP, EBD, EPI, GLD, HA,
HI, LD, MLD, PD, Phe, PH, PMLD,
PNI, SCD, SCLD, SLD, SPLD, VIS

Scotland

Aberdeen

VSA Linn Moor Campus
Peterculter, Aberdeen AB14 0PJ
Tel: 01224 732246
Age range: 5–18
No. of pupils: 25
Fees: Day £38,326
FB £76,650–£239,114
Special needs catered for:
ASC, AUT, CLD, GLD, LD,
MLD, SCD, SCLD, SPLD

Clackmannanshire

New Struan School
100 Smithfield Loan, Alloa,
Clackmannanshire FK10 1NP
Tel: 01259 222000
Age range: 5–17
Special needs catered for:
ASC, AUT

Glasgow

East Park
1092 Maryhill Road,
Glasgow G20 9TD
Tel: 0141 946 2050
Age range: 0–25
Fees: Day £12,298 FB £22,958
Special needs catered for:
AUT, CP, DEL, EPI, HI, MLD,
PH, PMLD, SLD, SP&LD, VIS

Perth & Kinross

Ochil Tower
140 High Street, Auchterarder,
Perth, Perth & Kinross PH3 1AD
Tel: 01764 662416
Age range: 5–18
No. of pupils: 35
Fees: Day £23,500 FB £41,100
Special needs catered for: ADD,
ADHD, ASC, BESD, CLD, EBD, EPI, LD,
MLD, MSI, PMLD, SCD, SCLD, SP&LD

THE NEW SCHOOL
For further details see p. 128
Butterstone, Dunkeld,
Perth & Kinross PH8 0HA
Tel: 01350 724216
Email: info@thenewschool.co.uk
Website:
www.thenewschool.co.uk
Head of School: Mr Bill Colley
Age range: 11–19
No. of pupils: 25
Special needs catered for: ADD,
ADHD, ASC, ASP, AUT, BESD,
CLD, DEL, DYS, DYSP, EBD, GLD,
HA, LD, MLD, SCD, SEMH, SPLD

Wales

Denbighshire

Cambian Pengwern College
Sarn Lane, Rhuddlan, Rhyl,
Denbighshire LL18 5UH
Tel: 0800 138 1184
Age range: 16–25
No. of pupils: 60
Special needs catered for: ADD,
ADHD, ASC, ASP, AUT, BESD, CLD,
CP, DYSP, EBD, EPI, GLD, HI, LD,
MLD, MSI, PD, Phe, PH, PMLD, SCD,
SCLD, SEMH, SLD, SP&LD, SLI, VIS

Gwynedd

Aran Hall School
Rhydymain, Dolgellau,
Gwynedd LL40 2AR
Tel: 01341 450641
Age range: B11–19
Fees: WB £230,100 FB £299,400
Special needs catered for:
ADHD, ASC, ASP, AUT, CLD,
EPI, GLD, LD, MLD, PMLD, SCD,
SCLD, SP&LD, SPLD, SLI

Pembrokeshire

Coleg Plas Dwbl
Mynachlog-ddu, Clunderwen,
Pembrokeshire SA66 7SE
Tel: 01453 837502
Age range: 16–25
Special needs catered for:
ASC, ASP, CLD, EBD

Vale of Glamorgan

Action for Children Headlands School
2 St Augustine's Road, Penarth,
Vale of Glamorgan CF64 1YY
Tel: 02920 709771
Age range: 8–19
Special needs catered for: ADD,
ADHD, ASC, ASP, AUT, BESD,
DYS, EBD, MLD, SP&LD, SPLD

Wrexham

Prospects School
12 Grosvenor Road,
Wrexham LL11 1BU
Tel: 01978 313777
Age range: 11–16
No. of pupils: 21
Special needs catered for:
MLD, SPLD

Schools and colleges specialising in sensory or physical impairment

Abbreviations

ACLD	Autism, Communication and Associated Learning Difficulties
ADD	Attention Deficit Disorder
ADHD	Attention Deficit and Hyperactive Disorder (Hyperkinetic Disorder)
ASC	Autistic Spectrum Conditions
ASP	Asperger Syndrome
AUT	Autism
BESD	Behavioural, Emotional and Social Difficulties
CCD	Complex Communication Difficulties
CLD	Complex Learning Difficulties
CP	Cerebral Palsy
D	Deaf
DEL	Delicate
DYS	Dyslexia
DYSP	Dyspraxia
EBD	Emotional and Behavioural Difficulties
EBSD	Emotional, Behavioural and/ or Social Difficulties
EPI	Epilepsy
GLD	General Learning Difficulties
HA	High Ability
HI	Hearing Impairment
HS	Hospital School
LD	Learning Difficulties
MLD	Moderate Learning Difficulties
MSI	Multi-sensory Impairment
OCD	Obsessive Compulsive Disorder
PD	Physical Difficulties
PH	Physical Impairment
Phe	Partially Hearing
PMLD	Profound and Multiple Learning Difficulties
PNI	Physical Neurological Impairment
PRU	Pupil Referral Unit
SCD	Social and Communication Difficulties
SCLD	Severe and Complex Learning Difficulties
SEBD	Severe Emotional and Behavioural Disorders
SEBN	Social, Emotional and Behavioural Needs
SLD	Severe Learning Difficulties
SLI	Specific Language Impairment
SPLD	Specific Learning Difficulties
SP&LD	Speech and Language Difficulties
SLCN	Speech Language & Communication Needs
VIS	Visually Impaired

Key to Symbols

Type of school:

(symbol)	Boys' school
(symbol)	Girls' school
(symbol)	International school

School offers:

(A)	A levels
(symbol)	Residential
(16+)	Entrance at 16+
(symbol)	Vocational qualifications
(symbol)	Learning support
(✓)	This is a DfE approved independent or non-maintained school under section 41 of the Children and Families Act 2014 or section 342 of the 1996 Education Act

Please note: Unless otherwise indicated, all schools are coeducational day schools. Single-sex and boarding schools will be indicated by the relevant icon.

Central & West

Buckinghamshire

THE PACE CENTRE
For further details see p. 131
Philip Green House,
Coventon Road, Aylesbury,
Buckinghamshire HP19 9JL
Tel: 01296 392739
Email: info@thepacecentre.org
Website:
www.thepacecentre.org
Head Teacher: Mrs Claire Smart
Age range: 1–16
Special needs catered for: CLD,
CP, DYSP, HI, LD, MLD, MSI, PD,
PNI, SCLD, SLD, SP&LD, VIS
✔

Gloucestershire

National Star College
Ullenwood, Cheltenham,
Gloucestershire GL53 9QU
Tel: 01242 527631
Age range: 16–25
No. of pupils: 178
Special needs catered for:
ASC, ASP, AUT, CLD, CP, DYS,
DYSP, EPI, GLD, HI, LD, MLD, MSI,
PD, Phe, PH, PMLD, PNI, SCD,
SCLD, SLD, SP&LD, SPLD, VIS
♿ 16

St Rose's School
Stratford Lawn, Stroud,
Gloucestershire GL5 4AP
Tel: 01453 763793
Age range: 2–25
No. of pupils: 54
Special needs catered for: CLD,
CP, D, DEL, DYS, DYSP, EPI, GLD, HI,
LD, MLD, MSI, PD, Phe, PH, PMLD,
PNI, SCD, SCLD, SLD, SP&LD, SLI, VIS
♿ 16 ✔

West Berkshire

Mary Hare Primary School
Mill Hall, Pigeons Farm Road,
Thatcham, Newbury, West
Berkshire RG19 8XA
Tel: 01635 573800
Age range: 5–12
Special needs catered for:
D, HI, SP&LD, SLI
♿

**MARY HARE
SECONDARY SCHOOL**
For further details see p. 130
Arlington Manor, Snelsmore
Common, Newbury, West
Berkshire RG14 3BQ
Tel: 01635 244200
Email: enquiries@
maryhare.org.uk
Website: www.maryhare.org.uk
Principal: Mr Peter Gale
Age range: 11–19
No. of pupils: 220
Special needs catered for: D, HI
♿ 16 ✔

East

Hertfordshire

**Aurora Meldreth
Manor School**
Fenny Lane, Meldreth, Royston,
Hertfordshire SG8 6LG
Tel: 01763 268 000
Age range: 9–19+
No. of pupils: 30
Special needs catered for: CP,
D, EPI, GLD, HI, LD, MLD, MSI, PD,
Phe, PH, PMLD, SCLD, SP&LD, VIS
♿ 16 ✔

St Elizabeth's School
South End, Much Hadham,
Hertfordshire SG10 6EW
Tel: 01279 844270
Age range: 5–19
Special needs catered for:
AUT, CP, DYS, DYSP, EBD, EPI,
MLD, SLD, SP&LD, SPLD
♿ 16 ✔

East Midlands

Derbyshire

**Royal School for
the Deaf Derby**
Ashbourne Road, Derby,
Derbyshire DE22 3BH
Tel: 01332 362512
Age range: 3–19
Special needs catered for: D, HI
♿ 16 ✔

Leicestershire

Homefield College
42 St Mary's Road,
Sileby, Loughborough,
Leicestershire LE12 7TL
Tel: 01509 815696
Age range: 16–25
No. of pupils: 54 VIth54
Special needs catered for:
ASC, BESD, LD, SCD
£

**RNIB COLLEGE
LOUGHBOROUGH**
For further details see p. 132
Radmoor Road, Loughborough,
Leicestershire LE11 3BS
Tel: 01509 611077
Email: enquiries@
rnibcollege.ac.uk
Website: www.rnibcollege.ac.uk
Principal: June Murray
Age range: 16–65
No. of pupils: 100
Special needs catered for:
ADD, ADHD, ASC, ASP, AUT,
BESD, CLD, CP, DYS, DYSP, EBD,
EPI, GLD, HA, HI, LD, MLD, MSI,
PD, Phe, PH, PNI, SCD, SCLD,
SEMH, SLD, SP&LD, SPLD, SLI, VIS
16 ♿ ✔

Nottinghamshire

Portland College
Nottingham Road,
Mansfield, Nottingham,
Nottinghamshire NG18 4TJ
Tel: 01623 499111
Age range: 16–59
No. of pupils: 230
Special needs catered for:
ASC, ASP, AUT, CP, D, DYS,
DYSP, EBD, EPI, GLD, HI, MLD,
MSI, PD, Phe, PH, PMLD, PNI,
SCLD, SP&LD, SPLD, SLI, VIS
♿

Rutland

The Shires School
Shires Lane, Stretton,
Rutland LE15 7GT
Tel: 01780 411944
Age range: 11–19
Special needs catered for:
ASC, AUT, SLD
♿ ✔

Greater London

Kent

Nash College
Croydon Road, Bromley,
Kent BR2 7AG
Tel: 020 8315 4844
Age range: 18–25
Special needs catered for: AUT,
CP, EPI, MLD, PH, PMLD, PNI, SCD,
SCLD, SLD, SP&LD, SPLD, VIS
♿

Middlesex

RNIB SUNSHINE HOUSE SCHOOL
For further details see p. 133
33 Dene Road, Northwood,
Middlesex HA6 2DD
Tel: 01923 822538
Email: sunshinehouse@
rnib.org.uk
Website:
www.rnib.org.uk/sunshinehouse
Head: Jackie Seaman
and Mark Fuel
Age range: 2–14
Special needs catered for: CLD,
CP, D, EPI, GLD, HI, LD, MSI, PD,
Phe, PH, PMLD, SCLD, SPLD, VIS
♿ ✔

London

North London

Woodstar School
143 Coppetts Road,
London N10 1JP
Tel: 020 8444 7242
Age range: 3–11
Special needs catered for: CP, PD
✔

North-East

Tyne & Wear

Hedleys College
Station Road, Forest Hall, Newcastle
upon Tyne, Tyne & Wear NE12 8YY
Tel: 0191 266 5491
Age range: 14–19
No. of pupils: 170
Fees: Day £19,944 FB £42,134
Special needs catered for: HI
♿ 16+ ✔

Hedleys Northern Counties School
Tankerville Terrace, Jesmond,
Newcastle upon Tyne,
Tyne & Wear NE12 7BH
Tel: 0191 281 5821
Age range: 3–19
Fees: Day £13,767–£29,772
FB £19,134–£33,162
Special needs catered for:
AUT, HI, PMLD, SLD, VIS
♿ 16+ ✔

Percy Hedley School
West Lane, Killingworth, Newcastle
upon Tyne, Tyne & Wear NE12 7BH
Tel: 0191 2161811
Age range: 3–14
Special needs catered for: CP, SCD
♿

North-West

Lancashire

Beaumont College
Slyne Road, Lancaster,
Lancashire LA2 6AP
Tel: 01524 541400
Age range: 16–25
No. of pupils: 77
Special needs catered for:
ASC, AUT, BESD, CLD, CP, DYS,
DYSP, EBD, EPI, GLD, HI, MSI,
PD, PH, PMLD, PNI, SCD, SCLD,
SEMH, SLD, SP&LD, SLI, VIS
16+ ♿

Merseyside

Royal School for the Blind
Church Road North, Wavertree,
Liverpool, Merseyside L15 6TQ
Tel: 0151 733 1012
Age range: 2–19
No. of pupils: 51
Special needs catered for: ASC,
AUT, BESD, CLD, CP, D, EBD, EPI, HI,
MLD, MSI, PD, Phe, PH, PMLD, PNI,
SCLD, SLD, SP&LD, SPLD, SLI, VIS
♿ 16+ ✔

St Vincent's School for the Visually Handicapped
Yew Tree Lane, West Derby,
Liverpool, Merseyside L12 9HN
Tel: 0151 228 9968
Age range: 3–17
Fees: Day £19,566 FB £27,363
Special needs catered for: MLD, VIS
♿ ✔

South-East

East Sussex

CHAILEY HERITAGE SCHOOL
For further details see p. 134
Haywards Heath Road,
North Chailey, Lewes,
East Sussex BN8 4EF
Tel: 01825 724444
Email: office@chf.org.uk
Website: www.chf.org.uk
Charity Chief Executive: Helen Hewitt
Age range: 3–19
No. of pupils: 95
Special needs catered for:
ASC, AUT, CLD, CP, D, EBD, EPI,
HI, MLD, MSI, PD, PH, PMLD,
PNI, SCLD, SLD, SP&LD, VIS

Hamilton Lodge School
9 Walpole Road, Brighton,
East Sussex BN2 0LS
Tel: 01273 682362
Age range: 5–16
Special needs catered for: D, HI

ST MARY'S SCHOOL & 6TH FORM COLLEGE
For further details see p. 135
Wrestwood Road, Bexhill-on-Sea, East Sussex TN40 2LU
Tel: 01424 730740
Email: admin@stmarysbexhill.org
Website: www.stmarysbexhill.org
Headteacher: Mark Bryant
Age range: 7–19
No. of pupils: 63
Special needs catered for:
ASC, ASP, AUT, CLD, CP, D,
DEL, DYS, DYSP, EPI, GLD, HI,
LD, MLD, MSI, PD, Phe, PH,
SCD, SP&LD, SPLD, SLI, VIS

Hampshire

TRELOAR SCHOOL
For further details see p. 137
Holybourne, Alton,
Hampshire GU34 4GL
Tel: 01420 547400
Email: admissions@treloar.org.uk
Website: www.treloar.org.uk
Age range: 2–19
No. of pupils: 80 VIth20
Special needs catered for:
CLD, CP, DEL, DYSP, EPI, HA,
HI, MLD, MSI, PD, Phe, PH, PNI,
SCLD, SP&LD, SPLD, SLI, VIS

Kent

Dorton College of Further Education
Seal Drive, Seal, Sevenoaks,
Kent TN15 0AH
Tel: 01732 592600
Age range: 16–19
No. of pupils: 60
Special needs catered for: VIS

Surrey

St Piers School and College
St Piers Lane, Lingfield,
Surrey RH7 6PW
Tel: 01342 832243
Age range: 5–25
No. of pupils: 181
Special needs catered for: ADD,
ADHD, ASP, AUT, CP, EPI, MLD,
PMLD, PNI, SCD, SCLD, SLD, SP&LD

Stepping Stones School
Tower Road, Hindhead,
Surrey GU26 6SU
Tel: 01428 609083
Age range: 8–19
No. of pupils: 40
Fees: Day £11,000–£14,800
Special needs catered for: ASC,
ASP, AUT, MLD, PD, SP&LD

THE CHILDREN'S TRUST SCHOOL
For further details see p. 136
Tadworth Court, Tadworth,
Surrey KT20 5RU
Tel: 01737 365810
Email: school@thechildrenstrust.org.uk
Website: www.thechildrenstrustschool.org.uk
Head Teacher: Samantha Newton
Age range: 2–19
No. of pupils: 44
Special needs catered for:
CLD, CP, EPI, HI, MSI, PD, PH,
PMLD, PNI, SLD, SP&LD, VIS

West Sussex

Ingfield Manor School
Five Oaks, Billingshurst,
West Sussex RH14 9AX
Tel: 01403 782294/784241
Age range: 3–16
Special needs catered for: CP

South-West

Devon

Dame Hannah Rogers School
Woodland Road, Ivybridge,
Devon PL21 9HQ
Tel: 01752 892461
Age range: 3–18
No. of pupils: 2
Special needs catered for:
ASC, MLD, PD, PMLD, SLD

Exeter Royal Academy for Deaf Education
50 Topsham Road, Exeter,
Devon EX2 4NF
Tel: 01392 267023
Age range: 5–25
No. of pupils: VIth68
Fees: Day £23,007–£39,195
WB £31,779–£46,800
FB £36,360–£48,990
Special needs catered for: AUT, CP,
D, EPI, HI, MLD, MSI, Phe, SP&LD, VIS

On Track Training Centre
Unit 8, Paragon Buildings, Ford
Road, Totnes, Devon TQ9 5LQ
Tel: 01803 866462
Age range: 11–18
No. of pupils: 24
Special needs catered for:
ADD, ADHD, ASC, ASP, AUT,
BESD, DEL, DYS, DYSP, EBD,
GLD, MLD, MSI, SCD, SPLD

Vranch House
Pinhoe Road, Exeter,
Devon EX4 8AD
Tel: 01392 468333
Age range: 2–12
Fees: Day £19,425
Special needs catered for: CP,
EPI, MLD, PD, PH, PMLD, SP&LD

WESC Foundation – The Specialist College for Visual Impairment
Countess Wear, Exeter,
Devon EX2 6HA
Tel: 01392 454200
Age range: 16+
Special needs catered for:
EPI, PH, PMLD, VIS

WESC Foundation – The Specialist School for Visual Impairment
Countess Wear, Exeter,
Devon EX2 6HA
Tel: 01392 454200
Age range: 5–16
Special needs catered for:
EPI, PH, PMLD, VIS

Dorset

Langside School
Langside Avenue, Parkstone,
Poole, Dorset BH12 5BN
Tel: 01202 518635
Age range: 2–19
No. of pupils: 23
Special needs catered for: CLD, CP,
EPI, MSI, PD, PMLD, SCD, SCLD, SLD

The Fortune Centre of Riding Therapy
Avon Tyrrell, Bransgore,
Christchurch, Dorset BH23 8EE
Tel: 01425 673297
Age range: 16–25
No. of pupils: 47
Special needs catered for: AUT,
CP, DEL, DYS, EBD, EPI, HI, MLD,
PH, PMLD, SLD, SP&LD, SPLD, VIS

Victoria Education Centre
12 Lindsay Road, Branksome
Park, Poole, Dorset BH13 6AS
Tel: 01202 763697
Age range: 3–19
No. of pupils: 90
Special needs catered for:
DEL, EPI, PH, SP&LD

West Midlands

Herefordshire

The Royal National College for the Blind (RNC)
Venns Lane, Hereford,
Herefordshire HR1 1DT
Tel: 01432 376621
Age range: 16–65
Special needs catered for: ASP,
AUT, DYS, HA, MLD, PD, Phe, VIS
16+ ♿

Shropshire

Derwen College
Oswestry, Shropshire SY11 3JA
Tel: 01691 661234
Age range: 16–25
No. of pupils: 160
Fees: FB £17,928
Special needs catered for:
CP, DEL, DYS, EPI, HI, MLD, PH,
PMLD, SLD, SP&LD, SPLD, VIS
♿

West Midlands

Hereward College of Further Education
Bramston Crescent, Tile Hill Lane,
Coventry, West Midlands CV4 9SW
Tel: 024 7646 1231
Age range: 16+
No. of pupils: 400
Special needs catered for: ASP,
AUT, CP, DEL, DYS, DYSP, EBD,
EPI, HA, HI, MLD, PH, SPLD, VIS
♿

National Institute for Conductive Education
Cannon Hill House, Russell
Road, Moseley, Birmingham,
West Midlands B13 8RD
Tel: 0121 449 1569
Age range: 0–11
No. of pupils: 18
Fees: Day £25,000
Special needs catered for:
CP, DYSP, PNI
✔

RNIB PEARS CENTRE FOR SPECIALIST LEARNING
For further details see p. 138
Wheelwright Lane, Ash
Green, Coventry, West
Midlands CV7 9RA
Tel: 024 7636 9500
Email: pearscentre@rnib.org.uk
Website:
www.rnib.org.uk/pearscentre
Principal: Robert Jones
Age range: 4–19
No. of pupils: 31
Special needs catered for:
ASC, AUT, BESD, CLD, CP, D,
EPI, GLD, HI, LD, MSI, PD, Phe,
PH, PMLD, SCLD, SPLD, VIS,
♿ 16+ ✔

Worcestershire

New College Worcester
Whittington Road, Worcester,
Worcestershire WR5 2JX
Tel: 01905 763933
Age range: usually 11–19
No. of pupils: 88
Fees: Day £30,049–£32,485
WB £40,076–£42,268
FB £44,366–£46,813
Special needs catered for: VIS
♿ 16+ ✔

Yorkshire & Humberside

North Yorkshire

Henshaws College
Bogs Lane, Harrogate,
North Yorkshire HG1 4ED
Tel: 01423 886451
Age range: 16–25
Special needs catered for: CLD,
CP, D, EPI, HI, LD, MLD, MSI, PD,
Phe, SCD, SLD, SP&LD, VIS
16+ ♿

South Yorkshire

Communication Specialist College
Leger Way, Doncaster,
South Yorkshire DN2 6AY
Tel: 01302 386700
Age range: 16–59
No. of pupils: 185
Special needs catered for: HI
♿

DONCASTER SCHOOL FOR THE DEAF
For further details see p. 139
Leger Way, Doncaster,
South Yorkshire DN2 6AY
Tel: 01302 386733
Email: jgoodman@
ddt-deaf.org.uk
Website:
www.deaf.school.org.uk
Executive Principal: Mr
Alan W Robinson
Age range: 4–19
No. of pupils: 32
Special needs catered for: BESD,
CP, D, DYS, GLD, HI, MLD, PH,
PMLD, SLD, SP&LD, SPLD, VIS
♿ ✔

Paces High Green School for Conductive Education
Paces High Green Centre, Pack
Horse Lane, High Green, Sheffield,
South Yorkshire S35 3HY
Tel: 0114 284 5298
Age range: 0–18
No. of pupils: 30
Fees: Day £27,452
Special needs catered for: CP, PD
16+ ✔

West Yorkshire

Holly Bank School
Roe Head, Far Common Road,
Mirfield, West Yorkshire WF14 0DQ
Tel: 01924 490833
Age range: 5–19
No. of pupils: 20 VIth10
Fees: Day £35,000–£45,000
WB £70,000–£75,000
FB £99,000–£105,000
Special needs catered for: CLD, CP,
MSI, PD, PH, PMLD, PNI, SCLD, SLD
♿ 16+

ST JOHN'S CATHOLIC SCHOOL FOR THE DEAF
For further details see p. 140
Church Street, Boston
Spa, Wetherby, West
Yorkshire LS23 6DF
Tel: 01937 842144
Email: info@stjohns.org.uk
Website: www.stjohns.org.uk
Headteacher: Mrs A Bradbury
BA(Hons), MSc, NPQH
Age range: 4–19
No. of pupils: 62
Special needs catered for: ADD,
ADHD, ASC, ASP, AUT, BESD,
CP, D, DEL, DYS, DYSP, EBD, EPI,
HI, LD, MLD, MSI, PD, Phe, PH,
PMLD, SCD, SLD, SP&LD, SLI, VIS
♿ 16+ ✔

Northern Ireland

County Antrim

Jordanstown School
85 Jordanstown Road,
Newtownabbey, County
Antrim BT37 0QE
Tel: 028 9086 3541
Age range: 4–19
No. of pupils: 79
Special needs catered for: ASC, D,
EBD, GLD, HI, LD, MSI, PD, SP&LD, VIS
16+

County Tyrone

Buddy Bear Trust Conductive Education School
Killyman Road, Dungannon,
County Tyrone BT71 6DE
Tel: 02887 752 025
Special needs catered for: CP

Scotland

Aberdeen

Camphill School Aberdeen
Murtle House, Bieldside,
Aberdeen AB15 9EP
Tel: 01224 867935
Age range: 3–19
Fees: Day 25,198–50,397
FB 50,397–100,794
Special needs catered for:
ADD, ADHD, ASC, ASP, AUT,
BESD, CLD, CP, D, DEL, DYS, DYSP,
EBD, EPI, GLD, LD, MLD, MSI, PD,
PMLD, PNI, SCD, SCLD, SEMH,
SLD, SP&LD, SPLD, SLI, VIS
♿ 16+

Edinburgh

THE ROYAL BLIND SCHOOL
For further details see p. 142
43 Canaan Lane,
Edinburgh EH10 4SG
Tel: 0131 446 3120
Email: office@
royalblindschool.org.uk
Website:
www.royalblind.org/education
Head Teacher: Elaine
Brackenridge (BEd)
Age range: 5–19
Special needs catered for:
AUT, CP, DEL, EPI, MLD, PH,
PMLD, SLD, SP&LD, SPLD, VIS
♿ ✎ 16+

Renfrewshire

Corseford School
Milliken Park, Johnstone,
Renfrewshire PA10 2NT
Tel: 01505 702141
Age range: 3–18
No. of pupils: 50
Special needs catered for:
CP, DEL, DYSP, EPI, HI, MLD,
PH, SP&LD, SPLD, VIS
♿ 16+

South Lanarkshire

Stanmore House School
Lanark, South Lanarkshire ML11 7RR
Tel: 01555 665041
Age range: 0–18
No. of pupils: 47
Special needs catered for:
CP, PH, SCLD, SP&LD, VIS
♿ 16+

West Lothian

Donaldson's School
Preston Road, Linlithgow,
West Lothian EH49 6HZ
Tel: 01506 841900
Age range: 2–19
No. of pupils: 12
Special needs catered for:
ASP, AUT, D, HI, Phe, PMLD,
SCD, SLD, SP&LD, SLI
♿ ✎ 16+

Wales

Glamorgan

Craig-y-Parc School
Pentyrch, Cardiff,
Glamorgan CF15 9NB
Tel: 029 2089 0397/2089 0361
Age range: 3–19
Special needs catered for: CP,
EPI, HI, LD, MLD, MSI, PD, Phe, PH,
PMLD, SCLD, SLD, SP&LD, VIS
♿

Special Educational Needs and the independent and non-maintained schools and colleges that cater for them

Schools and colleges by category

Attention Deficit Disorder (ADD)

Abingdon House School, London D171
Action for Children Headlands School, Vale of Glamorgan D176
Action for Children Parklands Campus, Oxfordshire D157
Appleford School, Wiltshire D173
Appletree School, Cumbria 97, D160
Avon Park School, Warwickshire D152
Belgrave School, Bristol D169
Belmont School, Lancashire D161
Birtenshaw School (Bolton), Greater Manchester D172
Bladon House School, Staffordshire D174
Blossom Lower School and Upper House, London 112, D171
Bramfield House School, Suffolk D158
Brantwood Specialist School, South Yorkshire D165
Breckenbrough School, North Yorkshire D164
Brewood School, Kent D162
Cambian Dilston College, Northumberland D171
Cambian Pengwern College, Denbighshire D176
Cambian Potterspury Lodge School, Northamptonshire D148
Camphill School Aberdeen, Aberdeen D183
Cedar House School, Lancashire D161
Centre Academy London, London D171
Chaigeley, Warrington D161
Chilworth House Upper School, Oxfordshire D157
Coleg Elidyr, Carmarthenshire D153
Copperfield School, Norfolk D169
Cotswold Chine School, Gloucestershire D157
Crookhey Hall School, Lancashire D161
Cruckton Hall, Shropshire 78, D151
Demeter House School, North Lincolnshire D152
Falkland House School, Fife D165
Farleigh College Mells, Somerset D151
Foxes Academy, Somerset 123, D173
Harmeny Education Trust Ltd, Edinburgh D165
Hillcrest Glebedale School, Staffordshire 103, D164
Hillcrest Jubilee School, Hampshire 99, D162
Hillcrest New Barn School, West Berkshire 92, D157
Hillcrest Park School, Oxfordshire 93, D157
Hillcrest Shifnal School, Shropshire 104, D164
Hillcrest Slinfold School, West Sussex 100, D163
Holme Court School, Cambridgeshire D169
Hope House School, Nottinghamshire D158
Hope View School, Kent D162
Horton House School, East Riding of Yorkshire D164
Insights School & Skills Academy, London D159
Kisharon School, London D171
Lakeside School, Merseyside D150
Learn 4 Life, Lancashire D161
Linkage College - Toynton Campus, Lincolnshire D170
Linkage College - Weelsby Campus, North-East Lincolnshire D174
Muntham House School Ltd, West Sussex D163
North Hill House School, Somerset D151
Northease Manor School, East Sussex D172
Ochil Tower, Perth & Kinross D175
Octavia House School, Kennington, London D171
Octavia House School, Vauxhall, London D159
Octavia House School, Walworth, London D159
On Track Training Centre, Devon D181
Orchard Hill College and Academy Trust, Surrey D173
Overley Hall School, West Midlands 124, D174
Owlswick School, East Sussex D172
Parayhouse School, London D171
Parkanaur College, County Tyrone D175
Philpots Manor School, West Sussex 101, D163
Queen Alexandra College (QAC), West Midlands 83, D152
Queenswood School, Herefordshire D164
Ripplevale School, Kent D162
RNIB College Loughborough, Leicestershire 132, D179
Rossendale School, Lancashire D149
Sheiling School, Thornbury, Bristol D169
Small Haven School, Kent D162
Springboard Education Senior, West Sussex D163
St Catherine's School, Isle of Wight 119, D172
St Dominic's School, Surrey D173
St Edward's School, Hampshire D162
St John's Catholic School for the Deaf, West Yorkshire 140, D182
St John's School & College, East Sussex 122, D172
St Piers School and College, Surrey D181
Sunfield School, West Midlands D174
Talbot House School, Tyne & Wear D159
Talocher School, Monmouthshire D166
The Linnet Independent Learning Centre, Derbyshire D158
The Loddon School, Hampshire D172
The Marchant-Holliday School, Somerset D163
The Mount Camphill Community, East Sussex D161
The New School, Perth & Kinross 128, D175
The Ryes College & Community, Essex D157
Underley Garden, Cumbria D160
Waterloo Lodge School, Lancashire D161
West Heath School, Kent 102, D162
William Henry Smith School, West Yorkshire D165
Wings School, Cumbria, Cumbria D160
Wings School, Nottinghamshire, Nottinghamshire D158
Woodcroft School, Essex D169
Woodlands, Wrexham D166

Attention Deficit and Hyperactive Disorder (ADHD)

3 Dimensions, Somerset D151
Abingdon House School, London D171
Action for Children Headlands School, Vale of Glamorgan D176
Action for Children Parklands Campus, Oxfordshire D157
Alderwasley Hall School & Sixth Form Centre, Derbyshire D170
Appleford School, Wiltshire D173
Appletree School, Cumbria 97, D160
Aran Hall School, Gwynedd D176
Arc School Ansley, Warwickshire D164
Arc School Napton, Warwickshire D164
Ashbrooke School, Tyne & Wear D149
Aurora Brambles East School, Lancashire D149
Avon Park School, Warwickshire D152
Beech Lodge School, Berkshire D161
Belmont School, Lancashire D161
Birtenshaw School (Bolton), Greater Manchester D172
Bladon House School, Staffordshire D174
Blossom Lower School and Upper House, London 112, D171
Bracken School, Lancashire D149
Bramfield House School, Suffolk D158
Brantridge School, West Sussex D162
Brantwood Specialist School, South Yorkshire D165
Breckenbrough School, North Yorkshire D164
Brewood School, Kent D162
Cambian Dilston College, Northumberland D171
Cambian Pengwern College, Denbighshire D176
Cambian Potterspury Lodge School, Northamptonshire D148
Cambian Red Rose School, Lancashire D161
Cambian Spring Hill School, North Yorkshire D164
Camphill Community Glencraig, County Down D165
Camphill School Aberdeen, Aberdeen D183
Cedar House School, Lancashire D161
Centre Academy East Anglia, Suffolk D170
Centre Academy London, London D171
Chaigeley, Warrington D161
Chilworth House School, Oxfordshire D157
Chilworth House Upper School, Oxfordshire D157
Coleg Elidyr, Carmarthenshire D153
Copperfield School, Norfolk D169
Cotswold Chine School, Gloucestershire D157
Crookhey Hall School, Lancashire D161
Cruckton Hall, Shropshire 78, D151
Cumberland School, Lancashire D161
Devon Education and Children's Services, Devon D151
Eden Grove School, Cumbria D160
Falkland House School, Fife D165
Farleigh College Mells, Somerset D151
Farney Close School, West Sussex D162
Foxes Academy, Somerset 123, D173
Frederick Hugh House, London D171

Autistic Spectrum Conditions (ASC) (also Autistic Spectrum Disorders – ASD)

Asperger Syndrome (ASP)

Autism (AUT)

Behaviour, Emotional and Social Difficulties (BESD) – see also EBSD and SEBD

Complex Learning Difficulties (CLD)

National Star College, Gloucestershire D179
Ochil Tower, Perth & Kinross D175
Options Higford, Shropshire 81, D151
Options Kinsale, Flintshire 90, D153
Options Trent Acres, Staffordshire 82, D152
Orchard Hill College and Academy Trust, Surrey D173
Overley Hall School, West Midlands................................124, D174
Parayhouse School, London D171
Parkanaur College, County Tyrone D175
Pegasus School, Derbyshire D170
Pennine Camphill Community, West Yorkshire D175
Pontville, Lancashire D172
Prior's Court School, West Berkshire 66, D147
Queen Alexandra College (QAC), West Midlands.............83, D152
Regent College, Staffordshire D174
Ripplevale School, Kent D162
RNIB College Loughborough, Leicestershire 132, D179
RNIB Pears Centre for Specialist Learning, West Midlands.........138, D182
RNIB Sunshine House School, Middlesex 133, D180
Rossendale School, Lancashire D149
Rowden House School, Herefordshire D174
Royal School for the Blind, Merseyside D180
Ruskin Mill College, Gloucestershire D169

Sheiling College, Hampshire D172
Sheiling School, Hampshire...D172
Sheiling School, Thornbury, Bristol......................................D169
Small Haven School, Kent D162
St Dominic's School, Surrey D173
St John's School & College, East Sussex.........................122, D172
St Joseph's Specialist School & College, Surrey 120, D173
St Mary's School & 6th Form College, East Sussex........................135, D181
St Rose's School, Gloucestershire D179
Strathmore College, Staffordshire D152
Sunfield School, West Midlands D174
The Children's Trust School, Surrey 136, D181
The Linnet Independent Learning Centre, Derbyshire D158
The Loddon School, Hampshire D158
The Mount Camphill Community, East Sussex D161
The New School, Perth & Kinross 128, D175
The Pace Centre, Buckinghamshire 131, D179
Treloar School, Hampshire 137, D181
VSA Linn Moor Campus, Aberdeen.....................................D175
William Henry Smith School, West Yorkshire D165
Wilsic Hall College, South Yorkshire 126, D175
Wilsic Hall School, South Yorkshire 127, D175
Woodcroft School, Essex D169

Cerebral Palsy (CP)

Aurora Meldreth Manor School, Hertfordshire D179
Aurora St Christopher's School, Bristol.................................D169
Beaumont College, Lancashire D180
Birtenshaw School (Bolton), Greater Manchester D172
Buddy Bear Trust Conductive Education School, County Tyrone...... D182
Cambian Dilston College, Northumberland...........................D171
Cambian Pengwern College, Denbighshire D176
Cambian Spring Hill School, North Yorkshire D164
Camphill Community Glencraig, County Down D165
Camphill School Aberdeen, Aberdeen D183
Chailey Heritage School, East Sussex.............................134, D181
Corseford School, Renfrewshire D183
Craig-y-Parc School, Glamorgan D183
Derwen College, Shropshire D182
Doncaster School for the Deaf, South Yorkshire 139, D182
East Park, Glasgow D175
Eden Grove School, Cumbria D160
Exeter Royal Academy for Deaf Education, Devon D181
Foxes Academy, Somerset 123, D173
Frederick Hugh House, London D171
Henshaws College, North Yorkshire D182
Hereward College of Further Education, West Midlands.................... D182
Holly Bank School, West Yorkshire D182
Ingfield Manor School, West Sussex.....................................D181
Kisharon School, London D171
Langside School, Dorset D181
Linkage College - Toynton Campus, Lincolnshire.................D170
Linkage College - Weelsby Campus, North-East Lincolnshire D174
Nash College, Kent D180
National Institute for Conductive Education, West Midlands D182
National Star College, Gloucestershire D179

Orchard Hill College and Academy Trust, Surrey D173
Paces High Green School for Conductive Education,
    South Yorkshire D182
Parayhouse School, London D171
Parkanaur College, County Tyrone D175
Percy Hedley School, Tyne & Wear D180
Portland College, Nottinghamshire D179
Queen Alexandra College (QAC), West Midlands.............83, D152
RNIB College Loughborough, Leicestershire 132, D179
RNIB Pears Centre for Specialist Learning, West Midlands.........138, D182
RNIB Sunshine House School, Middlesex 133, D180
Royal School for the Blind, Merseyside D180
Rutherford School, Surrey D170
Sheiling School, Thornbury, Bristol......................................D169
St Elizabeth's School, Hertfordshire D179
St John's Catholic School for the Deaf, West Yorkshire.............140, D182
St John's School & College, East Sussex.........................122, D172
St Mary's School & 6th Form College, East Sussex........................135, D181
St Piers School and College, Surrey D181
St Rose's School, Gloucestershire D179
Stanmore House School, South Lanarkshire........................ D183
The Children's Trust School, Surrey 136, D181
The David Lewis School, Cheshire D172
The Fortune Centre of Riding Therapy, Dorset.....................D181
The Mount Camphill Community, East Sussex D161
The Pace Centre, Buckinghamshire 131, D179
The Royal Blind School, Edinburgh...................................142, D183
Treloar School, Hampshire 137, D181
Vranch House, Devon D181
Woodcroft School, Essex D169
Woodstar School, London D180

Deaf (D) – see also Hearing Impairment (HI)

Aurora Meldreth Manor School, Hertfordshire D179
Camphill School Aberdeen, Aberdeen D183
Chailey Heritage School, East Sussex.............................134, D181
Donaldson's School, West Lothian....................................... D183
Doncaster School for the Deaf, South Yorkshire 139, D182
Exeter Royal Academy for Deaf Education, Devon D181
Hamilton Lodge School, East Sussex D181
Henshaws College, North Yorkshire D182
Jordanstown School, County Antrim D182
Kisharon School, London D171
Linkage College - Toynton Campus, Lincolnshire.................D170
Linkage College - Weelsby Campus, North-East Lincolnshire D174
Mary Hare Primary School, West Berkshire.....................130, D179
Mary Hare Secondary School, West Berkshire 130, D179

Portland College, Nottinghamshire D179
Queen Alexandra College (QAC), West Midlands.............83, D152
RNIB Pears Centre for Specialist Learning, West Midlands.........138, D182
RNIB Sunshine House School, Middlesex 133, D180
Royal College Manchester, Cheshire D149
Royal School for the Blind, Merseyside D180
Royal School for the Deaf Derby, Derbyshire D179
Royal School Manchester, Cheshire D149
Rutherford School, Surrey D170
St John's Catholic School for the Deaf, West Yorkshire.............140, D182
St John's School & College, East Sussex.........................122, D172
St Mary's School & 6th Form College, East Sussex........................135, D181
St Rose's School, Gloucestershire.......................................D179

Dyslexia (DYSL) – see also SPLD

Dyspraxia (DYSP)

Emotional, Behavioural Difficulties (EBD) – see also BESD and SEMH

Epilepsy (EPI)

General Learning Difficulties (GLD)

High Ability (HA)

Hearing Impairment (HI)

Learning Difficulties (LD)

Moderate Learning Difficulties (MLD)

Multi-sensory Impairment (MSI)

Partially Hearing (Phe)

Physical Difficulties (PD)

Physical Impairment (PH)

Profound and Multiple Learning Difficulties (PMLD)

Physical Neurological Impairment (PNI)

Social and Communication Difficulties (SCD)

Severe and Complex Learning Difficulties (SCLD)

Social, Emotional and Mental Health needs (SEMH) – see also BESD and EBD

Severe Learning Difficulties (SLD)

Speech and Language Difficulties (SP&LD)

Specific Learning Difficulties (SPLD)

Specific Language Impairment (SLI)

Visually Impaired (VIS)

Maintained special schools and colleges

BEDFORD
Borough Council

Bedford SEND Team, 5th Floor, Borough Hall, Cauldwell Street, Bedford, MK42 9AP
Tel: 01234 228375 Email: statass@bedford.gov.uk Website: www.bedford.gov.uk

BEDFORD
Ridgeway School
Hill Rise, Kempston,
BEDFORD MK42 7EB
Tel: 01234 402402
Category: PD (Coed 2-19) LD LDD

**St Johns Special
School & College**
Austin Cannons, Kempston,
BEDFORD MK42 8AA
Tel: 01234 345565
Category: SLD PMLD (Coed 2-19)

CENTRAL BEDFORDSHIRE
Council

Central Bedfordshire SEND Team, Priory House, Monks Walk, Chicksands Shefford, SG17 5TQ
Tel: 0300 300 8088 Email: cbcsendpypps@centralbedfordshire.gov.uk Website: www.centralbedfordshire.gov.uk

BIGGLESWADE
Ivel Valley Primary School
The Baulk, BIGGLESWADE,
Bedfordshire SG18 0PT
Tel: 01767 601010
Category: ASD PMLD SLD
SpEd(Coed 3-10)

**Ivel Valley Secondary
School**
Hitchmead Road, BIGGLESWADE,
Bedfordshire SG18 0NL
Tel: 01767 601010
Category: SLD PMLD ASD
SpEd (Coed 11-19)

DUNSTABLE
**The Chiltern
Primary School**
Beech Road, DUNSTABLE,
Bedfordshire LU6 3LY
Tel: 01582 667106
Category: ASC SLD
PMLD (Coed 3-11)

HOUGHTON REGIS
**The Chiltern
Secondary School**
Kingsland Campus, Parkside
Drive, HOUGHTON REGIS,
Bedfordshire LU5 5PX
Tel: 01582 866972
Category: ASC SLD
PMLD (Coed 12-19)

LEIGHTON BUZZARD
Oak Bank School
Sandy Lane, LEIGHTON BUZZARD,
Bedfordshire LU7 3BE
Tel: 01525 374559
Category: ADHD, ASD, ASP, BESD,
DYSL, OCD, ODD, PDA (Coed 9-16)

WEST BERKSHIRE
Council

West Berkshire FIS, The SEN Team, West Street House, West Street Newbury, Berkshire, RG14 1BD
Tel: 01635 503100 Email: fis@westberks.gov.uk Website: www.westberks.gov.uk

NEWBURY
The Castle School
Love Lane, Donnington,
NEWBURY, Berkshire RG14 2JG
Tel: 01635 42976
Category: ASD CLD SLD SpEd
SPLD GLD PH (Coed 2-19)

READING
**Brookfields School:
Specialist SEN School**
Sage Road, Tilehurst, READING,
Berkshire RG31 6SW
Tel: 01189 421382
Category: ADHD, AUT, CB, CP, HI,
MSI Complex Needs, SLCN, VIS

BLACKBURN WITH DARWEN
Borough Council

Blackburn SEND Team, 10 Duke Street, Floor 5, Blackburn, Lancashire, BB2 1DH
Tel: 01254 666739 Email: sendss@blackburn.gov.uk Website: www.blackburn.gov.uk

BLACKBURN

Crosshill Special School with BCHS
Haslingden Road, BLACKBURN,
Lancashire BB2 3HJ
Tel: 01254 667713
Category: ASD, GLD, HI, MLD, SEMH,
SLCN, SLD, VIS (Coed Day 11-16)

Newfield School
Old Bank Lane, BLACKBURN,
Lancashire BB1 2PW
Tel: 01254 588600
Category: ASC, ASD,
Complex (Coed Day 2-19)

St. Thomas's Centre
Lambeth Street, BLACKBURN,
Lancashire BB1 1NA
Tel: 01254 680523
Category: ADD, ADHD, Pupil
Referral Unit, SEMH (Coed Day 5-16)

DARWEN

Sunnyhurst Centre
Salisbury Road, DARWEN,
Lancashire BB3 1HZ
Tel: 01254 702317
Category: ADHD, ASD, ODD, Pupil
Referral Unit (Coed Day 5-11)

BLACKPOOL
Council

Blackpool SEN Team, PO Box 4, Town Hall, Municipal Buildings Blackpool, FY1 1NA
Tel: 01253 477100 Email: local.offer@blackpool.gov.uk Website: www.blackpool.gov.uk

BLACKPOOL

Highfurlong School
Blackpool Old Road, BLACKPOOL,
Lancashire FY3 7LR
Tel: 01253 392188
Category: ASD, HI, MLD,
MSI, PH (Coed 2-19)

Woodlands School
Whitegate Drive, BLACKPOOL,
Lancashire FY3 9HF
Tel: 01253 316722
Category: SLD PMLD
MSI (Coed 2-19)

BOURNEMOUTH
Borough Council

Bournemouth SEN Team, Bournemouth Council, St Stephen's Road, Bournemouth, Dorset, BH2 6DY
Tel: 01202 451451 Email: cs@bournemouth.gov.uk Website: www.bournemouth.gov.uk

BOURNEMOUTH

Linwood School
Alma Road, Winton,
BOURNEMOUTH, Dorset BH9 1AJ
Tel: 01202 525107
Category: ASD MLD SLD
PMLD (Coed 3-19)

Tregonwell Academy
Petersfield Road, BOURNEMOUTH,
Dorset BH7 6QP
Tel: 01202 424361
Category: ASC, ASD,
BESD (Coed 5-16)

BRACKNELL FOREST
Borough Council

Bracknell SENDIASS, Time Square, Market Street, Bracknell, Berkshire, RG12 1JD
Tel: 01344 354011 Email: send.support@bracknell-forest.gov.uk Website: www.bracknell-forest.gov.uk

BRACKNELL

Kennel Lane School
Kennel Lane, BRACKNELL,
Berkshire RG42 2EX
Tel: 01344 483872
Category: MLD SLD AUT PMLD

BRADFORD
Council

Bradford SENDIASS, Queen's House, Queen's Road, Bradford, West Yorkshire, BD8 7BS
Tel: 01274 481183 Email: bradfordsendiass@barnardos.org.uk

BRADFORD

Chellow Heights School
Thorn Lane, Bingley Road,
BRADFORD, West Yorkshire BD9 6AL
Tel: 01274 484242
Category: ADS, AUT, HI, MSI,
PMLD, SLD, VIS (Primary 2-11)

Delius Special School
Barkerend Road, BRADFORD,
West Yorkshire BD3 8QX
Tel: 01274 666472
Category: SLD PMLD ASD
(Nursery & Primary 2-11)

Hazelbeck School
Wagon Lane, Bingley, BRADFORD,
West Yorkshire BD16 1EE
Tel: 01274 777107
Category: SLD PMLD
ASD (Secondary)

High Park School
Thorn lane, BRADFORD,
West Yorkshire BD9 6RY
Tel: 01274 696740
Category: ASD (Primary
& Secondary)

Oastler's School
Flockton Road, BRADFORD,
West Yorkshire BD4 7RH
Tel: 01274 307456
Category: (Coed Day 11-19)

Southfield School
Haycliffe Lane, BRADFORD,
West Yorkshire BD5 9ET
Tel: 01274 779662
Category: SLD PMLD
ASD (Secondary)

KEIGHLEY

**Beckfood Phoenix
Primary Special School**
Braithwaite Avenue, KEIGHLEY,
West Yorkshire BD22 6HZ
Tel: 01535 607038
Category: ASD, HI, PMLD,
SLD, SP&LD, VIS (Primary)

Beechcliffe School
Greenhead Road, Utley, KEIGHLEY,
West Yorkshire BD20 6ED
Tel: 01535 603041
Category: SLD PMLD
ASD (Secondary)

BRIGHTON & HOVE
City Council

Brighton & Hove SEN Team, Kings House, Grand Avenue, Hove, East Sussex, BN3 2LS
Tel: 01273 293552 Fax: 01273 293547 Email: sen.team@brighton-hove.gov.uk Website: www.brighton-hove.gov.uk

BRIGHTON

Cedar Centre
Lynchet Close, Hollingdean,
BRIGHTON, East Sussex BN1 7FP
Tel: 01273 558622
Category: ADHD, ASC, MLD

Downs Park School
Foredown Road, Portslade,
BRIGHTON, East Sussex BN41 2FU
Tel: 01273 417448
Category: ASD (Coed 5-16)

Downs View School
Warren Road, BRIGHTON,
East Sussex BN2 6BB
Tel: 01273 601680
Category: ASD, HI, SLD, VIS (4-19)

Hillside Special School
Foredown Road, Portslade,
BRIGHTON, East Sussex BN41 2FU
Tel: 01273 416979
Category: ASC, MLD, SLD (4-16)

Homewood College
Queensdown Road, BRIGHTON,
East Sussex BN1 7LA
Tel: 01273 604472
Category: ADHD, SEBD,
SPLD, SP&LD (Coed 5-16)

Patcham House School
7 Old London Road, Patcham,
BRIGHTON, East Sussex BN1 8XR
Tel: 01273 551028
Category: PD Del ASP
MLD SPLD (11-16)

BRISTOL
City Council

Bristol SEN Team, Parkview Campus, P.O. Box 3176, Bristol, BS3 9FS
Tel: 0117 922 3700 Email: sen@bristol.gov.uk Website: www.bristol.gov.uk

BRISTOL

Briarwood School
Briar Way, Fishponds,
BRISTOL BS16 4EA
Tel: 01173 532651
Category: SLD PMLD
AUT (Coed 3-19)

Bristol Gateway School
Long Cross, Lawrence
Weston, BRISTOL BS11 0QA
Tel: 01173 772275
Category: SEMH (Coed 11-17)

Claremont School
Henleaze Park, Westbury-
on-Trym, BRISTOL BS9 4LR
Tel: 01173 533622
Category: MSI, PD, PMLD,
SLCN, SLD (Coed 2-19)

**Elmfield School for
Deaf Children**
Greystoke Avenue, Westbury-
on-Trym, BRISTOL BS10 6AY
Tel: 01179 030366
Category: D HI (Coed 2-16)

Kingsweston School
Napier Miles Road, Kingsweston,
BRISTOL BS11 0UT
Tel: 01179 030400
Category: MLD SLD AUT (Coed 3-19)

Knowle DGE Academy
Leinster Avenue, Knowle,
BRISTOL BS4 1NN
Tel: 01173 532011
Category: ASC, CLD, MLD, SEMH,
SLCN, Complex Needs (Coed 5-16)

New Fosseway School
Teyfant Road, Hartcliffe,
BRISTOL BS13 0RL
Tel: 01179 030220
Category: ASD, AUT, PMLD,
SLD (Coed 6-19)

Notton House School
28 Notton, Lacock,
BRISTOL SN15 2NF
Tel: 01249 730407
Category: SEMH (Boys 9-16)

Woodstock School
Rectory Gardens, Henbury,
BRISTOL BS10 7AH
Tel: 01173 772175
Category: SEMH (Primary)

BUCKINGHAMSHIRE
County Council

Buckinghamshire SENDIASS, County Hall, Walton Street, Aylesbury, Buckinghamshire, HP20 1UA
Tel: 01296 383754 Email: sendias@buckscc.gov.uk Website: www.buckscc.gov.uk

AMERSHAM

Stony Dean School
Orchard End Avenue, Off
Pineapple Road, AMERSHAM,
Buckinghamshire HP7 9JW
Tel: 01494 762538
Category: ASD, MLD Language &
Communication, SLCN (Coed 11-19)

AYLESBURY

Booker Park School
Stoke Leys Close, Kynaston
Avenue, AYLESBURY,
Buckinghamshire HP21 9ET
Tel: 01296 427221
Category: ASD MLD
SLD (Coed 3-11)

**Chiltern Way Federation -
Wendover House School**
Church Lane, Wendover,
AYLESBURY, Buckinghamshire
HP22 6NL
Tel: 01296 622157
Category: BESD (Boys
Day/boarding 11-16)

Pebble Brook School
Churchill Avenue, AYLESBURY,
Buckinghamshire HP21 8LZ
Tel: 01296 415761
Category: ADHD, ASC, MLD SLC
(Coed Day/boarding 11-19)

**Stocklake Park
Community School**
Stocklake, AYLESBURY,
Buckinghamshire HP20 1DP
Tel: 01296 423507
Category: SLD (Coed 11-19)

BEACONSFIELD

Alfriston School
Penn Road, Knotty
Green, BEACONSFIELD,
Buckinghamshire HP9 2TS
Tel: 01494 673740
Category: MLD (Girls Day/
boarding 11-19)

CHESHAM

Heritage House School
Cameron Road, CHESHAM,
Buckinghamshire HP5 3BP
Tel: 01494 771445
Category: SLD (Coed 2-19)

GREAT MISSENDEN

**Chiltern Way Federation
- Prestwood Campus**
Nairdwood Lane, Prestwood,
GREAT MISSENDEN,
Buckinghamshire HP16 0QQ
Tel: 01494 863514
Category: BESD (Boys
Day/boarding 11-16)

HIGH WYCOMBE

Chiltern Wood School
Verney Avenue, HIGH WYCOMBE,
Buckinghamshire HP12 3NE
Tel: 01494 532621
Category: ASD, SLCN (Coed 3-19)

The Downley School
Faulkner Way, Downley,
HIGH WYCOMBE,
Buckinghamshire HP13 5AL
Tel: 01494 525728
Category: EBSD, LD,
SPLD (Coed 2-19)

Westfield School
Highfield Road, Bourne
End, HIGH WYCOMBE,
Buckinghamshire SL8 5BE
Tel: 01628 533125
Category: ASD, ADHD,
BESD, SP&LD (Coed 4-11)

WINSLOW

Furze Down School
Verney Road, WINSLOW,
Buckinghamshire MK18 3BL
Tel: 01296 711380
Category: ASD, MLD, SLCN,
SPLD (Coed 2-19)

CAMBRIDGESHIRE
County Council

Cambridgeshire SEN Team, Box No. CC1101, Castle Court, Cambridge, CB3 0AP

Tel: 01223 699214 Email: pps@cambridgeshire.gov.uk Website: www.cambridgeshire.gov.uk

Samuel Pepys School
Cromwell Road, St. Neots, ,
Cambridgeshire PE19 2EZ
Tel: 01480 375012
Category: ASD HI PMLD SLD VIS
Complex needs (Coed 2-19)

CAMBRIDGE

Castle School
Courtney Way,
CAMBRIDGE CB4 2EE
Tel: 01223 442400
Category: ASC MLD PMLD
SLD SP&LD (Coed 3-19)

Granta School
Cambridge Road, Linton,
CAMBRIDGE CB21 4NN
Tel: 01223 896890
Category: ASD PMLD SLD
MLD (Coed 3-19)

TBAP Unity Academy
Almond Road, St.
Neots, CAMBRIDGE,
Cambridgeshire PE19 1EA
Tel: 020 3108 0345
Category: ACLD, EBSP,
SEAL (Coed 11-16)

COTTENHAM

The Centre School
High Street, COTTENHAM,
Cambridgeshire CB24 8UA
Tel: 01954 288789
Category: SEMH (Coed 11-16)

ELY

Highfield Ely Academy
Downham Road, ELY,
Cambridgeshire CB6 1BD
Tel: 01353 662085
Category: ASD MLD PD
PMLD SLD VIS (Coed 2-19)

The Harbour School
Station Road, Wilburton, ELY,
Cambridgeshire CB6 3RR
Tel: 01353 740229
Category: ADD EBD MLD
SEBN (Boys 5-16)

WISBECH

Meadowgate School
Meadowgate Lane, WISBECH,
Cambridgeshire PE13 2JH
Tel: 01945 461836
Category: AUT MLD SLD
SP&LD (Coed 2-19)

CHESHIRE EAST
Council

Cheshire East SENDIASS, c/o Municipal Buildings, Earle Street, Crewe, CW1 2BJ

Tel: 0300 123 5166 Email: ceias@cheshireeast.gov.uk Website: www.ceias.cheshireeast.gov.uk

CREWE

Springfield School
Crewe Green Road, CREWE,
Cheshire CW1 5HS
Tel: 01270 685446
Category: ASC PMLD
SLD (Coed 4-19)

MACCLESFIELD

Park Lane School
Park Lane, MACCLESFIELD,
Cheshire SK11 8JR
Tel: 01625 384040
Category: AUT HI SLD VIS
(Coed Day 2-19)

CHESHIRE WEST & CHESTER
Council

Chester SEN Assessment, Monitoring & Support Team, 4 Civic Way, Ellesmere Port, CH65 0BE

Tel: 0151 337 6505 Email: senteam@cheshirewestandchester.gov.uk Website: www.cheshirewestandchester.gov.uk

CHESTER

Dee Banks School
Dee Banks, Sandy Lane,
CHESTER, Cheshire CH3 5UX
Tel: 01244 981030
Category: ASD SLD PMLD
(Coed Day 2-19)

**Dorin Park School &
Specialist SEN College**
Wealstone Lane, Upton,
CHESTER, Cheshire CH2 1HD
Tel: 01244 981191
Category: PD Complex
needs (Coed Day 2-19)

ELLESMERE PORT

**Capenhurst
Grange School**
Chester Road, Great
Sutton, ELLESMERE PORT,
Cheshire CH66 2NA
Tel: 01513 382141
Category: BESD (Coed 11-16)

Hinderton School
Capenhurst Lane,
Whitby, ELLESMERE PORT,
Cheshire CH65 7AQ
Tel: 01513 382200
Category: ASD with complex
learning needs (Coed Day 3-11)

NORTHWICH

Greenbank School
Greenbank Lane, Hartford,
NORTHWICH, Cheshire CW8 1LD
Tel: 01606 288028
Category: ASD MLD
(Coed Day 11-18)

Rosebank School
Townfield Lane, Barnton,
NORTHWICH, Cheshire CW8 4QP
Tel: 01606 74975
Category: ASD with complex
learning needs (Coed Day 4-11)

The Russett School
Middlehurst Avenue, Weaverham,
NORTHWICH, Cheshire CW8 3BW
Tel: 01606 853005
Category: MSI PMLD SLD
(Coed Day 2-19)

WINSFORD

**Hebden Green
Community School**
Woodford Lane West,
WINSFORD, Cheshire CW7 4EJ
Tel: 01606 594221
Category: PD Complex needs
(Coed Day/Residential 6-19)

Oaklands School
Montgomery Way, WINSFORD,
Cheshire CW7 1NU
Tel: 01606 551048
Category: HI MLD SEMH
SP&LD (Coed Day 11-17)

CORNWALL
Council

Cornwall SEN Team, 3 West, New County Hall, Truro, Cornwall, TR1 3AY
Tel: 01872 324242 Email: specialeducation@cornwall.gov.uk Website: www.cornwall.gov.uk

PENZANCE

Nancealverne School
Madron Road, PENZANCE,
Cornwall TR20 8TP
Tel: 01736 365039
Category: HI PD PMLD
SLD VIS (Coed 2-19)

REDRUTH

Curnow School
Drump Road, REDRUTH,
Cornwall TR15 1LU
Tel: 01209 215432
Category: PMLD SLD (Coed 3-19)

ST AUSTELL

Doubletrees School
St Blazey Gate, St Blazey, Par, ST
AUSTELL, Cornwall PL24 2DS
Tel: 01726 812757
Category: ASD PD PMLD
SLD (Coed 2-19)

CUMBRIA
County Council

Cumbria SEND Team, Cumbria House, 117 Botchergate, Carlisle, Cumbria, CA1 1RD
Tel: 01228 226582 Email: localoffer@cumbria.gov.uk Website: www.cumbria.gov.uk

CARLISLE

James Rennie School
California Road, Kingstown,
CARLISLE, Cumbria CA3 0BX
Tel: 01228 554280
Category: MSI PMLD
SLD (3-19 Coed)

KENDAL

Sandgate School
Sandylands Road, KENDAL,
Cumbria LA9 6JG
Tel: 01539 792100
Category: PMLD SLD (3-19 Coed)

ULVERSTON

Sandside Lodge School
Sandside Road, ULVERSTON,
Cumbria LA12 9EF
Tel: 01229 588825
Category: PMLD SLD (2-19 Coed)

WHITEHAVEN

Mayfield School
Moresby Road, Hensingham,
WHITEHAVEN, Cumbria CA28 8TU
Tel: 01946 691253
Category: PMLD SLD (3-19 Coed)

DERBYSHIRE
County Council

Derbyshire Special Needs Section, County Hall, Matlock, Derbyshire, DE4 3AG
Tel: 01629 536539 Email: sen.admin@derbyshire.gov.uk Website: www.derbyshire.gov.uk

ALFRETON

**Alfreton Park Community
Special School**
Wingfield Road, Alfreton Park,
ALFRETON, Derbyshire DE55 7AL
Tel: 01773 832019
Category: ASD SLD (2-19)

**Swanwick School and
Sports College**
Hayes Lane, Swanwick,
ALFRETON, Derbyshire DE55 1AR
Tel: 01773 602198
Category: ASD MLD PD SEMH
SLCN SLD SpLD (5-16)

BELPER

Holbrook School for Autism
Port Way, Holbrook, BELPER,
Derbyshire DE56 0TE
Tel: 01332 880208
Category: AUT (4-19)

BUXTON

Peak School
Buxton Road, Chinley, High Peak,
BUXTON, Derbyshire SK23 6ES
Tel: 01663 750324
Category: PMLD SLD (2-19)

CHESTERFIELD

Ashgate Croft School
Ashgate Road, CHESTERFIELD,
Derbyshire S40 4BN
Tel: 01246 275111
Category: AUT EBD MLD
PMLD SLD (4-19)

Holly House School
Church Street North, Old
Whittington, CHESTERFIELD,
Derbyshire S41 9QR
Tel: 01246 450530
Category: EBD SEBD (7-14 Coed)

ILKESTON

**Bennerley Fields
Specialist Speech &
Language College**
Stratford Street, ILKESTON,
Derbyshire DE7 8QZ
Tel: 01159 326374
Category: ASD MLD SLCN SLD (2-16)

LONG EATON

Brackenfield School
Bracken Road, LONG
EATON NG10 4DA
Tel: 01159 733710
Category: ADHD ASD
MLD SEBN (4-16)

**Stanton Vale
Special School**
Thoresby Road, LONG
EATON NG10 3NP
Tel: 01159 72 9769
Category: ASD AUT CB MLD
MSI PH PMLD SLD (2-19)

SHIREBROOK

Stubbin Wood School
Common Lane, SHIREBROOK,
Derbyshire NG20 8QF
Tel: 01623 742795
Category: MLD PMLD SLD (2-19)

DERBY CITY
Council

Derby SENDIASS, The Council House, Corporation Street, Derby, Derbyshire, DE1 2FS
Tel: 01332 641414 Email: sendiass@derby.gov.uk Website: www.derby.gov.uk

DERBY

Ivy House School
Moorway Lane, Littleover,
DERBY DE23 2FS
Tel: 01332 777920
Category: SLD PMLD (Coed 2-19)

St Andrew's School
St Andrew's View, Breadsall
Hilltop, DERBY DE21 4EW
Tel: 01332 832746
Category: ASD MLD
SLD (Coed 11-19)

St Clare's School
Rough Heanor Road,
Mickleover, DERBY DE3 9AZ
Tel: 01332 511757
Category: AUT MLD HI PD SLD
SP&LD VIS (Coed 11-16)

St Giles' School
Hampshire Road, Chaddesden,
DERBY DE21 6BT
Tel: 01332 343039
Category: ASD CLD MLD
SLD (Coed 4-11)

St Martin's School
Bracknell Drive, Alvaston,
DERBY DE24 0BR
Tel: 01332 571151
Category: ASD CLD EBD
MLD SLD (Coed 11-16)

The Kingsmead School
Bridge Street, DERBY DE1 3LB
Tel: 01332 715970
Category: EBD (Coed 11-16)

DEVON
County Council

Devon 0-25 SEN Team, County Hall, Topsham Road, Exeter, Devon, EX2 4QD
Tel: 01392 383913 Email: specialeducation0-25-mailbox@devon.gov.uk Website: www.devon.gov.uk

BARNSTAPLE

Pathfield School
Abbey Road, Pilton,
BARNSTAPLE, Devon EX31 1JU
Tel: 01271 342423
Category: ASD PMLD SLD (3-19)

**The Lampard
Community School**
St John's Lane, BARNSTAPLE,
Devon EX32 9DD
Tel: 01271 345416
Category: Complex and
difficulties with communication
and interaction (including
SLCN and/or ASC) (5-16)

BUDLEIGH SALTERTON

**Mill Water Community
School**
Bicton, East Budleigh, BUDLEIGH
SALTERTON, Devon EX9 7BJ
Tel: 01395 568890
Category: ASC CD PD
PMLD SLD (3-19)

DAWLISH

Oaklands Park School
John Nash Drive, DAWLISH,
Devon EX7 9SF
Tel: 01626 862363
Category: SLD ASC PMLD
(Day/boarding 3-19)

Ratcliffe School
John Nash Drive, DAWLISH,
Devon EX7 9RZ
Tel: 01626 862939
Category: ASC and Associated
Social Development Needs (5-16)

EXETER

Barley Lane School
Barley Lane, St Thomas,
EXETER, Devon EX4 1TA
Tel: 01392 430774
Category: ADHD ASD BESD (7-16)

Ellen Tinkham School
Hollow Lane, EXETER,
Devon EX1 3RW
Tel: 01392 467168
Category: ASC PMLD SLD (3-19)

Southbrook School
Bishop Westall Road,
EXETER, Devon EX2 6JB
Tel: 01392 258373
Category: ASC EBSD MLD PD (11-16)

TORRINGTON

Marland School
Petersmarland, TORRINGTON,
Devon EX38 8QQ
Tel: 01805 601324
Category: BESD SEBD (10-16 boys)

TOTNES

Bidwell Brook School
Shinner's Bridge, Dartington,
TOTNES, Devon TQ9 6JU
Tel: 01803 864120
Category: SLD PMLD (3-19)

DORSET
County Council

Dorset SEN Team, County Hall, Dorchester, DT1 1XJ
Tel: 01305 224888 Fax: 01305 224547 Email: senteam@dorsetcc.gov.uk Website: https://www.dorsetforyou.gov.uk/

BEAMINSTER

Mountjoy School
Tunnel Road, BEAMINSTER,
Dorset DT8 3HB
Tel: 01308 861155
Category: ASD SLD MLD
PMLD Complex (2-19)

STURMINSTER NEWTON

Yewstock School
Honeymead Lane, STURMINSTER
NEWTON, Dorset DT10 1EW
Tel: 01258 472796
Category: ASC MLD/
Comlex PMLD SLD (3-19)

WEYMOUTH

Westfield Arts College
Littlemoor Road, Preston,
WEYMOUTH, Dorset DT3 6AA
Tel: 01305 833518
Category: ASD MLD/Complex (4-19)

Wyvern School
Dorchester Road, WEYMOUTH,
Dorset DT3 5AL
Tel: 01305 817917
Category: ASD PMLD
SLD Complex (2-19)

WIMBORNE

Beaucroft Foundation School
Wimborne Road, Colehill,
WIMBORNE, Dorset BH21 2SS
Tel: 01202 886083
Category: ASD MLD/Complex (4-19)

DURHAM
County Council

Durham SEN Team, Children and Adult Services, County Hall, Durham, County Durham, DH1 5UJ
Tel: 03000 265878 Website: www.durham.gov.uk

BISHOP AUCKLAND

Evergreen Primary School
Warwick Road, BISHOP
AUCKLAND, Durham DL14 6LS
Tel: 01388 459721
Category: MLD SLD PMLD AUT (2-11)

CONSETT

Villa Real School
Villa Real Road, CONSETT,
Durham DH8 6BH
Tel: 01207 503651
Category: AUC BESD
PMLD SLD (2-19)

DURHAM

Durham Trinity School and Sports College
Aykley Heads, DURHAM DH1 5TS
Tel: 01913 864612
Category: ASD ASP MLD
PMLD SLD SP&LD (2-19)

FERRYHILL

Windlestone School
Chilton, FERRYHILL,
Durham DL17 0HP
Tel: 01388 720337
Category: AUT ASP
SEBD SP&LD (11-16)

NEWTON AYCLIFFE

Walworth School
Bluebell Way, NEWTON
AYCLIFFE, Durham DL5 7LP
Tel: 01325 300194
Category: SEBD (4-11)

SHERBURN

Elemore Hall School
Pittington, SHERBURN,
Durham DH6 1QD
Tel: 01913 720275
Category: SEBD (11-16)

SPENNYMOOR

The Meadows School
Whitworth Lane, SPENNYMOOR,
Durham DL16 7QW
Tel: 01388 811178
Category: SEBD (11-16)

The Oaks Secondary School
Rock Road, SPENNYMOOR,
Durham DL16 7DB
Tel: 01388 827380
Category: ASD MLD PMLD
SLD (11-19 coed)

STANLEY

Croft Community School
Greencroft Road End, Annfield
Plain, STANLEY, Durham DH9 8PR
Tel: 01207 234547
Category: ASD MLD SLCN
SLD (4-16 coed)

EDINBURGH

Gorgie Mills Special School
97 Gorgie Park Road,
EDINBURGH EH11 2QL
Tel: 01313 133848

ESSEX
County Council

Essex SENDIASS, County Hall, Market Road, Chelmsford, Essex, CM1 1QH
Tel: 03330 138913 Email: send.iass@essex.gov.uk Website: www.essex.gov.uk

BASILDON

Castledon School
Bromfords Drive, Wickford,
BASILDON, Essex SS12 0PW
Tel: 01268 761252
Category: ASD MLD (5-16)

The Pioneer School
Ghyllgrove, BASILDON,
Essex SS14 2LA
Tel: 01268 243300
Category: CLD PMLD SLD (3-19)

BENFLEET

Cedar Hall School
Hart Road, Thundersley,
BENFLEET, Essex SS7 3UQ
Tel: 01268 774723
Category: AUT CD MLD (4-16)

Glenwood School
Rushbottom Lane, New
Thundersley, BENFLEET,
Essex SS7 4LW
Tel: 01268 792575
Category: ASD SLD (3-19)

BILLERICAY

Ramsden Hall School
Heath Road, Ramsden Heath,
BILLERICAY, Essex CM11 1HN
Tel: 01277 624580
Category: BESD (Boys 11-16)

BRAINTREE

The Edith Borthwick School
Springwood Drive, BRAINTREE,
Essex CM7 2YN
Tel: 01376 529300
Category: ASD MLD PH
SLD SP&LD (3-19)

BRENTWOOD

Grove House School
Sawyers Hall Lane, BRENTWOOD,
Essex CM15 9DA
Tel: 01277 361498
Category: SP&LD Communication
Difficulties (9-19)

The Endeavour School
Hogarth Avenue, BRENTWOOD,
Essex CM15 8BE
Tel: 01277 217330
Category: MLD (5-16)

CHELMSFORD

**The Columbus
School & College**
Oliver Way, CHELMSFORD,
Essex CM1 4ZB
Tel: 01245 491492
Category: SpLD (3-19 coed)

Thriftwood School
Slades Lane, Galleywood,
CHELMSFORD, Essex CM2 8RW
Tel: 01245 266880
Category: LD (5-13)

CHIGWELL

Wells Park School
School Lane, Lambourne Road,
CHIGWELL, Essex IG7 6NN
Tel: 02085 026442
Category: BESD (5-11 boys)

CLACTON ON SEA

Shorefields School
114 Holland Road, CLACTON
ON SEA, Essex CO15 6HF
Tel: 01255 424412
Category: ASD MLD SLD (3-19)

COLCHESTER

Kingswode Hoe School
Sussex Road, COLCHESTER,
Essex CO3 3QJ
Tel: 01206 576408
Category: ASD ASP MLD
PI SP&LD (5-16)

Langham Oaks School
School Road, Langham,
COLCHESTER, Essex CO4 5PA
Tel: 01206 271571
Category: SEMH (Boys 10-16)

Lexden Springs School
Halstead Road, Lexden,
COLCHESTER, Essex CO3 9AB
Tel: 01206 563321
Category: ASD MLD
PMLD SLD (3-19)

Market Field School
School Road, Elmstead Market,
COLCHESTER, Essex CO7 7ET
Tel: 01206 825195
Category: ASD MLD SLD (4-16)

HARLOW

**Harlow Fields School
& College**
Tendring Road, HARLOW,
Essex CM18 6RN
Tel: 01279 423670
Category: ASD HI MLD PD
SLD SP&LD VIS (3-19)

LOUGHTON

Oak View School
Whitehills Road, LOUGHTON,
Essex IG10 1TS
Tel: 02085 084293
Category: MLD SLD (3-19)

WITHAM

Southview School
Conrad Road, WITHAM,
Essex CM8 2TA
Tel: 01376 503505
Category: PNI (3-19 coed)

GLOUCESTERSHIRE
County Council

Gloucestershire SENDIASS, Messenger House (2nd Floor), 35 St. Michael's Square, Gloucester, GL1 1HX
Tel: 0800 158 3603 Email: sendiass@carersgloucestershire.org.uk Website: http://sendiassglos.org.uk/

CHELTENHAM

**Battledown Centre for
Children and Families**
Harp Hill, Battledown,
CHELTENHAM,
Gloucestershire GL52 6PZ
Tel: 01242 525472
Category: VI SLCN ASD SEMH
PD MLD SLD (Coed 2-7)

Belmont School
Warden Hill Road, CHELTENHAM,
Gloucestershire GL51 3AT
Tel: 01242 216180
Category: MLD (Coed 4-16)

Bettridge School
Warden Hill Road, CHELTENHAM,
Gloucestershire GL51 3AT
Tel: 01242 514934
Category: ASD PMLD SLCN
SLD VI (Coed 2-19)

CIRENCESTER

Paternoster School
Watermoor Road, CIRENCESTER,
Gloucestershire GL7 1JR
Tel: 01285 652480
Category: PMLD SLD (Coed 2-16)

COLEFORD

**Heart of the Forest
Community School**
Speech House, Coalway,
COLEFORD, Gloucestershire
GL16 7EJ
Tel: 01594 822175
Category: PMLD SLD (Coed 3-19)

GLOUCESTER

The Milestone School
Longford Lane, GLOUCESTER,
Gloucestershire GL2 9EU
Tel: 01452 874000
Category: ASD PD PMLD MLD
SEMH SLCN SLD VI (Coed 2-16)

STONEHOUSE

The Shrubberies School
Oldends Lane, STONEHOUSE,
Gloucestershire GL10 2DG
Tel: 01453 822155
Category: SLD (Coed 2-19)

TEWKESBURY

Alderman Knight School
Ashchurch Road, TEWKESBURY,
Gloucestershire GL20 8JJ
Tel: 01684 295639
Category: ASD MLD
SLD (Coed 5-19)

SOUTH GLOUCESTERSHIRE
Council

0-25 Service, Department for Children, Adults & Health, PO Box 298, Civic
Centre, High Street Bristol, South Gloucestershire, BS15 0DQ
Tel: 01454 863301 or 01454 863173 Website: www.southglos.gov.uk

DOWNEND

Pathways Learning Centre
Overndale Road, DOWNEND,
South Gloucestershire BS16 2RQ
Tel: 01454 862630
Category: (Day 4-16)

KINGSWOOD

**New Horizons
Learning Centre**
Mulberry Drive, KINGSWOOD,
South Gloucestershire BS15 4EA
Tel: 01454 865340
Category: BESD

THORNBURY

New Siblands School
Easton Hill Road, THORNBURY,
South Gloucestershire BS35 2JU
Tel: 01454 862888
Category: SLD

Sheiling School
Thornbury Park, Park
Road, THORNBURY, South
Gloucestershire BS35 1HP
Tel: 01454 412 194
Category: (Day & Boarding)

WARMLEY

Warmley Park School
Tower Road North, WARMLEY,
South Gloucestershire BS30 8XL
Tel: 01454 867272
Category: SLD (Day 3-19)

YATE

Culverhill School
Kelston Close, YATE, South
Gloucestershire BS37 8SZ
Tel: 01454 866930
Category: CLD (Day 7-16)

HALTON
Borough Council

Halton SEND Partnership, Rutland House, Halton Lea, Runcorn, Cheshire, WA7 2GW
Tel: 01515 117733 Email: sendpartnership@halton.gov.uk Website: www3.halton.gov.uk

WIDNES

Ashley School
Cawfield Avenue, WIDNES,
Cheshire WA8 7HG
Tel: 01514 244892
Category: MLD Complex
emotional needs (11-16)

Brookfields School
Moorfield Road, WIDNES,
Cheshire WA8 0JA
Tel: 01514 244329
Category: SLD (2-11)

**Chesnut Lodge School &
Specialist SEN College**
Green Lane, WIDNES,
Cheshire WA8 7HF
Tel: 01514 240679
Category: PH (2-16)

HAMPSHIRE

County Council

Children's Services Department, Elizabeth II Court, The Castle, Winchester, Hampshire, SO23 8UG
Tel: 03005 551384 Email: childrens.services@hants.gov.uk Website: www.hants.gov.uk

ANDOVER

Icknield School
River Way, ANDOVER,
Hampshire SP11 6LT
Tel: 01264 365297
Category: SLD (Coed 2-19)

Norman Gate School
Vigo Road, ANDOVER,
Hampshire SP10 1JZ
Tel: 01264 323423
Category: MLD ASD (Coed 2-11)

The Mark Way School
Batchelors Barn Road, ANDOVER,
Hampshire SP10 1HR
Tel: 01264 351835
Category: MLD ASD (Coed 11-16)

**Wolverdene
Special School**
22 Love Lane, ANDOVER,
Hampshire SP10 2AF
Tel: 01264 362350
Category: BESD (Coed 5-11)

BASINGSTOKE

Coppice Spring School
Pack Lane, BASINGSTOKE,
Hampshire RG22 5TH
Tel: 01256 336601
Category: BESD (Coed 11-16)

Dove House School
Sutton Road, BASINGSTOKE,
Hampshire RG21 5SU
Tel: 01256 351555
Category: MLD ASD (Coed 11-16)

Limington House School
St Andrews Road, BASINGSTOKE,
Hampshire RG22 6PS
Tel: 01256 322148
Category: SLD (Coed 2-19)

Maple Ridge School
Maple Crescent, BASINGSTOKE,
Hampshire RG21 5SX
Tel: 01256 323639
Category: MLD ASD (Coed 4-11)

Saxon Wood School
Rooksdown, Barron
Place, BASINGSTOKE,
Hampshire RG24 9NH
Tel: 01256 356635
Category: PD (Coed 2-11)

BORDON

Hollywater School
Mill Chase Road, BORDON,
Hampshire GU35 0HA
Tel: 01420 474396
Category: LD (Coed 2-19)

CHANDLERS FORD

Lakeside School
Winchester Road, CHANDLERS
FORD, Hampshire SO53 2DW
Tel: 02380 266633
Category: BESD (Boys 11-16)

FAREHAM

Baycroft School
Gosport Road, Stubbington,
FAREHAM, Hampshire PO14 2AE
Tel: 01329 664151
Category: MLD ASD (Coed 11-16)

Heathfield School
Oldbury Way, FAREHAM,
Hampshire PO14 3BN
Tel: 01329 845150
Category: MLD ASD PD (Coed 2-11)

St Francis Special School
Patchway Drive, Oldbury Way,
FAREHAM, Hampshire PO14 3BN
Tel: 01329 845730
Category: SLD (Coed 2-19)

FARNBOROUGH

Henry Tyndale School
Ship Lane, FARNBOROUGH,
Hampshire GU14 8BX
Tel: 01252 544577
Category: LD ASD (Coed 2-19)

**Samuel Cody Specialist
Sports College**
Ballantyne Road, FARNBOROUGH,
Hampshire GU14 8SS
Tel: 01252 514194
Category: MLD ASD (Coed 11-16)

HAVANT

Prospect School
Freeley Road, HAVANT,
Hampshire PO9 4AQ
Tel: 02392 485140
Category: BESD (Boys 11-16)

PORTSMOUTH

Glenwood School
Washington Road,
Emsworth, PORTSMOUTH,
Hampshire PO10 7NN
Tel: 01243 373120
Category: MLD ASD (Coed 11-16)

SOUTHAMPTON

Forest Park School
Ringwood Road,
Totton, SOUTHAMPTON,
Hampshire SO40 8DZ
Tel: 02380 864949
Category: LD (Coed 2-19)

Oak Lodge School
Roman Road, Dibden
Purlieu, SOUTHAMPTON,
Hampshire SO45 4RQ
Tel: 02380 847213
Category: MLD ASD (Coed 11-16)

WATERLOOVILLE

Rachel Madocks School
Eagle Avenue, Cowplain,
WATERLOOVILLE,
Hampshire PO8 9XP
Tel: 02392 241818
Category: SLD (Coed 2-19)

**Riverside Community
Special School**
Scratchface Lane,
Purbrook, WATERLOOVILLE,
Hampshire PO7 5QD
Tel: 02392 250138
Category: MLD ASD (Coed 3-11)

The Waterloo School
Warfield Avenue, WATERLOOVILLE,
Hampshire PO7 7JJ
Tel: 02392 255956
Category: BESD (Boys 4-11)

WINCHESTER

Osborne School
Athelstan Road, WINCHESTER,
Hampshire SO23 7GA
Tel: 01962 854537
Category: LD ASD (Coed 11-19)

**Shepherds Down
Special School**
Shepherds Lane, Compton,
WINCHESTER, Hampshire SO21 2AJ
Tel: 01962 713445
Category: LD ASD (Coed 4-11)

HARTLEPOOL

Borough Council

Hartlepool SEN Team, IASS, Civic Centre, Victoria Road, Hartlepool, TS24 8AY
Tel: 01429 284866 Email: hartlepooliass@hartlepool.gov.uk Website: www.hartlepool.gov.uk

HARTLEPOOL

Springwell School
Wiltshire Way, HARTLEPOOL TS26 0TB
Tel: 01429 280600
Category: MLD SLD PMLD
ASD BESD (Coed 3-11)

HEREFORDSHIRE

Council

Herefordshire SENDIAS, Herefordshire Council, Plough Lane, Hereford, Herefordshire, HR4 0LE
Tel: 01432 260955 Email: sendias@herefordshire.gov.uk Website: www.herefordshire.gov.uk

HEREFORD

Barrs Court School
Barrs Court Road,
HEREFORD HR1 1EQ
Tel: 01432 265035
Category: CLD PMLD MSI PD ADHD
ASD OCD SP&LD SLD (Coed 11-19)

Blackmarston School
Honddu Close, HEREFORD HR2 7NX
Tel: 01432 272376
Category: SLD ASD
PMLD(Coed 3-11)

LEOMINSTER

Westfield School
Westfield Walk,
LEOMINSTER HR6 8NZ
Tel: 01568 613147
Category: SLD ASD
PMLD (Coed 2-19)

HERTFORDSHIRE

County Council

Hertfordshire SENDIASS, County Hall, Pegs Lane, Hertford, SG13 8DQ
Tel: 01992 555847 Email: sendiass@hertfordshire.gov.uk Website: www.hertsdirect.org

BALDOCK

Brandles School
Weston Way, BALDOCK,
Hertfordshire SG7 6EY
Tel: 01462 892189
Category: EBD (Boys 11-16)

BUSHEY

Meadow Wood School
Cold Harbour Lane, BUSHEY,
Hertfordshire WD23 4NN
Tel: 02084 204720
Category: PI (Coed Day 3-12)

HATFIELD

Southfield School
Woods Avenue, HATFIELD,
Hertfordshire AL10 8NN
Tel: 01707 276504
Category: MLD (Coed Day 3-11)

HEMEL HEMPSTEAD

Haywood Grove School
St Agnells Lane, HEMEL HEMPSTEAD,
Hertfordshire HP2 7BG
Tel: 01442 250077
Category: EBD (Coed Day 5-11)

The Collett School
Lockers Park Lane, HEMEL
HEMPSTEAD, Hertfordshire HP1 1TQ
Tel: 01442 398988
Category: MLD AUT (Coed 4-16)

Woodfield School
Malmes Croft, Leverstock
Green, HEMEL HEMPSTEAD,
Hertfordshire HP3 8RL
Tel: 01442 253476
Category: SLD AUT (Coed Day 3-19)

HERTFORD

Hailey Hall School
Hailey Lane, HERTFORD,
Hertfordshire SG13 7PB
Tel: 01992 465208
Category: EBD (Boys 11-16)

RADLETT

**Forest House
Education Centre**
9 Forest Lane, Kingsley Green,
Harper Lane, RADLETT,
Hertfordshire WD7 9HQ
Tel: 01923 633241
Category: (13-18)

REDBOURN

St Luke's School
Crouch Hall Lane, REDBOURN,
Hertfordshire AL3 7ET
Tel: 01582 626727
Category: MLD (Coed Day 9-16)

ST ALBANS

Batchwood School
Townsend Drive, ST ALBANS,
Hertfordshire AL3 5RP
Tel: 01727 868021
Category: EBD (Coed 11-16)

Heathlands School
Heathlands Drive, ST ALBANS,
Hertfordshire AL3 5AY
Tel: 01727 807807
Category: HI (Coed Day
& boarding 3-16)

Watling View School
Watling View, ST ALBANS,
Hertfordshire AL1 2NU
Tel: 01727 850560
Category: SLD (Coed Day 2-19)

STEVENAGE

Greenside School
Shephall Green, STEVENAGE,
Hertfordshire SG2 9XS
Tel: 01438 315356
Category: SLD AUT (Coed Day 2-19)

Larwood School
Webb Rise, STEVENAGE,
Hertfordshire SG1 5QU
Tel: 01438 236333
Category: EBD (Coed
Day & boarding 5-11)

Lonsdale School
Brittain Way, STEVENAGE,
Hertfordshire SG2 8UT
Tel: 01438 726999
Category: PH (Coed Day
& boarding 5-19)

The Valley School
Valley Way, STEVENAGE,
Hertfordshire SG2 9AB
Tel: 01438 747274
Category: MLD (Coed Day 11-19)

WARE

**Amwell View School &
Specialist Sports College**
Stanstead Abbotts, WARE,
Hertfordshire SG12 8EH
Tel: 01920 870027
Category: SLD AUT (Coed Day 2-19)

Middleton School
Walnut Tree Walk, WARE,
Hertfordshire SG12 9PD
Tel: 01920 485152
Category: MLD AUT
(Coed Day 5-11)

Pinewood School
Hoe Lane, WARE,
Hertfordshire SG12 9PB
Tel: 01920 412211
Category: MLD (Coed
Residential 11-16)

WATFORD

Breakspeare School
Gallows Hill Lane, Abbots Langley,
WATFORD, Hertfordshire WD5 0BU
Tel: 01923 263645
Category: SLD (Coed Day 3-19)

Colnbrook School
Hayling Road, WATFORD,
Hertfordshire WD19 7UY
Tel: 02084 281281
Category: MLD AUT
(Coed Day 4-11)

Falconer School
Falconer Road, Bushey, WATFORD,
Hertfordshire WD23 3AT
Tel: 02089 502505
Category: EBD (Boys Day/
boarding 10-19)

Garston Manor School
Horseshoe Lane, Garston,
WATFORD, Hertfordshire WD25 7HR
Tel: 01923 673757
Category: MLD (Coed Day 11-16)

WELWYN GARDEN CITY

Knightsfield School
Knightsfield, WELWYN GARDEN
CITY, Hertfordshire AL8 7LW
Tel: 01707 376874
Category: HI (Coed Day
& boarding 10-19)

Lakeside School
Stanfield, Lemsford Lane,
WELWYN GARDEN CITY,
Hertfordshire AL8 6YN
Tel: 01707 327410
Category: SLD PD (Coed Day 2-19)

ISLE OF WIGHT
Council

Isle of Wight SEN Service, Thompson House, Sandy Lane, Newport, Isle of Wight, PO30 3NA
Tel: 01983 823470 Website: www.iwight.com

NEWPORT

Medina House School
School Lane, NEWPORT,
Isle of Wight PO30 2HS
Tel: 01983 522917
Category: Severe & complex
needs (Coed 2-11)

St George's School
Watergate Road, NEWPORT,
Isle of Wight PO30 1XW
Tel: 01983 524634
Category: Severe complex
needs (Coed 11-19)

KENT
County Council

Kent SENDIASS, Shepway Centre, Oxford Road, Maidstone, Kent, ME15 8AW
Tel: 03000 412412 Email: iask@kent.gov.uk Website: www.kent.gov.uk

ASHFORD

Goldwyn School
Godinton Lane, Great Chart,
ASHFORD, Kent TN23 3BT
Tel: 01233 622958
Category: BESD (Coed 11-16)

The Wyvern School
Great Chart Bypass,
ASHFORD, Kent TN23 4ER
Tel: 01233 621468
Category: PMLD SLD
CLD PD (Coed 3-19)

BROADSTAIRS

Stone Bay School
70 Stone Road, BROADSTAIRS,
Kent CT10 1EB
Tel: 01843 863421
Category: SLD AUT SLCN MLD C&I
(Coed Day & Residential 11-19)

CANTERBURY

St Nicholas' School
Holme Oak Close, Nunnery Fields,
CANTERBURY, Kent CT1 3JJ
Tel: 01227 464316
Category: PMLD SLD CLD
PSCN (Coed 3-19)

The Orchard School
Cambridge Road,
CANTERBURY, Kent CT1 3QQ
Tel: 01227 769220
Category: MLD CLD
B&L (Coed 11-16)

DARTFORD

Rowhill School
Main Road, Longfield,
DARTFORD, Kent DA3 7PW
Tel: 01474 705377
Category: B&L AUT LD
Complex needs Behavioural
difficulties (Coed Day 4-16)

DOVER

Elms School
Elms Vale Road, DOVER,
Kent CT17 9PS
Tel: 01304 201964
Category: BESD ASD MLD
B&L (Coed 4-16)

Portal House School
Sea Street, St Margarets-at-
Cliffe, DOVER, Kent CT15 6SS
Tel: 01304 853033
Category: BESD (Coed 11-16)

FOLKESTONE

The Beacon School
Park Farm Road, FOLKESTONE,
Kent CT19 5DN
Tel: 01303 847555
Category: MLD CLD Complex
needs (Coed 4-17)

GRAVESEND

The Ifield School
Cedar Avenue, GRAVESEND,
Kent DA12 5JT
Tel: 01474 365485
Category: CLD PMLD SLD
MLD PSCN (Coed 4-18)

MAIDSTONE

Bower Grove School
Fant Lane, MAIDSTONE,
Kent ME16 8NL
Tel: 01622 726773
Category: BESD MLD ASD
B&L (Coed Day 5-16)

Five Acre Wood School
Boughton Lane, Loose Valley,
MAIDSTONE, Kent ME15 9QF
Tel: 01622 743925
Category: ASD PMLD SLD PD
CLD PSCN (Coed 4-19)

MARGATE

St Anthony's School
St Anthony's Way, MARGATE,
Kent CT9 3RA
Tel: 01843 292015
Category: MLD ASD LD SEBD
SLCN B&L (Coed 3-11)

RAMSGATE

Foreland Fields School
Newlands Lane, RAMSGATE,
Kent CT12 6RH
Tel: 01843 863891
Category: ASD PMLD SLD
PSCN (Coed 2-19)

Laleham Gap School
Ozengell Place, RAMSGATE,
Kent CT12 6FH
Tel: 01843 570598
Category: AUT ABD PD SLCN C&I
(CoedDay & Residential 3-16)

SEVENOAKS

Grange Park School
Borough Green Road, Wrotham,
SEVENOAKS, Kent TN15 7RD
Tel: 01732 882111
Category: AUT C&I
(Coed Day 11-19)

SITTINGBOURNE

Meadowfield School
Swanstree Avenue,
SITTINGBOURNE, Kent ME10 4NL
Tel: 01795 477788
Category: CLD PMLD SLD ASD
SP&LD PSCN (Coed 4-19)

SWANLEY

**Broomhill Bank
School (North)**
Rowhill Road, Hextable,
SWANLEY, Kent BR8 7RP
Tel: 01322 662937
Category: MLD SP&LD CLD AUT C&I
(Coed Day & Residential 11-19)

TONBRIDGE

Nexus School
Upper Haysden Lane,
TONBRIDGE, Kent TN11 8AA
Tel: 01732 771384
Category: PMLD ASD (Coed 2-19)

**Oakley School -
Tonbridge Site**
Waveney Road, TONBRIDGE,
Kent TN10 3JU
Tel: 01892 823096
Category: PMLD ASD MLD
PSCN (Coed 3-19)

TUNBRIDGE WELLS

**Broomhill Bank
School (West)**
Broomhill Road, Rusthall,
TUNBRIDGE WELLS, Kent TN3 0TB
Tel: 01892 510440
Category: MLD SP&LD CLD AUT C&I
(Coed Day & Residential 11-19)

**Oakley School -
Tunbridge Wells Site**
Pembury Road, TUNBRIDGE
WELLS, Kent TN2 4NE
Tel: 01892 823096
Category: PMLD ASD MLD
PSCN (Coed 3-19)

WESTERHAM

Valence School
Westerham Road, WESTERHAM,
Kent TN16 1QN
Tel: 01959 562156
Category: PD Sensory Medical
(Coed Day & Residential 4-19)

KINGSTON UPON HULL

City Council

0-25 Integrated SEN Team, Hull City Council, Children & Young People's
Services, Brunswick House, Strand Close Hull, HU2 9DB
Tel: 01482 300300 Email: send@hullcc.gov.uk Website: www.hullcc.gov.uk

KINGSTON UPON HULL

Bridgeview School
262a Pickering Road, KINGSTON
UPON HULL HU4 7AB
Tel: 01482 303300
Category: BESD

Frederick Holmes School
Inglemire Lane, KINGSTON
UPON HULL HU6 8JJ
Tel: 01482 804766
Category: PH

Ganton Primary School
The Compass, 1 Burnham Road,
KINGSTON UPON HULL HU4 7EB
Tel: 01482 564 646
Category: SLD

Ganton Secondary School
294 Anlaby Park Road South,
KINGSTON UPON HULL HU4 7JB
Tel: 01482 564646
Category: SLD

Northcott School
Dulverton Close, Bransholme,
KINGSTON UPON HULL HU7 4EL
Tel: 01482 825311
Category: Vulnerable ASD

Oakfield School
Hopewell Road, KINGSTON
UPON HULL HU9 4HD
Tel: 01482 854588
Category: BESD

Tweendykes School
Midmere Avenue, Leads Road,
KINGSTON UPON HULL HU7 4PW
Tel: 01482 826508
Category: SLD

LANCASHIRE

County Council

Lancashire SENDIASS, PO Box 78, County Hall, Fishergate Preston, Lancashire, PR1 8XJ
Tel: 03001 236706 Email: information.lineteam@lancashire.gov.uk Website: www.lancashire.gov.uk

ACCRINGTON

**Broadfield Specialist
School for SEN**
Fielding Lane, Oswaldtwistle,
ACCRINGTON, Lancashire BB5 3BE
Tel: 01254 381782
Category: AUT SLCN PD
PMLD VI HI (Coed 11-19)

White Ash School
Thwaites Road, Oswaldtwistle,
ACCRINGTON, Lancashire BB5 4QG
Tel: 01254 235772
Category: GLD (Coed 2-11)

BURNLEY

Holly Grove School
Burnley Campus, Barden Lane,
BURNLEY, Lancashire BB10 1JD
Tel: 01282 682278
Category: SLD MLD PMLD ASD
Medical needs (Coed 2-11)

**Ridgewood Community
High School**
Eastern Avenue, BURNLEY,
Lancashire BB10 2AT
Tel: 01282 682316
Category: MSI PD LD (Coed 11-19)

The Rose School
Greenock Street, BURNLEY,
Lancashire BB11 4DT
Tel: 01282 683050
Category: SEMH (Coed 11-16)

CARNFORTH

Bleasdale School
27 Emesgate Lane, Silverdale,
CARNFORTH, Lancashire LA5 0RG
Tel: 01524 701217
Category: PMLD (Coed 2-19)

CHORLEY

Astley Park School
Harrington Road, CHORLEY,
Lancashire PR7 1JZ
Tel: 01257 262227
Category: MLD SLD AUT
SLCN (Coed 4-16)

Mayfield Specialist School
Gloucester Road, CHORLEY,
Lancashire PR7 3HN
Tel: 01257 263063
Category: SLD PMLD AUT
SLCN PD MSI (Coed 2-19)

COLNE

**Pendle View
Primary School**
Gibfield Road, COLNE,
Lancashire BB8 8JT
Tel: 01282 865011
Category: PMLD (Coed 2-11)

HASLINGDEN

Tor View Community Special School
Clod Lane, HASLINGDEN,
Lancashire BB4 6LR
Tel: 01706 214640
Category: AUT (Coed 3-19)

KIRKHAM

Pear Tree School
29 Station Road, KIRKHAM,
Lancashire PR4 2HA
Tel: 01772 683609
Category: SLD PMLD (Coed 2-19)

LANCASTER

The Loyne Specialist School
Sefton Drive, LANCASTER,
Lancashire LA1 2PZ
Tel: 01524 64543
Category: SLD PMLD AUT (2-19)

Wennington Hall School
Lodge Lane, Wennington,
LANCASTER, Lancashire LA2 8NS
Tel: 01524 221333
Category: SEMH (Boys
Day or resident 11-16)

MORECAMBE

Morecambe Road School
Morecambe Road, MORECAMBE,
Lancashire LA3 3AB
Tel: 01524 414384
Category: PD HI VI AUT MLD
PMLD SLD (Coed 3-16)

NELSON

Pendle Community High School and College
Oxford Road, NELSON,
Lancashire BB9 8LF
Tel: 01282 682260
Category: MLD BESD
ASD (Coed 11-19)

POULTON-LE-FYLDE

Brookfield School
Fouldrey Avenue, POULTON-
LE-FYLDE, Lancashire FY6 7HE
Tel: 01253 886895
Category: SEMH (Coed 11-16)

PRESTON

Acorns Primary School
Blackpool Road, Moor Park,
PRESTON, Lancashire PR1 6AU
Tel: 01772 792681
Category: AUT SLD
PMLD (Coed 2-11)

Hillside Specialist School & College
Ribchester Road, Longridge,
PRESTON, Lancashire PR3 3XB
Tel: 01772 782205
Category: AUT (Coed 3-19)

Moor Hey School
Far Croft, off Leyland Road, Lostock
Hall, PRESTON, Lancashire PR5 5SS
Tel: 01772 336976
Category: GLD (4-16)

Moorbrook School
Ainslie Road, Fulwood, PRESTON,
Lancashire PR2 3DB
Tel: 01772 774752
Category: SEMH (11-16)

Royal Cross Primary School
Elswick Road, Ashton-on-Ribble,
PRESTON, Lancashire PR2 1NT
Tel: 01772 729705
Category: Deaf (Coed 4-11)

Sir Tom Finney Community High School
Ribbleton Hall Drive, PRESTON,
Lancashire PR2 6EE
Tel: 01772 795749
Category: GLD (Coed 11-19)

The Coppice School
Ash Grove, Bamber Bridge,
PRESTON, Lancashire PR5 6GY
Tel: 01772 336342
Category: SLD PMLD AUT
MLD VI HI MSI (Coed 2-19)

RAWTENSTALL

Cribden House Community Special School
Haslingden Road, RAWTENSTALL,
Lancashire BB4 6RX
Tel: 01706 213048
Category: SEMH (Coed 5-11)

SKELMERSDALE

Elm Tree Community Primary School
Elmers Wood Road, SKELMERSDALE,
Lancashire WN8 6SA
Tel: 01695 50924
Category: SEMH (Coed 5-11)

Hope High School
Clay Brow, SKELMERSDALE,
Lancashire WN8 9DP
Tel: 01695 721066
Category: SEMH (Coed 11-16)

Kingsbury Primary School
School Lane, Chapel
House, SKELMERSDALE,
Lancashire WN8 8EH
Tel: 01695 722991
Category: GLD (Coed 2-11)

West Lancashire Community High School
School Lane, Chapel
House, SKELMERSDALE,
Lancashire WN8 8EH
Tel: 01695 721487
Category: MLD SLD PMLD
AUT VI HI (Coed 11-19)

THORNTON-CLEVELEYS

Great Arley School
Holly Road, THORNTON-
CLEVELEYS, Lancashire FY5 4HH
Tel: 01253 821072
Category: MLD CLD
(Coed Day 4-16)

Red Marsh School
Holly Road, THORNTON-
CLEVELEYS, Lancashire FY5 4HH
Tel: 01253 868451
Category: MLD SLD AUT
PMLD (Coed 2-19)

LEICESTER CITY

Council

Leicester SEND Team, City Hall, 115 Charles Street, Leicester, LE1 1FZ
Tel: 01164 541000 Email: localoffer@leicester.gov.uk Website: www.leicester.gov.uk

LEICESTER

Ellesmere College
40 Braunstone Lane East,
LEICESTER LE3 2FD
Tel: 0116 289 4242

Keyham Lodge School
Keyham Lane, LEICESTER LE5 1FG
Tel: 0116 241 6852
Category: EBD (Boys Secondary)

Leicester Partnership School
Braunstone Skills Centre, 35 Fullhurst
Avenue, LEICESTER LE3 1BL
Tel: 0116 303 3281
Category: PRU

Millgate School
18 Scott Street, LEICESTER LE2 6DW
Tel: 0116 270 4922

Nether Hall School
Keyham Lane West,
LEICESTER LE5 1RT
Tel: 0116 241 7258

Oaklands School
Whitehall Road, LEICESTER LE5 6GJ
Tel: 0116 241 5921
Category: MLD (Primary)

The Children's Hospital School
Leicester Royal Infirmary, Infirmary
Square, LEICESTER LE1 5WW
Tel: 0116 229 8137
Category: HS

West Gate School
Glenfield Road, LEICESTER LE3 6DG
Tel: 0116 255 2187
Category: SLD MLD

LEICESTERSHIRE
County Council

Leicestershire FIS, Abington House, 85 Station Road, Wigston, Leicestershire, LE18 2DP
Tel: 0116 305 6545 Email: family@leics.gov.uk Website: www.leics.gov.uk

HINCKLEY

Sketchley Hill Menphys Nursery School, Burbage
Sketchley Road, Burbage, HINCKLEY, Leicestershire LE10 2DY
Tel: 01455 890684

Sketchley School
Manor Way, Burbage, HINCKLEY, Leicestershire LE10 3HT
Tel: 01455 890023
Category: AUT, ASP, ASD (Coed 8-19)

LOUGHBOROUGH

Ashmount School
Thorpe Hill, LOUGHBOROUGH, Leicestershire LE11 4SQ
Tel: 01509 268506
Category: SLD PMLD (2-18)

Maplewell Hall School
Maplewell Road, Woodhouse Eaves, LOUGHBOROUGH, Leicestershire LE12 8QY
Tel: 01509 890237
Category: MLD AUT (10-15)

MELTON MOWBRAY

Birch Wood (Melton Area Special School)
Grange Drive, MELTON MOWBRAY, Leicestershire LE13 1HA
Tel: 01664 483340
Category: MLD SLD AUT (5-19)

WIGSTON

Wigston Birkett House Community Special School
Launceston Road, WIGSTON, Leicestershire LE18 2DT
Tel: 01162 885802
Category: SLD PMLD (2-18)

Wigston Menphys Nursery School
Launceston Road, WIGSTON, Leicestershire LE18 2FR
Tel: 01162 889977
Category: (2-5)

LINCOLNSHIRE
County Council

Lincolnshire SENDIASS, County Offices, Newland, Lincoln, Lincolnshire, LN1 1YL
Tel: 01522 553332 Email: iass@lincolnshire.gov.uk Website: www.lincolnshire.gov.uk

BOURNE

Willoughby School
South Road, BOURNE, Lincolnshire PE10 9JE
Tel: 01778 425203
Category: SLD (2-19)

GRANTHAM

The Phoenix School
Great North Road, GRANTHAM, Lincolnshire NG31 7US
Tel: 01476 574112
Category: EBD (11-16)

SLEAFORD

The Ash Villa School
Willoughby Road, Greylees, SLEAFORD, Lincolnshire NG34 8QA
Tel: 01529 488066
Category: HS (8-16)

GAINSBOROUGH

Aegir Community School
Sweyn Lane, GAINSBOROUGH, Lincolnshire DN21 1PB
Tel: 01427 619360
Category: SLD

LINCOLN

St Christopher's School
Hykeham Road, LINCOLN, Lincolnshire LN6 8AR
Tel: 01522 528378
Category: MLD (3-16)

NORTH LINCOLNSHIRE
Council

North Lincolnshire SENDIASS, Hewson House, PO Box 35, Station Road Brigg, North Lincolnshire, DN20 8XJ
Tel: 01724 277665 Email: help@nlsendiass.org.uk Website: www.northlincs.gov.uk

SCUNTHORPE

St Hugh's Communication & Interaction Specialist College
Bushfield Road, SCUNTHORPE, North Lincolnshire DN16 1NB
Tel: 01724 842960
Category: MLD SLD PMLD (Coed 11-19)

St Luke's Primary School
Grange Lane North, SCUNTHORPE, North Lincolnshire DN16 1BN
Tel: 01724 844560
Category: PMLD SLD MLD (Coed 3-11)

London

BARKING & DAGENHAM
Council

Barking & Dagenham Education Inclusion Team, 2nd Floor, Town Hall, 1 Town Square, Barking, Essex, IG11 8LU
Tel: 020 8227 2636 Website: www.lbbd.gov.uk

BARKING

Riverside Bridge School
Renwick Road, BARKING,
Essex IG11 0FU
Tel: 02039 465888

DAGENHAM

Hopewell School
Baden Powell Close,
DAGENHAM, Essex RM9 6XN
Tel: 02085 936610

Trinity School
Heathway, DAGENHAM,
Essex RM10 7SJ
Tel: 02034 355955
Category: SLD ASD
PMLD (Coed 3-19)

London

BARNET
Council

Barnet SENDIASS, North London Business Park, Oakleigh Road South, London, N11 1NP
Tel: 020 8359 7637 Fax: 020 8359 2480 Email: sendiass@barnet.gov.uk Website: www.barnet.gov.uk

LONDON

Mapledown School
Claremont Road, Golders
Green, LONDON NW2 1TR
Tel: 02084 554111
Category: SLD CLD (Mixed 11-19)

Northway School
The Fairway, Mill Hill,
LONDON NW7 3HS
Tel: 02083 595450
Category: CLD AUT (Mixed 5-11)

Oak Lodge School
Heath View, Off East End
Road, LONDON N2 0QY
Tel: 02084 446711
Category: MLD ASD SCLN
EBD (Mixed 11-19)

Oakleigh School
Oakleigh Road North,
Whetstone, LONDON N20 0DH
Tel: 02083 685336
Category: SLD AUT
PMLD (Mixed 3-11)

London

LONDON BOROUGH OF BEXLEY
Council

Bexley Local Offer, Civic Offices, 2 Watling Street, Bexleyheath, Kent, DA6 7AT
Tel: 020 3045 5677 Email: localoffer@bexley.gov.uk Website: www.bexley.gov.uk

BEXLEYHEATH

**Endeavour Academy
Bexley**
Woodside Road, BEXLEYHEATH,
Kent DA7 6LB
Tel: 01322 553787
Category: BESD (Coed 11-16)

CRAYFORD

Shenstone School
94 Old Road, CRAYFORD,
Kent DA1 4DZ
Tel: 01322 524145
Category: SLD (2-11)

ERITH

Woodside School
Colyers Lane, ERITH, Kent DA8 3PB
Tel: 01322 350123
Category: MLD (Primary/
Secondary)

SIDCUP

Marlborough School
Marlborough Park Avenue,
SIDCUP, Kent DA15 9DP
Tel: 02083 006896
Category: SLD (11-19)

WELLING

Aspire Academy Bexley
Gypsy Road South,
WELLING, Kent DA16 1JB
Tel: 02083 041320
Category: BESD (5-11)

London

BRENT
Council

Brent SENDIASS, Brent Civic Centre, Engineers Way, Wembley, Middlesex, HA9 0FJ
Tel: 020 8937 3434 Email: sendias@brent.gov.uk Website: www.brent.gov.uk

KENSALE RISE

Manor School
Chamberlayne Road, KENSALE RISE, London NW10 3NT
Tel: 02089 683160
Category: MLD SLD CLD ASD (Coed 4-11)

KINGSBURY

The Village School
Grove Park, KINGSBURY, London NW9 0JY
Tel: 02082 045396
Category: LD DD VIS Medical needs (Coed 2-19)

Woodfield School
Glenwood Avenue, KINGSBURY, London NW9 7LY
Tel: 02082 051977
Category: MLD BESD ASD (Coed 11-16)

NEASDEN

Phoenix Arch School
Drury Way, NEASDEN, London NW10 0NQ
Tel: 02084 516961
Category: BESD LD ADHD ASD (Coed 5-11)

London

BROMLEY
Council

Bromley SENDIASS, 6th Floor, Central Library, High Street, Bromley, Kent, BR1 1EX
Tel: 020 8461 7630 Email: iass@bromley.gov.uk Website: www.bromley.gov.uk

BECKENHAM

Riverside School Beckenham (ASD Centre)
2 Hayne Road, BECKENHAM, Kent BR3 4HY
Tel: 020 8639 0079
Category: ASD (Coed 4-19)

CHISLEHURST

Marjorie McClure School
Hawkwood Lane, CHISLEHURST, Kent BR7 5PS
Tel: 02084 670174
Category: PD SLD Medical needs (Coed 3-18)

ORPINGTON

Riverside School
Main Road, St Paul's Cray, ORPINGTON, Kent BR5 3HS
Tel: 01689 870519
Category: ASD (Coed 4-19)

WEST WICKHAM

Glebe School
117 Hawes Lane, WEST WICKHAM, Kent BR4 9AE
Tel: 02087 774540
Category: Complex needs SCD ASD SLD (Coed 11-16)

London Borough

CAMDEN
Council

Camden SENDIASS, 10th Floor, 5 Pancras Square, c/o Town Hall, Judd Street London, WC1H 9JE
Tel: 020 7974 6500 Email: sendiass@camden.gov.uk Website: www.camden.gov.uk

LONDON

Cpotential
143 Coppetts Road, LONDON N10 1JP
Tel: 02084 447242
Category: CP

Frank Barnes Primary School for Deaf Children
4 Wollstonecraft Street, LONDON N1C 4BT
Tel: 02073 917040
Category: HI (Coed 2-11)

Hampstead School
Westbere Road, LONDON NW2 3RT
Tel: 02077 948133

SEBD Special School
Harmood Street, LONDON NW1 8DP
Tel: 02079 748906
Category: BESD (Coed 11-16)

Swiss Cottage School
80 Avenue Road, LONDON NW8 6HX
Tel: 02076 818080
Category: LD (2-16)

The Children's Hospital School
Great Ormond Street, LONDON WC1N 3JH
Tel: 02078 138269
Category: HS (Coed 0-19)

The Royal Free Hospital Children's School
Royal Free Hospital, Pond Street, LONDON NW3 2QG
Tel: 02074 726298
Category: HS (5-16)

London

CROYDON
Council

KIDS Croydon SENDIAS, Carers Support Centre, 24 George Street, Croydon, Surrey, CR0 1PB
Tel: 020 8663 5630 Email: croydon@kids.org.uk Website: www.croydon.gov.uk

BECKENHAM

Beckmead School
Monks Orchard Road,
BECKENHAM, Kent BR3 3BZ
Tel: 020 8777 9311
Category: BESD (Boys 5-16)

CROYDON

**Bramley Bank Short
Stay School**
170 Sanderstead Road,
CROYDON, Surrey CR2 0LY
Tel: 020 8686 0393
Category: Behaviour
Support (Coed 5-11)

Chaffinch Brook School
32 Morland Road, CROYDON,
Surrey CR0 6NA
Tel: 020 8325 4612
Category: AUT (Coed 5-11)

Red Gates
Farnborough Avenue,
CROYDON, Surrey CR2 8HD
Tel: 020 8651 6540
Category: SLD AUT (Coed 4-12)

St Giles School
207 Pampisford Road,
CROYDON, Surrey CR2 6DF
Tel: 020 8680 2141
Category: PD PMLD
MLD (Coed 4-19)

PURLEY

St Nicholas School
Reedham Drive, PURLEY,
Surrey CR8 4DS
Tel: 020 8660 4861
Category: MLD AUT (Coed 4-11)

THORNTON HEATH

Bensham Manor School
Ecclesbourne Road, THORNTON
HEATH, Surrey CR7 7BN
Tel: 020 8684 0116
Category: MLD AUT (Coed 11-16)

UPPER NORWOOD

Priory School
Hermitage Road, UPPER
NORWOOD, Surrey SE19 3QN
Tel: 020 8653 7879
Category: SLD AUT (Coed 11-19)

London

EALING
Council

Ealing SEN Team, 2nd Floor NE, Perceval House, 14-16 Uxbridge Road London, W5 2HL
Tel: 02088 255533 Email: education@ealing.gov.uk Website: www.ealing.gov.uk

EALING

Castlebar School
Hathaway Gardens, EALING,
London W13 0DH
Tel: 02089 983135
Category: MLD SLD ASD
(Coed Day 4-11)

Springhallow School
Compton Close, Cavendish
Ave, EALING, London W13 0JG
Tel: 02088 328979
Category: ASD (Coed Day 4-16/17)

GREENFORD

Mandeville School
Horsenden Lane North,
GREENFORD, Middlesex UB6 0PA
Tel: 02088 644921
Category: SLD ASD PMLD
(Coed Day 2-12)

HANWELL

St Ann's School
Springfield Road, HANWELL,
London W7 3JP
Tel: 02085 676291
Category: SLD MSI PNLD
SLCN Complex medical
conditions (Coed Day 11-19)

NORTHOLT

Belvue School
Rowdell Road, NORTHOLT,
London UB5 6AG
Tel: 02088 455766
Category: MLD SLD ASD
(Coed Day 11-18)

John Chilton School
Compton Crescent, NORTHOLT,
London UB5 5LD
Tel: 02088 421329
Category: PH/Medical
(Coed Day 2-18)

London

ENFIELD

Council

Enfield SEN Team, Civic Centre, Silver Street, Enfield, Middlesex, EN1 3XY
Tel: 020 8379 5667 Email: sen@enfield.gov.uk Website: www.enfield.gov.uk

EDMONTON

West Lea School
Haselbury Road, EDMONTON,
London N9 9TU
Tel: 02088 072656
Category: HA ASD PD
LD (Coed 5-19)

ENFIELD

Aylands School
Keswick Drive, ENFIELD,
London EN3 6NY
Tel: 01992 761229
Category: EBD (Coed 7-19)

Durants School
4 Pitfield Way, ENFIELD,
London EN3 5BY
Tel: 02088 041980
Category: CLD ASD (Coed 11-19)

Russet House School
11 Autumn Close, ENFIELD,
London EN1 4JA
Tel: 02083 500650
Category: AUT (Coed 3-11)

Waverley School
105 The Ride, ENFIELD,
London EN2 7DL
Tel: 02088 051858
Category: PMLD SLD (Coed 3-19)

SOUTHGATE

Oaktree School
Chase Side, SOUTHGATE,
London N14 4HN
Tel: 02084 403100
Category: Complex
needs (Coed 7-19)

London

ROYAL BOROUGH OF GREENWICH

Council

Greenwich SEN Team, The Woolwich Centre, 35 Wellington Street, Woolwich London, SE18 6HQ
Tel: 020 8921 8044 Email: special-needs@royalgreenwich.gov.uk Website: www.royalgreenwich.gov.uk

LONDON

Moatbridge School
Eltham Palace Road,
LONDON SE9 5LX
Tel: 02088 508081
Category: BESD (Boys 11-19)

Waterside School
Robert Street, Plumstead,
LONDON SE18 7NB
Tel: 02083 177659
Category: BESD (Coed 5-11)

Willow Dene School
Swingate Lane, Plumstead,
LONDON SE18 2JD
Tel: 02088 549841
Category: SCLD CLD PMLD
PD ASD (Coed 3-11)

London

HACKNEY

Council

Hackney SEN Team, Hackney Learning Trust, 1 Reading Lane, London, E8 1GQ
Tel: 02088 207000 Fax: 02088 207001 Email: localoffer@learningtrust.co.uk Website: www.hackneylocaloffer.co.uk

LONDON

Ickburgh School
Kenworthy Road, LONDON E9 5RB
Tel: 02088 064638
Category: SLD PMLD (3-19)

**New Regents
College (PRU)**
Ickburgh Road, LONDON E5 8AD
Tel: 02089 856833

Stormont House School
Downs Park Road, LONDON E5 8NP
Tel: 02089 854245
Category: Complex
needs (Secondary)

The Garden School
Wordsworth Road,
LONDON N16 8BZ
Tel: 02072 548096
Category: MLD ASD (2-16)

London

HAMMERSMITH & FULHAM
Council

Hammersmith & Fulham SEN Team, 3rd Floor, 145 King Street, Hammersmith London, W6 9XY
Tel: 020 8753 1021 Email: sen@rbkc.gov.uk Website: www.lbhf.gov.uk

LONDON

Cambridge School
61 Bryony Road, Hammersmith,
LONDON W12 0SP
Tel: 02087 350980
Category: MLD (11-16)

Jack Tizard School
South Africa Road,
LONDON W12 7PA
Tel: 02087 353590
Category: SLD PMLD
(Coed Day 3-19)

Queensmill School
1 Askham Road, Shepherds
Bush, LONDON W12 0NW
Tel: 02073 842330
Category: ASD (Coed 3-25)

**The Courtyard at
Langford Primary**
The Courtyard, Langford Primary,
Gilstead Road, LONDON SW6 2LG
Tel: 02076 108075
Category: BESD (5-11)

Woodlane High School
Du Cane Road, LONDON W12 0TN
Tel: 02087 435668
Category: SCLN SPLD SEBD MSI
Medical difficulties (Coed 11-16)

London

HARINGEY
Council

Haringey Additional Needs & Disabilities, Alexandra House, 2nd Floor, 10 Station Road, Wood Green London, N22 7TR
Tel: 020 8489 1913 Email: sen@haringey.gov.uk Website: www.haringey.gov.uk

MUSWELL HILL

**Blanche Nevile
Secondary School**
Burlington Road, MUSWELL
HILL, London N10 1NJ
Tel: 02084 422750
Category: HI (Coed Day 11-18)

NORTH HILL

**Blanche Nevile
Primary School**
Storey Road, NORTH HILL,
London N6 4ED
Tel: 02083 473760
Category: HI (Coed Day 3-10)

TOTTENHAM

Riverside School
Wood Green Inclusive Learning
Campus, White Hart Lane,
TOTTENHAM, London N22 5QJ
Tel: 02088 897814
Category: PMLD ASD
(Coed Day 11-16)

The Brook on Broadwaters
Adams Road, TOTTENHAM,
London N17 6HW
Tel: 02088 087120
Category: CP EPI (Coed Day 4-11)

WEST GREEN

The Vale School
Northumberland Park Community
School, Trulock Road, WEST
GREEN, London N17 0PG
Tel: 02088 016111
Category: PD (Coed Day 2-16)

London

BOROUGH OF HARROW
Council

Harrow SEN Team, Alexandra Avenue Health & Social Care Centre, 275 Alexandra Avenue, South Harrow, Middlesex, HA2 9DX

Tel: 020 8966 6483 Fax: 020 8966 6489 Email: senassessment.reviewservice@ harrow.gov.uk Website: www.harrow.gov.uk

EDGWARE
Woodlands School
Bransgrove Road, EDGWARE,
Middlesex HA8 6JP
Tel: 02083 812188
Category: SLD PMLD
ASD (Coed 3-11)

HARROW
Alexandra School
Alexandra Avenue, HARROW,
Middlesex HA2 9DX
Tel: 02088 642739
Category: MLD EBD
ASD (Coed 4-11)

Kingsley High School
Whittlesea Road, HARROW,
Middlesex HA3 6ND
Tel: 02084 213676
Category: SLD PMLD (Coed 11-19)

Shaftesbury High School
Long Elmes, Harrow Weald,
HARROW, Middlesex HA3 6LE
Tel: 02084 282482
Category: MLD EBD
ASD (Coed 11-19)

London Borough of

HAVERING
Council

Havering SENDIASS, Mercury House, Romford, Essex, RM1 3DW

Tel: 01708 433 885 Email: sendiass@havering.gov.uk Website: www.havering.gov.uk

ROMFORD
Dycorts School
Settle Road, Harold Hill,
ROMFORD, Essex RM3 9YA
Tel: 01708 343649
Category: MLD

Ravensbourne School
Neave Cres, Faringdon Ave, Harold
Hill, ROMFORD, Essex RM3 8HN
Tel: 01708 341800
Category: SLD PMLD

UPMINSTER
Corbets Tey School
Harwood Hall Lane, Corbets Tey,
UPMINSTER, Essex RM14 2YQ
Tel: 01708 225888
Category: MLD/SLD/
Complex Needs

London

HILLINGDON
Council

Hillingdon SEN Team, 4E/05, Civic Centre, High Street, Uxbridge, Middlesex, UB8 1UW

Tel: 01895 250244 Fax: 01895 250878 Email: cmoses@hillingdon.gov.uk Website: www.hillingdon.gov.uk

HAYES
**Hedgewood
Special School**
Weymouth Road, HAYES,
Middlesex UB4 8NF
Tel: 02088 456756
Category: MLD ASD
Complex moderate learning
needs (Coed 5-11)

ICKENHAM
Pentland Field School
Pentland Way, ICKENHAM,
Middlesex UB10 8TS
Tel: 01895 609120
Category: MLD SLD (Coed 4-19)

PINNER
Grangewood School
Fore Street, Eastcote, PINNER,
Middlesex HA5 2JQ
Tel: 01895 676401
Category: SLD PMLD
AUT (Coed 3-11)

UXBRIDGE
Meadow High School
Royal Lane, Hillingdon,
UXBRIDGE, Middlesex UB8 3QU
Tel: 01895 443310
Category: CLD ASD
Complex moderate learning
needs (Coed 11-19)

London

HOUNSLOW
Council

Hounslow SENDIASS, Civic Centre, Lampton Road, Hounslow, TW3 4DN
Tel: 020 8583 2607 Email: sendiass@hounslow.gov.uk Website: www.hounslow.gov.uk

BEDFONT

Marjory Kinnon School
Hatton Road, BEDFONT,
London TW14 9QZ
Tel: 02088 908890
Category: MLD AUT (5-16)

FELTHAM

The Rise School
Browells Lane, FELTHAM,
London TW13 7EF
Tel: 02080 990640
Category: AUT (4-18)

ISLEWORTH

Oaklands School
Woodlands Road, ISLEWORTH,
London TW7 6JZ
Tel: 02085 603569
Category: SLD (Secondary)

CRANFORD

The Cedars Primary School
High Street, CRANFORD,
London TW5 9RU
Tel: 02082 300015
Category: EBD (Primary)

HANWORTH

The Lindon Bennett School
Main Street, HANWORTH,
London TW13 6ST
Tel: 02088 980479
Category: SLD (3-11)

London

ISLINGTON
Council

Islington SEN Team, First Floor, 222 Upper Street, London, N1 1XR
Tel: 0-13: 020 7527 5518; 14-25: 020 7527 4860 Email: sen@islington.gov.uk Website: www.islington.gov.uk

LONDON

Richard Cloudesley Primary School
Golden Lane Campus,
101 Whitecross Street,
LONDON EC1Y 8JA
Tel: 020 7786 4800
Category: PD (Coed 2-11)

Richard Cloudesley Secondary School
Tudor Rose Building, 1 Prebend
Street, LONDON N1 8RE
Tel: 020 7704 8127
Category: PD (Coed 11-19)

Samuel Rhodes Primary School
Montem Community Campus,
Hornsey Road, LONDON N7 7QT
Tel: 020 7281 5114
Category: MLD ASD
BESD (Coed 5-11)

Samuel Rhodes Secondary School
11 Highbury New Park,
LONDON N5 2EG
Tel: 020 7704 7490
Category: MLD ASD
BESD (Coed 11-18)

The Bridge Primary School
251 Hungerford Road,
LONDON N7 9LD
Tel: 020 7619 1000
Category: ASD SLD
PMLD (Coed 2-11)

The Bridge Secondary School
28 Carleton Road, LONDON N7 0EQ
Tel: 020 7715 0320
Category: ASD SLD
PMLD (Coed 11-19)

London

ROYAL BOROUGH OF KINGSTON UPON THAMES
Council

Richmond & Kingston SENDIASS, Moor Lane Centre, Chessington Kingston upon Thames, Surrey, KT9 2AA
Tel: 020 8831 6179 Email: richmondkingston@kids.org.uk Website: www.kingston.gov.uk

CHESSINGTON

St Philip's School & Post 16
Harrow Close, Leatherhead Road,
CHESSINGTON, Surrey KT9 2HR
Tel: 02083 972672
Category: MLD SLD ASD (11-19)

KINGSTON UPON THAMES

Bedelsford School
Grange Road, KINGSTON UPON
THAMES, Surrey KT1 2QZ
Tel: 02085 469838
Category: PD PMLD MSI CLD (2-19)

SURBITON

Dysart School
190 Ewell Road, SURBITON,
Surrey KT6 6HL
Tel: 02084 122600
Category: SLD ASD PMLD (5-19)

London

LAMBETH
Council

Lambeth SEN Team, 10th Floor, International House, Canterbury Crescent, Brixton London, SW9 7QE
Tel: 020 7926 9460 Email: sendsupport@lambeth.gov.uk Website: www.lambeth.gov.uk

RUSKIN PARK

The Michael Tippet School
Heron Road, RUSKIN PARK,
London SE24 0HZ
Tel: 02073 265898
Category: CLD AUT PD
SLD PMLD (Coed 11-18)

STREATHAM

The Livity School
Adare walk, STREATHAM,
London SW16 2PW
Tel: 02087 691009
Category: SLD PMLD
ASD (Coed 2-11)

WEST NORWOOD

Elm Court School
96 Elm Park, WEST NORWOOD,
London SW2 2EF
Tel: 02086 743412
Category: SEBN SLCN (Coed 6-16)

STOCKWELL

Lansdowne School
Argyll Close, Dalyell Road,
STOCKWELL, London SW9 9QL
Tel: 02077 373713
Category: MLD SEBD ASD
CLD SLD (Coed 11-15)

WEST DULWICH

Turney School
Turney Road, WEST DULWICH,
London SE21 8LX
Tel: 02086 707220
Category: MLD SLD CLD
ASD (Coed 5-10)

London

LEWISHAM
Council

Lewisham SEN Team, Kaleidoscope Child Development Centre, 32 Rushey Green, London, SE6 4JF
Tel: 02030 491475 Email: sen@lewisham.gov.uk Website: www.lewisham.gov.uk

BROMLEY

Drumbeat School
Roundtable Road, Downham,
BROMLEY, Kent BR1 5LE
Tel: 02086 989738
Category: ASD (5-19)

DOWNHAM

New Woodlands School
49 Shroffold Road,
DOWNHAM, Kent BR1 5PD
Tel: 02086 952380
Category: BESD (Coed 5-14)

LONDON

Abbey Manor College
40 Falmouth Close, Lee,
LONDON SE12 8PJ
Tel: 02082 977060
Category: BESD (Coed 11-19)

Brent Knoll School
Mayow Road, Forest Hill,
LONDON SE23 2XH
Tel: 02086 991047
Category: AUT ASP SLCN
Emotionally Vulnerable (Coed 4-16)

Greenvale School
Waters Road, LONDON SE6 1UF
Tel: 02084 650740
Category: SLD PMLD (Coed 11-19)

Watergate School
Lushington Road, Bellingham,
LONDON SE6 3WG
Tel: 02086 956555
Category: SLD PMLD (Coed 3-11)

London

MERTON
Council

Merton SENDIS, Merton Civic Centre, London Road, Morden, SM4 5DX
Tel: 020 8545 4811 Email: sen@merton.gov.uk Website: www.merton.gov.uk

MITCHAM

Cricket Green School
Lower Green West, MITCHAM,
Surrey CR4 3AF
Tel: 02086 401177
Category: CLD (Coed 5-19)

Melrose School
Church Road, MITCHAM,
Surrey CR4 3BE
Tel: 02086 462620
Category: SEBD (Coed 11-16)

MORDEN

Perseid School
Bordesley Road, MORDEN,
Surrey SM4 5LT
Tel: 02086 489737
Category: PMLD (Coed 3-19)

London

NEWHAM
Council

Newham SEN Team, Newham Dockside, 1000 Dockside Road, London, E16 2QU
Tel: 02084 302000 Website: www.newham.gov.uk

BECKTON

**Eleanor Smith KS3
Annexe (Secondary)**
90a Lawson Close, BECKTON,
London E16 3LU
Tel: 020 7511 3222
Category: SEBD (11-16)

PLAISTOW

**Eleanor Smith
School (Primary)**
North Street, PLAISTOW,
London E13 9HN
Tel: 020 8471 0018
Category: SEBD (5-10)

STRATFORD

John F Kennedy School
Pitchford Street, STRATFORD,
London E15 4RZ
Tel: 020 8534 8544
Category: SLD PMLD ASD Complex
medical needs (Coed 2-19)

London

REDBRIDGE
Council

Redbridge SEN Team, Lynton House, 255-259 High Road, Ilford, Essex, IG1 1NN
Tel: 02085 545000 Email: customer.cc@redbridge.gov.uk Website: www.redbridge.gov.uk

GOODMAYES

Newbridge School - Barley Lane Campus
258 Barley Lane, GOODMAYES, Essex IG3 8XS
Tel: 02085 991768
Category: SLD PMLD ASD Complex medical needs (11-19)

HAINAULT

New Rush Hall School
Fencepiece Road, HAINAULT, Essex IG6 2LB
Tel: 02085 013951
Category: SEMH (5-15)

ROMFORD

Little Heath Foundation School
Hainault Road, Little Heath, ROMFORD, Essex RM6 5RX
Tel: 02085 994864
Category: MLD Learning difficulties & complex needs (11-19)

Newbridge School - Gresham Drive Campus
161 Gresham Drive, Chadwell Heath, ROMFORD, Essex RM6 4TR
Tel: 02085 907272
Category: SLD PMLD ASD Complex medical needs (2-11)

WOODFORD GREEN

Hatton School
Roding Lane South, WOODFORD GREEN, Essex IG8 8EU
Tel: 02085 514131
Category: AUT SP&LD (3-11)

London

RICHMOND UPON THAMES
Council

Richmond SEN Team, Parent Partnership Service, Croft Centre, Windham Road, Richmond, Middlesex, TW9 2HP
Tel: 020 8891 7541 Website: www.richmond.gov.uk

HAMPTON

Clarendon School
Hanworth Road, HAMPTON, Surrey TW12 3DH
Tel: 02089 791165
Category: MLD (7-16) (offsite EBD 7-11)

RICHMOND

Strathmore School
Meadlands Drive, Petersham, RICHMOND, Surrey TW10 7ED
Tel: 02089 480047
Category: SLD PMLD (7-19)

London

SOUTHWARK
Council

Southwark SEN Team, PO Box 64529, London, SE1P 5LX
Tel: 02075 254278 Email: sen@southwark.gov.uk Website: www.southwark.gov.uk

BERMONDSEY

Beormund Primary School
Crosby Row, Long Lane, BERMONDSEY SE1 3PS
Tel: 02075 259027
Category: EBD (Boys 5-11)

Cherry Garden School
Macks Road, BERMONDSEY SE16 3XU
Tel: 02072 374050
Category: SCLD (Coed 2-11)

Spa School
Monnow Road, BERMONDSEY SE1 5RN
Tel: 02072 373714
Category: MLD AUT ASP SLD SCD (Coed 11-19)

PECKHAM

Highshore Secondary School
Bellenden Road, PECKHAM SE15 5BB
Tel: 02076 397211
Category: DYS PD SLCN EBD Complex needs (Coed 11-16)

Newlands School
Stuart Road, PECKHAM SE15 3AZ
Tel: 02076 392541
Category: SEBD (Boys 11-16)

Tuke Secondary School
Daniels Gardens, PECKHAM SE15 6ER
Tel: 02076 395584
Category: SLD PMLD ASD (Coed 11-19)

London

SUTTON

Council

Sutton SENDIASS, Civic Offices, St Nicholas Way, Sutton, Surrey, SM5 3AL
Tel: 020 8770 4541 Email: spps@sutton.gov.uk Website: www.sutton.gov.uk

WALLINGTON

Sherwood Park School
Streeters Lane, WALLINGTON,
Surrey SM6 7NP
Tel: 02087 739930
Category: SLD PMLD
ASD (Coed 2-19)

London

TOWER HAMLETS

Council

Tower Hamlets SEN Team, 30 Greatorex Street, London, E1 5NP
Tel: 020 7364 6486 Email: fis@towerhamlets.gov.uk Website: www.towerhamlets.gov.uk

BOW

Cherry Trees School
68 Campbell Road, BOW,
London E3 4EA
Tel: 02089 834344
Category: SEBD (Boys Day 5-11)

Phoenix School
49 Bow Road, BOW, London E3 2AD
Tel: 02089 804740
Category: ASD (Coed Day 3-19)

BROMLEY-BY-BOW

Ian Mikardo High School
60 William Guy Gardens,
Talwin Street, BROMLEY-BY-
BOW, London E3 3LF
Tel: 02089 812413
Category: SEBD (Boys Day 11-16)

LIMEHOUSE

Stephen Hawking School
2 Brunton Place, LIMEHOUSE,
London E14 7LL
Tel: 02074 239848
Category: PMLD (Coed Day 2-11)

MILE END

Beatrice Tate School
Poplar Day Centre, 40 Southern
Grove, MILE END, London E3 4PX
Tel: 02089 833760
Category: PMLD SLD
(Coed Day 11-19)

SEAFORD

Bowden House School
Firle Road, SEAFORD BN25 2JB
Tel: 01323 893138
Category: SEMH (Weekly
Residential)

London

WALTHAM FOREST
Council

Waltham Forest SENDIASS, 220 Hoe Street, Walthamstow London, E17 3AY
Tel: 020 3233 0251 Email: wfsendiass@walthamforestcab.org.uk Website: www.walthamforest.gov.uk

HALE END

Joseph Clarke School
31 Vincent Road, Highams Park,
HALE END, London E4 9PP
Tel: 02085 234833
Category: VIS Complex
needs (Coed 2-18)

LEYTON

Belmont Park School
101 Leyton Green Road,
LEYTON, London E10 6DB
Tel: 02085 560006
Category: Challenging
behaviour (Coed 7-19)

WALTHAMSTOW

Whitefield Schools
Macdonald Road, WALTHAMSTOW,
London E17 4AZ
Tel: 02085 313426
Category: LD MSI SP&LD
(Coed 3-19)

London

WANDSWORTH
Council

Wandsworth SEN Team, The Town Hall, High Street, Wandsworth London, SW18 3LL
Tel: 020 8871 7899 Email: fis@wandsworth.gov.uk Website: fis.wandsworth.gov.uk

BALHAM

Oak Lodge School
101 Nightingale Lane, BALHAM,
London SW12 8NA
Tel: 02086 733453
Category: D (Coed, Day/
boarding 11-19)

BROADSTAIRS

Bradstow School
34 Dumpton Park Drive,
BROADSTAIRS, Kent CT10 1BY
Tel: 01843 862123
Category: PD AUT Challenging
behaviour (Coed 5-19)

EARLSFIELD

Garratt Park School
Waldron Road, EARLSFIELD,
London SW18 3BT
Tel: 02089 465769
Category: MLD SP&LD (Coed 11-18)

PUTNEY

Greenmead School
St Margaret's Crescent,
PUTNEY, London SW15 6HL
Tel: 02087 891466
Category: PD PMLD (Coed 3-11)

Paddock Primary School
St Margaret's Crescent,
PUTNEY, London SW15 6HL
Tel: 02087 885648
Category: ASD MLD
SLD (Coed 3-11)

ROEHAMPTON

**Paddock Secondary
School**
Priory Lane, ROEHAMPTON,
London SW15 5RT
Tel: 02088 781521
Category: SCLD ASD with
SLD (Coed 11-19)

SOUTHFIELDS

Linden Lodge School
61 Princes Way, SOUTHFIELDS,
London SW19 6JB
Tel: 02087 880107
Category: VIS PMLD MSI (Coed 3-11)

TOOTING

Nightingale School
Beechcroft Road, TOOTING,
London SW17 7DF
Tel: 02088 749096
Category: BESD (Boys 11-19)

London

CITY OF WESTMINSTER
Council

Westminster SEN Team, The Town Hall, 2nd Floor, Green Zone, Hornton Street London, W8 7NX
Tel: 02073 613311 Website: www.westminster.gov.uk

LONDON

College Park School
Garway Road, LONDON W2 4PH
Tel: 020 7221 3454
Category: MLD (Coed 4-19)

**Queen Elizabeth II
Jubilee School**
Kennet Road, LONDON W9 3LG
Tel: 020 7641 5825
Category: SLD (Coed 5-19)

LUTON

Borough Council

Luton SENDIAS, Futures House, The Moakes, Luton, LU3 3QB

Tel: 01525 719754 Email: parentpartnership@luton.gov.uk Website: www.luton.gov.uk

LUTON

Lady Zia Werner School
Ashcroft Road, LUTON,
Bedfordshire LU2 9AY
Tel: 01582 728705
Category: SLD PMLD (Yr 1-6 & Early Years)

Richmond Hill School
Sunridge Avenue, LUTON,
Bedfordshire LU2 7JL
Tel: 01582 721019
Category: SLD PMLD (Primary Yr 1-6)

Woodlands School
Northwell Drive, LUTON,
Bedfordshire LU3 3SP
Tel: 01582 572880
Category: SLD PMLD (11-19)

Greater Manchester

BOLTON

Council

Bolton SENDIASS, Lowndes Street Day Nursery, Bolton, BL1 4QB

Tel: 01204 848722 Email: pps@boltoncog.co.uk Website: www.bolton.gov.uk

BOLTON

Firwood School
Stitch Mi Lane, BOLTON BL2 4HU
Tel: 01204 333044
Category: SLD PMLD ASD (Coed 11-19)

Ladywood School
Masefield Road, Little
Lever, BOLTON BL3 1NG
Tel: 01204 333400
Category: MLD with Complex needs incl ASD PD MSI (Coed 4-11)

Rumworth School
Armadale Road, Ladybridge,
BOLTON BL3 4TP
Tel: 01204 333600
Category: MLD with Complex needs incl ASD PD MSI (Coed 11-19)

Thomasson Memorial School
Devonshire Road, BOLTON BL1 4PJ
Tel: 01204 333118
Category: HI (Coed 2-16)

FARNWORTH

Green Fold School
Highfield Road,
FARNWORTH BL4 0RA
Tel: 01204 335883
Category: SLD ASD PMLD (Coed 2-11)

HORWICH

Lever Park School
Stocks Park Drive,
HORWICH BL6 6DE
Tel: 01204 332666
Category: SEBD (Coed 11-16)

Greater Manchester

BURY

Council

Bury SENDIASS, Red Centre, Morley St, Bury, Lancashire, BL9 9JQ

Tel: 0161 761 0401 Email: iass.bury@togethertrust.org.uk Website: www.bury.gov.uk

BURY

Elms Bank Specialist Arts College
Ripon Avenue, Whitefield,
BURY M45 8PJ
Tel: 01617 661597
Category: LD (Coed 11-19)

Millwood School
School Street, Radcliffe,
BURY M26 3BW
Tel: 01617 242266
Category: SLD PMLD ASD AUT Complex needs (Coed 2-11)

PRESTWICH

Cloughside College (Hospital Special School)
Bury New Road,
PRESTWICH M25 3BL
Tel: 01617 724625
Category: HS (Coed 11-19)

Greater Manchester

MANCHESTER
City Council

Manchester SEN Team, Children's Services, 1st Floor, Universal Square,
Devonshire Street North Manchester, Lancashire, M12 6JH
Tel: 01612 457459 Fax: 01612 747084 Email: sen@manchester.gov.uk Website: www.manchester.gov.uk

CONGLETON

Buglawton Hall
Buxton Road, CONGLETON,
Cheshire CW12 3PQ
Tel: 01260 274492
Category: SEBD
(Residential Boys 8-16)

MANCHESTER

Ashgate School
Crossacres Road, Peel
Hall, Wythenshawe,
MANCHESTER M22 5DR
Tel: 01612 196642
Category: SLD (5-11)

Camberwell Park
Bank House Road, Blackley,
MANCHESTER M9 8LT
Tel: 01617 401897
Category: SLD (5-11)

Grange School
Matthews Lane, Longsight,
MANCHESTER M12 4GR
Tel: 01612 312590
Category: ASD CLD (4-19)

Lancasterian School
Elizabeth Springer Road, West
Didsbury, MANCHESTER M20 2XA
Tel: 01614 450123
Category: PD (2-16)

Manchester Hospital Schools & Home Teaching Service
Third Floor School, Royal
Manchester Children's
Hospital, Oxford Road,
MANCHESTER M13 9WL
Tel: 01617 010684
Category: HS

Meade Hill School
Chain Road, Higher Blackley,
MANCHESTER M9 6GN
Tel: 01612 343925
Category: SEBD (11-16)

Melland High School
Gorton Education Village,
50 Wembley Road, Gorton,
MANCHESTER M18 7DT
Tel: 01612 239915
Category: SLD (11-19)

North Ridge High School
Higher Blackley Education
Village, Alworth Road,
MANCHESTER M9 0RP
Tel: 01612 343588
Category: MLD (11-19)

Piper Hill High School
Firbank Road, Newall Green,
MANCHESTER M23 2YS
Tel: 01614 363009
Category: SLD (11-19)

Rodney House School
Albert Grove, Longsight,
MANCHESTER M12 4WF
Tel: 0161 230 6854
Category: ASD (2-7)

Southern Cross School
Barlow Hall Road, Chorlton,
MANCHESTER M21 7JJ
Tel: 01618 812695
Category: SEBD (11-16)

The Birches
Newholme Road, West Didsbury,
MANCHESTER M20 2XZ
Tel: 01614 488895
Category: SLD (5-11)

Greater Manchester

OLDHAM
Council

Oldham SENDIASS, Chadderton Court, 451 Middleton Road, Chadderton Oldham, Greater Manchester, OL9 9LB
Tel: 0161 503 1540 Email: iass@pointoldham.co.uk Website: www.oldham.gov.uk

OLDHAM

Bright Futures School
164 Oldham Road,
Grasscroft, OLDHAM, Greater
Manchester OL4 4DW
Tel: 01457 878738
Category: AUT ASD (5-16)

Elland House School Royton
Roman Road, Royton, OLDHAM,
Greater Manchester OL2 5PJ
Tel: 7841 615 159
Category: (11-18)

Great Howarth School
Great Howarth Road,
Rochdale, OLDHAM, Greater
Manchester OL12 9HJ
Tel: 01706 631804
Category: SEMH ADHD ASD (7-18)

New Bridge Learning Centre
St Martin's Road, Fitton
Hill, OLDHAM, Greater
Manchester OL8 2PZ
Tel: 01618 832402
Category: (Coed 16-19)

New Bridge School
Roman Road, Hollinwood,
OLDHAM, Greater
Manchester OL8 3PH
Tel: 01618 832401
Category: PMLD SLD MLD
ASD PD (Coed 11-19)

Spring Brook Academy - Upper School
Dean Street, Failsworth, OLDHAM,
Greater Manchester M35 0DQ
Tel: 0161 883 3431
Category: BESD (11-16)

The Kingfisher Community Special School
Foxdenton Lane, Chadderton,
OLDHAM, Greater
Manchester OL9 9QR
Tel: 01617 705910
Category: PMLD SLD
ASD (Coed 4-11)

Greater Manchester

ROCHDALE
Metropolitan Borough Council

Rochdale SEN Assessment Team, Number One Riverside, Smith Street, Rochdale, OL16 1XU
Tel: 01706 925981 Email: sen@rochdale.gov.uk Website: www.rochdale.gov.uk

MIDDLETON

Newlands School
Waverley Road,
MIDDLETON M24 6JG
Tel: 01616 550220
Category: Generic Primary
Special School (Coed 3-11)

ROCHDALE

Brownhill School
Heights Lane, ROCHDALE OL12 0PZ
Tel: 03003 038384
Category: EBD (Coed 7-16)

Redwood School
Hudson's Walk, ROCHDALE OL11 5EF
Tel: 01706 750815
Category: Generic Secondary
Special School (Coed 11-19)

Springside School
Albert Royds Street,
ROCHDALE OL16 2SU
Tel: 01706 764451
Category: Generic Primary
Special School (Coed 3-11)

Greater Manchester

SALFORD
City Council

Salford SENDIASS, Salford Civic Centre, Chorley Road, Swinton Salford, M27 5AW
Tel: 0161 778 0343 Email: siass@salford.gov.uk Website: www.salford.gov.uk

ECCLES

Chatsworth High School
Chatsworth Road, Ellesmere
Park, ECCLES M30 9DY
Tel: 01619 211405
Category: SLD PMLD
ASD (Coed 11-19)

New Park High School
Green Lane, ECCLES M30 0RW
Tel: 01619 212000
Category: SEBD LD (Coed 8-16)

SWINTON

**Springwood
Primary School**
Barton Road, SWINTON M27 5LP
Tel: 01617 780022
Category: ASD MLD SLD
PMLD (Coed 2-11)

Greater Manchester

STOCKPORT
Metropolitan Borough Council

Stockport SEN Team, Town Hall, Edward Street, Stockport, SK1 3XE
Tel: 0161 474 2525 Email: sen@stockport.gov.uk Website: www.stockport.gov.uk

STOCKPORT

Castle Hill High School
The Fairway, Offerton,
STOCKPORT SK2 5DS
Tel: 01612 853925
Category: EBD GLD
CLD (Coed 11-16)

Heaton School
St James Road, Heaton Moor,
STOCKPORT SK4 4RE
Tel: 01614 321931
Category: SLD PMLD (Coed 10-19)

Lisburne School
Half Moon Lane, Offerton,
STOCKPORT SK2 5LB
Tel: 01614 835045
Category: CLD (Coed 4-11)

Oakgrove School
Matlock Road, Heald Green,
STOCKPORT SK8 3BU
Tel: 01614 374956
Category: SEBD (Coed 5-11)

Valley School
Whitehaven Road, Bramhall,
STOCKPORT SK7 1EN
Tel: 01614 397343
Category: PMLD ASD
SLD (Coed 2-11)

Windlehurst School
Windlehurst Road, Hawk Green,
Marple, STOCKPORT SK6 7HZ
Tel: 01614 274788
Category: EBD (Coed 11-16)

Greater Manchester

TAMESIDE
Metropolitan Borough Council

Tameside SENDIASS, Jubilee Gardens, Gardenfold Way, Droylsden, Tameside, M43 7XU
Tel: 0161 342 3383 Website: www.tameside.gov.uk

ASHTON-UNDER LYNE

Samuel Laycock School
Broadoak Road, ASHTON-UNDER LYNE, Tameside OL6 8RF
Tel: 01613 441992
Category: MLD (Secondary)

AUDENSHAW

Hawthorns School
Sunnyside Moss Campus, Lumb Lane, AUDENSHAW, Tameside M34 5SF
Tel: 01613 701312
Category: MLD (Primary)

DUKINFIELD

Cromwell School
Yew Tree Lane, DUKINFIELD, Tameside SK16 5BJ
Tel: 01613 389730
Category: SLD PMLD MLD (Secondary)

Oakdale School
Cheetham Hill Road, DUKINFIELD, Tameside SK16 5LD
Tel: 01613 679299
Category: SLD PMLD (Primary)

White Bridge College
Globe Lane, DUKINFIELD, Tameside SK16 4UJ
Tel: 0161 214 8484
Category: (Secondary)

HYDE

Thomas Ashton School
Bennett Street, HYDE, Tameside SK14 4SS
Tel: 01613 686208
Category: BESD (Primary)

Greater Manchester

TRAFFORD
Council

Trafford FIS, 2nd Floor, Waterside House, Sale, Manchester, M33 72F
Tel: 01619 121053 Email: fis@trafford.gov.uk Website: www.trafford.gov.uk/localoffer

ALTRINCHAM

Pictor School
Grove Lane, Timperley, ALTRINCHAM, Cheshire WA15 6PH
Tel: 01619 123082
Category: SLCN SPLD ASD PD MLD (Coed 2-11)

FLIXTON

Delamere School
Irlam Road, FLIXTON, Greater Manchester M41 6AP
Tel: 01617 475893
Category: ASD SLD (Coed 2-11)

Nexus Education Centre (Pupil Referral Unit)
Lydney Road, FLIXTON, Manchester M41 8RN
Tel: 01619 121479
Category: (Coed 5-16)

Trafford Medical Education Service (Pupil Referral Unit)
The Flixton Centre, 350 Flixton Road, FLIXTON, Manchester M41 5GW
Tel: 01619 124766

SALE

Brentwood High School & Community College
Cherry Lane, SALE, Cheshire M33 4GY
Tel: 01619 052371
Category: ASD SLD (Coed 11-19)

STRETFORD

Longford Park School
74 Cromwell Road, STRETFORD, Greater Manchester M32 8QJ
Tel: 01619 121895
Category: SEMH MLD ASD (Coed 5-11)

URMSTON

Egerton High School
Kingsway Park, URMSTON, Greater Manchester
Tel: 01617 497094
Category: SEMH (Coed 5-16)

Greater Manchester

WIGAN
Council

Wigan SENDIASS, Embrace Wigan and Leigh, 81 RibMANWIG, Rowan Tree Primary School Green Hall Close, ATHERTON
Tel: Greater Manchester Fax: M46 9HP Email: 01942 883928 Website: Head

WIGAN

Hope School & College
Kelvin Grove, Marus Bridge,
WIGAN WN3 6SP
Tel: 01942 824150
Category: ASD SLD
PMLD (Coed 2-19)

Landgate School
Landgate Lane, Bryn,
WIGAN WN4 0EP
Tel: 01942 776688
Category: AUT SP&LD (Coed 4-19)

Newbridge Learning Community School
Moss Lane, Platt Bridge,
WIGAN WN2 3TL
Tel: 01942 776020

Oakfield High School & College
Long Lane, Hindley Green,
WIGAN WN2 4XA
Tel: 01942 776142
Category: MLD SLD PD
SEBD (Coed 11-19)

Willow Grove Primary School
Willow Grove, Ashton-in-
Makerfield, WIGAN WN4 8XF
Tel: 01942 727717
Category: SEBD (Coed 5-11)

MEDWAY
Council

Medway SEN Team, Family Information Service, Gun Wharf, Dock Road Chatham, ME4 4TR
Tel: 01634 332195 Email: familyinfo@medway.gov.uk Website: www.medway.gov.uk

GILLINGHAM

Danecourt School
Hotel Road, Watling Street,
GILLINGHAM, Kent ME8 6AA
Tel: 01634 232589
Category: ASD SLD (Coed 4-11)

Rivermead School
Forge Lane, GILLINGHAM,
Kent ME7 1UG
Tel: 01634 338348
Category: ASD Complex
emotional needs (Coed 11-19)

STROOD

Abbey Court School
Rede Court Road,
STROOD, Kent ME2 3SP
Tel: 01634 338220
Category: SLD PMLD (Coed 4-19)

Merseyside

KNOWSLEY
Metropolitan Borough Council

Liverpool & Knowsley SENDIASS, Stoneycroft Childrenís Centre, 38 Scotia Road, Liverpool, Merseyside, L13 6QJ
Tel: 0800 012 9066 Email: liverpoolandknowsleysend@wired.me.uk Website: www.knowsley.gov.uk

HALEWOOD

Finch Woods Academy
Baileys Lane, HALEWOOD,
Merseyside L26 0TY
Tel: 01512 888930
Category: SEBD (Coed 6-16)

Yew Tree Community Primary School
The Avenue, Wood Road,
HALEWOOD L26 1UU
Tel: 0151 477 8950
Category: (3-11)

HUYTON

Alt Bridge Secondary Support Centre
Wellcroft Road, HUYTON,
Merseyside L36 7TA
Tel: 01514 778310
Category: MLD SPLD CLD
ASD SLD PD (Coed 11-16)

Knowsley Central Primary Support Centre
Mossbrow Road, HUYTON,
Merseyside L36 7SY
Tel: 01514 778450
Category: CLD SEBD (Coed 2-11)

KIRKBY

Bluebell Park School
Cawthorne Walk, Southdene,
KIRKBY, Merseyside L32 3XP
Tel: 01514 778350
Category: PD PMLD SLD
MLD (Coed 2-19)

Northwood Community Primary School
Roughwood Drive, Northwood,
KIRKBY, Merseyside L33 8XD
Tel: 01514 778630
Category: (0-11)

STOCKBRIDGE VILLAGE

Meadow Park School
Haswell Drive, STOCKBRIDGE
VILLAGE, Merseyside L28 1RX
Tel: 01514 778100
Category: (7-16)

Merseyside

LIVERPOOL
City Council

Liverpool Children's Services (Education), Municipal Buildings, Dale Street, Liverpool, L2 2DH
Tel: 01512 333000 Email: liverpool.direct@liverpool.gov.uk Website: www.liverpool.gov.uk

LIVERPOOL

Abbot's Lea School
Beaconsfield Road, Woolton,
LIVERPOOL, Merseyside L25 6EE
Tel: 01514 281161
Category: AUT (Coed 5-19)

Bank View High School
177 Long Ln, LIVERPOOL,
Merseyside L9 6AD
Tel: 01512 336120
Category: CLD (Coed 11-18)

Childwall Abbey School
Childwall Abbey Rd, LIVERPOOL,
Merseyside L16 5EY
Tel: 01517 221995
Category: CLD ASD

Clifford Holroyde School
Thingwall Lane, LIVERPOOL,
Merseyside L14 7NX
Tel: 01512 289500
Category: EBD (Coed 7-16)

Ernest Cookson School
54 Bankfield Road, West Derby,
LIVERPOOL, Merseyside L13 0BQ
Tel: 01512 201874
Category: EBD (Boys 5-16)

Hope School
Naylorsfield Drive, LIVERPOOL,
Merseyside L27 0YD
Tel: 01514 984055
Category: EBD (Boys 5-16)

**Millstead Special
Needs Primary**
Iliad St, Everton, LIVERPOOL,
Merseyside L5 3LU
Tel: 01512 074656
Category: SLD (Coed 2-11)

Palmerston School
Beaconsfield Road, Woolton,
LIVERPOOL, Merseyside L25 6EE
Tel: 01514 282128
Category: SLD (Coed 11-19)

Princes Primary School
Selborne Street, LIVERPOOL,
Merseyside L8 1YQ
Tel: 01517 092602
Category: SLD (Coed 2-11)

Redbridge High School
Long Ln, LIVERPOOL,
Merseyside L9 6AD
Tel: 01512 336170
Category: SLD (Coed 11-19)

Sandfield Park School
Sandfield Walk, West Derby,
LIVERPOOL, Merseyside L12 1LH
Tel: 01512 280324
Category: PD HS (Coed 11-19)

Woolton High School
Woolton Hill Road, Woolton,
LIVERPOOL, Merseyside L25 6JA
Tel: 01514 284071
Category: (Coed 11-16)

Merseyside

SEFTON
Council

Sefton SENDIASS, Redgate Annexe, Redgate, Formby, Merseyside, L37 4EW
Tel: 0151 934 3334 Email: seftonsendiass@sefton.gov.uk Website: www.sefton.gov.uk

BOOTLE

Rowan Park School
Sterrix Lane, Litherland,
BOOTLE, Merseyside L21 0DB
Tel: 01512 224894
Category: SLD (Coed 3-18)

CROSBY

Crosby High School
De Villiers Avenue, CROSBY,
Merseyside L23 2TH
Tel: 01519 243671
Category: MLD (Coed 11-16)

Newfield School
Edge Lane, Thornton, CROSBY,
Merseyside L23 4TG
Tel: 01519 342991
Category: BESD (Coed 5-17)

SOUTHPORT

Merefield School
Westminster Drive, SOUTHPORT,
Merseyside PR8 2QZ
Tel: 01704 577163
Category: SLD (Coed 3-16)

**Presfield High School
and Specialist College**
Preston New Road, SOUTHPORT,
Merseyside PR9 8PA
Tel: 01704 227831
Category: ASD (Coed 11-16)

Merseyside

ST HELENS

Council

St Helens SENDIASS, Sutton Children's Centre, Ellamsbridge Road, St Helens, Merseyside, WA10 6RW
Tel: 01744 822160 Website: www.sthelens.gov.uk

NEWTON-LE-WILLOWS

Penkford School
Wharf Road, Earlestown, NEWTON-LE-WILLOWS, Merseyside WA12 9XZ
Tel: 01744 678745
Category: SEBD (9-16)

ST HELENS

Lansbury Bridge School
Lansbury Avenue, Parr, ST HELENS, Merseyside WA9 1TB
Tel: 01744 678579
Category: CLD PD MLD
ASD (Coed 3-16)

Mill Green School
Lansbury Avenue, Parr, ST HELENS, Merseyside WA9 1BU
Tel: 01744 678760
Category: SLD CLD PMLD
ASD (Coed 14-19)

Merseyside

WIRRAL

Council

Wirral SEN Team, Conway Street, Birkenhead Wirral, CH41 4FD
Tel: 01516664306 Email: paularista@wirral.gov.uk Website: www.wirral.gov.uk

BIRKENHEAD

Kilgarth School
Cavendish Street, BIRKENHEAD, Merseyside CH41 8BA
Tel: 01516 528071
Category: EBD ADHD (Boys 11-16)

PRENTON

The Observatory School
Bidston Village Road, Bidston, PRENTON, Merseyside CH43 7QT
Tel: 01516 527093
Category: SEBD LD (Coed 11-16)

WALLASEY

Elleray Park School
Elleray Park Road, WALLASEY, Merseyside CH45 0LH
Tel: 01516 393594
Category: CLD SLD PD
AUT PMLD (Coed 2-11)

WIRRAL

Clare Mount Specialist Sports College
Fender Lane, Moreton, WIRRAL, Merseyside CH46 9PA
Tel: 01516 069440
Category: MLD (Coed 11-19)

Gilbrook School
Glebe Hey Road, Woodchurch, WIRRAL, Merseyside CH49 8HE
Tel: 01515 223900
Category: EBD DYS (Coed 4-11)

Hayfield School
Manor Drive, Upton, WIRRAL, Merseyside CH49 4LN
Tel: 01516 779303
Category: MLD CLD
ASD (Coed 4-11)

Meadowside School
Pool Lane, Woodchurch, WIRRAL, Merseyside CH49 5LA
Tel: 01516 787711
Category: CLD SLD (Coed 11-19)

Orrets Meadow School
Chapelhill Road, Moreton, WIRRAL, Merseyside CH46 9QQ
Tel: 01516 788070
Category: SPLD SP&LD LD
AUT ASD EBD (Coed 5-11)

Stanley School
Greenbank Drive, WIRRAL, Merseyside CH61 5UE
Tel: 01513 426741
Category: (2-11)

Wirral Hospitals School
Joseph Paxton Campus, 157 Park Road North, Claughton, WIRRAL, Merseyside CH41 0EZ
Tel: 01514 887680
Category: HS (Coed 2-19)

WOODCHURCH

Foxfield School
New Hey Road, Moreton, WOODCHURCH, Merseyside CH49 5LF
Tel: 01516 418810
Category: ADHD SLD
ASD PD (Coed 11-19)

MIDDLESBROUGH
Council

Middlesbrough SENDIASS, 16 High Force Road, Riverside Park, Middlesbrough, TS2 1RH
Tel: 01642 608012 Email: main_sendiassmiddlesbrough@iammain.org.uk Website: www.middlesbrough.gov.uk

MIDDLESBROUGH

Beverley School
Saltersgill Avenue,
MIDDLESBROUGH,
Cleveland TS4 3JS
Tel: 01642 811350
Category: AUT (Coed 3-19)

Holmwood School
Saltersgill Avenue, Easterside,
MIDDLESBROUGH,
Cleveland TS4 3PT
Tel: 01642 819157
Category: EBD (Coed 4-11)

Priory Woods School
Tothill Avenue, Netherfields,
MIDDLESBROUGH,
Cleveland TS3 0RH
Tel: 01642 770540
Category: SLD PMLD (Coed 4-19)

MILTON KEYNES
Council

Milton Keynes SENDIASS, Civic Offices, 1 Saxon Gate, Milton Keynes, MK9 3EJ
Tel: 01908 254518 Email: mksendias@milton-keynes.gov.uk Website: www.milton-keynes.gov.uk

MILTON KEYNES

Romans Field School
Shenley Road, Bletchley, MILTON
KEYNES, Buckinghamshire MK3 7AW
Tel: 01908 376011
Category: SEBD (Coed
Day/boarding 5-12)

Slated Row School
Old Wolverton Road,
Wolverton, MILTON KEYNES,
Buckinghamshire MK12 5NJ
Tel: 01908 316017
Category: MLD Complex
needs (Coed Day 4-19)

The Redway School
Farmborough, Netherfield, MILTON
KEYNES, Buckinghamshire MK6 4HG
Tel: 01908 206400
Category: PMLD CLD SCD
AUT (Coed Day 2-19)

The Walnuts School
Admiral Drive, Hazeley, MILTON
KEYNES, Buckinghamshire MK8 0PU
Tel: 01908 563885
Category: ASD SCD (Coed
Day/boarding 4-19)

White Spire School
Rickley Lane, Bletchley, MILTON
KEYNES, Buckinghamshire MK3 6EW
Tel: 01908 373266
Category: MLD (Coed
Day & boarding 5-19)

NORFOLK
County Council

Norfolk SEN Team, County Hall, Martineau Lane, Norwich, Norfolk, NR1 2DH
Tel: 03448 008020 Email: send@norfolk.gov.uk Website: www.norfolk.gov.uk

ATTLEBOROUGH

Chapel Green School
Attleborough Road, Old
Buckenham, ATTLEBOROUGH,
Norfolk NR17 1RF
Tel: 01953 453116
Category: Complex
needs (Coed 3-19)

CROMER

Sidestrand Hall School
Cromer Road, Sidestrand,
CROMER, Norfolk NR27 0NH
Tel: 01263 578144
Category: Complex
Needs (Coed 7-19)

DEREHAM

Fred Nicholson School
Westfield Road, DEREHAM,
Norfolk NR19 1JB
Tel: 01362 693915
Category: Complex
Needs (Coed 7-16)

GREAT YARMOUTH

John Grant School
St George's Drive, Caister-
on-Sea, GREAT YARMOUTH,
Norfolk NR30 5QW
Tel: 01493 720158
Category: Complex
Needs (Coed 3-19)

KING'S LYNN

Churchill Park School
Winston Churchill Drive, Fairstead,
KING'S LYNN, Norfolk PE30 4RP
Tel: 01553 763679
Category: Complex
Needs (Day 2-19)

NORWICH

Hall School
St Faith's Road, NORWICH,
Norfolk NR6 7AD
Tel: 01603 466467
Category: Complex
Needs (Coed 3-19)

Harford Manor School
43 Ipswich Road, NORWICH,
Norfolk NR2 2LN
Tel: 01603 451809
Category: Complex
Needs (Coed 3-19)

The Clare School
South Park Avenue, NORWICH,
Norfolk NR4 7AU
Tel: 01603 454199
Category: MSI Complex
Needs (Coed 3-19)

The Parkside School
College Road, NORWICH,
Norfolk NR2 3JA
Tel: 01603 441126
Category: Complex
Needs (Coed 3-19)

SHERINGHAM

**Sheringham
Woodfields School**
Holt Road, SHERINGHAM,
Norfolk NR26 8ND
Tel: 01263 820520
Category: Complex
Needs (Coed 3-19)

NORTHAMPTONSHIRE
County Council

Northamptonshire CYPS, John Dryden House, 8-10 The Lakes, Northampton, NN4 7YD
Tel: 01001 261000 Email: education@northamptonshire.gov.uk Website: www.northamptonshire.gov.uk

KETTERING

**Isebrook SEN Cognition
& Learning College**
Eastleigh Road, KETTERING,
Northamptonshire NN15 6PT
Tel: 01536 500030
Category: MLD ASD SLD
SP&LD PH (11-19)

**Wren Spinney Community
Special School**
Westover Road, KETTERING,
Northamptonshire NN15 7LB
Tel: 01536 481939
Category: SLD PMLD ASD MSI (11-19)

NORTHAMPTON

Fairfields School
Trinity Avenue, NORTHAMPTON,
Northamptonshire NN2 6JN
Tel: 01604 714777
Category: PMLD PH
MSI SLD ASD (3-11)

**Greenfields School
and Sports College**
Prentice Court, Lings Way,
Goldings, NORTHAMPTON,
Northamptonshire NN3 8XS
Tel: 01604 741960
Category: PMLD SLD ASD MSI (11-19)

Kings Meadow School
Manning Road, Moulton
Leys, NORTHAMPTON,
Northamptonshire NN3 7AR
Tel: 01604 673730
Category: BESD (4-11)

**Northgate School
Arts College**
Queens Park Parade,
NORTHAMPTON,
Northamptonshire NN2 6LR
Tel: 01604 714098
Category: MLD SLD ASD (11-19)

TIFFIELD

The Gateway School
St Johns Road, TIFFIELD,
Northamptonshire NN12 8AA
Tel: 01604 878977
Category: BESD (11-19)

WELLINGBOROUGH

**Rowan Gate
Primary School**
Finedon Road, WELLINGBOROUGH,
Northamptonshire NN8 4NS
Tel: 01933 304970
Category: PMLD ASD (3-11)

NORTHUMBERLAND
County Council

Northumberland SENDIASS, County Hall, Morpeth, Northumberland, NE61 2EF
Tel: 01670 623555 Email: sen@northumberland.gov.uk Website: www.northumberland.gov.uk

ALNWICK

Barndale House School
Howling Lane, ALNWICK,
Northumberland NE66 1DQ
Tel: 01665 602541
Category: SLD

BERWICK UPON TWEED

The Grove Special School
Grove Gardens, Tweedmouth,
BERWICK UPON TWEED,
Northumberland TD15 2EN
Tel: 01289 306390
Category: SLD

BLYTH

The Dales School
Cowpen Road, BLYTH,
Northumberland NE24 4RE
Tel: 01670 352556
Category: MLD CLD PH EBD

CHOPPINGTON

Cleaswell Hill School
School Avenue, Guide
Post, CHOPPINGTON,
Northumberland NE62 5DJ
Tel: 01670 823182
Category: MLD

CRAMLINGTON

Atkinson House School
North Terrace, Seghill,
CRAMLINGTON,
Northumberland NE23 7EB
Tel: 0191 2980838
Category: EBD

**Cramlington
Hillcrest School**
East View Avenue, CRAMLINGTON,
Northumberland NE23 1DY
Tel: 01670 713632
Category: MLD

HEXHAM

Hexham Priory School
Corbridge Road, HEXHAM,
Northumberland NE46 1UY
Tel: 01434 605021
Category: SLD

MORPETH

**Collingwood School &
Media Arts College**
Stobhillgate, MORPETH,
Northumberland NE61 2HA
Tel: 01670 516374
Category: MLD CLD AUT
SP&LD PH Emotionally fragile
Specific medical conditions

NOTTINGHAM
City Council

Nottingham SEN Team, Glenbrook Management Centre, Wigman Road, Bilborough Nottingham, NG8 4PD
Tel: 01158 764300 Email: special.needs@nottinghamcity.gov.uk Website: www.nottinghamcity.gov.uk

NOTTINGHAM

Oak Field School and Specialist Sports College
Wigman Road, Bilborough,
NOTTINGHAM NG8 3HW
Tel: 01159 153265
Category: SCD ASD SPLI
(Coed Day 3-19)

Rosehill Special School
St Matthias Road, St Ann's,
NOTTINGHAM NG3 2FE
Tel: 01159 155815
Category: AUT (Coed Day 4-19)

Westbury School
Chingford Road, Bilborough,
NOTTINGHAM NG8 3BT
Tel: 01159 155858
Category: EBD (Coed Day 7-16)

Woodlands Special School
Beechdale Road, Aspley,
NOTTINGHAM NG8 3EZ
Tel: 01159 155734
Category: MLD (Coed Day 3-16)

NOTTINGHAMSHIRE
County Council

Integrated Children's Disability Service (ICDS), Meadow House, Littleworth, Mansfield, Nottinghamshire, NG18 2TB
Tel: 0115 8041275 Email: icds.duty@nottscc.gov.uk Website: www.nottinghamshire.sendlocaloffer.org.uk

ASHFIELD

Bracken Hill School
Chartwell Road, ASHFIELD,
Nottinghamshire NG17 7HZ
Tel: 01623 477268
Category: (Coed Day 3-19)

GEDLING

Carlton Digby School
Digby Avenue, Mapperley,
GEDLING, Nottingham NG3 6DS
Tel: 01159 568289
Category: (Coed 3-19)

Derrymount School (Lower)
Churchmoor Lane, Arnold,
GEDLING, Nottingham NG5 8HN
Tel: 01159 534015
Category: (Coed 3-13)

Derrymount School (Upper)
Sherbrook Road, Daybrook,
GEDLING, Nottingham NG5 6AT
Category: (Coed 14-19)

MANSFIELD

Fountaindale School
Nottingham Road, MANSFIELD,
Nottinghamshire NG18 5BA
Tel: 01623 792671
Category: PD (Coed 3-19)

Redgate School
Somersall Street, MANSFIELD,
Nottinghamshire NG19 6EL
Tel: 01623 455944
Category: (Coed Day 3-11)

Yeoman Park School
Park Hall Road, Mansfield
Woodhouse, MANSFIELD,
Nottinghamshire NG19 8PS
Tel: 01623 459540
Category: (Coed Day 3-19)

NEWARK

The Newark Orchard School (Lower)
Appleton Gate, NEWARK,
Nottinghamshire NG24 1JR
Tel: 01636 682255
Category: (Coed 3-14)

The Newark Orchard School (Upper)
London Road, New
Balderton, NEWARK,
Nottinghamshire NG24 3AL
Tel: 01636 682256
Category: (Coed 14-19)

RETFORD

St Giles School
North Road, RETFORD,
Nottinghamshire DN22 7XN
Tel: 01777 703683
Category: (Coed 3-19)

RUSHCLIFFE

Ash Lea School
Owthorpe Road, RUSHCLIFFE,
Nottinghamshire NG12 3PA
Tel: 01159 892744
Category: (Coed Day 3-19)

OXFORDSHIRE
County Council

Oxfordshire SENDIASS, Freepost SCE11489, Oxford, OX1 1ZS
Tel: 01865 810516 Website: www.oxfordshire.gov.uk/localoffer

BANBURY

Frank Wise School
Hornbeam Close, BANBURY,
Oxfordshire OX16 9RL
Tel: 01295 263520
Category: SLD PMLD (Coed 2-19)

BICESTER

Bardwell School
Hendon Place, Sunderland Drive,
BICESTER, Oxfordshire OX26 4RZ
Tel: 01869 242182
Category: SLD PMLD (Coed 2-19)

OXFORD

John Watson School
Littleworth Road, Wheatley,
OXFORD OX33 1NN
Tel: 01865 452725
Category: SLD PMLD (Coed 2-19)

Mabel Prichard School
Cuddesdon Way, OXFORD OX4 6SB
Tel: 01865 777878
Category: SLD PMLD (Coed 2-19)

Northfield School
Knights Road, Blackbird
Leys, OXFORD OX4 6DQ
Tel: 01865 771703
Category: BESD (Boys 11-18)

Oxfordshire Hospital School
c/o St Nicholasí Primary School, Raymund Road, Old Marston, OXFORD OX3 OPJ
Tel: 01865 957480
Category: HS (Coed 3-18)

Woodeaton Manor School
Woodeaton, OXFORD OX3 9TS
Tel: 01865 558722
Category: SEMH (Coed 7-18 Day/residential weekday boarding)

SONNING COMMON

Bishopswood Special School
Grove Road, SONNING COMMON, Oxfordshire RG4 9RH
Tel: 01189 724311
Category: SLD PMLD (Coed 2-16)

WITNEY

Springfield School
The Bronze Barrow, Cedar Drive, Madley Park, WITNEY, Oxfordshire OX28 1AR
Tel: 01993 703963
Category: SLD (Coed 2-16)

PETERBOROUGH

City Council

Peterborough SEN Team, Town Hall, Bridge Street, Peterborough, PE1 1HF
Tel: 01733 863979 Email: pps@peterborough.gov.uk Website: www.peterborough.gov.uk

PETERBOROUGH

Heltwate School
North Bretton, PETERBOROUGH, Cambridgeshire PE3 8RL
Tel: 01733 262878
Category: MLD SLD AUT PD SCD (Coed 4-16)

Marshfields School
Eastern Close, Dogsthorpe, PETERBOROUGH, Cambridgeshire PE1 4PP
Tel: 01733 568058
Category: MLD SCD SEBD SLD (Coed 11-19)

NeneGate School
Park Lane, Eastfield, PETERBOROUGH, Cambridgeshire PE1 5GZ
Tel: 01733 349438
Category: EBD (Coed 11-16)

Phoenix School
Clayton, Orton Goldhay, PETERBOROUGH, Cambridgeshire PE2 5SD
Tel: 01733 391666
Category: SLD PMLD PD SCN ASD MSI (Coed 2-19)

PLYMOUTH

City Council

Plymouth SENDIASS, Ballard House, West Hoe Road, Plymouth, Devon, PL1 3BJ
Tel: 01752 258933 Email: pias@plymouth.gov.uk Website: www.plymouth.gov.uk

PLYMOUTH

Brook Green Centre for Learning
Bodmin Road, Whitleigh, PLYMOUTH, Devon PL5 4DZ
Tel: 01752 773875
Category: MLD BESD (11-16)

Cann Bridge School
Miller Way, Estover, PLYMOUTH, Devon PL6 8UN
Tel: 01752 207909
Category: SLD (3-19)

Courtlands School
Widey Lane, Crownhill, PLYMOUTH, Devon PL6 5JS
Tel: 01752 776848
Category: MLD BESD (4-11)

Longcause Community Special School
Longcause, Plympton, PLYMOUTH, Devon PL7 1JB
Tel: 01752 336881
Category: MLD (5-17)

Mill Ford Community Special School
Rochford Crescent, Ernesettle, PLYMOUTH, Devon PL5 2PY
Tel: 01752 300270
Category: SLD PMLD (3-19)

Mount Tamar School
Row Lane, Higher St Budeaux, PLYMOUTH, Devon PL5 2EF
Tel: 01752 365128
Category: BESD (5-16)

Woodlands School
Picklecombe Drive, Off Tamerton Foliot Road, Whitleigh, PLYMOUTH, Devon PL6 5ES
Tel: 01752 300101
Category: PD PMLD MSI (2-19)

BOROUGH OF POOLE

Borough Council

Poole SENDIASS, Quay Advice Centre, 18 Hill Street, Poole, Dorset, BH15 1NR
Tel: 01202 261933 Email: sendiass@poole.gov.uk Website: www.poole.gov.uk

POOLE

Winchelsea School
Guernsey Road, Parkstone, POOLE, Dorset BH12 4LL
Tel: 01202 746240
Category: ADHD ASD ASP MLD (3-16)

PORTSMOUTH
City Council

Portsmouth SENDIASS, Frank Sorrell Centre, Prince Albert Road, Portsmouth, Hampshire, PO4 9HR
Tel: 0300 303 2000 Email: portsmouthiass@roseroad.org.uk Website: www.portsmouthlocaloffer.org

PORTSMOUTH

Mary Rose School
Gisors Road, Southsea,
PORTSMOUTH, Hampshire PO4 8GT
Tel: 02392 852330
Category: SCN ASD
PMLD (Coed 2-19)

Redwood Park School
Wembley Grove, Cosham,
PORTSMOUTH, Hampshire PO6 2RY
Tel: 02392 377500
Category: CLD ASD (Coed 11-16)

The Harbour School
151 Locksway Road, Milton,
PORTSMOUTH, Hampshire PO4 8LD
Tel: 023 92818547
Category: BESD

READING
Borough Council

Reading SENDIASS, First Floor, Hamilton Centre, 135 Bulmershe Road, Reading, Berkshire, RG1 5SG
Tel: 0118 937 3421 Email: iass@reading.gov.uk Website: www.reading.gov.uk/servicesguide

READING

Phoenix College
40 Christchurch Road,
READING, Berkshire RG2 7AY
Tel: 01189 375524
Category: BESD (Coed 11-16)

The Holy Brook School
145 Ashampstead Road,
Southcote, READING,
Berkshire RG30 3LJ
Tel: 01189 375489
Category: BESD (Coed 5-11)

REDCAR & CLEVELAND
Borough Council

Redcar & Cleveland SENDIASS, Redcar & Cleveland House, Kirkleatham Street, Redcar, Middlesborough, TS10 1RT
Tel: 01642 444527 Email: sendiass@redcar-cleveland.gov.uk Website: www.redcar-cleveland.gov.uk

MIDDLESBROUGH

Pathways School
Tennyson Avenue, Grangetown,
MIDDLESBROUGH TS6 7NP
Tel: 01642 779292
Category: SEBD (Coed Day 7-15)

REDCAR

Kirkleatham Hall School
Kirkleatham Village, REDCAR,
Cleveland TS10 4QR
Tel: 01642 483009
Category: SLD PMLD SLCN ASC
PD CLDD (Coed Day 4-19)

RUTLAND

County Council

Rutland SENDIASS, Catmose House, Catmose Street, Oakham, Rutland, LE15 6HP
Tel: 07977 015 674 Email: info@sendiassrutland.org.uk Website: www.rutland.gov.uk

OAKHAM

**The Parks at Oakham
CE Primary School**
Burley Road, OAKHAM,
Rutland LE15 6GY
Tel: 01572 722404
Category: AUT MLD PMLD
SP&LD VIS SEBD (Coed 2-5)

SHROPSHIRE

Council

Shropshire SEN Team, The Shirehall, Abbey Foregate, Shrewsbury, Shropshire, SY2 6ND
Tel: 01743 254366 Email: senteam@shropshire.gov.uk Website: www.shropshire.gov.uk

OSWESTRY

Acorns Centre
Middleton Road, OSWESTRY,
Shropshire SY11 2LF
Category: SEMH (Coed 9-11)

SHREWSBURY

Woodlands School
Tilley Green, Wem, SHREWSBURY,
Shropshire SY4 5PJ
Tel: 01939 232372
Category: SEMH (Coed 11-16)

SLOUGH

Borough Council

Slough SENDASS, St Martins Place, 51 Bath Rd, Slough, Berkshire, SL1 3UF
Tel: 01753 787693 Email: sendass@scstrust.co.uk Website: www.slough.gov.uk

SLOUGH

Arbour Vale School
Farnham Road, SLOUGH,
Berkshire SL2 3AE
Tel: 01753 515560
Category: SLD ASD
MLD (Coed 2-19)

Littledown School
Queen's Road, SLOUGH,
Berkshire SL1 3QW
Tel: 01753 521734
Category: BESD (Coed 5-11)

Millside School
112 Burnham Lane, SLOUGH,
Berkshire SL1 6LZ
Tel: 01628 696061
Category: BESD (Coed 11-16)

SOMERSET
County Council

Somerset SEN Team, County Hall, Taunton, Somerset, TA1 4DY

Tel: 0300 123 2224 Email: somersetdirect@somerset.gov.uk Website: www.somerset.gov.uk

BRIDGWATER

Elmwood School
Hamp Avenue, BRIDGWATER,
Somerset TA6 6AW
Tel: 01278 456243
Category: SLD MLD ASD
EBD (Coed Day 11-16)

Penrose School
Albert Street, Willow Brook,
BRIDGWATER, Somerset TA6 7ET
Tel: 01278 423660
Category: CLD ASD SLD
(4-10 and Post-16)

FROME

Critchill School
Nunney Road, FROME,
Somerset BA11 4LB
Tel: 01373 464148
Category: SLD MLD CLD
(Coed Day 4-16)

STREET

Avalon Special School
Brooks Road, STREET,
Somerset BA16 0PS
Tel: 01458 443081
Category: SLD MLD PMLD
ASD (Coed Day 3-16)

TAUNTON

Selworthy School
Selworthy Road, TAUNTON,
Somerset TA2 8HD
Tel: 01823 284970
Category: SLD PMLD MLD
ASD BESD (Coed Day 4-19)

**Sky College (formerly
The Priory School)**
Pickeridge Close, TAUNTON,
Somerset TA2 7HW
Tel: 01823 275569
Category: EBD (Boys
Boarding 11-16)

YEOVIL

Fairmead School
Mudford Road, YEOVIL,
Somerset BA21 4NZ
Tel: 01935 421295
Category: MLD SEBD AUT
SLD (Coed Day 4-16)

Fiveways Special School
Victoria Road, YEOVIL,
Somerset BA21 5AZ
Tel: 01935 476227
Category: SLD PMLD ASD
(Coed Day 4-19)

NORTH SOMERSET
Council

North Somerset SEN Team, Town Hall, Room 119, Weston-Super-Mare, North Somerset, BS23 1UJ

Tel: 01275 888297 Website: www.n-somerset.gov.uk

NAILSEA

Ravenswood School
Pound Lane, NAILSEA, North
Somerset BS48 2NN
Tel: 01275 854134
Category: CLD SLD (3-19)

WESTON-SUPER-MARE

Baytree School
The Campus, Highlands
Lane, WESTON-SUPER-MARE,
North Somerset BS24 7DX
Tel: 01934 427555
Category: SLD (3-19)

Westhaven School
Ellesmere Road, Uphill,
WESTON-SUPER-MARE,
North Somerset BS23 4UT
Tel: 01934 632171
Category: CLD (7-16)

SOUTHAMPTON
City Council

Southampton SEN Team, Civic Centre (North Block), Southampton, Hampshire, SO14 7LY

Tel: 023 8083 3270 Email: sen.team@southampton.gov.uk Website: www.southampton.gov.uk

SOUTHAMPTON

Great Oaks School
Vermont Close, off Winchester
Rd, SOUTHAMPTON,
Hampshire SO16 7LT
Tel: 02380 767660
Category: MLD AUT ASP SLD (11-16)

Springwell School
Hinkler Road, Thornhill,
SOUTHAMPTON,
Hampshire SO19 6DH
Tel: 02380 445981
Category: CLD SP&LD AUT SLD
Challenging behaviour (4-11)

The Cedar School
Redbridge Lane,
Nursling, SOUTHAMPTON,
Hampshire SO16 0NX
Tel: 02380 734205
Category: PD (2-16)

The Polygon School
Handel Terrace, SOUTHAMPTON,
Hampshire SO15 2FH
Tel: 02380 636776
Category: EBD (Boys 11-16)

Vermont School
Vermont Close, Off Winchester
Rd, SOUTHAMPTON,
Hampshire SO16 7LT
Tel: 02380 767988
Category: EBD (Boys 5-11)

STAFFORDSHIRE

County Council

The SEN Team, Tipping Street, Stafford, Staffordshire, ST16 2DH
Tel: 03001 118000 Email: education@staffordshire.gov.uk Website: www.staffordshire.gov.uk

BURNTWOOD

Chasetown Community School
Church Street, Chasetown, BURNTWOOD, Staffordshire WS7 3QL
Tel: 01543 686315
Category: SEBD (Coed Day 4-11)

BURTON UPON TRENT

The Fountains High School
Bitham Lane, Stretton, BURTON UPON TRENT, Staffordshire DE13 0HB
Tel: 01283 239161
Category: Generic (Coed Day 11-19)

The Fountains Primary School
Bitham Lane, Stretton, BURTON UPON TRENT, Staffordshire DE13 0HB
Tel: 01283 239700
Category: Generic (Coed Day 2-11)

CANNOCK

Hednesford Valley High School
Stanley Road, Hednesford, CANNOCK, Staffordshire WS12 4JS
Tel: 01543 423714
Category: Generic (Coed Day 11-19)

Sherbrook Primary School
Brunswick Road, CANNOCK, Staffordshire WS11 5SF
Tel: 01543 510216
Category: Generic (Coed Day 2-11)

LEEK

Horton Lodge Community Special School & Key Learning Centre
Reacliffe Road, Rudyard, LEEK, Staffordshire ST13 8RB
Tel: 01538 306214
Category: PD MSI SP&LD (Coed Day/Boarding 2-11)

Meadows Special School
Springfield Road, LEEK, Staffordshire ST13 6EU
Tel: 01538 225050
Category: Generic (Coed Day 11-19)

Springfield Community Special School
Springfield Road, LEEK, Staffordshire ST13 6LQ
Tel: 01538 383558
Category: Generic (Coed Day 2-11)

LICHFIELD

Queen's Croft High School
Birmingham Road, LICHFIELD, Staffordshire WS13 6PJ
Tel: 01543 510669
Category: Generic (Coed Day11-19)

Rocklands School
Purcell Avenue, LICHFIELD, Staffordshire WS13 7PH
Tel: 01543 510760
Category: ASD MLD PMLD SLD (Coed Day 2-11)

NEWCASTLE UNDER LYME

Merryfields School
Hoon Avenue, NEWCASTLE UNDER LYME, Staffordshire ST5 9NY
Tel: 01782 296076
Category: Generic (Coed Day 2-11)

STAFFORD

Greenhall Nursery
Second Avenue, Holmcroft, STAFFORD, Staffordshire ST16 1PS
Tel: 01785 246159
Category: PD (Coed Day 2-5)

Marshlands Special School
Second Avenue, STAFFORD, Staffordshire ST16 1PS
Tel: 01785 356385
Category: Generic (Coed Day 2-11)

TAMWORTH

Two Rivers High School
Deltic, off Silver Link Road, Glascote, TAMWORTH, Staffordshire B77 2HJ
Tel: 01827 475690
Category: Generic (Coed Day 11-19)

Two Rivers Primary School
Quince, Amington Heath, TAMWORTH, Staffordshire B77 4EN
Tel: 01827 475740
Category: Generic (Coed Day 2-11)

WOLVERHAMPTON

Cherry Trees School
Giggetty Lane, Wombourne, WOLVERHAMPTON, West Midlands WV5 0AX
Tel: 01902 894484
Category: Generic (Coed Day 2-11)

Wightwick Hall School
Tinacre Hill, Wightwick, WOLVERHAMPTON, West Midlands WV6 8DA
Tel: 01902 761889
Category: Generic (Coed Day 11-19)

STOCKTON-ON-TEES

Borough Council

Stockton-on-Tees SEN Team, 4th Floor, Queensway House, West Precinct Billingham, TS23 2YQ
Tel: 01642 527145 Email: sensection@stockton.gov.uk Website: www.stockton.gov.uk

STOCKTON-ON-TEES

Horizons Specialist Academy Trust, Abbey Hill Academy & Sixth Form
Ketton Road, Hardwick Green, STOCKTON-ON-TEES TS19 8BU
Tel: 01642 677113
Category: SLD PMLD AUT (Coed 11-19)

Horizons Specialist Academy Trust, Westlands at Green Gates
Melton Road, Elmtree, STOCKTON-ON-TEES TS19 0JD
Tel: 01642 570104
Category: BESD (Coed Residential 5-11)

STOKE-ON-TRENT
City Council

Stoke-on-Trent SEND Services, Floor 2, Civic Centre, Glebe Street, Stoke-on-Trent, Staffordshire, ST4 1HH
Tel: 01782 233198 Email: localoffer@stoke.gov.uk Website: www.stoke.gov.uk

BLURTON
Kemball Special School
Beconsfield Drive, BLURTON,
Stoke-on-Trent ST3 3JD
Tel: 01782 883120
Category: PMLD SLD ASD
CLD (Coed Day 2-19)

BLYTHE BRIDGE
Portland School and Specialist College
Uttoxeter Road, BLYTHE BRIDGE,
Staffordshire ST11 9JG
Tel: 01782 882020
Category: MLD SEBD
(Coed Day 3-16)

STOKE-ON-TRENT
Abbey Hill School and Performing Arts College
Box Lane, Meir, STOKE-ON-TRENT, Staffordshire ST3 5PP
Tel: 01782 882882
Category: MLD AUT
(Coed Day 2-18)

TUNSTALL
Watermill Special School
Turnhurst Road, Packmoor,
TUNSTALL, Stoke-on-Trent ST6 6JZ
Tel: 01782 883737
Category: MLD (Coed Day 5-16)

SUFFOLK
County Council

Suffolk SENDIASS, Endeavour House, 8 Russell Road, Ipswich, Suffolk, IP1 2BX
Tel: 01473 265210 Email: sendiass@suffolk.gov.uk Website: www.suffolk.gov.uk

BURY ST EDMUNDS
Riverwalk School
Chevington Close, BURY ST
EDMUNDS, Suffolk IP33 3JZ
Tel: 01284 764280
Category: SLD (Coed Day 3-19)

IPSWICH
The Bridge School (Primary Campus)
Sprites Lane, IPSWICH,
Suffolk IP8 3ND
Tel: 01473 556200
Category: SLD PMLD
(Coed Day 3-11)

The Bridge School (Secondary Campus)
Sprites Lane, IPSWICH,
Suffolk IP8 3ND
Tel: 01473 556200
Category: SLD PMLD
(Coed Day 11-16)

LOWESTOFT
Warren School
Clarkes Lane, Oulton Broad,
LOWESTOFT, Suffolk NR33 8HT
Tel: 01502 561893
Category: SLD PMLD
(Coed Day 3-19)

SUDBURY
Hillside School
Hitchcock Place, SUDBURY,
Suffolk CO10 1NN
Tel: 01787 372808
Category: SLD PMLD
(Coed day 3-19)

SURREY
County Council

Surrey SENDIASS, Third Floor, Consort House, 5-7 Queensway, Redhill, Surrey, RH1 1BY
Tel: 01737 737300 Email: ssiass@surreycc.gov.uk Website: www.surreycc.gov.uk

ADDLESTONE
Philip Southcote School
Addlestone Moor, ADDLESTONE,
Surrey KT15 2QH
Tel: 01932 562326
Category: HI LD (11-19)

CAMBERLEY
Portesbery School
Newfoundland Road, Deepcut,
CAMBERLEY, Surrey GU16 6TA
Tel: 01252 832100
Category: SLD (2-19)

CATERHAM
Clifton Hill School
Chaldon Road, CATERHAM,
Surrey CR3 5PH
Tel: 01883 347740
Category: SLD (11-19)

Sunnydown School
Portley House, 152 Whyteleafe
Road, CATERHAM, Surrey CR3 5ED
Tel: 01883 342281
Category: ASD SLCN
(Boarding & day 11-16)

FARNHAM
The Abbey School
Menin Way, FARNHAM,
Surrey GU9 8DY
Tel: 01252 725059
Category: LD (11-16)

GUILDFORD
Gosden House School
Horsham Road, Bramley,
GUILDFORD, Surrey GU5 0AH
Tel: 01483 892008
Category: LD (Day 5-16)

Wey House School
Horsham Road, Bramley,
GUILDFORD, Surrey GU5 0BJ
Tel: 01483 898130
Category: BESD (Day only 7-11)

OXTED
Limpsfield Grange School
89 Bluehouse Lane, Limpsfield,
OXTED, Surrey RH8 0RZ
Tel: 01883 713928
Category: ELD (Boarding
& day 11-16)

REIGATE

Brooklands School
27 Wray Park Road,
REIGATE, Surrey RH2 0DF
Tel: 01737 249941
Category: SLD (2-11)

SHEPPERTON

Manor Mead School
Laleham Road, SHEPPERTON,
Middlesex TW17 8EL
Tel: 01932 241834
Category: SLD (2-11)

WALTON-ON-THAMES

Walton Leigh School
Queens Road, WALTON-ON-THAMES, Surrey KT12 5AB
Tel: 01932 223243
Category: SLD (11-19)

WOKING

Freemantles School
Smarts Heath Road, Mayford
Green, WOKING, Surrey GU22 0AN
Tel: 01483 545680
Category: CLD (4-19)

The Park School
Onslow Crescent, WOKING,
Surrey GU22 7AT
Tel: 01483 772057
Category: LD (11-16)

EAST SUSSEX

County Council

East Sussex ISEND, PO Box 4, County Hall, St Anne's Crescent Lewes, East Sussex, BN7 1UE
Email: isend.comms@eastsussex.gov.uk Website: www.eastsussex.gov.uk

CROWBOROUGH

Grove Park School
Church Road, CROWBOROUGH,
East Sussex TN6 1BN
Tel: 01892 663018
Category: CLD/ASD (Coed 2-19)

EASTBOURNE

Hazel Court Special School
Larkspur Drive, EASTBOURNE,
East Sussex BN23 8EJ
Tel: 01323 465720
Category: CLD/ASD (Coed 11-19)

WEST SUSSEX

County Council

West Sussex SEN Team, County Hall, West Street, Chichester, West Sussex, PO19 1RQ
Tel: 0330 222 8555 Email: localoffer@westsussex.gov.uk Website: www.westsussex.gov.uk

BURGESS HILL

Woodlands Meed
Chanctonbury Road, BURGESS
HILL, West Sussex RH15 9EY
Tel: 01444 244133
Category: LD (Coed 2-19)

CHICHESTER

Fordwater School
Summersdale Road, CHICHESTER,
West Sussex PO19 6PP
Tel: 01243 782475
Category: SLD (Coed 2-19)

Littlegreen School
Compton, CHICHESTER,
West Sussex PO18 9NW
Tel: 02392 631259
Category: SEBD (Boys 7-16)

St Anthony's School
Woodlands Lane, CHICHESTER,
West Sussex PO19 5PA
Tel: 01243 785965
Category: MLD (Coed 4-16)

CRAWLEY

Manor Green College
Lady Margaret Road, Ifield,
CRAWLEY, West Sussex RH11 0DX
Tel: 01293 520351
Category: LD (Coed 11-19)

Manor Green Primary School
Lady Margaret Road, Ifield,
CRAWLEY, West Sussex RH11 0DU
Tel: 01293 526873
Category: LD (Coed 2-11)

HORSHAM

Queen Elizabeth II Silver Jubilee School
Compton's Lane, HORSHAM,
West Sussex RH13 5NW
Tel: 01403 266215
Category: SLD AUT
PMLD (Coed 2-19)

LITTLEHAMPTON

Cornfield School
Cornfield Close, Wick,
LITTLEHAMPTON, West
Sussex BN17 6HY
Tel: 01903 731277
Category: SEBD (Coed 7-16)

SHOREHAM-BY-SEA

Herons Dale Primary School
Hawkins Crescent, SHOREHAM-BY-SEA, West Sussex BN43 6TN
Tel: 01273 596904
Category: LD (Coed 4-11)

WORTHING

Oak Grove College
The Boulevard, WORTHING,
West Sussex BN13 1JX
Tel: 01903 708870
Category: LD (Coed 11-19)

Palatine Primary School
Palatine Road, Goring-By-Sea,
WORTHING, West Sussex BN12 6JP
Tel: 01903 242835
Category: LD (Coed 3-11)

SWINDON
Borough Council

Swindon SENDIASS, Civic Offices, Euclid Street, Swindon, Wiltshire, SN1 2JH
Email: parentpartnership@swindon.gov.uk Website: www.swindon.gov.uk

SWINDON

Brimble Hill School
Tadpole Lane, North Swindon
Learning Campus, Redhouse,
SWINDON, Wiltshire SN25 2NB
Tel: 01793 493900
Category: SLD (5-11)

Chalet School
Liden Drive, Liden, SWINDON,
Wiltshire SN3 6EX
Tel: 01793 534537
Category: CLD including ASD (3-11)

Crowdys Hill School
Jefferies Avenue, Cricklade Road,
SWINDON, Wiltshire SN2 7HJ
Tel: 01793 332400
Category: CLD & other
difficulties (11-16)

Nyland Campus
Nyland Road, Nythe,
SWINDON, Wiltshire SN3 3RD
Tel: 01793 535023
Category: BESD (5-11)

St Luke's School
Cricklade Road, SWINDON,
Wiltshire SN2 7AS
Tel: 01793 705566
Category: BESD (11-16)

Uplands School
The Learning Campus, Tadpole
Lane, Redhouse, SWINDON,
Wiltshire SN25 2NB
Tel: 01793 493910
Category: SLD (11-19)

TELFORD & WREKIN
Council

Telford & Wrekin SENDIASS, The Glebe Centre, Glebe Street, Wellington Telford, TF1 1JP
Tel: 01952 457176 Email: info@iass.org.uk Website: www.telford.gov.uk

TELFORD

Haughton School
Queen Street, Madeley,
TELFORD, Shropshire TF7 4BW
Tel: 01952 387540
Category: MLD ASD SLD
SP&LD BESD (Coed 5-11)

Mount Gilbert School
Hinkshay Road, Dawley,
TELFORD, Shropshire TF4 3PP
Tel: 01952 387670
Category: SEBD SPLD
AUT (Coed 11-16)

Queensway HLC
Hadley, TELFORD, Shropshire TF1 6AJ
Tel: 01952 388555
Category: ASD (11-18)

Southall School
Off Rowan Avenue, Dawley,
TELFORD, Shropshire TF4 3PN
Tel: 01952 387600
Category: MLD ASD
SEBD (Coed 11-16)

The Bridge Special School
HLC, Waterloo Road, Hadley,
TELFORD, Shropshire TF1 5NQ
Tel: 01952 387108
Category: (3-16)

THURROCK
Council

Thurrock SENDIASS, Parent Advisory Team Thurrock (PATT), The Beehive, West Street Grays, Essex, RM17 6XP
Tel: 01375 389 894 Email: info@patt.org.uk Website: www.thurrock.gov.uk

GRAYS

**Beacon Hill Academy
(Post 16 Provision)**
Buxton Road, GRAYS,
Essex RM16 2WU
Tel: 01375 898656
Category: SLD PNI PMLD
(Coed 16-19)

Treetops School (6th Form)
Buxton Road, GRAYS,
Essex RM16 2WU
Tel: 01375 372723
Category: MLD ASD (Coed 16-18)

TORBAY
Council

Torbay SEN Team, Tor Hill House, c/o Torquay Town Hall, Torquay, Devon, TQ1 3DR
Tel: 01803 208274 Email: sensection@torbay.gov.uk Website: www.torbay.gov.uk

PAIGNTON

Torbay School
170b Torquay Road, Preston,
PAIGNTON, Devon TQ3 2AL
Tel: 01803 665522
Category: BESD (11-16)

TORQUAY

Mayfield School
Moor Lane, Watcombe,
TORQUAY, Devon TQ2 8NH
Tel: 01803 328375
Category: SLD PMLD PH
AUT (3-19) BESD (5-11)

Tyne & Wear
GATESHEAD
Council

Gateshead SEND Team, Civic Centre, Regent Street, Gateshead, Tyne & Wear, NE8 1HH
Tel: 0191 433 3626 Email: senteam@gateshead.gov.uk Website: www.gateshead.gov.uk

GATESHEAD

**Dryden School Business
& Enterprise College**
Shotley Gardens, Low Fell,
GATESHEAD, Tyne & Wear NE9 5UR
Tel: 01914 203811
Category: SLD (Coed 11-19)

Eslington Primary School
Hazel Road, GATESHEAD,
Tyne & Wear NE8 2EP
Tel: 01914 334131
Category: EBD (Coed 4-11)

Furrowfield School
Whitehill Drive, Felling, GATESHEAD,
Tyne & Wear NE10 9RZ
Tel: 01914 954700
Category: EBD (Boys 11-16)

**Hill Top Specialist
Arts College**
Wealcroft, Leam Lane Estate,
GATESHEAD, Tyne & Wear NE10 8LT
Tel: 01914 692462
Category: MLD AUT (Coed 11-19)

NEWCASTLE
UPON TYNE

Gibside School
Burnthouse Lane, Whickham,
NEWCASTLE UPON TYNE,
Tyne & Wear NE16 5AT
Tel: 01914 410123
Category: SLD MLD AUT
LD (Coed 3-11)

NEWCASTLE UPON TYNE
City Council

Newcastle SEN Assessment Service, Room 213, Civic Centre, Newcastle upon Tyne, Tyne & Wear, NE1 8QH
Tel: 01912 774650 Email: localoffer@newcastle.gov.uk Website: www.newcastlechildrenservices.org.uk

NEWCASTLE
UPON TYNE

Hadrian School
Bertram Crescent, Pendower,
NEWCASTLE UPON TYNE,
Tyne & Wear NE15 6PY
Tel: 01912 734440
Category: PMLD SLD
(Coed Day 2-11)

Linhope Pupil Referral Unit
Linhope Centre, Linhope
Road, NEWCASTLE UPON TYNE,
Tyne & Wear NE5 2NW
Tel: 01912 674447
Category: (Coed Day 5-16)

Newcastle Bridges School
c/o Kenton College, Drayton
Road, Kenton, NEWCASTLE UPON
TYNE, Tyne & Wear NE3 3RU
Tel: 01918 267086
Category: HS (Coed 2-19)

Sir Charles Parson School
Westbourne Avenue, NEWCASTLE
UPON TYNE, Tyne & Wear NE6 4ED
Tel: 01912 952280
Category: SLD PD PMLD
(Coed Day 11-19)

Thomas Bewick School
Linhope Road, West Denton,
NEWCASTLE UPON TYNE,
Tyne & Wear NE5 2LW
Tel: 01912 296020
Category: AUT (Coed
Day/boarding 3-19)

Trinity School
Condercum Road, NEWCASTLE
UPON TYNE, Tyne & Wear NE4 8XJ
Tel: 01912 986950
Category: SEBD (Coed Day 7-16)

Tyne & Wear

SUNDERLAND
City Council

Sunderland SENDIASS, Civic Centre, Burdon Road, Sunderland, Tyne & Wear, SR2 7DN
Tel: 0191 5615643 Email: caroline.comer@sunderland.gov.uk Website: www.sunderland.gov.uk

SUNDERLAND

Sunningdale School
Shaftoe Road, Springwell,
SUNDERLAND, Tyne & Wear SR3 4HA
Tel: 01915 280440
Category: PMLD SLD
(Coed Day 2-11)

WASHINGTON

Columbia Grange School
Oxclose Road, Columbia,
WASHINGTON, Tyne &
Wear NE38 7NY
Tel: 01912 193860
Category: SLD ASD (Coed Day 3-11)

Tyne & Wear

NORTH TYNESIDE
Council

North Tyneside SENDIASS, Floor 2, Quadrant West, Cobalt Business Park,
Silverlink North North Tyneside, Tyne & Wear, NE27 0BY
Tel: 01916 438317 Email: sendiass@northtyneside.gov.uk Website: www.northtyneside.gov.uk

LONGBENTON

Benton Dene School
Hailsham Avenue, LONGBENTON,
Tyne & Wear NE12 8FD
Tel: 01916 432730
Category: MLD ASD (Coed 5-11+)

NORTH SHIELDS

Southlands School
Beach Road, Tynemouth, NORTH
SHIELDS, Tyne & Wear NE30 2QR
Tel: 01912 006348
Category: MLD BESD (Coed 11-16+)

WALLSEND

Beacon Hill School
Rising Sun Cottages, High Farm,
WALLSEND, Tyne & Wear NE28 9JW
Tel: 01916 433000
Category: ASD SLD
PMLD (Coed 2-16)

Silverdale School
Langdale Gardens, WALLSEND,
Tyne & Wear NE28 0HG
Tel: 01912 005982
Category: BESD (Coed 7-16)

WHITLEY BAY

Woodlawn School
Drumoyne Gardens, West
Monkseaton, WHITLEY BAY,
Tyne & Wear NE25 9DL
Tel: 01916 432590
Category: PD MSI Medical
needs (Coed 2-16)

Tyne & Wear

SOUTH TYNESIDE
Council

South Tynesdie SEN Team, Children, Adults & Families, Level 0, Town Hall & Civic
Offices, Westoe Road South Shields, Tyne & Wear, NE33 2RL
Tel: 01914 247808 Email: tracey.wilson@southtyneside.gov.uk Website: www.southtyneside.info

HEBBURN

**Hebburn Lakes
Primary School**
Campbell Park Road, HEBBURN,
Tyne & Wear NE31 1QY
Tel: 01914 839122
Category: BESD LD Complex
medical needs

Keelman's Way School
Campbell Park Road, HEBBURN,
Tyne & Wear NE31 1QY
Tel: 01914 897480
Category: PMLD SLD
(Coed Day 2-19)

JARROW

**Epinay Business &
Enterprise School**
Clervaux Terrace, JARROW,
Tyne & Wear NE32 5UP
Tel: 01914 898949
Category: MLD EBD (Coed 5-17)

Fellgate Autistic Unit
Oxford Way, Fellgate Estate,
JARROW, Tyne & Wear NE32 4XA
Tel: 01914 894801
Category: AUT (Coed 3-11)

**Hedworthfield Language
Development Unit**
Linkway, Hedworth Estate,
JARROW, Tyne & Wear NE32 4QF
Tel: 01915 373373
Category: SP&LD (Coed)

Jarrow School
Field Terrace, JARROW,
Tyne & Wear NE32 5PR
Tel: 01914 283200
Category: HI ASD

Simonside Primary School
Glasgow Road, JARROW,
Tyne & Wear NE32 4AU
Tel: 01914 898315
Category: HI

SOUTH SHIELDS

Ashley Child Development Centre
Temple Park Road, SOUTH
SHIELDS, Tyne & Wear NE34 0QA
Tel: 01914 564977
Category: Other Early Years

Bamburgh School
Horsley Hill Community
Campus, SOUTH SHIELDS,
Tyne & Wear NE34 7TD
Tel: 01914 274330
Category: PD MED VIS HI
MLD (Coed Day 2-17)

Harton Speech and Language and ASD Resource Bases
c/o Harton Technology College,
Lisle Road, SOUTH SHIELDS,
Tyne & Wear NE34 6DL
Tel: 01914 274050
Category: Speech and
language ASD

Park View School
Temple Park Road, SOUTH
SHIELDS, Tyne & Wear NE34 0QA
Tel: 01914 541568
Category: BESD (Coed Day 11-16)

WARRINGTON
Borough Council

Warrington Pupil Assessment Support Team, New Town House, Buttermarket Street, Warrington, WA1 2NH
Tel: 01925 443322 Email: contact@warrington.gov.uk Website: www.warrington.gov.uk

WARRINGTON

Fox Wood School
Holes Lane, Woolston,
WARRINGTON, Cheshire WA1 4LS
Tel: 01925 818534
Category: SLD (Coed Day 4-19)

Green Lane Community Special School
Holes Lane, Woolston,
WARRINGTON, Cheshire WA1 4LS
Tel: 01925 811617
Category: MLD CLD
(Coed Day 4-19)

Woolston Brook School
Green Lane, Padgate,
WARRINGTON, Cheshire WA1 4JL
Tel: 01925 818549
Category: BESD (Coed Day 7-16)

WARWICKSHIRE
County Council

Warwickshire SENDIASS, Canterbury House, Exhall Grange Campus,
Easter Way, Ash Green Coventry, Warwickshire, CV7 9HP
Tel: 024 7636 6054 Email: wias@family-action.org.uk Website: www.warwickshire.gov.uk

ASH GREEN

Exhall Grange School & Science College
Easter Way, ASH GREEN,
Warwickshire CV7 9HP
Tel: 02476 364200
Category: VIS PD Med
(Coed Day 2-19)

WARWICK

Ridgeway School
Deansway, WARWICK,
Warwickshire CV34 5DF
Tel: 01926 491987
Category: Generic SLD VIS HI AUT
MSI PD MLD PMLD (Coed Day 2-11)

Round Oak School, Support Service & Sports College
Brittain Lane, off Myton Road,
WARWICK, Warwickshire CV34 6DX
Tel: 01926 423311
Category: Generic SLD VIS HI AUT
MSI PD MLD PMLD (Coed Day 11-19)

West Midlands

BIRMINGHAM
City Council

Birmingham SENDIASS Team, Lancaster Circus, PO Box 16289, Birmingham, B2 2XN
Tel: 0121 303 5004 Email: sendiass@birmingham.gov.uk Website: www.birmingham.gov.uk

BROMSGROVE

Hunters Hill College
Spirehouse Lane,
Blackwell, BROMSGROVE,
Worcestershire B60 1QD
Tel: 01214 451320
Category: BESD MLD (Coed 11-16)

EDGBASTON

Baskerville School
Fellows Lane, Harborne,
EDGBASTON, Birmingham B17 9TS
Tel: 01214 273191
Category: ASD (Coed
boarding 11-19)

ERDINGTON

Queensbury School
Wood End Road, ERDINGTON,
Birmingham B24 8BL
Tel: 01213 735731
Category: MLD AUT SLD
(Coed Day 11-19)

The Pines Special School
Marsh Hill, ERDINGTON,
Birmingham B23 7EY
Tel: 01214 646136
Category: ASD SLCN
(Coed Day 2-12)

HALL GREEN

**Fox Hollies School &
Performing Arts College**
Highbury Community Campus,
Queensbridge Road, Moseley,
HALL GREEN, Birmingham B13 8QB
Tel: 01214 646566
Category: SLD PD CLD
MSI (Coed Day 11-19)

Uffculme School
Queensbridge Road, Moseley,
HALL GREEN, Birmingham B13 8QB
Tel: 01214 645250
Category: ASD (Coed day 3-19)

HODGE HILL

Beaufort School
Stechford Road, HODGE
HILL, Birmingham B34 6BJ
Tel: 01216 758500
Category: SLD PMLD ASD
(Coed Day 2-11)

Braidwood School
Bromford Road, HODGE
HILL, Birmingham B36 8AF
Tel: 01214 645558
Category: Deaf HI (Coed Day 11-19)

NORTHFIELD

**Longwill Primary School
for Deaf Children**
Bell Hill, NORTHFIELD,
Birmingham B31 1LD
Tel: 01214 753923
Category: HI Deaf (Coed Day 2-12)

Victoria School
Bell Hill, NORTHFIELD,
Birmingham B31 1LD
Tel: 01214 769478
Category: PD (Coed Day 2-19)

PERRY BARR

Hamilton School
Hamilton Road, Handsworth,
PERRY BARR, Birmingham B21 8AH
Tel: 01214 641676
Category: ASD SLCN
(Coed Day 4-11)

Mayfield School
Heathfield Road, Handsworth,
PERRY BARR, Birmingham B19 1HJ
Tel: 0121 5237321
Category: ASD BESD MLD
PMLD SLD (Coed Day 3-19)

Oscott Manor School
Old Oscott Hill, Kingstanding,
PERRY BARR, Birmingham B44 9SP
Tel: 01213 608222
Category: ASD SLCN
(Coed Day 11-19)

Priestley Smith School
Beeches Road, Great Barr, PERRY
BARR, Birmingham B42 2PY
Tel: 01213 253900
Category: VI (Coed Day 2-19)

REDDITCH

Skilts School
Gorcott Hill, REDDITCH,
Worcestershire B98 9ET
Tel: 01527 853851
Category: BESD (Boys 5-11)

SELLY OAK

Cherry Oak School
60 Frederick Road, SELLY
OAK, Birmingham B29 6PB
Tel: 01214 642037
Category: ASD SLD SLCN
(Coed Day 3-11)

Lindsworth School
Monyhull Hall Road, Kings Norton,
SELLY OAK, Birmingham B30 3QA
Tel: 01216 935363
Category: BESD (Coed
Boarding 9-16)

Selly Oak Trust School
Oak Tree Lane, SELLY OAK,
Birmingham B29 6HZ
Tel: 01214 720876
Category: MLD (Coed Day 11-19)

**The Dame Ellen
Pinsent School**
Ardencote Road, SELLY OAK,
Birmingham B13 0RW
Tel: 01216 752487
Category: MLD ASD SLCN
SLD (Coed day 5-11)

SOLIHULL

**Springfield House
Community Special School**
Kenilworth Road, Knowle,
SOLIHULL, West Midlands B93 0AJ
Tel: 01564 772772
Category: ASD MLD BESD
(Coed Boarding 4-11)

SUTTON COLDFIELD

Langley School
Trinity Road, SUTTON COLDFIELD,
West Midlands B75 6TJ
Tel: 01216 752929
Category: MLD ASD
(Coed Day 3-11)

West Midlands

COVENTRY
City Council

Coventry SEN & Inclusion, Civic Centre 2.3, Earl Street, Coventry, West Midlands, CV1 5RS
Tel: 02476 831624 Website: www.coventry.gov.uk

COVENTRY

**Baginton Fields
Secondary School**
Sedgemoor Road, COVENTRY,
West Midlands CV3 4EA
Tel: 02476 303854
Category: SLD (Coed Day 11-19)

Castle Wood
Deedmore Road, COVENTRY,
West Midlands CV2 1EQ
Tel: 02476 709060
Category: (Coed Day 3-11)

Corley Centre
Church Lane, Fillongley, COVENTRY,
West Midlands CV7 8AZ
Tel: 01676 540218
Category: Complex
SCD (Coed 11-19)

River Bank Academy
Ashington Grove, COVENTRY,
West Midlands CV3 4DE
Tel: 02476 303776
Category: (Coed Day 11-19)

**Sherbourne Fields Primary
& Secondary School**
Rowington Close, Off
Kingsbury Road, COVENTRY,
West Midlands CV6 1PS
Tel: 02476 591501
Category: PD (Coed Day 2-19)

Tiverton Primary
Rowington Close, Off
Kingsbury Road, COVENTRY,
West Midlands CV6 1PS
Tel: 02476 594954
Category: SLD (Coed Day 3-11)

Woodfield School
Hawthorn Lane Secondary Site,
COVENTRY, West Midlands CV4 9PB
Tel: 02476 462335
Category: EBD (Boys Day 11-16)

Woodfield School
Stoneleigh Road Primary Site,
COVENTRY, West Midlands CV4 7AB
Tel: 02476 418755
Category: ESBD (Coed Day 5-11)

West Midlands

DUDLEY
Council

Dudley SENDIASS, Saltwells Education Centre, Bowling Green Road, Netherton Dudley, West Midlands, DY2 9LY
Tel: 01384 817373 Website: www.dudley.gov.uk

DUDLEY

Old Park School
Thorns Road, Quarry Bank,
DUDLEY, West Midlands DY5 2JY
Tel: 01384 818905
Category: SLD (4-19)

Rosewood School
Bell Street, Coseley, DUDLEY,
West Midlands WV14 8XJ
Tel: 01384 816800
Category: EBD (11-16)

The Brier School
Bromley Lane, Kingswinford,
DUDLEY, West Midlands DY6 8QN
Tel: 01384 816000
Category: MLD (4-16)

**The Sutton School &
Specialist College**
Scotts Green Close, Russells
Hall Estate, DUDLEY, West
Midlands DY1 2DU
Tel: 01384 818670
Category: MLD (11-16)

The Woodsetton School
Tipton Road, Woodsetton,
DUDLEY, West Midlands DY3 1BY
Tel: 01384 818265
Category: MLD (4-11)

HALESOWEN

Halesbury School
Feldon Lane, HALESOWEN,
West Midlands B62 9DR
Tel: 01384 818630
Category: MLD (4-16)

STOURBRIDGE

Pens Meadow School
Ridge Hill, Brierley Hill Road,
Wordsley, STOURBRIDGE,
West Midlands DY8 5ST
Tel: 01384 818945
Category: SLD (3-19)

West Midlands

SANDWELL
Council

Sandwell SEN Service, PO Box 16230, Sandwell Council House, Freeth Street Oldbury, West Midlands, B69 9EX
Tel: 01215 698240 Email: children_families@sandwell.gov.uk Website: www.sandwell.gov.uk

LICHFIELD

Shenstone Lodge School
Birmingham Road, Shenstone,
LICHFIELD, Staffordshire WS14 0LB
Tel: 01543 480369
Category: EBD (Coed Day 4-16)

OLDBURY

**The Meadows
Sports College**
Dudley Road East, OLDBURY,
West Midlands B69 3BU
Tel: 01215 697080
Category: PMLD (Coed Day 11-19)

The Orchard School
Causeway Green Road, OLDBURY,
West Midlands B68 8LD
Tel: 01215 697040
Category: PMLD(Coed Day 2-11)

ROWLEY REGIS

The Westminster School
Curral Road, ROWLEY REGIS,
West Midlands B65 9AN
Tel: 01215 616884
Category: MLD (Coed Day 11-19)

West Midlands

SOLIHULL
Metropolitan Borough Council

Solihull SENDIASS, Sans Souci, Tanworth Lane, Shirley Solihull, West Midlands, B90 4D
Tel: 0121 5165173 Email: solihullsendias@family-action.org.uk Website: www.solihull.gov.uk

BIRMINGHAM

Forest Oak School
Windward Way, Smith's
Wood, BIRMINGHAM, West
Midlands B36 0UE
Tel: 01217 170088
Category: MLD (Coed Day 4-18)

Merstone School
Windward Way, Smith's
Wood, BIRMINGHAM, West
Midlands B36 0UE
Tel: 01217 171040
Category: SLD (Coed Day 2-19)

SOLIHULL

Hazel Oak School
Hazel Oak Road, Shirley, SOLIHULL,
West Midlands B90 2AZ
Tel: 01217 444162
Category: MLD (Coed Day 4-18)

Reynalds Cross School
Kineton Green Road, SOLIHULL,
West Midlands B92 7ER
Tel: 01217 073012
Category: SLD (Coed Day 2-19)

West Midlands

WALSALL
Council

Walsall SENDIASS, Blakenhall Village Centre, Thames Road, Blakenhall Walsall, West Midlands, WS3 1LZ
Tel: 01922 650330 Email: iasssend@walsall.gov.uk Website: www.walsall.gov.uk

WALSALL

**Castle Business &
Enterprise College**
Odell Road, Leamore, WALSALL,
West Midlands WS3 2ED
Tel: 01922 710129
Category: MLD, Additional
Needs (Coed Day 7-19)

Elmwood School
King George Crescent, Rushall,
WALSALL, West MIdlands WS4 1EG
Tel: 01922 721081
Category: EBD (Coed Day 11-16)

Mary Elliot Special School
Leamore Lane, WALSALL,
West Midlands WS2 7NR
Tel: 01922 490190
Category: SLD PMLD AUT
(Coed day 11-19)

Oakwood School
Druids Walk, Walsall Wood,
WALSALL, West Midlands WS9 9JS
Tel: 01543 452040
Category: SLD CLD PMLD
ASD Challenging behaviour
(Coed Day 3-11)

Old Hall School
Bentley Lane, WALSALL,
West Midlands WS2 7LU
Tel: 01902 368045
Category: SLD PMLD AUT
(Coed day 3-11)

The Jane Lane School
Churchill Road, Bentley, WALSALL,
West Midlands WS2 0JH
Tel: 01922 721161
Category: MLD, Additional
Needs (Coed Day 7-19)

West Midlands

WOLVERHAMPTON
City Council

Wolverhampton SENDIASS, The Gem Centre, Neachells Lane, Wolverhampton, West Midlands, WV11 3PG
Tel: 01902 556945 Email: ias.service@wolverhampton.gov.uk Website: www.wolverhampton.gov.uk

WOLVERHAMPTON

Green Park School
The Willows, Green Park Avenue,
Bilston, WOLVERHAMPTON,
West Midlands WV14 6EH
Tel: 01902 556429
Category: PMLD SLD
(Coed Day 4-19)

Penn Fields Special School
Boundary Way, Penn,
WOLVERHAMPTON, West
Midlands WV4 4NT
Tel: 01902 558640
Category: MLD SLD ASD
(Coed Day 4-19)

Penn Hall School
Vicarage Road, Penn,
WOLVERHAMPTON, West
Midlands WV4 5HP
Tel: 01902 558355
Category: PD SLD MLD
(Coed Day 3-19)

Tettenhall Wood School
Regis Road, Tettenhall,
WOLVERHAMPTON, West
Midlands WV6 8XF
Tel: 01902 556519
Category: ASD (Coed Day 5-19)

**Wolverhampton
Vocational Training
Centre (WVTC)**
Millfield Road, Ettingshall,
WOLVERHAMPTON, West
Midlands WV4 6JP
Tel: 01902 552274
Category: MLD SLD ASD
ADHD (Coed Day 16-18)

WILTSHIRE
Council

Wiltshire SEN/Disability 0-25 Service, County Hall, Bythesea Road, Trowbridge, Wiltshire, BA14 8JN
Tel: 01225 757985 Email: Statutorysen.service@wiltshire.gov.uk Website: www.wiltshirelocaloffer.org.uk

CHIPPENHAM

St Nicholas School
Malmesbury Road, CHIPPENHAM,
Wiltshire SN15 1QF
Tel: 01249 650435
Category: SLD PMLD
(Coed Day 3-19)

DEVIZES

Downland School
Downlands Road, DEVIZES,
Wiltshire SN10 5EF
Tel: 01380 724193
Category: BESD SPLD
(Boys Boarding 11-16)

Rowdeford School
Rowde, DEVIZES, Wiltshire SN10 2QQ
Tel: 01380 850309
Category: MLD (Coed
Boarding 11-16)

TROWBRIDGE

Larkrise School
Ashton Street, TROWBRIDGE,
Wiltshire BA14 7EB
Tel: 01225 761434
Category: SLD MLD
(Coed Day 3-19)

WINDSOR & MAIDENHEAD
Borough Council

Windsor & Maidenhead SENDIASS, Riverside Children's Centre, West Dean, Maidenhead, Berkshire, SL6 7JB
Tel: 01628 683182 Email: ias@rbwm.gov.uk Website: www.rbwm.gov.uk

MAIDENHEAD

Manor Green School
Cannon Road, MAIDENHEAD,
Berkshire SL6 3LE
Tel: 01628 513800
Category: SLD PMLD ASD
MLD (Coed 2-19)

WOKINGHAM
Borough Council

Wokingham SEN Team, Highwood Annexe, Fairwater Drive, Woodley Wokingham, Berkshire, RG5 3RU
Tel: 01189 746216 Email: sen@wokingham.gov.uk Website: www.wokingham.gov.uk

WOKINGHAM

Addington School
Woodlands Avenue, Woodley,
WOKINGHAM, Berkshire RG5 3EU
Tel: 01189 669073
Category: SLD PMLD ASD
MLD (Coed 4-18)

Northern House School
Gipsy Lane, WOKINGHAM,
Berkshire RG40 2HR
Tel: 01189 771293
Category: BESD (Coed 7-16)

WORCESTERSHIRE
County Council

Worcestershire SENDIASS, WCC Young People's Support Services, Tolladine Road, Worcester, WR4 9NB
Tel: 01905 768153 Email: sendiass@worcestershire.gov.uk Website: www.worcestershire.gov.uk

BROMSGROVE

Chadsgrove School & Specialist Sports College
Meadow Road,
Catshill, BROMSGROVE,
Worcestershire B61 0JL
Tel: 01527 871511
Category: PD PMLD MSI LD (2-19)

Rigby Hall School
19 Rigby Lane, Astonfields,
BROMSGROVE,
Worcestershire B60 2EP
Tel: 01527 875475
Category: SLD MLD ASD (3-19)

EVESHAM

Vale of Evesham School
Four Pools Lane, EVESHAM,
Worcestershire WR11 1BN
Tel: 01386 443367
Category: SLD MLD PMLD ASD (4-19)

KIDDERMINSTER

Wyre Forest School
Habberley Road, KIDDERMINSTER,
Worcestershire DY11 6FA
Tel: 01562 827785
Category: MLD SLD ASD
BESD (Coed 7-16)

REDDITCH

Kingfisher School
Clifton Close, Matchborough,
REDDITCH, Worcestershire B98 0HF
Tel: 01527 502486
Category: BESD (Coed 7-16)

Pitcheroak School
Willow Way, Brockhill, REDDITCH,
Worcestershire B97 6PQ
Tel: 01527 65576
Category: SLD MLD AUT (2-19)

WORCESTER

Fort Royal Community Primary School
Wylds Lane, WORCESTER WR5 1DR
Tel: 01905 355525
Category: MLD PD SLD (2-11)

Regency High School
Carnforth Drive,
WORCESTER WR4 9JL
Tel: 01905 454828
Category: PD MLD SLD (11-19)

Riversides School
Thorneloe Road,
WORCESTER WR1 3HZ
Tel: 01905 21261
Category: BESD (Coed 7-16)

CITY OF YORK
Council

York SENDIASS, West Offices, Station Rise, York, YO1 6GA
Tel: 01904 554319 Email: yorksendiass@york.gov.uk Website: www.yorksendiass.org.uk

YORK

Applefields School
Bad Bargain Lane, YORK YO31 0LW
Tel: 01904 553900
Category: MLD AUT
SLD PMLD (11-19)

Danesgate School
Fulford Cross, YORK YO10 4PB
Tel: 01904 642611
Category: (5-16)

Hob Moor Oaks School
Green Lane, Acomb,
YORK YO24 4PS
Tel: 01904 555000
Category: MLD AUT SLD PMLD (3-11)

EAST RIDING OF YORKSHIRE

Council

E Riding of Yorkshire SENDIASS, Families Information Service Hub (FISH),
County Hall, Beverley, East Riding of Yorkshire, HU17 9BA
Tel: 01482 396469 Email: sendiass@eastriding.gov.uk Website: www.eastriding.gov.uk

BROUGH

**St Anne's School &
Sixth Form College**
St Helen's Drive, Welton, BROUGH,
East Riding of Yorkshire HU15 1NR
Tel: 01482 667379
Category: SLD

DRIFFIELD

Kings Mill School & Nursery
Victoria Road, DRIFFIELD, East
Riding of Yorkshire YO25 6UG
Tel: 01377 253375
Category: SLD

GOOLE

Riverside Special School
Ainsty Street, GOOLE, East
Riding of Yorkshire DN14 5JS
Tel: 01405 763925
Category: MLD and other
complex needs

NORTH YORKSHIRE

County Council

North Yorkshire SENDIASS, County Hall, Northallerton, North Yorkshire, DL7 8AD
Tel: 01609 536923 Website: www.northyorks.gov.uk

BEDALE

Mowbray School
Masham Road, BEDALE,
North Yorkshire DL8 2SD
Tel: 01677 422446
Category: MLD SP&LD (2-16)

HARROGATE

Forest Moor School
Menwith Hill Road, Darley,
HARROGATE, North
Yorkshire HG3 2RA
Tel: 01423 779232
Category: BESD (Boys 11-16)

Springwater School
High Street, Starbeck, HARROGATE,
North Yorkshire HG2 7LW
Tel: 01423 883214
Category: SLD PMLD (2-19)

KIRKBYMOORSIDE

Welburn Hall School
KIRKBYMOORSIDE, York YO62 7HQ
Tel: 01751 431218
Category: PHLD (8-18)

KNARESBOROUGH

The Forest School
Park Lane, KNARESBOROUGH,
North Yorkshire HG5 0DG
Tel: 01423 864583
Category: MLD (2-16)

NORTHALLERTON

The Dales School
Morton-on-Swale,
NORTHALLERTON, North
Yorkshire DL7 9QW
Tel: 01609 772932
Category: SLD PMLD (2-19)

SCARBOROUGH

Brompton Hall School
High Street, Brompton-by-
Sawdon, SCARBOROUGH,
North Yorkshire YO13 9DB
Tel: 01723 859121
Category: BESD (Boys 8-16)

Springhead School
Barry's Lane, Seamer Road,
SCARBOROUGH, North
Yorkshire YO12 4HA
Tel: 01723 367829
Category: SLD PMLD (2-19)

SKIPTON

Brooklands School
Burnside Avenue, SKIPTON,
North Yorkshire BD23 2DB
Tel: 01756 794028
Category: MLD SLD PMLD (2-19)

South Yorkshire

BARNSLEY

Council

Barnsley SENDIASS, PO Box 634, Barnsley, South Yorkshire, S70 9GG
Tel: 01226 787234 Email: parentpartners@barnsley.gov.uk Website: www.barnsley.gov.uk

BARNSLEY

Greenacre School
Keresforth Hill Road, BARNSLEY,
South Yorkshire S70 6RG
Tel: 01226 287165
Category: SLD CLD PMLD
MSI AUT (Coed Day 2-19)

**Springwell Learning
Community**
St Helen's Boulevard, Carlton Road,
BARNSLEY, South Yorkshire S71 2AY
Tel: 01226 291133

South Yorkshire

DONCASTER
Council

Doncaster SEN Team, Civic Office, Waterdale, Doncaster, DN1 3BU
Tel: 01302 737209 Email: sen@doncaster.gov.uk Website: www.doncaster.gov.uk

DONCASTER

Coppice School
Ash Hill Road, Hatfield,
DONCASTER, South
Yorkshire DN7 6JH
Tel: 01302 844883
Category: SLD ASD BESD
(Coed Day 3-19)

Heatherwood School
Leger Way, DONCASTER,
South Yorkshire DN2 6HQ
Tel: 01302 322044
Category: SLD PD (Coed Day 3-19)

**North Ridge
Community School**
Tenter Balk Lane, Adwick-
le-Street, DONCASTER,
South Yorkshire DN6 7EF
Tel: 01302 720790
Category: SLD (Coed Day 3-19)

Stone Hill School
Barnsley Road, Scawsby,
DONCASTER, South
Yorkshire DN5 7UB
Tel: 01302 800090
Category: MLD (Coed 6-16)

South Yorkshire

ROTHERHAM
Metropolitan Borough Council

Rotherham SENDIASS, Riverside House, Main Street, Rotherham, South Yorkshire, S60 1AE
Tel: 01709 823627 Email: parentpartnership@rotherham.gov.uk Website: www.rotherhamsendiass.org.uk

MEXBOROUGH

Milton School
Storey Street, Swinton,
MEXBOROUGH, South
Yorkshire S64 8QG
Tel: 01709 570246
Category: MLD (5-16) ASD (5-11)

ROTHERHAM

Abbey School
Little Common Lane,
Kimberworth, ROTHERHAM,
South Yorkshire S61 2RA
Tel: 01709 740074
Category: MLD

Hilltop School
Larch Road, Maltby, ROTHERHAM,
South Yorkshire S66 8AZ
Tel: 01709 813386
Category: SLD

Kelford School
Oakdale Road, Kimberworth,
ROTHERHAM, South
Yorkshire S61 2NU
Tel: 01709 512088
Category: SLD

Newman School
East Bawtry Road, Whiston,
ROTHERHAM, South
Yorkshire S60 3LX
Tel: 01709 828262
Category: PH Medical needs

The Willows School
Locksley Drive, Thurcroft,
ROTHERHAM, South
Yorkshire S66 9NT
Tel: 01709 542539
Category: MLD

South Yorkshire

SHEFFIELD
City Council

Sheffield SENDIASS, Floor 6, North Wing, Moorfoot Building, Sheffield, S1 4PL
Tel: 0114 273 6009 Email: ed-parent.partnership@sheffield.gov.uk Website: www.sheffield.gov.uk

SHEFFIELD

Becton School
Beighton Community Hospital,
Sevenairs Road, SHEFFIELD,
South Yorkshire S20 1NZ
Tel: 01143 053121
Category: LD EBD SCD ADHD
Speech&LangD (Coed 5-18)

Bents Green School
Ringinglow Road, SHEFFIELD,
South Yorkshire S11 7TB
Tel: 01142 363545
Category: AUT ASD
SCD (Coed 11-19)

**Heritage Park
Foundation School**
Norfolk Park Road, SHEFFIELD,
South Yorkshire S2 2RU
Tel: 01142 796850
Category: BESD (KS 2/3/4)

**Holgate Meadows
Foundation School**
Lindsay Road, SHEFFIELD,
South Yorkshire S5 7WE
Tel: 01142 456305
Category: BESD (KS 2/3/4)

Mossbrook Special School
Bochum Parkway, SHEFFIELD,
South Yorkshire S8 8JR
Tel: 01142 372768
Category: AUT SCD (Coed 4-11)

Norfolk Park School
Archdale Road, SHEFFIELD,
South Yorkshire S2 1PL
Tel: 01142 726165
Category: LD Complex
Needs (Coed 3-11)

Rowan School
4 Durvale Court, Dore, SHEFFIELD,
South Yorkshire S17 3PT
Tel: 01142 350479
Category: AUT SCD (Primary)

Seven Hills School
Granville Road, SHEFFIELD,
South Yorkshire S2 2RJ
Tel: 01142 743560
Category: LD Complex Needs

Talbot Specialist School
Lees Hall Road, SHEFFIELD,
South Yorkshire S8 9JP
Tel: 01142 507394
Category: LD Complex
Needs (Coed 11-19)

Woolley Wood Community Primary School
Chaucer Road, SHEFFIELD,
South Yorkshire S5 9QN
Tel: 01142 327160
Category: LD Complex Needs

West Yorkshire

CALDERDALE
Council

Calderdale SEN Team, Town Hall, PO Box 51, Halifax, West Yorkshire, HX1 1TP
Tel: 01422 394141 Email: sen.team@calderdale.gov.uk Website: www.calderdale.gov.uk

BRIGHOUSE

Highbury School
Lower Edge Road, Rastrick,
BRIGHOUSE, West Yorkshire HD6 3LD
Tel: 01484 716319
Category: All (3-11)

HALIFAX

Ravenscliffe High School
Skircoat Green, HALIFAX,
West Yorkshire HX3 0RZ
Tel: 01422 358621
Category: All (11-18)

Wood Bank School
Dene View, Luddendenfoot,
HALIFAX, West Yorkshire HX2 6PB
Tel: 01422 884170
Category: All (4-11)

West Yorkshire

KIRKLEES
Council

Kirklees SEN Team, Kirkgate Building, Byram Street, Huddersfield, West Yorkshire, HD1 1BY
Tel: 01484 456888 Email: senact@kirklees.gov.uk Website: www.kirklees.gov.uk

BATLEY

Fairfield School
White Lee Road, BATLEY,
West Yorkshire WF17 8AS
Tel: 01924 326103
Category: SLD (Coed Day 3-19)

HOLMFIRTH

Lydgate School
Kirkroyds Lane, New Mill,
HOLMFIRTH, West Yorkshire HD9 1LS
Tel: 01484 222484
Category: MLD (Coed Day 5-16)

Woodley School & College
Dog Kennel Bank, HUDDERSFIELD,
West Yorkshire HD5 8JE
Tel: 01484 223937
Category: MLD AUT SEMH
(Coed Day 5-16)

DEWSBURY

Ravenshall School
Ravensthorpe Road, Thornhill Lees,
DEWSBURY, West Yorkshire WF12 9EE
Tel: 01924 456811
Category: MLD (Coed Day 5-16)

HUDDERSFIELD

Castle Hill School
Newsome Road South,
Newsome, HUDDERSFIELD,
West Yorkshire HD4 6JL
Tel: 01484 226659
Category: SLD AUT PMLD
(Coed Day 3-19)

West Yorkshire

LEEDS

City Council

Leeds SENDIASS, 9 Harrogate Road, Chapel Allerton, Leeds, West Yorkshire, LS7 3NB
Tel: 0113 378 5020 Email: sendiass@leeds.gov.uk Website: www.educationleeds.co.uk

LEEDS

East SILC - John Jamieson (main site)
Hollin Hill Drive, Oakwood, LEEDS, West Yorkshire LS8 2PW
Tel: 01132 930236
Category: Complex physical, learning and care needs (Coed 2-19)

North West SILC - Penny Field (main site)
Tongue Lane, Meanwood, LEEDS, West Yorkshire LS6 4QD
Tel: 01133 368270
Category: Complex physical, learning and care needs (Coed 2-19)

South SILC - Broomfield (main site)
Broom Place, Belle Isle, LEEDS, West Yorkshire LS10 3JP
Tel: 01132 771603
Category: Complex physical, learning and care needs (Coed 2-19)

West Oaks SEN Specialist School & College
Westwood Way, Boston Spa, Wetherby, LEEDS, West Yorkshire LS23 6DX
Tel: 01937 844772
Category: Complex physical, learning and care needs (Coed 2-19)

West Yorkshire

WAKEFIELD

Council

Wakefield SEN Team, Wakefield One, PO Box 700, Burton Street Wakefield, WF1 2EB
Tel: 01924 379015 Email: wesail@kids.org.uk Website: www.wakefield.gov.uk

CASTLEFORD

Kingsland School Castleford
Poplar Avenue, Townville, CASTLEFORD, West Yorkshire WF10 3QJ
Tel: 01977 723085
Category: SLD MLD (Coed 4-11)

OSSETT

Highfield School
Gawthorpe Lane, Gawthorpe, OSSETT, West Yorkshire WF5 9BS
Tel: 01924 302980
Category: MLD (Coed 11-16)

PONTEFRACT

High Well School
Rookhill Road, PONTEFRACT, West Yorkshire WF8 2DD
Tel: 01924 572100
Category: EBD (Coed 11-16)

Oakfield Park School
Barnsley Road, Ackworth, PONTEFRACT, West Yorkshire WF7 7DT
Tel: 01977 613423
Category: SLD PMLD (Coed 11-19)

WAKEFIELD

Kingsland School Stanley
Aberford Road, Stanley, WAKEFIELD, West Yorkshire WF3 4BA
Tel: 01924 303100
Category: SLD PMLD (Coed 2-11)

CHELTENHAM

The Ridge Primary Academy
Clyde Crescent, CHELTENHAM, Gloucestershire GL52 5QH
Tel: 01242 512680
Category: SEBD (Coed 5-11)

DURSLEY

Greenfield Academy
Drake Lane, DURSLEY, Gloucestershire GL11 5HD
Tel: 01453 542130
Category: SEBD (Coed Day 11-16)

Peak Academy
Drake Lane, DURSLEY, Gloucestershire GL11 5HD
Tel: 01453 542130
Category: SEBD (Boys Day 11-16)

CHANNEL ISLANDS

GUERNSEY

Council

Guernsey SEN Team, PO Box 32, Grange Road, St Peter Port, Guernsey, GY1 3AU
Tel: 01481 733000 Email: office@education.gov.gg Website: www.education.gg

FOREST

**Le Rondin School
and Centre**
Rue des Landes, FOREST,
Guernsey GY8 0DP
Tel: 01481 268300
Category: MLD SLD PMLD (3-11)

ST SAMPSON'S

Le Murier School
Rue de Dol, ST SAMPSON'S,
Guernsey GY2 4DA
Tel: 01481 246660
Category: MLD PMLD
SLD (Coed 11-16)

ST. PETER PORT

Les Voies School
Collings Road, ST. PETER
PORT, Guernsey GY1 1FW
Tel: 01481 710721
Category: SEBD (Coed 4-16)

JERSEY

Council

Jersey SEN Team, PO Box 142, Highlands Campus, St. Saviour, Jersey, JE4 8QJ
Tel: 01534 449424 Email: education@gov.je Website: www.gov.je/esc

ST HELIER

Mont a l'Abbe School
La Grande Route de St
Jean, La Pouquelaye, ST
HELIER, Jersey JE2 3FN
Tel: 01534 875801
Category: LD (3-19)

ST SAVIOUR

D'Hautree House
St Saviour's Hill, ST SAVIOUR,
Jersey JE2 7LF
Tel: 01534 618042
Category: SEBD (Coed 11-16)

The Alternative Curriculum
Oakside House, La Grande
Route de St Martin, Five Oaks,
ST SAVIOUR, Jersey JE2 7GS
Tel: 01534 872840
Category: EBD

NORTHERN IRELAND

BELFAST

NI Education Authority

Education Authority, SEN Team, Belfast Office, 40 Academy Street, Belfast, Northern Ireland, BT1 2NQ
Tel: +44 (0)28 9056 4000 Email: info@eani.org.uk Website: www.eani.org.uk

BELFAST

Belfast Hospital School
Royal Belfast Hospital School
for Sick Children, Falls Road,
BELFAST, Co Antrim BT12 6BE
Tel: 02890 633498
Category: HS (Coed 4-19)

Cedar Lodge School
24 Lansdowne Park North,
BELFAST, Co Antrim BT15 4AE
Tel: 02890 777292
Category: EPI ASD ADHD
Medical needs (Coed 4-16)

Clarawood School
Clarawood Park, BELFAST,
Co Antrim BT5 6FR
Tel: 02890 472736
Category: SEBD (Coed 8-12)

Fleming Fulton School
35 Upper Malone Road,
BELFAST, Co Antrim BT9 6TY
Tel: 02890 613877
Category: PH MLD (Coed 3-19)

Glenveagh School
Harberton Park, BELFAST,
Co Antrim BT9 6TX
Tel: 02890 669907
Category: SLD (Coed 8-19)

Greenwood House Assessment Centre
Greenwood Avenue, Upper
Newtownards Road, BELFAST,
Co Antrim BT4 3JJ
Tel: 02890 471000
Category: SP&LD MLD EBD SLD
Medical needs (Coed 4-7)

Harberton Special School
Haberton Park, BELFAST,
Co Antrim BT9 6TX
Tel: 02890 381525
Category: AUT ASP SP&LD EBD
Medical needs (Coed 4-11)

Loughshore Educational Resource Centre
889 Shore Road, BELFAST,
Co Antrim BT36 7DH
Tel: 02890 773062

Mitchell House School
Marmont Park, Holywood Road,
BELFAST, Co Antrim BT4 2GT
Tel: 02890 768407
Category: PD MSI (Coed 3-18)

Oakwood Assessment Centre
Harberton Park, BELFAST,
Co Antrim BT9 6TX
Tel: 02890 605116
Category: SLD PMLD
ASD (Coed 3-8)

Park Education Resource Centre
145 Ravenhill Road, BELFAST,
Co Antrim BT6 8GH
Tel: 02890 450513
Category: MLD (Coed 11-16)

St Gerard's School & Support Services
Blacks Road, BELFAST,
Co Antrim BT10 0NB
Tel: 02890 600330
Category: MLD (Coed 4-16)

St Teresa's Speech, Language & Communication Centre
St Teresaís Primary School, Glen
Road, BELFAST, Co Antrim BT11 8BL
Tel: 02890 611943

St Vincent's Centre
6 Willowfield Drive, BELFAST,
Co Antrim BT6 8HN
Tel: 02890 461444

NORTH EASTERN

NI Education Authority

Education Authority, SEN Team, Antrim Office, County Hall, 182 Galgorm Rd Ballymena, Northern Ireland, BT42 1HN
Tel: +44 (0)28 2565 3333 Email: info@eani.org.uk Website: www.eani.org.uk

ANTRIM

Riverside School
Fennel Road, ANTRIM,
Co Antrim BT41 4PB
Tel: 02894 428946
Category: SLD

BALLYMENA

Castle Tower School
50 Larne Road Link, BALLYMENA,
Co Antrim BT42 3GA
Tel: 02825 633400
Category: MLD SLD PD SEBD

COLERAINE

Sandelford Special School
4 Rugby Avenue, COLERAINE,
Co Londonderry BT52 1JL
Tel: 02870 343062
Category: SLD

MAGHERAFELT

Kilronan School
46 Ballyronan Road, MAGHERAFELT,
Co Londonderry BT45 6EN
Tel: 02879 632168
Category: SLD

NEWTOWNABBEY

Hill Croft School
3 Manse Way, NEWTOWNABBEY,
Co Antrim BT36 5UW
Tel: 02890 837488
Category: SLD

Jordanstown Special School
85 Jordanstown Road,
NEWTOWNABBEY, Co
Antrim BT37 0QE
Tel: 02890 863541
Category: HI VIS (Coed 4-19)

Rosstulla Special School
2 Jordanstown Road,
NEWTOWNABBEY, Co
Antrim BT37 0QS
Tel: 02890 862743
Category: MLD (Coed 5-16)

Maintained special schools and colleges

SOUTH EASTERN
NI Education Authority

Education Authority, SEN Team, Dundonald Office, Grahamsbridge Road, Dundonald, Northern Ireland, BT16 2HS
Tel: +44 (0)28 9056 6200 Email: info@eani.org.uk Website: www.eani.org.uk

BANGOR

Clifton Special School
292a Old Belfast Road,
BANGOR, Co Down BT19 1RH
Tel: 02891 270210
Category: SLD

Lakewood Special School
96 Newtownards Road,
BANGOR, Co Down BT19 1GZ
Tel: 02891 456227

BELFAST

Longstone Special School
Millars Lane, Dundonald,
BELFAST, Co Down BT16 2DA
Tel: 02890 480071
Category: MLD

Tor Bank School
5 Dunlady Road, Dundonald,
BELFAST, Co Down BT16 1TT
Tel: 02890 484147
Category: SLD

CRAIGAVON

Brookfield School
65 Halfpenny Gate Road, Moira,
CRAIGAVON, Co Armagh BT67 0HP
Tel: 02892 622978
Category: MLD (Coed 5-11)

DONAGHADEE

Killard House School
Cannyreagh Road, DONAGHADEE,
Co Down BT21 0AU
Tel: 02891 882361
Category: MLD

DOWNPATRICK

Ardmore House
95a Saul Street, DOWNPATRICK,
Co Down BT30 6NJ
Tel: 02844 614881
Category: EBD

Knockevin Special School
33 Racecourse Hill, DOWNPATRICK,
Co Down BT30 6PU
Tel: 02844 612167
Category: SLD

HILLSBOROUGH

Beechlawn School
3 Dromore Road, HILLSBOROUGH,
Co Down BT26 6PA
Tel: 02892 682302
Category: MLD

LISBURN

Parkview Special School
2 Brokerstown Road, LISBURN,
Co Antrim BT28 2EE
Tel: 02892 601197
Category: SLD

SOUTHERN
NI Education Authority

Education Authority, SEN Team, Armagh Office, 3 Charlemont Place, The Mall Armagh, Northern Ireland, BT61 9AX
Tel: +44 (0)28 3751 2200 Email: info@eani.org.uk Website: www.eani.org.uk

ARMAGH

Lisanally Special School
85 Lisanally Lane, ARMAGH,
Co Armagh BT61 7HF
Tel: 02837 523563
Category: SLD (Coed)

BANBRIDGE

Donard School
22a Castlewellan Road,
BANBRIDGE, Co Down BT32 4XY
Tel: 02840 662357
Category: SLD (Coed)

CRAIGAVON

Ceara School
Sloan Street, Lurgan, CRAIGAVON,
Co Armagh BT66 8NY
Tel: 02838 323312
Category: SLD (Coed)

NEWRY

Rathore School
23 Martin's Lane, Carnagat,
NEWRY, Co Down BT35 8PJ
Tel: 02830 261617
Category: SLD (Coed)

WESTERN
NI Education Authority

Education Authority, SEN Team, Omagh Office, 1 Hospital Road, Omagh, Northern Ireland, BT79 0AW
Tel: +44 (0)28 8241 1411 Email: info@eani.org.uk Website: www.eani.org.uk

ENNISKILLEN

Willowbridge School
8 Lough Shore Road, Drumlyon,
ENNISKILLEN, Co Fermanagh BT74 7EY
Tel: 02866 329947
Category: SLD MLD (Coed)

LIMAVADY

Rossmar School
2 Ballyquin Road, LIMAVADY,
Co Londonderry BT49 9ET
Tel: 02877 762351
Category: MLD (Coed)

LONDONDERRY

**Ardnashee School
& College**
15-17 Racecourse Road,
LONDONDERRY, Co
Londonderry BT48 7RE
Tel: 02871 263270
Category: SLD (Coed)

OMAGH

**Arvalee School &
Resource Centre**
Strule Campus, Gortin Road,
OMAGH, Co Tyrone BT79 7DH
Tel: 02882 255710
Category: MLD SLD (Coed)

STRABANE

**Knockavoe School &
Resource Centre**
10a Melmount Gardens,
STRABANE, Co Tyrone BT82 9EB
Tel: 02871 883319
Category: SLD MLD (Coed)

SCOTLAND

ABERDEEN
Council

Aberdeen ASN Team, Business Hub 13, Second Floor North, Marischal College, Broad Street Aberdeen, AB10 1AB
Tel: 03000 200293 Email: fis@aberdeencity.gov.uk Website: www.aberdeencity.gov.uk

ABERDEEN

**Aberdeen School
for the Deaf**
c/o Sunnybank School, Sunnybank
Road, ABERDEEN AB24 3NJ
Tel: 01224 261722
Category: HI

Cordyce School
Riverview Drive, Dyce,
ABERDEEN AB21 7NF
Tel: 01224 724215
Category: EBD

**Hospital and Home
Tuition Service**
Royal Aberdeen Children's
Hospital, Lowit Unit, Westburn
Road, ABERDEEN AB25 2ZG
Tel: 01224 550317
Category: HS

Orchard Brae School
Howes Road, ABERDEEN AB16 7RW
Tel: 01224 788950
Category: SCLD

ABERDEENSHIRE
Council

Aberdeenshire ASN Team, St Leonards, Sandyhill Road, Banff, AB45 1BH
Tel: 01261 813340 Email: education.development@aberdeenshire.gov.uk Website: www.aberdeenshire.gov.uk

FRASERBURGH

Westfield School
Argyll Road, FRASERBURGH,
Aberdeenshire AB43 9BL
Tel: 01346 518699
Category: PMLD SCLD
(Coed 5-18, 0-3 Nursery)

INVERURIE

St Andrew's School
St Andrew's Garden, INVERURIE,
Aberdeenshire AB51 3XT
Tel: 01467 536940
Category: PMLD SCLD (Coed 3-18)

PETERHEAD

Anna Ritchie School
Grange Gardens, PETERHEAD,
Aberdeenshire AB42 2AP
Tel: 01779 403670
Category: PMLD SCLD (Coed 3-18)

STONEHAVEN

Carronhill School
Mill of Forest Road, STONEHAVEN,
Kincardineshire AB39 2GZ
Tel: 01569 763886
Category: PMLD SCLD (Coed 3-18)

EAST AYRSHIRE
Council

East Ayrshire Support Team (EAST), Crosshouse Campus, Playingfield Road, Crosshouse, KA2 0JJ
Tel: 01563 554974 Email: catherine.rodger@east-ayrshire.gov.uk Website: www.east-ayrshire.gov.uk

CUMNOCK

Hillside School
Dalgleish Avenue, Drumbrochan,
CUMNOCK, East Ayrshire KA18 1QQ
Tel: 01290 423239
Category: SLD PMLD (Coed 6-17)

KILMARNOCK

Park School
Beech Avenue, Grange,
KILMARNOCK, East
Ayrshire KA1 2EW
Tel: 01563 549988
Category: LD PD (Coed 5-18)

Willowbank School
Grassyards Road, New Farm Loch,
KILMARNOCK, East Ayrshire KA3 7BB
Tel: 01563 526115
Category: SLD PMLD

SOUTH AYRSHIRE
Council

South Ayrshire ASN Team, County Buildings, Wellington Square, Ayr, KA7 1DR
Tel: 03001 230900 Website: www.south-ayrshire.gov.uk

AYR
Southcraig Campus
Belmont Avenue, AYR,
South Ayrshire KA7 2ND
Tel: 01292 612146
Category: SLD CLD (Coed 1-5)

GIRVAN
Invergarven School
15 Henrietta Street, GIRVAN,
South Ayrshire KA26 9EB
Tel: 01465 716808
Category: SLD CLD PD
MSI (Coed 3-16)

CLACKMANNANSHIRE
Council

Clackmannanshire Educational Service, Kilncraigs, Greenside Street, Alloa, Clackmannanshire, FK10 1EB
Tel: 01259 450000 Fax: 01259 452440 Email: education@clacks.gov.uk Website: www.clacksweb.org.uk

ALLOA
**Primary Schools'
Support Service**
Park Primary School, East
Castle Street, ALLOA,
Clackmannanshire FK10 1BB
Tel: 01259 212151

**Secondary Schools'
Support Service**
Bedford Place, ALLOA,
Clackmannanshire FK10 1LJ
Tel: 01259 724345

SAUCHIE
Lochies School
Gartmorn Road, SAUCHIE,
Clackmannanshire FK10 3PB
Tel: 01259 452312
Category: CLD SLD (Coed 5-11)

COMHAIRLE NAN EILEAN SIAR
Council

Comhairle Nan Eilean Siar ASN Team, Sandwick Road, Stornoway, Isle of Lewis, HS1 2BW
Tel: 08456 007090 Email: enquiries@cne-siar.gov.uk Website: www.cne-siar.gov.uk

STORNOWAY
Stornoway Primary School
Jamieson Drive, STORNOWAY,
Isle of Lewis HS1 2LF
Tel: 01851 703418

EAST DUNBARTONSHIRE
Council

East Dunbartonshire ASN Team, 12 Strathkelvin Place, Kirkintilloch, Glasgow, Lanarkshire, G66 1TJ
Tel: 0300 123 4510 Email: education@eastdunbarton.gov.uk Website: www.eastdunbarton.gov.uk

KIRKINTILLOCH
Merkland School
Langmuir Road, KIRKINTILLOCH,
East Dunbartonshire G66 2QF
Tel: 01419 552336
Category: MLD PH

LENZIE
Campsie View School
Boghead Road, LENZIE, East
Dunbartonshire G66 4DP
Tel: 01419 552339
Category: SCLD

WEST DUNBARTONSHIRE
Council

West Dunbartonshire ASN Team, Educational Services, Council Offices, Garshake Road Dunbarton, G82 3PU
Tel: 01389 737374 Email: contact.centre@west-dunbarton.gov.uk Website: www.west-dunbarton.gov.uk

CLYDEBANK

Cunard School
Cochno Street, Whitecrook,
CLYDEBANK, West
Dunbartonshire G81 1RQ
Tel: 01419 521621
Category: SEBD (Primary)

Kilpatrick School
Mountblow Road,
Dalmuir, CLYDEBANK, West
Dunbartonshire G81 4SW
Tel: 01389 804430
Category: SCLD (Primary/
Secondary)

CITY OF EDINBURGH
Council

Edinburgh ASN Team, Waverley Court, 4 East Market Street, Edinburgh, Midlothian, EH8 8BG
Tel: 0131 200 2000 Website: www.edingburgh.gov.uk

EDINBURGH

Braidburn Special School
107 Oxgangs Road North,
EDINBURGH EH14 1ED
Tel: 01313 122320
Category: EPI PH (Coed 2-18)

Kaimes School
140 Lasswade Road,
EDINBURGH EH16 6RT
Tel: 01316 648241
Category: SP&LD ASD (Coed 5-18)

Oaklands School
750 Ferry Road,
EDINBURGH EH4 4PQ
Tel: 01313 158100
Category: SLD CLD PD MSI

Panmure St Ann's
6 South Grays Close,
EDINBURGH EH1 1TQ
Tel: 01315 568833

Pilrig Park Special School
12 Balfour Place,
EDINBURGH EH6 5DW
Tel: 01314 677960
Category: MLD SLD (Coed 11-16)

**Prospect Bank
Special School**
81 Restalrig Road,
EDINBURGH EH6 8BQ
Tel: 01315 532239
Category: LD SP&LD (Coed 5-12)

Redhall Special School
3c Redhall Grove,
EDINBURGH EH14 2DU
Tel: 01314 431256
Category: LD (Coed 4-11)

Rowanfield Special School
67c Groathill Road North,
EDINBURGH EH4 2SA
Tel: 01313 436116
Category: EBD

St Crispin's Special School
19 Watertoun Road,
EDINBURGH EH9 3HZ
Tel: 01316 674831
Category: SLD AUT (Coed 5-16)

Woodlands Special School
36 Dolphin Avenue,
EDINBURGH EH14 5RD
Tel: 01314 493447

FALKIRK
Council

Falkirk Additional Support for Learning, Sealock House, 2 Inchyra Road, Grangemouth, FK3 9XB
Tel: 01324 506649 Email: additionalsupport@falkirk.gov.uk Website: www.falkirk.gov.uk

FALKIRK

Mariner Support Service
Laurieston Campus, Bog
Road, FALKIRK FK2 9PB
Tel: 01324 501090
Category: SEBD (Secondary)

Windsor Park School
Bantaskine Road, FALKIRK FK1 5HT
Tel: 01324 508640
Category: Deaf (Coed 3-16)

GRANGEMOUTH

Carrongrange School
Oxgang Road,
GRANGEMOUTH FK3 9HP
Tel: 01324 492592
Category: CLD MLD (Secondary)

Oxgang School
c/o Moray Primary School, Moray
Place, GRANGEMOUTH FK3 9DL
Tel: 01324 501311
Category: BESD (5-11)

FIFE

Council

Fife ASN Team, Rothesay House, Rothesay Place, Glenrothes, Fife, KY7 5PQ
Tel: 03451 555555 (Ext 442126) Email: jennifer.allan@fife.gov.uk Website: www.fifedirect.org.uk/fifecouncil

CUPAR

Kilmaron School
Balgarvie Road, CUPAR,
Fife KY15 4PE
Tel: 01334 659480
Category: CLD PD (Coed 3-18)

DUNFERMLINE

Calaiswood School
Nightingale Place,
DUNFERMLINE, Fife KY11 8LW
Tel: 01383 602481
Category: CLD (Coed 3-18)

Woodmill High School ASN
Shields Road, DUNFERMLINE,
Fife KY11 4ER
Tel: 01383 602406
Category: SEBD

GLENROTHES

John Fergus School
Erskine Place, GLENROTHES,
Fife KY7 4JB
Tel: 01592 583489
Category: CD PD (Coed Day 3-18)

KIRKCALDY

Rosslyn School
Windmill Community
Campus, Windmill Road,
KIRKCALDY, Fife KY1 3AL
Tel: 01592 583482
Category: SLD PMLD PD (Coed 3-19)

LEVEN

Hyndhead School
Barncraig Street, Buckhaven,
LEVEN, Fife KY8 1JE
Tel: 01592 583480
Category: SLD ASD (Coed 5-18)

GLASGOW

City Council

Glasgow ASN Team, 40 John Street, Glasgow, G1 1JL
Tel: 01412 872000 Website: www.glasgow.gov.uk

GLASGOW

Abercorn Secondary School
195 Garscube Road,
GLASGOW G4 9QH
Tel: 01413 326212
Category: MLD

Ashton Secondary School
100 Avenue End Road,
GLASGOW G33 3SW
Tel: 01417 743428
Category: PH VIS CLD

Broomlea Primary School
Keppoch Campus, 65 Stonyhurst
Street, GLASGOW G22 5AX
Tel: 01413 368428
Category: CLD

Cardinal Winning Secondary School
30 Fullarton Avenue,
GLASGOW G32 8NJ
Tel: 01417 783714
Category: MLD

Cartvale Secondary School
3 Burndyke Court,
GLASGOW G51 2BG
Tel: 01414 451767
Category: SEBN

Croftcroighn Primary School
290 Mossvale Road,
GLASGOW G33 5NY
Tel: 01417 743760
Category: CLD

Drummore Primary School
129 Drummore Road,
GLASGOW G15 7NH
Tel: 01419 441323
Category: MLD

Eastmuir Primary School
211 Hallhill Road,
GLASGOW G33 4QL
Tel: 01417 713464
Category: MLD

Greenview Learning Centre
384 Drakemire Drive,
GLASGOW G45 9SR
Tel: 01416 341551
Category: SEBN

Hampden Primary School
18 Logan Gardens,
GLASGOW G5 0LJ
Tel: 01414 296095
Category: CLD

Hazelwood School
50 Dumbreck Court,
GLASGOW G41 5DQ
Tel: 01414 279334
Category: HI VIS CLD (2-19)

Howford Primary School
487 Crookston Road,
GLASGOW G53 7TX
Tel: 01418 822605
Category: MLD

John Paul II Primary School
29 Dunagoil Road,
GLASGOW G45 9UR
Tel: 01416 345219

Kelbourne Park Primary School
109 Hotspur Street,
GLASGOW G20 8LH
Tel: 01419 461405
Category: PH CLD

Kirkriggs Primary School
500 Croftfoot Road,
GLASGOW G45 0NJ
Tel: 01416 347158
Category: MLD

Langlands Primary School
Glenside Avenue,
GLASGOW G53 5FD
Tel: 01418 920952
Category: CLD

Lourdes Primary School
150 Berryknowes Road,
GLASGOW G52 2DE
Tel: 01418 822305

Middlefield School
80 Ardnahoe Avenue,
GLASGOW G42 0DL
Tel: 01416 431399
Category: ASD (Day)

Newhills Secondary School
42 Newhills Road,
GLASGOW G33 4HJ
Tel: 01417 731296
Category: CLD

Parkhill Secondary School
375 Cumbernauld Road,
GLASGOW G31 3LP
Tel: 01415 542765
Category: MLD

St Albert's Primary School
36 Maxwell Drive,
GLASGOW G41 5DU
Tel: 01414 291983

St Kevin's Primary School
25 Fountainwell Road,
GLASGOW G21 1TN
Tel: 01415 573722
Category: MLD

St Oswald's Secondary School
9 Birgidale Road,
GLASGOW G45 9NJ
Tel: 01416 373952
Category: MLD

Westmuir High School
255 Rigby Street,
GLASGOW G32 6DJ
Tel: 01415 566276
Category: SEBN

HIGHLAND
Council
Highland ASN Team, Glenurquhart Road, Inverness, IV3 5NX
Tel: 01463 702801 Website: www.highland.gov.uk

INVERNESS

Drummond School
Drummond Road, INVERNESS,
Highland IV2 4NZ
Tel: 01463 701050
Category: SLD PMLD
CLD (Coed 3-16)

The Bridge
14 Seafield Road, INVERNESS,
Highland IV1 1SG
Tel: 01463 256600

ROSS-SHIRE

St Clement's School
Tulloch Street, Dingwall, ROSS-
SHIRE, Highland IV15 9JZ
Tel: 01349 863284
Category: SP&LD VIS
HI PD (Coed 5-11)

St Duthus School
Academy Street, Tain, ROSS-
SHIRE, Highland IV19 1ED
Tel: 01862 894407
Category: SLD PLD CLD (Coed 3-18)

INVERCLYDE
Council
Inverclyde ASN Team, Wallace Place, Greenock, PA15 1JB
Tel: 01475 717171 Email: admin.educationhq@inverclyde.gov.uk Website: www.inverclyde.gov.uk

GOUROCK

Garvel Deaf Centre
c/o Moorfoot Primary School,
GOUROCK, Inverclyde PA19 1ES
Tel: 01475 715642
Category: Deaf

PORT GLASGOW

Craigmarloch School
New Port Glasgow Community
Campus, Kilmacolm Road, PORT
GLASGOW, Inverclyde PA14 6PP
Tel: 01475 715345
Category: (Coed Day 6-18)

NORTH LANARKSHIRE
Council
North Lanarkshire ASN Team, Learning and Leisure Services, Municipal Buildings, Kildonan Street Coatbridge, ML5 3BT
Tel: 01236 812790 Website: www.northlan.gov.uk

AIRDRIE

**Mavisbank School
and Nursery**
Mitchell Street, AIRDRIE, North
Lanarkshire ML6 0EB
Tel: 01236 632108
Category: PMLD (Coed 3-18)

COATBRIDGE

Buchanan High School
67 Townhead Road, COATBRIDGE,
North Lanarkshire ML5 2HT
Tel: 01236 632052
Category: (Coed Day 12-18)

Drumpark School
Albert Street, COATBRIDGE,
North Lanarkshire ML5 3ET
Tel: 01236 794884
Category: MLD PH SP&LD (3-18)

Pentland School
Tay Street, COATBRIDGE,
North Lanarkshire ML5 2NA
Tel: 01236 794833
Category: SEBD (Coed 5-11)

Portland High School
31-33 Kildonan Street, COATBRIDGE,
North Lanarkshire ML5 3LG
Tel: 01236 632060
Category: SEBD (Coed 11-16)

Willowbank School
299 Bank Street, COATBRIDGE,
North Lanarkshire ML5 1EG
Tel: 01236 632078
Category: SEBD (Coed 11-18)

CUMBERNAULD

Glencryan School
Greenfaulds Road, CUMBERNAULD,
North Lanarkshire G67 2XJ
Tel: 01236 794866
Category: MLD PH ASD (Coed 5-18)

**Redburn School
and Nursery**
Kildrum Ring Road, CUMBERNAULD,
North Lanarkshire G67 2EL
Tel: 01236 736904
Category: SLD CLD PH (Coed 2-18)

MOTHERWELL

Bothwellpark High School
Annan Street, MOTHERWELL,
North Lanarkshire ML1 2DL
Tel: 01698 274939
Category: SLD (Coed 11-18)

**Clydeview School
and Nursery**
Magna Street, MOTHERWELL,
North Lanarkshire ML1 3QZ
Tel: 01698 264843
Category: SLD (Coed 5-11)

Firpark Primary School
177 Milton Street, MOTHERWELL,
North Lanarkshire ML1 1DL
Tel: 01698 274933
Category: (Coed Day 3-10)

Firpark Secondary School
Firpark Street, MOTHERWELL,
North Lanarkshire ML1 2PR
Tel: 01698 251313
Category: MLD PH (Coed 11-18)

UDDINGSTON

Fallside Secondary School
Sanderson Avenue,
Viewpark, UDDINGSTON,
North Lanarkshire G71 6JZ
Tel: 01698 274986
Category: EBD (Coed 11-16)

SOUTH LANARKSHIRE
Council

South Lanarkshire ASN Team, Inclusion service, Almada Street, Hamilton, ML3 0AA
Tel: 0303 123 1023 Email: education.inclusion@southlanarkshire.gov.uk Website: www.southlanarkshire.gov.uk

BLANTYRE

KEAR Campus School
Bardykes Road, BLANTYRE,
South Lanarkshire G72 9UJ
Tel: 01698 722120
Category: SEBD

CAMBUSLANG

Rutherglen High School
Langlea Road, CAMBUSLANG,
South Lanarkshire G72 8ES
Tel: 01416 433480

CARLUKE

Victoria Park School
Market Road, CARLUKE,
South Lanarkshire ML8 4BE
Tel: 01555 750591
Category: PMLD SLD

EAST KILBRIDE

Greenburn School
Calderwood Road, EAST KILBRIDE,
South Lanarkshire G74 3DP
Tel: 01355 237278
Category: PMLD

Sanderson High School
High Common Road, EAST
KILBRIDE, South Lanarkshire G74 2LP
Tel: 01355 588625

West Mains School
Logie Park, EAST KILBRIDE,
South Lanarkshire G74 4BU
Tel: 01355 249938
Category: SLD

HAMILTON

**Hamilton School
for the Deaf**
Anderson Street, HAMILTON,
South Lanarkshire ML3 0QL
Tel: 01698 823377
Category: Deaf

MIDLOTHIAN
Council

Midlothian ASN Team, Fairfield House, 8 Lothian Road, Dalkeith, Midlothian, EH22 3ZG
Tel: 01312 713689 Email: asl.officer@midlothian.gov.uk Website: www.midlothian.gov.uk

DALKEITH

Saltersgate School
3 Cousland Road, DALKEITH,
Midlothian EH22 2PS
Tel: 01316 544703
Category: GLD (Coed Secondary)

WEST LOTHIAN
Council

West Lothian ASN Team, West Lothian Civic Centre, Howden South Road, Livingston, West Lothian, EH54 6FF
Tel: 01506 282634 Email: alison.raeburn@westlothian.gov.uk Website: www.westlothian.gov.uk

BATHGATE

Pinewood Special School
Elm Grove, Blackburn, BATHGATE,
West Lothian EH47 7QX
Tel: 01506 656374
Category: SCLD (Primary/
Secondary)

BLACKBURN

Connolly School Campus
Hopefield Road, BLACKBURN,
West Lothian EH47 7HZ
Tel: 01506 283888
Category: SEBN (Primary)

LIVINGSTON

Beatlie School Campus
The Mall, Craigshill, LIVINGSTON,
West Lothian EH54 5EJ
Tel: 01506 777598
Category: SCLD MSI PD
(Nursery - Secondary)

Cedarbank School
Cedarbank, Ladywell East,
LIVINGSTON, West Lothian EH54 6DR
Tel: 01506 442172
Category: ASD LD (Secondary)

Ogilvie School Campus
Ogilvie Way, Knightsridge,
LIVINGSTON, West Lothian EH54 8HL
Tel: 01506 441430
Category: SCLD (Primary)

PERTH & KINROSS
Council

Perth & Kinross ASN Team, 2 High Street, 35 Kinnoull Street, Perth, PH1 5PH
Tel: 01738 476200 Email: ecsschools@pkc.gov.uk Website: www.pkc.gov.uk

PERTH

Fairview School
Oakbank Crescent, PERTH,
Perthshire & Kinross PH1 1DF
Tel: 01738 473050
Category: SLD CLD (Coed 2-18)

RENFREWSHIRE
Council

Renfrewshire ASN Team, Renfrewshire House, Cotton Street, Paisley, PA1 1UJ
Tel: 03003 000170 Email: asn.els@renfrewshire.gov.uk Website: www.renfrewshire.gov.uk

LINWOOD

Clippens School
Brediland Road, LINWOOD,
Renfrewshire PA3 3RX
Tel: 01505 325333
Category: ASD CLD PI
MSI (Coed 5-19)

PAISLEY

Kersland School
Ben Nevis Road, PAISLEY,
Renfrewshire PA2 7LA
Tel: 01418 898251
Category: SLD (Coed 5-18)

Mary Russell School
Hawkhead Road, PAISLEY,
Renfrewshire PA2 7BE
Tel: 01418 897628
Category: MLD (Coed 5-18)

EAST RENFREWSHIRE
Council

East Renfrewshire ASN Team, Council Offices, 211 Main Street, Barrhead, East Renfrewshire, G78 1SY
Tel: 0141 577 3001 Email: customerservices@eastrenfrewshire.gov.uk Website: www.eastrenfrewshire.gov.uk

NEWTON MEARNS

The Isobel Mair School
58 Stewarton Road, NEWTON
MEARNS, East Renfrewshire G77 6NB
Tel: 0141 577 7600
Category: CLD (Coed 5-18)

STIRLING
Council

Stirling ASN Team, Teith House, Kerse Road, Stirling, FK7 7QA
Tel: 01786 233212 Email: additionalsupportneeds@stirling.gov.uk Website: www.stirling.gov.uk

STIRLING

Castleview School
Raploch Community Campus,
Drip Road, STIRLING FK8 1SD
Tel: 01786 272326
Category: PD PMLD

WALES

BLAENAU GWENT

County Borough Council

SNAP Cymru, Head Office, 10 Coopers Yard, Curran Road Cardiff, CF10 5NB
Tel: 0845 1203730 Email: gwent@snapcymru.org Website: www.snapcymru.org

EBBW VALE

Pen-y-Cwm Special School
Ebbw Fawr Learning Community,
Strand Annealing Lane, EBBW
VALE, Blaenau Gwent NP23 5QD
Tel: 01495 304031
Category: SLD PMLD

BRIDGEND

County Borough Council

SNAP Cymru, Head Office, 10 Coopers Yard, Curran Road Cardiff, CF10 5NB
Tel: 0808 801 0608 Email: enquiries@snapcymru.org Website: www.snapcymru.org

BRIDGEND

Heronsbridge School
Ewenny Road, BRIDGEND CF31 3HT
Tel: 01656 815725
Category: PMLD VIS AUT (Coed
Day & boarding 3-18)

Ysgol Bryn Castell
Llangewydd Road, Cefn
Glas, BRIDGEND CF31 4JP
Tel: 01656 815595
Category: EBD LD HI ASD MLD
SLD SP&LD (Coed 3-19)

CAERPHILLY

County Borough Council

SNAP Cymru, Head Office, 10 Coopers Yard, Curran Road Cardiff, CF10 5NB
Tel: 0808 801 0608 Email: enquiries@snapcymru.org Website: www.snapcymru.org

CAERPHILLY

**Trinity Fields
Special School**
Caerphilly Road, Ystrad Mynach,
CAERPHILLY CF82 7XW
Tel: 01443 866000
Category: SLD VIS HI CLD
SP&LD (Coed 3-19)

CARDIFF
Council

SNAP Cymru, Head Office, 10 Coopers Yard, Curran Road Cardiff, CF10 5NB
Tel: 0808 801 0608 Email: enquiries@snapcymru.org Website: www.cardiff.gov.uk

CARDIFF

Greenhill School
Heol Brynglas, Rhiwbina,
CARDIFF CF14 6UJ
Tel: 02920 693786
Category: SEBD (Coed 11-16)

Meadowbank School
Colwill Road, Gabalfa,
CARDIFF CF14 2QQ
Tel: 02920 616018
Category: SLCD (Coed 4-11)

Riverbank School
Vincent Road, Caerau,
CARDIFF CF5 5AQ
Tel: 02920 563860
Category: MLD SLD (Coed 4-11)

The Court School
Station Road, Llanishen,
CARDIFF CF14 5UX
Tel: 02920 752713
Category: SEBD (Coed 4-11)

The Hollies School
Brynheulog, Pentwyn,
CARDIFF CF23 7XG
Tel: 02920 734411
Category: ASD PMED (Coed 4-11)

Ty Gwyn School
Vincent Road, Caerau,
CARDIFF CF5 5AQ
Tel: 02920 838560
Category: PMLD ASD (Coed 4-19)

Woodlands High School
Vincent Road, Caerau,
CARDIFF CF5 5AQ
Tel: 02920 561279
Category: MLD SLD (Coed 11-19)

CARMARTHENSHIRE
County Council

SNAP Cymru, Head Office, 10 Coopers Yard, Curran Road Cardiff, CF10 5NB
Tel: 0808 801 0608 Email: enquiries@snapcymru.org Website: www.snapcymru.org

CARMARTHEN

Rhydygors School
Rhyd-y-gors, Johnstown,
CARMARTHEN,
Carmarthenshire SA31 3NQ
Tel: 01267 231171
Category: EBD

LLANELLI

Ysgol Heol Goffa
Heol Goffa, LLANELLI,
Carmarthenshire SA15 3LS
Tel: 01554 759465
Category: SLD PMLD

CONWY
County Borough Council

SNAP Cymru, Head Office, 10 Coopers Yard, Curran Road Cardiff, CF10 5NB
Tel: 0808 801 0608 Email: enquiries@snapcymru.org Website: www.snapcymru.org

LLANDUDNO

Ysgol Y Gogarth
Ffordd Nant y Gamar, Craig y Don,
LLANDUDNO, Conwy LL30 1YE
Tel: 01492 860077
Category: General SEN (2-19)

DENBIGHSHIRE
County Council

SNAP Cymru, Head Office, 10 Coopers Yard, Curran Road Cardiff, CF10 5NB
Tel: 0808 801 0608 Email: enquiries@snapcymru.org Website: www.snapcymru.org

DENBIGH

Ysgol Plas Brondyffryn
Park Street, DENBIGH,
Denbighshire LL16 3DR
Tel: 01745 813914
Category: AUT SLD (Coed 4-19)

RHYL

Ysgol Tir Morfa
Derwen Road, RHYL,
Denbighshire LL18 2RN
Tel: 01745 350388
Category: MLD SLD (Coed 4-19)

FLINTSHIRE
County Council

SNAP Cymru, Head Office, 10 Coopers Yard, Curran Road Cardiff, CF10 5NB
Tel: 0808 801 0608 Email: enquiries@snapcymru.org Website: www.snapcymru.org

FLINT

Ysgol Maes Hyfryd
Fifth Avenue, FLINT,
Flintshire CH6 5QL
Tel: 01352 792720
Category: (Coed 11-16)

Ysgol Pen Coch
Prince of Wales Avenue,
FLINT, Flintshire CH6 5NF
Tel: 01352 792730
Category: (Coed 5-11)

GWYNEDD
Council

SNAP Cymru, Head Office, 10 Coopers Yard, Curran Road Cardiff, CF10 5NB
Tel: 0808 801 0608 Email: enquiries@snapcymru.org Website: www.snapcymru.org

CAERNARFON

Ysgol Pendalar
Ffordd Bethel, CAERNARFON,
Gwynedd LL55 1DU
Tel: 01248 672141
Category: SLD (3-18)

PENRHYNDEUDRAETH

Ysgol Hafod Lon
Parc Busnes Eryri,
PENRHYNDEUDRAETH,
Gwynedd LL48 6LD
Tel: 01766 772140
Category: SLD (3-18)

MERTHYR TYDFIL
County Borough Council

SNAP Cymru, Head Office, 10 Coopers Yard, Curran Road Cardiff, CF10 5NB
Tel: 0808 801 0608 Email: enquiries@snapcymru.org Website: www.snapcymru.org

MERTHYR TYDFIL

Greenfield Special School
Duffryn Road, Pentrebach,
MERTHYR TYDFIL CF48 4BJ
Tel: 01443 690468
Category: SLD MLD PMLD ASD
EBD MSI SP&LD (Coed 3-19)

MONMOUTHSHIRE
County Council

SNAP Cymru, Head Office, 10 Coopers Yard, Curran Road Cardiff, CF10 5NB
Tel: 0808 801 0608 Email: enquiries@snapcymru.org Website: www.snapcymru.org

CHEPSTOW

Mounton House School
Pwyllmeyric, CHEPSTOW,
Monmouthshire NP16 6LA
Tel: 01291 635050
Category: BESD (Boys
Day/Boarding 11-16)

NEATH PORT TALBOT
County Borough Council

SNAP Cymru, Head Office, 10 Coopers Yard, Curran Road Cardiff, CF10 5NB
Tel: 0808 801 0608 Email: enquiries@snapcymru.org Website: www.snapcymru.org

NEATH

Ysgol Hendrefelin
Heol Hendre, Bryncoch,
NEATH SA10 7TY
Tel: 01639 642786
Category: GLD (Coed 3-16)

Ysgol Maes Y Coed
Heol Hendre, Bryncoch,
NEATH SA10 7TY
Tel: 01639 643648
Category: GLD (Coed 2-19)

NEWPORT
City Council

SNAP Cymru, Head Office, 10 Coopers Yard, Curran Road Cardiff, CF10 5NB
Tel: 0808 801 0608 Email: enquiries@snapcymru.org Website: www.snapcymru.org

NEWPORT

Maes Ebbw School
Maesglas Road, Maesglas,
NEWPORT, Newport NP20 3DG
Tel: 01633 815480
Category: SLD PMLD AUT PH

PEMBROKESHIRE
County Council

SNAP Cymru, Head Office, 10 Coopers Yard, Curran Road Cardiff, CF10 5NB
Tel: 0808 801 0608 Email: enquiries@snapcymru.org Website: www.snapcymru.org

HAVERFORDWEST

Portfield School
off Portfield, HAVERFORDWEST,
Pembrokeshire SA61 1BS
Tel: 01437 762701
Category: SLD PMLD CLD
ASC (Coed 4-18+)

POWYS
County Council

SNAP Cymru, Head Office, 10 Coopers Yard, Curran Road Cardiff, CF10 5NB
Tel: 0808 801 0608 Email: enquiries@snapcymru.org Website: www.snapcymru.org

BRECON
Ysgol Penmaes
Canal Road, BRECON,
Powys LD3 7HL
Tel: 01874 623508
Category: SLD ASD PMLD
(Coed Day/Residential 3-19)

NEWTOWN
Brynllywarch Hall School
Kerry, NEWTOWN, Powys SY16 4PB
Tel: 01686 670276
Category: MLD EBD

Ysgol Cedewain
Maesyrhandir, NEWTOWN,
Powys SY16 1LH
Tel: 01686 627454
Category: SLD ASD PMLD
(Coed Day 3-19)

RHONDDA CYNON TAFF
County Borough Council

SNAP Cymru, Head Office, 10 Coopers Yard, Curran Road Cardiff, CF10 5NB
Tel: 0808 801 0608 Email: enquiries@snapcymru.org Website: www.snapcymru.org

ABERDARE
Maesgwyn Special School
Cwmdare Road, Cwmdare,
ABERDARE, Rhondda
Cynon Taf CF44 8RE
Tel: 01685 873933
Category: MLD (Coed 11-18)

Park Lane Special School
Park Lane, Trecynon, ABERDARE,
Rhondda Cynon Taf CF44 8HN
Tel: 01685 874489
Category: SLD (3-19)

PENTRE
Ysgol Hen Felin
Gelligaled Park, Ystrad, PENTRE,
Rhondda Cynon Taf CF41 7SZ
Tel: 01443 431571
Category: SLD (3-19)

PONTYPRIDD
Ysgol Ty Coch
Lansdale Drive, Tonteg,
PONTYPRIDD, Rhondda
Cynon Taf CF38 1PG
Tel: 01443 203471
Category: SLD (3-19)

Ysgol Ty Coch - Buarth y Capel
Ynysybwl, PONTYPRIDD,
Rhondda Cynon Taf CF37 3PA
Tel: 01443 791424

SWANSEA
City and County of
Council

SNAP Cymru, Head Office, 10 Coopers Yard, Curran Road Cardiff, CF10 5NB
Tel: 0808 801 0608 Email: enquiries@snapcymru.org Website: www.snapcymru.org

SWANSEA
Pen-y-Bryn Lower
Mynydd Garnllwyd Road,
Morriston, SWANSEA SA6 7QG
Tel: 01792 799064
Category: MLD SLD AUT

Ysgol Crug Glas
Croft Street, SWANSEA SA1 1QA
Tel: 01792 652388
Category: SLD PMLD

Ysgol Pen-y-Bryn
Glasbury Road, Morriston,
SWANSEA SA6 7PA
Tel: 01792 799064
Category: MLD SLD AUT

TORFAEN
County Borough Council

SNAP Cymru, Head Office, 10 Coopers Yard, Curran Road Cardiff, CF10 5NB
Tel: 0808 801 0608 Email: enquiries@snapcymru.org Website: www.snapcymru.org

CWMBRAN

Crownbridge School
Turnpike Road, Croesyceiliog,
CWMBRAN, Torfaen NP44 2BJ
Tel: 01633 624201
Category: SLD (2-19)

VALE OF GLAMORGAN
Council

SNAP Cymru, Head Office, 10 Coopers Yard, Curran Road Cardiff, CF10 5NB
Tel: 0808 801 0608 Email: enquiries@snapcymru.org Website: www.snapcymru.org

PENARTH

Ysgol Y Deri
Sully Road, PENARTH, Vale
of Glamorgan CF64 2TP
Tel: 02920 352280
Category: AUT PMLD MLD SLD
(Coed 5 Day/Residential 3-19)

WREXHAM
County Borough Council

SNAP Cymru, Head Office, 10 Coopers Yard, Curran Road Cardiff, CF10 5NB
Tel: 0808 801 0608 Email: enquiries@snapcymru.org Website: www.snapcymru.org

WREXHAM

St Christopher's School
Stockwell Grove,
WREXHAM LL13 7BW
Tel: 01978 346910
Category: MLD SLD
PMLD (Coed 6-19)

ACADEMIES

BATH & NORTH EAST SOMERSET

Bath

Aspire Academy
Frome Road, Odd Down,
BATH BA2 5RF
Tel: 01225 832212
Category: EBD (Coed 4-16)

Fosse Way School
Longfellow Road, Midsomer
Norton, BATH BA3 3AL
Tel: 01761 412198
Category: PH SLD SPLD ASD
MLD MSI CLD (Coed 3-19)

Three Ways School
180 Frome Road, Odd
Down, BATH BA2 5RF
Tel: 01225 838070
Category: PH SLD SPLD ASD
MLD MSI CLD (Coed 2-19)

BEDFORD

Grange Academy
Halsey Road, Kempston, BEDFORD,
Bedfordshire MK42 8AU
Tel: 01234 407100
Category: MLD with provision
for ASD (Coed 5-16)

CENTRAL BEDFORDSHIRE

Dunstable

Weatherfield Academy
Brewers Hill Road, DUNSTABLE,
Bedfordshire LU6 1AF
Tel: 01582 605632
Category: MLD (7-18)

BLACKPOOL

Park Community Academy
158 Whitegate Drive, BLACKPOOL,
Lancashire FY3 9HF
Tel: 01253 764130
Category: MLD CLD
SEBD (Coed 4-16)

BRISTOL

Venturers' Academy
Withywood Road, BRISTOL BS13 9AX
Tel: 0117 3010819
Category: ASC (4-16)

CAMBRIDGESHIRE

Huntingdon

Spring Common Academy
American Lane, HUNTINGDON,
Cambridgeshire PE29 1TQ
Tel: 01480 377403
Category: ASD EBD MLD
PMLD SLD (Coed 2-19)

CHESHIRE EAST

Crewe

Adelaide School
Adelaide Street, CREWE,
Cheshire CW1 3DT
Tel: 01270 685151
Category: AUT ADHD BESD
DYSL (Coed 9-18)

Knutsford

St John's Wood Academy
Longridge, KNUTSFORD,
Cheshire WA16 8PA
Tel: 01625 383045
Category: BESD (Coed Day 11-16)

CORNWALL

Truro

Pencalenick School
St Clement, TRURO, Cornwall TR1 1TE
Tel: 01872 520385
Category: SCLD (Coed 9-16)

CUMBRIA

Barrow In Furness

George Hastwell School
Moor Tarn Lane, Walney, BARROW
IN FURNESS, Cumbria LA14 3LW
Tel: 01229 475253
Category: ASC PMLD SLD (2-19)

DURHAM

Peterlee

Hopewood Academy (Ascent Trust)
Crawlaw Road, Easington Colliery,
PETERLEE, Durham SR8 3LP
Tel: 01915 691420
Category: ASD HI MLD
PMLD SLD (2-19)

HALTON

Runcorn

Cavendish High Academy
Lincoln Close, RUNCORN,
Cheshire WA7 4YX
Tel: 01928 561706
Category: SLD (11-19)

HARTLEPOOL

Catcote Academy
Catcote Road,
HARTLEPOOL TS25 4EZ
Tel: 01429 264036
Category: MLD SLD PMLD
ASD BESD (Coed 11-25)

HEREFORDSHIRE

Hereford

The Brookfield School & Specialist College
Grandstand Road,
HEREFORD HR4 9NG
Tel: 01432 265153
Category: BESD MLD ASD
ADHD (Coed 7-16)

HERTFORDSHIRE

Letchworth Garden City

Woolgrove School Special Needs Academy
Pryor Way, LETCHWORTH GARDEN
CITY, Hertfordshire SG6 2PT
Tel: 01462 622422
Category: MLD AUT
(Coed Day 5-11)

KENT

Dartford

Milestone Academy
Ash Road, New Ash Green,
DARTFORD, Kent DA3 8JZ
Tel: 01474 709420
Category: PMLD SLD AUT
MLD PSCN (Coed 2-19)

LEICESTERSHIRE

Coalville

Forest Way School
Warren Hills Road, COALVILLE,
Leicestershire LE67 4UU
Tel: 01530 831899
Category: SLD PMLD (2-18)

Hinckley

Dorothy Goodman School Hinckley
Stoke Road, HINCKLEY,
Leicestershire LE10 0EA
Tel: 01455 634582
Category: (2-18)

LINCOLNSHIRE

Boston

John Fielding School
Ashlawn Drive, BOSTON,
Lincolnshire PE21 9PX
Tel: 01205 363395
Category: SLD (2-19)

Gainsborough

Warren Wood Community School
Middlefield Lane, GAINSBOROUGH,
Lincolnshire DN21 1PU
Tel: 01427 615498
Category: SLD

Gosberton

Gosberton House School
11 Westhorpe Road, GOSBERTON,
Lincolnshire PE11 4EW
Tel: 01775 840250
Category: MLD (3-11)

Grantham

Sandon School
Sandon Close, GRANTHAM,
Lincolnshire NG31 9AX
Tel: 01476 564994
Category: SLD (2-19)

The Ambergate Sports College Specialist Education Centre
Dysart Road, GRANTHAM,
Lincolnshire NG31 7LP
Tel: 01476 564957
Category: MLD (5-16)

Horncastle

St Lawrence School
Bowl Alley Lane, HORNCASTLE,
Lincolnshire LN9 5EJ
Tel: 01507 522563
Category: MLD (5-16)

Lincoln

Athena School
South Park, LINCOLN,
Lincolnshire LN5 8EL
Tel: 01522 534559
Category: EBD, SEMH

St Francis School
Wickenby Crescent, Ermine Estate,
LINCOLN, Lincolnshire LN1 3TJ
Tel: 01522 526498
Category: PD Sensory (2-19)

The Fortuna Primary School
Kingsdown Road, Doddington
Park, LINCOLN, Lincolnshire LN6 0FB
Tel: 01522 705561
Category: EBD (4-11)

The Pilgrim School
Carrington Drive, LINCOLN,
Lincolnshire LN6 ODE
Tel: 01522 682319
Category: HS (4-16)

Louth

St Bernard's School
Wood Lane, LOUTH,
Lincolnshire LN11 8RS
Tel: 01507 603776
Category: SLD (2-19)

Spalding

The Garth School
Pinchbeck Road, SPALDING,
Lincolnshire PE11 1QF
Tel: 01775 725566
Category: SLD (2-19)

The Priory School
Neville Avenue, SPALDING,
Lincolnshire PE11 2EH
Tel: 01775 724080
Category: MLD (11-16)

Spilsby

Woodlands Academy
Partney Road, SPILSBY,
Lincolnshire PE23 5EJ
Tel: 01790 753902
Category: EBD

NORTH-EAST LINCOLNSHIRE

Grimsby

Humberston Park Special School
St Thomas Close, GRIMSBY, N
E Lincolnshire DN36 4HS
Tel: 01472 590645
Category: SLD PMLD PD
CLD MSI (Coed 3-19)

The Cambridge Park Academy
Cambridge Road, GRIMSBY,
N E Lincolnshire DN34 5EB
Tel: 01472 230110
Category: ASD SLCN MLD
SLD (Coed 3-19)

LONDON – BROMLEY

Bromley

Bromley Beacon Academy (Bromley Campus)
Old Homesdale Road,
BROMLEY, Kent BR2 9LJ
Tel: 020 3319 0503
Category: SEMH (Coed 7-18)

Orpington

Bromley Beacon Academy (Orpington Campus)
Avalon Road, ORPINGTON,
Kent BR6 9BD
Tel: 01689 821205
Category: SEMH (Coed 7-14)

LONDON – ROYAL BOROUGH OF GREENWICH

Charlton Park Academy
Charlton Park Road,
LONDON SE7 8HX
Tel: 02082 496844
Category: SCLD SCD PMLD
PD ASD (Coed 11-19)

LONDON – HILLINGDON

Hayes

The Willows School Academy Trust
Stipularis Drive, HAYES,
Middlesex UB4 9QB
Tel: 02088 417176
Category: SEBD ASD ADHD
Challenging behaviour (Coed 3-11)

Uxbridge

Moorcroft (Eden Academy)
Bramble Close, Hillingdon,
UXBRIDGE, Middlesex UB8 3BF
Tel: 01895 437799
Category: SLD PMLD
AUT (Coed 11-19)

West Drayton

Young People's Academy
Falling Lane, Yiewsley, WEST
DRAYTON, Middlesex UB7 8AB
Tel: 01895 446747
Category: BESD AUT
ADHD (Coed 11-16)

LONDON – SUTTON

Carshalton

Wandle Valley School
Welbeck Road, CARSHALTON,
Surrey SM5 1LW
Tel: 02086 481365
Category: SEBD (Coed 5-16)

Wallington

Carew Academy
Church Road, WALLINGTON,
Surrey SM6 7NH
Tel: 02086 478349
Category: MLD BESD
ASD PD (Coed 7-18)

LONDON – WALTHAM FOREST

Walthamstow

Hornbeam Academy - William Morris Campus
Folly Lane, WALTHAMSTOW, London E17 5NT
Tel: 02085 032225
Category: MLD SLD PMLD (Coed 11-16)

Woodford Green

Hornbeam Academy - Brookfield House Campus
Alders Avenue, WOODFORD GREEN, Essex IG8 9PY
Tel: 02085 272464
Category: HI PD Complex medical needs (Coed 2-16)

GREATER MANCHESTER – OLDHAM

Hollinwood Academy
Roman Road, Hollinwood, OLDHAM, Greater Manchester OL8 3PT
Tel: 0161 883 2404
Category: ASD SCD (4-19)

Spring Brook Academy - Lower School
Heron Street, OLDHAM, Greater Manchester OL8 4JD
Tel: 0161 883 2431
Category: BESD (Coed 4-11)

GREATER MANCHESTER – SALFORD

Eccles

Oakwood Academy
Chatsworth Road, Ellesmere Park, ECCLES M30 9DY
Tel: 01619 212880
Category: MLD HI VIS SEBD Complex needs (Coed 10-19)

GREATER MANCHESTER – TRAFFORD

Sale

Manor Academy
Manor Avenue, SALE, Cheshire M33 5JX
Tel: 01619 761553
Category: ASD SEMH MLD (Coed 11-18)

MEDWAY

Chatham

Bradfields Academy
Churchill Avenue, CHATHAM, Kent ME5 0LB
Tel: 01634 683990
Category: MLD SLD ASD (Coed 11-19)

MILTON KEYNES

Stephenson Academy
Crosslands, Stantonbury, MILTON KEYNES, Buckinghamshire MK14 6AX
Tel: 01908 889400
Category: EBD (Boys Day/ boarding 12-16)

NORFOLK

Norwich

Eaton Hall Specialist Academy
Pettus Road, NORWICH, Norfolk NR4 7BU
Tel: 01603 457480
Category: SEBD (Boys 7-16)

NORTHAMPTONSHIRE

Corby

Maplefields School
Tower Hill Road, CORBY, Northamptonshire NN18 0TH
Tel: 01536 424090
Category: BESD (5-19)

Kettering

Kingsley Special Academy Trust
Churchill Way, KETTERING, Northamptonshire NN15 5DP
Tel: 01536 316880
Category: PMLD SLD ASD (3-11)

Northampton

Billing Brook Special Academy Trust School
Penistone Road, NORTHAMPTON, Northamptonshire NN3 8EZ
Tel: 01604 773910
Category: MLD ASD SLD SPLD PH (3-19)

Wellingborough

Friars Academy
Friar's Close, WELLINGBOROUGH, Northamptonshire NN8 2LA
Tel: 01933 304950
Category: MLD SLD ASD (11-19)

NOTTINGHAM

Nethergate School
Swansdowne Drive, Clifton, NOTTINGHAM NG11 8HX
Tel: 01159 152959

NOTTINGHAMSHIRE

Broxtowe

Foxwood Academy
Off Derby Road, Bramcote Hills, Beeston, BROXTOWE, Nottingham NG9 3GF
Tel: 01159 177202
Category: (Coed 3-19)

Mansfield

The Beech Academy
Fairholme Drive, MANSFIELD, Nottinghamshire NG19 6DX
Tel: 01623 626008
Category: (Coed 11-19)

OXFORDSHIRE

Abingdon

Kingfisher School
Radley Road, ABINGDON, Oxfordshire OX14 3RR
Tel: 01235 555512
Category: SLD PMLD (Coed 2-19)

Oxford

Endeavour Academy
Waynflete Road, Headington, OXFORD OX3 8DD
Tel: 01865 767766
Category: AUT SLD (Coed Day/residential 9-19)

Iffley Academy
Iffley Turn, OXFORD OX4 4DU
Tel: 01865 747606
Category: MLD CLD BESD (Coed 5-18)

Northern House School
South Parade, Summertown, OXFORD OX2 7JN
Tel: 01865 557 004
Category: BESD (Coed 5-11)

Wantage

Fitzwaryn School
Denchworth Road, WANTAGE, Oxfordshire OX12 9ET
Tel: 01235 764504
Category: MLD CLD PMLD (Coed 3-19)

PETERBOROUGH

City of Peterborough Special School
Reeves Way, PETERBOROUGH,
Cambridgeshire PE1 5LQ
Tel: 01733 821403
Category: (Coed 4-18)

POOLE

Longspee Academy
Learoyd Road, Canford Heath,
POOLE, Dorset BH17 8PJ
Tel: 01202 380266
Category: BESD (5-14)

Montacute School
3 Canford Heath Road,
POOLE, Dorset BH17 9NG
Tel: 01202 693239
Category: PMLD SLD CLD
PH Medical needs (3-19)

PORTSMOUTH

Cliffdale Primary Academy
Battenburg Avenue, North End,
PORTSMOUTH, Hampshire PO2 0SN
Tel: 02392 662601
Category: CLD ASD (Coed 4-11)

READING

The Avenue School
Conwy Close, Tilehurst,
READING, Berkshire RG30 4BZ
Tel: 01189 375554
Category: AUT Complex
Needs (Coed 2-19)

REDCAR & CLEVELAND

Saltburn-By-Sea

KTS Academy
Marshall Drive, Brotton, SALTBURN-
BY-SEA, Cleveland TS12 2UW
Tel: 01287 677265
Category: SLD PMLD SLCN ASC
PD CLDD (Coed day 2-19)

SHROPSHIRE

Shrewsbury

Severndale Specialist Academy
Monkmoor Campus, Woodcote
Way, Monkmoor, SHREWSBURY,
Shropshire SY2 5SL
Tel: 01743 281600
Category: PMLD SLD MLD
CLDD (Coed Day 2-19)

SOUTHEND-ON-SEA

Kingsdown School
Snakes Lane, SOUTHEND-
ON-SEA, Essex SS2 6XT
Tel: 01702 527486
Category: SLD PMLD PNI
PD (Coed Day 3-14)

St Nicholas School
Philpott Avenue, SOUTHEND-
ON-SEA, Essex SS2 4RL
Tel: 01702 462322
Category: MLD AUT SEMH
(Coed Day 11-16)

Westcliff-On-Sea

Lancaster School
Prittlewell Chase, WESTCLIFF-
ON-SEA, Essex SS0 0RT
Tel: 01702 342543
Category: SLD PMLD PNI
PD (Coed Day 14-19)

STAFFORDSHIRE

Lichfield

Saxon Hill Special School
Kings Hill Road, LICHFIELD,
Staffordshire WS14 9DE
Tel: 01543 414892
Category: Generic (Coed
Day/Boarding 2-19)

Newcastle Under Lyme

Blackfriars Academy
Priory Road, NEWCASTLE UNDER
LYME, Staffordshire ST5 2TF
Tel: 01782 297780
Category: Generic
(Coed Day 11-19)

The Coppice Academy
Abbots Way, NEWCASTLE UNDER
LYME, Staffordshire ST5 2EY
Tel: 01782 297490
Category: Generic
(Coed Day 11-16)

Stafford

Walton Hall Academy
Stafford Road, Eccleshall,
STAFFORD, Staffordshire ST21 6JR
Tel: 01785 850420
Category: Generic (Coed
Day/Boarding 11-19)

Stoke On Trent

Cicely Haughton Community Special School
Westwood Manor, Wetley
Rocks, STOKE ON TRENT,
Staffordshire ST9 0BX
Tel: 01782 297780
Category: SEBD (Coed
Boarding 4-11)

Uttoxeter

Loxley Hall School
Stafford Road, Loxley, UTTOXETER,
Staffordshire ST14 8RS
Tel: 01889 256390
Category: SEBD (Coed
Boarding 11-16)

STOCKTON-ON-TEES

Billingham

Ash Trees Academy
Bowes Road, BILLINGHAM,
Stockton-on-Tees TS23 2BU
Tel: 01642 563712
Category: SLD PMLD
AUT (Coed 4-11)

Thornaby-On-Tees

Horizons Specialist Academy Trust, Westlands School
Eltham Crescent, THORNABY-
ON-TEES TS17 9RA
Tel: 01642 883030
Category: BESD (Coed
Residential 11-16)

SUFFOLK

Bury St Edmunds

Priory School
Mount Road, BURY ST
EDMUNDS, Suffolk IP32 7BH
Tel: 01284 761934
Category: MLD (Coed
Day & boarding 8-16)

Ipswich

Stone Lodge Academy
Stone Lodge Lane West,
IPSWICH, Suffolk IP2 9HW
Tel: 01473 601175
Category: MLD ASD
(Coed Day 5-11)

Thomas Wolsey School
Defoe Road, IPSWICH,
Suffolk IP1 6SG
Tel: 01473 467600
Category: PD/Comunication
(Coed Day 3-16)

Lowestoft

The Ashley School Academy Trust
Ashley Downs, LOWESTOFT,
Suffolk NR32 4EU
Tel: 01502 565439
Category: MLD (Coed
Day & boarding 7-16)

SURREY

Camberley

Carwarden House Community School
118 Upper Chobham Road,
CAMBERLEY, Surrey GU15 1EJ
Tel: 01276 709080
Category: LD (11-19)

Chobham

Wishmore Cross School
Alpha Road, CHOBHAM,
Surrey GU24 8NE
Tel: 01276 857555
Category: BESD (Boarding & day 11-16)

Farnham

The Ridgeway School
Frensham Road, FARNHAM,
Surrey GU9 8HB
Tel: 01252 724562
Category: SLD (2-19)

Guildford

Pond Meadow School
Larch Avenue, GUILDFORD,
Surrey GU1 1DR
Tel: 01483 532239
Category: SLD (2-19)

Leatherhead

West Hill School
Kingston Road, LEATHERHEAD,
Surrey KT22 7PW
Tel: 01372 814714
Category: LD (11-16)

Worcester Park

Linden Bridge School
Grafton Road, WORCESTER
PARK, Surrey KT4 7JW
Tel: 02083 303009
Category: ASD (Residential & day 4-19)

EAST SUSSEX

Bexhill-On-Sea

Glyne Gap Academy School
Hastings Road, BEXHILL-ON-
SEA, East Sussex TN40 2PU
Tel: 01424 217720
Category: CLD/ASD (Coed 2-19)

Eastbourne

The Lindfield Academy
Lindfield Road, EASTBOURNE,
East Sussex BN22 0BQ
Tel: 01323 502988
Category: ACLD (Coed 11-16)

The South Downs Academy
(West Site), Beechy Avenue,
EASTBOURNE, East Sussex BN20 8NU
Tel: 01323 730302
Category: ACLD CLD (Coed 4-11)

Hastings

Torfield School
Croft Road, HASTINGS,
East Sussex TN34 3JT
Tel: 01424 428228
Category: ACLD (Coed 3-11)

Heathfield

St Mary's School
Maynards Green, Horam,
HEATHFIELD, East Sussex TN21 0BT
Tel: 01435 812278
Category: SEBD (Boys 9-16)

Seaford

Cuckmere House School
Eastbourne Road, SEAFORD,
East Sussex BN25 4BA
Tel: 01323 893319
Category: SEBD (Boys 9-16)

St Leonards-On-Sea

New Horizons School
Beauchamp Road, ST LEONARDS-
ON-SEA, East Sussex TN38 9JU
Tel: 01424 855665
Category: SEBD (Coed 7-16)

Saxon Mount School
Edinburgh Road, ST LEONARDS-
ON-SEA, East Sussex TN38 8DA
Tel: 01424 426303
Category: ACLD (Coed 11-16)

THURROCK

Grays

Treetops School
Buxton Road, GRAYS,
Essex RM16 2WU
Tel: 01375 372723
Category: MLD ASD (Coed 3-16)

South Ockendon

Beacon Hill Academy (Main Site)
Erriff Drive, SOUTH OCKENDON,
Essex RM15 5AY
Tel: 01708 852006
Category: PNI PMLD
SLD (Coed 3-16)

TORBAY

Torquay

Combe Pafford School
Steps Lane, Watcombe,
TORQUAY TQ2 8NL
Tel: 01803 327902

TYNE & WEAR – GATESHEAD

Cedars Academy
Ivy Lane, Low Fell, GATESHEAD,
Tyne & Wear NE9 6QD
Tel: 01914 874595
Category: PD (Coed 2-16)

TYNE & WEAR – SUNDERLAND

Barbara Priestman Academy
Meadowside, SUNDERLAND,
Tyne & Wear SR2 7QN
Tel: 01915 536000
Category: ASD CLD
(Coed Day 11-19)

North View Academy
St Lukes Road, South Hylton,
SUNDERLAND, Tyne & Wear SR4 0HB
Tel: 01915 534580
Category: SEMH ASD (4-11)

Portland Academy
Weymouth Road,
Chapelgarth, SUNDERLAND,
Tyne & Wear SR3 2NQ
Tel: 01915 536050
Category: SLD (Coed Day 11-19)

The New Bridge Academy
Craigshaw Road, Hylton Castle,
SUNDERLAND, Tyne & Wear SR5 3NF
Tel: 01915 536067
Category: SEBD (Coed Day 11-19)

WARWICKSHIRE

Coleshill

Woodlands School
Packington Lane, COLESHILL,
West Midlands B46 3JE
Tel: 01675 463590
Category: Generic SLD VIS HI AUT
MSI PD MLD PMLD (Coed Day 2-19)

Nuneaton

Discovery Academy
Vernons Lane, NUNEATON,
Warwickshire CV11 5SS
Tel: 07494 457314
Category: (Coed 9-19)

Oak Wood Primary School
Morris Drive, NUNEATON,
Warwickshire CV11 4QH
Tel: 02476 740907
Category: Generic SLD MLD VIS HI
AUT MSI PD PMLD (Coed Day 2-11)

Oak Wood Secondary School
Morris Drive, NUNEATON,
Warwickshire CV11 4QH
Tel: 02476 740901
Category: Generic SLD MLD VIS HI
AUT MSI PD PMLD (Coed Day 11-19)

Quest Academy
St Davids Way, Bermuda Park,
NUNEATON, Warwickshire CV10 7SD
Tel: 01788 593112
Category: (9-19)

Rugby

Brooke School
Overslade Lane, RUGBY,
Warwickshire CV22 6DY
Tel: 01788 812324
Category: Generic SLD VIS HI AUT
MSI PD MLD PMLD (Coed Day 2-19)

Stratford-Upon-Avon

Welcombe Hills School
Blue Cap Road, STRATFORD-UPON-AVON, Warwickshire CV37 6TQ
Tel: 01789 266845
Category: Generic SLD VIS HI AUT MSI PD MLD PMLD (Coed Day 2-19)

WEST MIDLANDS – BIRMINGHAM

Erdington

Wilson Stuart School
Perry Common Road, ERDINGTON, Birmingham B23 7AT
Tel: 01213 734475
Category: PD (Coed Day 2-19)

Kitts Green

Hallmoor School
Scholars Gate, KITTS GREEN, Birmingham B33 0DL
Tel: 01217 833972
Category: MLD MSI SP&LD (Coed Day 4-19)

Ladywood

Calthorpe Teaching Academy
Darwin Street, Highgate, LADYWOOD, Birmingham B12 0TP
Tel: 01217 734637
Category: SLD MLD CLD PD MSI AUT (Coed Day 2-19)

James Brindley School
Bell Barn Road, Edgbaston, LADYWOOD, Birmingham B15 2AF
Tel: 01216 666409
Category: HS (Coed Day 2-19)

Sutton Coldfield

The Bridge School
Coppice View Road, SUTTON COLDFIELD, Birmingham B73 6UE
Tel: 01214 648265
Category: ASD PMLD SLD (Coed 2-11)

Yardley

Brays School
Brays Road, Sheldon, YARDLEY, Birmingham B26 1NS
Tel: 01217 435730
Category: PD ASD (Coed 2-11)

WEST MIDLANDS – COVENTRY

Coventry

RNIB Three Spires Academy
Kingsbury Road, COVENTRY, West Midlands CV6 1PJ
Tel: 02476 594952
Category: MLD (Coed Day 3-11)

WEST MIDLANDS – SOLIHULL

Northern House School
Lanchester Way, Castle Bromwich, BIRMINGHAM, West Midlands B36 9LF
Tel: 01217 489760
Category: SEMH (Coed Day 11-16)

WEST MIDLANDS – WALSALL

Phoenix Academy
Odell Road, Leamore, WALSALL, West Midlands WS3 2ED
Tel: 01922 712834
Category: EBD (Coed Day 4-11)

WEST MIDLANDS – WOLVERHAMPTON

Broadmeadow Special School
Lansdowne Road, WOLVERHAMPTON, West Midlands WV1 4AL
Tel: 01902 558330
Category: SLD ASD PMLD (Coed Day 2-6)

Northern House School
Cromer Gardens, Whitmore Reans, WOLVERHAMPTON, West Midlands WV6 0UB
Tel: 01902 551564
Category: BESD ADHD (Coed Day 8-16)

Westcroft School
Greenacres Avenue, Underhill, WOLVERHAMPTON, West Midlands WV10 8NZ
Tel: 01902 558350
Category: CLD (Coed Day 4-16)

WILTSHIRE

SALISBURY

Exeter House Special School
Somerset Road, SALISBURY, Wiltshire SP1 3BL
Tel: 01722 334168
Category: SLD PMLD SPLD Del (Coed Day 2-19)

NORTH YORKSHIRE

Scarborough

The Woodlands Academy
Woodlands Drive, SCARBOROUGH, North Yorkshire YO12 6QN
Tel: 01723 373260
Category: MLD (2-16)

Doncaster

Pennine View School
Old Road, Conisbrough, DONCASTER, South Yorkshire DN12 3LR
Tel: 01709 864978
Category: MLD (Coed Day 7-16)

WEST YORKSHIRE

Huddersfield

Joseph Norton Academy
Busker Lane, Scissett, HUDDERSFIELD, West Yorkshire HD8 9JU
Tel: 01484 868218
Category: SEMH (Coed Day 7-16)

Leeds

Springwell Leeds East
Brooklands View, Seacroft, LEEDS, West Yorkshire LS14 6XR
Tel: 0113 4870450
Category: SEMH

Springwell Leeds Primary
Oakwood Primary Site, Oakwood Lane, LEEDS, West Yorkshire LS8 3LF
Tel: 0113 8270063
Category: SEMH

Springwell Leeds South
Middleton Road, LEEDS, West Yorkshire LS10 3JA
Tel: 0113 4870500
Category: SEMH

SCOTLAND
GLASGOW

Hollybrook Academy
135 Hollybrook Street, GLASGOW G42 7HU
Tel: 01414 235937
Category: MLD (Secondary)

John Paul Academy
2 Arrochar Street, GLASGOW G23 5LY
Tel: 01415 820140

Linburn Academy
77 Linburn Road, GLASGOW G52 4EX
Tel: 01418 832082
Category: CLD (Secondary)

Rosshall Academy
131 Crookston Road, GLASGOW G52 3PD
Tel: 01415 820200

GREENOCK

Lomond View Academy
Ingleston Street, GREENOCK, Inverclyde PA15 4UQ
Tel: 01475 714414

Useful associations
and websites

AbilityNet

Freephone & text phone helpline: 0800 269 545
Email: enquiries@abilitynet.org.uk
Website: www.itcanhelp.org.uk
Twitter: @AbilityNet
Facebook: @AbilityNet

Helps people of any age and with any disability to use technology to achieve their goals at home, at work and in education. Provides specialist advice services and free information resources.

Action for Sick Children

10 Ravenoak Road
Cheadle Hulme
Stockport SK8 7DL
Tel: 0161 486 6788
Helpline: 0800 0744 519
Email: enquiries@actionforsickchildren.org
Website: www.actionforsickchildren.org
Twitter: @Action4SickCh
Facebook: @ActionforSickChildren

A charity specially formed to ensure that sick children receive the highest standard of care possible.

Action on Hearing Loss

19-23 Featherstone Street
London EC1Y 8SL
Tel: 0808 808 0123 (freephone)
Textphone: 0808 808 9000 (freephone)
SMS: 0780 0000 360
Email: informationline@hearingloss.org.uk
Website: www.actiononhearingloss.org.uk
Twitter: @ActionOnHearing
Facebook: @actiononhearingloss

Action on Hearing Loss, formerly the Royal National Institute for Deaf People, is the largest national charity representing the 11 million confronting deafness and hearing loss in the UK.

Action on Hearing Loss Cymru

Ground Floor
Anchor Court (North)
Keen Road
Cardiff
CF24 5JW
Tel: 02920 333 034
Text: 02920 333 036
Fax: 02920 333 035
Email: cymru@hearingloss.org.uk

See main entry above.

Action on Hearing Loss Northern Ireland

Harvester House
4-8 Adelaide Street
Belfast
BT2 8GA
Tel: 028 9023 9619
Fax: 028 9031 2032
Textphone: 028 9024 9462
Email: information.nireland@hearingloss.org.uk
Twitter: @hearinglossNI

See main entry above.

Action on Hearing Loss Scotland

Empire House
131 West Nile Street
Glasgow
G1 2RXJ
Tel: 0141 341 5330
Textphone: 0141 341 5347
Fax: 0141 354 0176
Email: scotland@hearingloss.org.uk

See main entry above.

ADDISS – National Attention Deficit Disorder Information & Support Service

PO Box 340
Edgware
Middlesex HA8 9HL
Tel: 020 8952 2800
Fax: 020 8952 2909
Email: info@addiss.co.uk
Website: www.addiss.co.uk

ADDISS provides information and assistance for those affected by ADHD.

Advisory Centre for Education – (ACE)

72 Durnsford Road
London
N11 2EJ
Tel: 0300 0115 142
Email: enquiries@ace-ed.org.uk
Website: www.ace-ed.org.uk
Twitter: @ACEducationUK

ACE is an independent national advice centre for parents/carers of children aged 5 to 16. Advice booklets can be downloaded or ordered from the website. Training courses and seminars for LA officers, schools and governors are available. As well as a training package for community groups advising parents on education matters. Has Facebook page and you can follow them on Twitter.

AFASIC – Unlocking Speech and Language

20 Bowling Green Lane
London EC1R 0BD
Tel: 020 7490 9410
Fax: 020 7251 2834
Helpline: 0300 666 9410
Website: www.afasicengland.org.uk
Twitter: @Afasic
Facebook: @Afasic.Charity

Helps children and young people with speech and language impairments. Provides: training/conferences for parents and professionals; a range of publications; support through local groups; and expertise in developing good practice. Has a Facebook page.

AFASIC – Cymru

Titan House
Cardiff Bay Business Centre
Lewis Road
Ocean Park
Cardiff CF24 5BS
Tel: 029 2046 5854
Fax: 029 2046 5854
Website: www.afasiccymru.org.uk
See main entry above.

AFASIC – Northern Ireland

Cranogue House
19 Derry Courtney Road
Caledon
County Tyrone BT68 4UF
Tel: 028 3756 9611 (M-F 10.30am-2.30pm)
Email: mary@afasicnorthernireland.org.uk
Website: www.afasicnorthernireland.org.uk

See main entry above.

AFASIC – Scotland

42-44 Castle Street
Dundee DD1 3AQ
Tel: 01382 250060
Fax: 01382 568391
Email: info@afasicscotland.org.uk
Website: www.afasicscotland.org.uk

See main entry above.

Association of Blind and Partially-Sighted Teachers and Students (ABAPSTAS)

BM Box 6727
London
WC1N 3XX
Tel: 0117 966 4839
Website: www.abapstas.org.uk

National organisation of visually impaired people that focuses on education and employment issues.

Association of Sign Language Interpreters (ASLI)

Derngate Mews
Derngate
Northampton
NN1 1UE
Tel: 01604 320834
Textphone: 18001 0871 474 0522
Fax: 08451 70 80 61
Email: office@asli.org.uk
Website: www.asli.org.uk
Twitter: @ASLIuk
Facebook: @ASLIuk

Has a useful online directory of sign language interpreters.

Asthma UK

18 Mansell St
London E1 8AA
Tel: 0300 222 5800
Email: info@asthma.org.uk
Website: www.asthma.org.uk
Twitter: @AsthmaUK
Facebook: @AsthmaUK

Charity dedicated to helping the 5.2 million people in the UK who are affected by asthma.

Ataxia (UK)

12 Broadbent Close
London N6 5JW
Tel: 020 7582 1444
Helpline: 0845 644 0606
Email: office@ataxia.org.uk
Website: www.ataxia.org.uk
Twitter: @AtaxiaUK
Facebook: @ataxiauk

Aims to support all people affected by ataxia. Has a Facebook page and you can follow them on Twitter.

BIBIC (British Institute for Brain Injured Children)

Old Kelways
Somerton Road
Langport
Somerset TA10 9SJ
Tel: 01458 253344
Fax: 01278 685573
Email: info@bibic.org.uk
Website: www.bibic.org.uk
Twitter: @bibic_charity

BIBIC helps children with a disability or learning difficulty caused by conditions such as cerebral palsy, Down's syndrome and other genetic disorders; acquired brain injury caused by trauma or illness; and developmental disorders such as autism, ADHD, Asperger syndrome and dyspraxia.

All children are assessed by a multi-professional team who put together a report and a therapy plan that is taught to the family by the child's key worker. This provides support for the family to learn about their child and how they can make a positive difference to their development. Sections of the plan are designed to be shared with the child's school and social groups to ensure a consistent approach in areas such as communication, behaviour and learning. Families return on a regular basis for reassessments and updated therapy programmes.

Brain and Spine Foundation

LG01, Lincoln House
Kennington Park
1-3 Brixton Road
London SW9 6DE
Tel: 020 7793 5900
Helpline: 0808 808 1000
Fax: 020 7793 5939
Fax helpline: 020 7793 5939
Email: info@brainandspine.org.uk
Website: www.brainandspine.org.uk
Twitter: @brainspine
Facebook: @brainandspine

A charity founded in 1992 to help those people affected by brain and spine conditions.

British Blind Sport (BBS)

Pure Offices
Plato Close
Tachbrook Park
Leamington Spa
Warwickshire CV34 6WE
Tel: 01926 424247
Fax: 01926 427775
Email: info@britishblindsport.org.uk
Website: www.britishblindsport.org.uk
Twitter: @BritBlindSport
Facebook: @BritishBlindSport

BBS provide sport and recreation for blind and partially sighted people.

British Deaf Association England

356 Holloway Road
London N7 6PA
Tel: 020 7697 4140
Textphone: 07795 410724
Fax: 01772 561610
Email: bda@bda.org.uk
Website: www.bda.org.uk
Twitter: @BDA_Deaf
Facebook: @BritishDeafAssociation

The BDA is a democratic, membership-led national charity campaigning on behalf of deaf sign language users in the UK. It exists to advance and protect the interests of the deaf community, to increase deaf people's access to facilities and lifestyles that most hearing people take for granted and to ensure greater awareness of their rights and responsibilities as members of society. The association has several main service areas, with teams covering education and youth, information, health promotions, video production and community services, offering advice and help. There is a national helpline that provides information and advice on a range of subjects such as welfare rights, the Disability Discrimination Act (DDA) and education.

British Deaf Association Northern Ireland

Unit 5c, Weavers Court
Linfield Road
Belfast BT12 5GH
Tel: 02890 437480
Textphone: 02890 437486
Fax: 02890 437487
Email: northernireland@bda.org
Website: www.bda.org.uk

See main entry under British Deaf Association England.

British Deaf Association Scotland

1st Floor Central Chambers, Suite 58
93 Hope Street
Glasgow G2 6LD
Tel: 0141 248 5565
Fax: 0141 248 5554
Email: scotland@bda.org.uk
Website: www.bda.org.uk

See main entry under British Deaf Association England.

British Deaf Association Wales

GAVO Offices
Church Road
Newport NP19 7EJ
Email: bdm.waleseng@bda.org.uk
Website: www.bda.org.uk

See main entry under British Deaf Association England.

British Dyslexia Association

Unit 8, Bracknell Beeches
Old Bracknell Lane
Bracknell RG12 7BW
Tel: 0333 405 4567 (Helpline) or
0333 405 4555 (Admin)
Fax: 0845 251 9005
Email: helpline@bdadyslexia.org.uk
Website: www.bdadyslexia.org.uk
Twitter: @BDAdyslexia
Facebook: @bdadyslexia

Helpline/information service open between 10am and 4pm (M-F) also open late on Wednesdays 5-7pm. Has a Facebook page.

British Institute of Learning Disabilities (BILD)

Birmingham Research Park
97 Vincent Drive
Edgbaston
Birmingham B15 2SQ
Tel: 0121 415 6960
Fax: 0121 415 6999
Email: enquiries@bild.org.uk
Website: www.bild.org.uk

BILD are committed to improving the quality of life of people with learning disabilities. They do this by advancing education, research and practice and by promoting better ways of working with children and adults with learning disabilities. BILD provides education, training, information, publications, journals, membership services, research and consultancy. Has a Facebook page and you can follow them on Twitter.

British Psychological Society

St Andrews House
48 Princess Road East
Leicester LE1 7DR
Tel: 0116 254 9568
Fax: 0116 227 1314
Email: enquiries@bps.org.uk
Website: www.bps.org.uk
Twitter: @BPSofficial
Facebook: @OfficialBPS

The representative body for psychology and psychologists in the UK. Has search facility for details on psychologists.

Butterfly AVM Charity

Unit C2 Crispin Industrial Centre,
Angel Road Works
Advent Way
London
N18 3AH
Tel: 07811 400633
Fax: 0208 8037600
Email: support@butterflyavmcharity.org.uk
Website: www.butterflyavmcharity.org.uk
Twitter: @Butterfly080666
Facebook: @ButterflyAvmCharity

Offers advice and support to anyone affected by an AVM

CALL Scotland

University of Edinburgh
Paterson's Land
Holyrood Road
Edinburgh
Midlothian EH8 8AQ
Tel: 0131 651 6235
Fax: 0131 651 6234
Email: call.scotland@ed.ac.uk
Website: www.callscotland.org.uk
Twitter: @CallScotland
Facebook: @CallScotland1983

CALL Scotland provides services and carries out research and development projects across Scotland for people, particularly children, with severe communication disabilities, their families and people who work with them in augmentative communication techniques and technology, and specialised computer use.

Cambian Group

Helpline: 0800 138 1418
Email: education@cambiangroup.com
Website: www.cambiangroup.com
Twitter:@Cambian_Group
Facebook: @cambiangroup

Cambian Group is one of the UK's leading providers of specialist services in education, care, mental health and learning disabilities. Works with 140 public authorities.

Capability Scotland (ASCS)

Osborne House
1 Osborne Terrace
Edinburgh EH12 5HG
Tel: 0131 337 9876
Textphone: 0131 346 2529
Fax: 0131 346 7864
Website: www.capability-scotland.org.uk
Twitter: @capability_scot
Facebook: @CapabilityScotland

ASCS is a national disability advice and information service, which provides free confidential advice and information on a range of disability issues including advice on cerebral palsy.

Carers UK

20 Great Dover Street
London SE1 4LX
Tel: 020 7378 4999
Fax: 020 7378 9781
Adviceline: 0808 808 7777 or Email: advice@carersuk.org
Email: info@carersuk.org
Website: www.carersuk.org
Twitter: @CarersUK
Facebook: @carersuk

For carers run by carers.

Carers Northern Ireland

58 Howard Street
Belfast BT1 6PJ
Tel: 028 9043 9843
Email: info@carersni.org
Website: www.carersuk.org/northern-ireland
Twitter: @CarersNI
Facebook: @carersuk

See main entry under Carers UK.

Carers Scotland

The Cottage
21 Pearce Street
Glasgow G51 3UT
Tel: 0141 445 3070
Email: info@carersscotland.org
Website: www.carersuk.org/scotland
Twitter: @CarersScotland
Facebook: @carersuk

See main entry under Carers UK.

Carers Wales

Unit 5
Ynys Bridge Court
Cardiff
CF15 9SS
Tel: 029 2081 1370
Email: info@carerswales.org
Website: www.carersuk.org/wales
Twitter: @carerswales
Facebook: @carersuk

See main entry under Carers UK.

Centre for Studies on Inclusive Education (CSIE)

The Park
Daventry Road
Knowle
Bristol BS4 1DQ
Tel: 0117 353 3150
Fax: 0117 353 3151
Email: admin@csie.org.uk
Website: www.csie.org.uk
Twitter: @CSIE_UK
Facebook: @csie.uk

Promoting inclusion for all children in restructured mainstream schools.

Challenging Behaviour Foundation

c/o The Old Courthouse
New Road Avenue
Chatham
Kent ME4 6BE
Tel: 01634 838739
Family support line: 0300 666 0126
Email: info@thecbf.org.uk
Website: www.challengingbehaviour.org.uk
Twitter: @CBFdn
Facebook: @thecbf

Supports families, professionals and stakeholders who live/work with people with severe learning disabilities who have challenging behaviour.

Child Brain Injury Trust (CBIT)

Unit 1, The Great Barn
Baynards Green Farm
Bicester
Oxfordshire OX27 7SG
Tel: 01869 341075
Email: info@cbituk.org
Website: www.childbraininjurytrust.org.uk
Twitter: @CBITUK
Facebook: @childbraininjurytrust

Formerly known as the Children's Head Injury Trust (CHIT) this organisation was originally set up in 1991. It offers support to children and families affected by brain injuries that happen after birth. Registered charity nos. 1113326 & SCO39703. Has Facebook page and you can follow them on Twitter.

Communication Matters

Leeds Innovation Centre
103 Clarendon Road
Leeds LS2 9DF
Tel/Fax: 0845 456 8211
Email: admin@communications.org.uk
Website: www.communicationmatters.org.uk
Twitter: @Comm_Matters
Facebook: @communicationmattersuk

Support for people who find communication difficult.

Contact a Family

209-211 City Road
London EC1V 1JN
Tel: 020 7608 8700
Helpline: 0808 808 3555 Textphone: 0808 808 3556
Fax: 020 7608 8701
Email: helpline@cafamily.org.uk
Website: www.cafamily.org.uk
Twitter: @ContactAFamily
Facebook: @contactafamily

A charity that provides support, advice and information to families with disabled children. Has a Facebook page and you can follow them on Twitter.

Coram Children's Legal Centre

Riverside Office Centre
Century House North, North Station Road
Colchester,
Essex CO1 1RE
Tel: 01206 714 650
Fax: 01206 714 660
Email: info@coramclc.org.uk
Website: www.childrenslegalcentre.com
Twitter: @CCLCUK
Facebook: @CCLCUK

The Children's Legal Centre is an independent national charity concerned with law and policy affecting children and young people. The centre runs a free and confidential legal advice and information service covering all aspects of law and the service is open to children, young people and anyone with concerns about them. The Education Legal Advocacy unit provides advice and representation to children and/or parents involved in education disputes with a school or a local education authority.

Council for Disabled Children

8 Wakley Street
London EC1V 7QE
Tel: 020 7843 1900
Fax: 020 7843 6313
Email: cdc@ncb.org.uk
Website: www.councilfordisabledchildren.org.uk
Twitter: @CDC_tweets
Facebook: @councilfordisabledchildren

The council promotes collaborative work and partnership between voluntary and non-voluntary agencies, parents and children and provides a national forum for the discussion, development and dissemination of a wide range of policy and practice issues relating to service provision and support for children and young people with disabilities and special educational needs. Has a particular interest in inclusive education, special education needs, parent partnership services, play and leisure and transition.

Council for the Registration of Schools Teaching Dyslexic Pupils (CReSTeD)

C/o Helen Arkell Dyslexia Centre,
Arkell Lane,
Frensham,
Farnham,
Surrey,
GU10 3BL
Email: admin@crested.org.uk
Website: www.crested.org.uk

CReSTeD's aim is to help parents and also those who advise them choose an educational establishment for children with Specific Learning Difficulties (SpLD). It maintains a register of schools and teaching centres which meets its criteria for the teaching of pupils with Specific Learning Difficulties.

All schools and centres included in the Register are visited regularly to ensure they continue to meet the criteria set by CReSTeD. CReSTeD acts as a source of names for educational establishments which parents can use as their first step towards making a placement decision which will be critical to their child's educational future.

CPotential

143 Coppetts Road
London
N10 1JP
Tel: 020 8444 7242
Fax: 020 8444 7241
Email: info@cplondon.org.uk
Website: www.cplondon.org.uk
Twitter: @C_Potential
Facebook: @CPotentialTrust

Provides education for young children with cerebral palsy using the system of Conductive Education.

Cystic Fibrosis Trust

One Aldgate
Second floor
London EC3N 1RE
Tel: 020 3795 1555
Helpline: 0300 373 1000 or 0203 795 2184
Fax: 020 8313 0472
Email: enquiries@cftrust.org.uk
Website: www.cftrust.org.uk
Twitter: @CFtrust
Facebook: @cftrust

The Cystic Fibrosis Trust is a national charity established in 1964. It offers information and support to people with cystic fibrosis, their families, their carers and anyone affected by cystic fibrosis. It funds research, offers some financial support to people with cystic fibrosis and campaigns for improved services. It provides a wide range of information including fact sheets, publications and expert concensus documents on treatment and care for people with cystic fibrosis.

Disabled Living Foundation

Unit 1, 34 Chatfield Road
Wandsworth
London SW11 3SE
Tel: 020 7289 6111
Helpline: 0300 999 0004
Email: info@dlf.org.uk
Website: www.dlf.org.uk
Twitter: @DLFUK
Facebook: @dlfuk

This foundation provides free, impartial advice about products for disabled people.

Down's Syndrome Education International

6 Underley Business Centre
Kirkby, Lonsdale
Cumbria LA6 2DY
Tel: 0300 330 0750
Fax: 0300 330 0754
Email: enquiries@downsed.org
Website: www.dseinternational.org
Twitter: @dseint
Facebook: @dseinternational

Down's Syndrome Education International works around the world to improve the development, education and social achievements of many thousands of people living with Down's syndrome. We undertake and support scientific research and disseminate quality information and advice widely through our websites, books, films and training courses.

Our education services support families and professionals to help people with Down's syndrome achieve sustained gains in all areas of their development.

For 30 years, we have disseminated the latest research findings in practical and accessible formats to the widest audiences, from birth to adulthood. Please visit our website for more information. We have a Facebook page and you can follow us on Twitter.

Down's Syndrome Association

Langdon Down Centre
2a Langdon Park
Teddington TW11 9PS
Tel: 0333 1212 300
Email: info@downs-syndrome.org.uk
Website: www.downs-syndrome.org.uk
Twitter: @DSAInfo
Facebook: @downssyndromeassociation

We provide information and support for people with Down's syndrome, their families and carers, and the professionals who work with them. We strive to improve knowledge of the condition. We champion the rights of people with Down's syndrome.

Down's Syndrome Association Northern Ireland

Unit 2, Marlborough House
348 Lisburn Road
Belfast BT9 6GH
Tel: 028 90666 5260
Fax: 028 9066 7674
Email: enquiriesni@downs-syndrome.org.uk

See main entry above.

Down's Syndrome Association Wales

Suite 1, 206 Whitchurch Road
Heath
Cardiff CF14 3NB
Tel: 0333 1212 300
Email: wales@downs-syndrome.org.uk

See main entry above.

Dyslexia Scotland

2nd floor – East Suite
Wallace House
17-21 Maxwell Place
Stirling FK8 1JU
Tel: 01786 446 650
Helpline: 0344 800 8484
Fax: 01786 471235
Email: info@dyslexiascotland.org.uk
Website: www.dyslexiascotland.org.uk
Twitter: @DyslexiaScotlan

Scottish association set up to support and campaign on behalf of people affected by dyslexia. They have a useful and easy to use website.

Dyspraxia Foundation

8 West Alley
Hitchin
Hertfordshire SG5 1EG
Tel: 01462 455016
Helpline: 01462 454 986
Fax: 01462 455052
Email: dyspraxia@dyspraxiafoundation.org.uk
Website: www.dyspraxiafoundation.org.uk
Twitter: @DYSPRAXIAFDTN
Facebook: @dyspraxiafoundation

The foundation exists to support individuals and families affected by dyspraxia; to promote better diagnostic and treatment facilities for those who have dyspraxia; to help professionals in health and education to assist those with dyspraxia; and to promote awareness and understanding of dyspraxia. As well as various publications, the Dyspraxia Foundation organises conferences and talks and supports a network of local groups across the United Kingdom.

Education Scotland

Denholm House
Almondvale Business Park
Almondvale Way
Livingston EH54 6GA
Tel: 0131 244 4330
Textphone: 18001+ 0131 244 4330
Email: enquiries@educationscotland.org.uk
Website: education.gov.scot
Twitter: @EducationScot
Facebook: @EducationScot

Education Scotland is an executive non-departmental public body sponsored by the Scottish government. It is the main organisation for the development and support of the Scottish curriculum and is at the heart of all major developments in Scottish education, moving education forward with its partners.

ENABLE Scotland

Inspire House
3 Renshaw Place
Eurocentral
Lanarkshire ML1 4UF
Tel: 01698 737 000
Fax: 0844 854 9748
Helpline: 0300 0200 101
Email: enabledirect@enable.org.uk
Website: www.enable.org.uk
Twitter: @ENABLEScotland
Facebook: @enablescotland

Contact the ENABLE Scotland Information Service about any aspect of learning disability. They offer jobs, training, respite breaks, day services, supported living, housing and support for people with learning disabilities in different parts of Scotland. Its legal service can assist families with wills and trusts.

English Federation of Disability Sport

Sport Park, Loughborough University
3 Oakwood Drive
Loughborough
Leicestershire LE11 3QF
Tel: 01509 227750
Fax: 0509 227777
Email: info@efds.co.uk
Website: www.efds.co.uk
Twitter: @Eng_Dis_Sport
Facebook: @EnglishDisabilitySport

A charity that creates opportunities for disabled people to participate in sporting activities.

Epilepsy Action

New Anstey House
Gate Way Drive,
Yeadon
Leeds LS19 7XY
Tel: 0113 210 880
Helpline: 0808 800 5050
Fax: 0113 391 0300
Email: epilepsy@epilepsy.org.uk
Website: www.epilepsy.org.uk
Twitter: @epilepsyaction
Facebook: @epilepsyaction

Epilepsy Action is the UK's leading epilepsy organisation and exists to improve the lives of everyone affected by the condition. As a member-led association, it is led by and represent people with epilepsy, their friends, families and healthcare professionals.

Epilepsy Society

Chesham Lane
Chalfont St Peter
Gerrards Cross,
Buckinghamshire SL9 0RJ
Tel: 01494 601300
Helpline: 01494 601400
Fax: 01494 871927
Website: www.epilepsysociety.org.uk
Twitter: @epilepsysociety
Facebook: @EpilepsySociety

The Epilepsy Society provides information and support to those affected by epilepsy.

GIFT

7 Tower Road
Writtle
Chelmsford
Essex CM1 3NR
Tel: 01245 830321
Email: enquiries@giftcourses.co.uk
Website: www.giftcourses.co.uk
Twitter: @giftcourses
Facebook: @giftcourses

GIFT aims to offer a value-for-money education consultancy of quality, which meets the needs of gifted and talented children and those working to support them in the excitement and challenge of achieving their full potential as human beings. Residential and non-residential courses are organised for exceptionally able children aged five to 18 throughout the year (see our website). INSET courses for schools on provision, identification and school policy are provided with a special emphasis on workshops for practical activities.

Haringey Association for Independent Living (HAIL)

Tottenham Town Hall
Town Hall Approach Road
Tottenham
London N15 4RY
Tel: 020 8275 6550
Fax: 020 8275 6559
Email: admin@hailltd.org
Website: www.hailltd.org
Twitter: @HAIL_tweets
Facebook: @HAIL6650

Haringey Association for Independent Living is a support service for adults with learning difficulties moving towards independent living. You can follow them on Twitter.

Headway

Bradbury House
190 Bagnall Road
Old Basford
Nottingham NG6 8SF
Tel: 0115 924 0800
Helpline: 0808 800 2244
Fax: 0115 958 4446
Email: enquiries@headway.org.uk
Website: www.headway.org.uk
Twitter: @HeadwayUK
Facebook: @headwayuk

A charity that supports people with brain injuries and their carers.

Helen Arkell Dyslexia Centre

Arkell Lane
Frensham
Farnham
Surrey GU10 3BL
Tel: 01252 792400
Email: enquiries@arkellcentre.org.uk
Website: www.arkellcentre.org.uk
Twitter: @ArkellDyslexia

A registered charity providing comprehensive help and care for children with specific learning difficulties, including assessment, specialist tuition, speech and language therapy, summer schools and short courses. Initial consultations can be arranged in order to give advice on options for support. Professional teacher-training programmes and schools' support. Financial help available in cases of need.

Huntington's Disease Association

Suite 24
Liverpool Science Park IC1
131 Mount Pleasant
Liverpool L3 5TF
Tel: 0151 331 5444
Fax: 0151 331 5441
Email: info@hda.org.uk
Website: www.hda.org.uk
Twitter: @HDA_tweeting
Facebook: @hdauk

Registered charity offering support to people affected by Huntington's Disease (HD); which is sometimes referred to as Huntington's Chorea. Has a Facebook page.

Independent Panel for Special Education Advice (IPSEA)

24 Gold Street
Saffron Walden CB10 1EJ
Tel: 01799 582030
Adviceline: 0800 018 4016
Email: info@ipsea.org.uk
Website: www.ipsea.org.uk
Twitter: @IPSEAcharity

IPSEA offers free and independent advice and support to parents of children with special educational needs including: free advice on LAs' legal duties towards children with free accompanied visits where necessary, free support and possible representation for those parents appealing to the Special Educational Needs Tribunal, free second opinions on a child's needs and the provision required to meet those needs.

Institute for Neuro-Physiological Psychology (INPP)

1 Stanley Street
Chester
Cheshire CH1 2LR
Tel: 01244 311414
Fax: 01244 311414
Email: mail@inpp.org.uk
Website: www.inpp.org.uk
Twitter: @INPPLtd
Facebook: @INPPLtd

Established in 1975 to research into the effect central nervous system (CNS) dysfunctions have on children with learning difficulties, to develop appropriate CNS remedial and rehabilitation programmes, and to correct underlying physical dysfunctions in dyslexia, dyspraxia and attention deficit disorder (ADD).

Ivemark Syndrome Association

18 French Road
Poole
Dorset BH17 7HB
Tel: 01202 699824
Email: marcus.fisher@virgin.net

Support group for families with children affected by Ivemark Syndrome (also know as right atrial isomerism).

Jeans for Genes

199 Victoria Street
London SW1E 5NE
Tel: 0800 980 4800
Email: hello@jeanforgenes.com
Website: www.jeansforgenes.com
Twitter: @JeansforGenes
Facebook: @JeansforGenesUK

The first Friday of every October is Jeans for Genes Day. Their aim is to raise money to fund research into genetic disorders and their target figure is £3million each year.

KIDS

7-9 Elliott's Place
London, N1 8HX
Tel: 020 7359 3635
Website: www.kids.org.uk
Twitter: @KIDScharity
Facebook: @KIDScharity

KIDS was established in 1970 to help disabled children in their development and communication skills. Has a Facebook page and you can follow them on Twitter.

Leonard Cheshire Disability England

66 South Lambeth Road
London SW8 1RL
Tel: 020 3242 0200
Fax: 020 3242 0250
Email: info@leonardcheshire.org
Website: www.leonardcheshire.org
Twitter: @LeonardCheshire
Facebook: @LeonardCheshireDisability

Leonard Cheshire – the UK's largest voluntary-sector provider of support services for disabled people. They also support disabled people in 52 countries around the world.

Leonard Cheshire Disability Northern Ireland

Unit 5, Boucher Plaza
Boucher Road
Belfast BT12 6HR
Tel: 028 9024 6247
Fax: 028 9024 6395
Email: northernirelandoffice@leonardcheshire.org

See main entry – Leonard Cheshire Disability England.

Leonard Cheshire Disability Scotland

Murrayburgh House
17 Corstorphine Road
Edinburgh EH12 6DD
Tel: 0131 346 9040
Fax: 0131 346 9050
Email: scotlandoffice@leonardcheshire.org

See main entry – Leonard Cheshire Disability England.

Leonard Cheshire Disability Wales

Llanhennock Lodge
Llanhennock
Nr Caerleon
NP18 1LT
Tel: 01633 422583
Email: walesoffice@leonardcheshire.org

See main entry – Leonard Cheshire Disability England.

Leukaemia Care UK

1 Birch Court
Blackpole East
Worcester WR3 8SG
Tel: 01905 755977 Careline: 08088 010 444
Fax: 01905 755 166
Email: care@leukaemiacare.org.uk
Website: www.leukaemiacare.org.uk
Twitter: @LeukaemiaCareUK
Facebook: @LeukaemiaCARE

Registered charity that exists to provide care and support to anyone affected by leukaemia.

Leukaemia Care Scotland

Regus Management
Maxim 1, Maxim Office Park
2 Parklands Way, Eurocentral
Motherwell ML1 4WR
Tel: 01698 209073
Email: scotland@leukaemiacare.org.uk

See main entry on Leukaemia Care UK.

Listening Books

12 Lant Street
London SE1 1QH
Tel: 020 7407 9417
Fax: 020 7403 1377
Email: info@listening-books.org.uk
Website: www.listening-books.org.uk
Twitter: @ListeningBooks
Facebook: @ListeningBooks12

A charity that provides a postal and internet based audio library service to anyone who is unable to read in the usual way due to an illness, disability or learning difficulty such as dyslexia.

Has a range of educational audio material to support all aspects of the National Curriculum, as well as thousands of general fiction and non-fiction titles for all ages. There is no limit to the number of titles you may borrow during the year.

Manx Dyslexia Association

Coan Aalin
Greeba Bridge
Greba
Isle of Man IM4 3LD
Tel: 07624 315724
Email: manxdyslexia@gmail.com
Website: www.manxdyslexia.com

Charity (no. IM706) founded in 1993 to help raise the awareness of dyslexia on the Isle of Man.

MENCAP England

123 Golden Lane
London EC1Y 0RT
Tel: 020 7454 0454
Helpline: 0808 808 1111
Fax: 020 7608 3254
Email: information@mencap.org.uk
Website: www.mencap.org.uk
Twitter: @mencap_charity
Facebook: @Mencap

The Royal MENCAP Society is a registered charity that offers services to adults and children with learning disabilities. We offer help and advice in benefits, housing and employment via our helpline.

Helplines are open from Monday to Friday 9.30am-4.30pm; Wednesday – subject to change: (open am-closed pm). Language line is also used. Our office is open Monday-Friday 9-5pm.

We also offer help and advice to anyone who has any other issues or we can signpost them in the right direction. We can also provide information and support for leisure, recreational services (Gateway Clubs) residential services and holidays.

MENCAP Northern Ireland

5 School Road
Newtownbreda
Belfast BT8 6BT
Tel: 028 9069 1351
Email: helpline.ni@mencap.org.uk
Twitter: @Mencap_NI

See main entry – MENCAP England.

MENCAP Cymru

31 Lambourne Crescent
Cardiff Business Park
Llanishen, Cardiff CF14 5GF
Helpline: 02920 747588
Email: helpline.wales@mencap.org.uk
Twitter: @MencapCymru

See main entry – MENCAP England.

MENSA

British Mensa Ltd
St John's House
St John's Square
Wolverhampton WV2 4AH
Tel: 01902 772771
Fax: 01902 392500
Email: enquiries@mensa.org.uk
Website: www.mensa.org.uk
Twitter: @BritishMensa
Facebook: @BritishMensa

MENSA aims to bring about awareness that giftedness in a child is frequently a specific learning difficulty and should be recognised and treated as such, train teachers to recognise giftedness in a child, train teachers to teach gifted children, establish mutually beneficial relationships with other organisations having similar aims to our own and to devise and implement strategies aimed, at ministerial and senior civil servant levels, at bringing about recognition of the importance of catering for the needs of gifted children.

Mind, the National Association for Mental Health

15-19 Broadway
Stratford
London E15 4BQ
Tel: 020 8519 2122
Fax: 020 8522 1725
Email: suppoterservices@mind.org.uk
Website: www.mind.org.uk
Twitter: @MindCharity
Facebook: @mindforbettermentalhealth

Mind (the National Association for Mental Health) is the leading mental health charity in England and Wales. Mind works for a better life for everyone with experience of mental or emotional stress. It does this by: advancing the views, needs and ambitions of people experiencing mental distress; promoting inclusion and challenging discrimination; influencing policy through effective campaigning and education; providing quality services that meet the expressed needs of people experiencing mental distress and which reflect the requirements of a diverse community; achieving equal legal and civil rights through campaigning and education.

With over 60 years of experience, Mind is a major national network consisting of over 200 local Mind associations, which cover most major towns and rural areas in England and Wales. These are separately registered charities operating under the Mind brand. The Mind network is the largest charitable provider of mental health services in the community. The work of the local associations is strengthened and supported by staff and activities through its many offices in England and Wales. This ensures that, as a national charity, Mind keeps a distinct local perspective to their work.

Mind believes in the individual and equipping them to make informed choices about options open to them. Mind's mental health telephone information service (Mindinfoline) deals with thousands of calls each year. We offer a vital lifeline to people in distress, their relatives and carers, as well as providing mental health information to members of the public, professionals and students.

Mind Cymru

3rd Floor, Quebec House
Castlebridge
5-19 Cowbridge Road East
Cardiff CF11 9AB
Tel: 029 2039 5123
Fax: 029 2034 6585
Email: contactwales@mind.org.uk

See main entry above.

Motability

City Gate House
22 Southwark Bridge Road
London SE1 9HB
Tel: 0300 4564566
Minicom/textphone: 0300 037 0100
Fax: 01279 632000
Website: www.motability.co.uk
Facebook: @motability

Motability helps disabled people to use their mobility allowance to obtain new transport.

MS Society

MS National Centre
372 Edgware Road
London NW2 6ND
Tel: 020 8438 0700
Fax: 020 8438 0701
Website: www.mssociety.org.uk
Twitter: @MSSocietyUK
Facebook: @MSSociety

Multiple Sclerosis Society.

MS Society Cymru

Temple Court
Cathedral Road
Cardiff CF11 9HA
Tel: 029 2078 6676
See main entry above.

MS Society Northern Ireland

The Resource Centre
34 Annadale Avenue
Belfast BT7 3JJ
Tel: 02890 802 802
See main entry above.

MS Society Scotland

National Office, Ratho Park
88 Glasgow Road
Ratho Station
Newbridge EH28 8PP
Tel: 0131 335 4050
Fax: 0131 335 4051
See main entry on MS Society.

Muscular Dystrophy Campaign

61A Great Suffolk Street
London SE1 0BU
Tel: 020 7803 4800
Helpline: 0800 652 6352
Email: info@musculardystrophyuk.org
Website: www.musculardystrophyuk.org
Twitter: @MDUK_News
Facebook: @musculardystrophyuk

Provides information and advice for families affected by muscular dystrophy and other neuromuscular conditions.

NAS – The National Autistic Society – England

393 City Road
London EC1V 1NG
Tel: 020 7833 2299
Helpline: 0800 800 4104
Fax: 020 7833 9666
Email: nas@nas.org.uk
Website: www.autism.org.uk
Twitter: @Autism
Facebook: @NationalAutisticSociety

The National Autistic Society is the UK's leading charity for people who are affected by autism. For more than 50 years we have worked to support children and young people with autism (including Asperger syndrome) to reach their goals. A well-rounded education, tailored to the needs of the individual, can help people to reach their full potential.

NAS Cymru

6/7 Village Way,
Greenmeadow Springs Business Park
Tongwynlais
Cardiff CF15 7NE
Tel: 02920 629 312
Fax: 02920 629 317
Email: wales@nas.org.uk

See main entry NAS – England.

NAS Northern Ireland

59 Malone Road
Belfast BT9 6SA
Tel: 02890 687 066
Fax: 02890 688 518
Email: northern.ireland@nas.org.uk

See main entry NAS – England.

NAS Scotland

Central Chambers
1st Floor
109 Hope Street
Glasgow G2 6LL
Tel: 0141 221 8090
Fax: 0141 221 8118
Email: scotland@nas.org.uk

See main entry NAS – England.

Nasen

4/5 Amber Business Village
Amber Close
Amington
Tamworth
Staffordshire B77 4RP
Tel: 01827 311500
Fax: 01827 313005
Email: welcome@nasen.org.uk
Website: www.nasen.org.uk
Twitter: @nasen_org
Facebook: @nasen.org

nasen promotes the interests of children and young people with exceptional learning needs and influences the quality of provision through strong and cohesive policies and strategies for parents and professionals.

Membership offers a number of journals, professional development and publications at a reduced cost, and provides a forum for members to share concerns and disseminate expertise and knowledge.

National Association for Able Children in Education (NACE)

NACE National Office
Horticulture House
Manor Court
Chilton
Didcot
Oxfordshire OX11 0RN
Tel: 01235 425000
Email: info@nace.co.uk
Website: www.nace.co.uk
Twitter: @naceuk

NACE works with teachers to support able children in schools. The organisation also provides, publications, journals, booklets, courses and conferences.

National Association of Independent Schools and Non-Maintained Special Schools (NASS)

PO Box 705
York YO30 6WW
Tel: 01904 624446
Email: krippon@nasschools.org.uk
Website: www.nasschools.org.uk
Twitter: @NASSCHOOLS

NASS is a voluntary organisation that represents the interests of those special schools outside the maintained sector of the education system.

Our commitment is to achieve excellence and to attain the highest professional standards in working with unique children and young people who have physical, sensory and intellectual difficulties. We exist to promote, develop and maintain the highest professional standards for non-maintained and independent special schools. We offer free information and advice on our member schools to families and professionals.

National Federation of the Blind of the UK

St John Wilson House
215 Kirkgate
Wakefield
Yorkshire WF1 1JG
Tel: 01924 291313
Fax: 01924 200244
Email: admin@nfbuk.org
Website: www.nfbuk.org
Twitter: @NFBUK

A charity that was set up to better the understanding between blind and sighted people.

Natspec

Robins Wood House
Robins Wood Road
Aspley
Nottingham NG8 3NH
Tel: 0115 854 1322
Email: info@natspec.org.uk
Website: www.natspec.org.uk
Twitter: @Natspec

Natspec represents independent specialist colleges across England, Wales and Northern Ireland, providing for over 3000 learners with learning difficulties and/or disabilities, often with complex or additional needs. Most colleges offer residential provision. Member colleges support learners in their transition to adult life, participation in the community and where possible, employment.

Natspec acts as a national voice for its member colleges and works in partnership with a range of other providers, agencies and organisations. You can contact colleges directly, via the website, or through your connexions/careers service.

NDCS – The National Deaf Children's Society

Ground Floor South, Castle House
37-45 Paul Street
London
EC2A 4LS
Tel: 020 7490 8656
Minicom: 020 7490 8656
Fax: 020 7251 5020
Email: ndcs@ndcs.org.uk
Website: www.ndcs.org.uk
Twitter: @NDCS_UK
Facebook: @NDCS.UK

Leading provider of information, advice, advocacy and support for deaf children, their parents and professionals on all aspects of childhood deafness. This includes advice and information on education, including further and higher education, and support at Special Educational Needs Tribunals.

NDCS also provides advice on equipment and technology for deaf children at home and at school.

NDCS Cmyru

Ty-Nant Court, Morganstown, Cardiff, South
Glamorgan CF15 8LW
Tel: 029 2037 3474
Minicom: 029 20811861
Fax: 029 2081 4900
Email: ndcswales@ndcs.org.uk

See main entry above.

NDCS Northern Ireland

38-42 Hill Street
Belfast BT1 2LB
Tel: 028 9031 3170
Text: 028 9027 8177
Fax: 028 9027 8205
Email: nioffice@ndcs.org.uk

See main entry above.

NDCS Scotland

Second Floor, Empire House
131 West Nile Street
Glasgow G1 2RX
Tel: 0141 354 7850
Textphone: 0141 332 6133
Fax: 0141 331 2780
Email: ndcs.scotland@ndcs.org.uk

See main entry above.

Network 81

10 Boleyn Way
West Clacton
Essex CO15 2NJ
Tel: 0845 077 4056 (Admin)
Helpline: 0845 077 4055
Fax: 0845 077 4058
Email: Network81@hotmail.co.uk
Website: www.network81.org.uk

Network 81 offers practical help and support to parents throughout all stages of assessment and statementing as outlined in the Education Act 1996. Their national helpline offers an individual service to parents linked to a national network of local contacts.

NIACE – National Learning and Work Institute

Chetwynd House
21 DeMontfort Street
Leicester LE1 7GE
Tel: 0116 204 4200
Fax: 0116 204 6988
Email: enquiries@learningandwork.org.uk
Website: www.learningandwork.org.uk
Twitter: @LearnWorkUK
Facebook: @festivaloflearning

Works across sectors and age groups to raise national standards and encourage adults in achieving literacy, numeracy and language skills. You can follow them on Twitter.

NOFAS – UK (National Organisation for Fetal Alcohol Syndrome)

022 Southbank House
Black Prince Road, Lambeth
London SE1 7SJ
Tel: 0208 458 5951
Email: info@nofas-uk.org
Website: www.nofas-uk.org
Twitter: @NOFASUK
Facebook: @nofasuk

Offers advice, support and information about Foetal Alcohol Spectrum Disorder.

Paget Gorman Signed Speech

PGS Administrative Secretary
43 Westover Road
Fleet GU51 3DB
Tel: 01252 621 183
Website: www.pagetgorman.org

Advice and information for parents and professionals concerned with speech and language-impaired children.

Parents for Inclusion (PI)

336 Brixton Road
London SW9 7AA
Tel: 020 7738 3888
Helpline: 0800 652 3145
Email: info@parentsforinclusion.org
Website: www.parentsforinclusion.org

A network of parents of disabled children and children with special needs.

Physically Disabled and Able Bodied (PHAB Ltd)

Summit House
50 Wandle Road
Croydon
CR0 1DF
Tel: 020 8667 9443
Fax: 020 8681 1399
Email: info@phab.org.uk
Website: www.phab.org.uk
Twitter: @phab_charity
Facebook: @PhabCharity

A charity that works to promote and encourage people with and without physical disabilities to work together to achieve inclusion for all in the wider community.

Potential Plus UK

Suite 1-2
Challenge House
Sherwood Drive
Bletchley
Milton Keynes MK3 6DP
Tel: 01908 646433
Fax: 0870 770 3219
Email: amazingchildren@potentialplusuk.org
Website: www.potentialplusuk.org
Twitter: @PPUK_
Facebook: @PotentialPlusUK

A mutually supportive self-help organisation offering services both through local branches and nationally. Membership is open to individuals, families, education professionals and schools.

Royal National Institute of Blind People (RNIB)

105 Judd Street
London WC1H 9NE
Tel: 020 7388 1266
Helpline: 0303 123 9999
Email: helpline@rnib.org.uk
Website: www.rnib.org.uk
Twitter: @RNIB
Facebook: @rnibuk

We're RNIB (Royal National Institute of Blind People) and we're here for everyone affected by sight loss. Whether you're losing your sight or you're blind or partially sighted, our practical and emotional support can help you face the future with confidence.

We raise awareness of sight problems, and how to prevent sight loss, and we campaign for better services and a more inclusive society.

We offer a wide range of services for blind and partially sighted children and young people, their families and the professionals who work with them. This includes children and young people with additional disabilities and multiple complex needs.

As well as our specialist schools, college and residences we offer:
- Equipment, toys and games
- Accessible books
- Family support
- Teaching and learning guidance and resources
- Information and networks for young people
- Research and campaigns

Scope

6 Market Road
London N7 9PW
Helpline: 0808 800 3333 (Scope response)
Tel: 020 7619 7100
Text SCOPE plus message to 80039
Email: helpline@scope.org.uk
Website: www.scope.org.uk
Twitter: @Scope
Facebook: @Scope

Scope is a national disability organisation whose focus is people with cerebral palsy. We provide a range of support, information and campaigning services both locally and nationally in addition to providing opportunities in early years, education, employment and daily living. For more information about cerebral palsy and Scope services, contact Scope Response, which provides free information, advice and initial counselling. Open 9am-7pm weekdays and 10am-2pm Saturdays.

Scope Cymru

4 Ty Nant Court
Morganstown
Cardiff CF15 8LW
Tel: 029 20 815 450
Email: helpline@scope.org.uk

See main entry above.

Scottish Society for Autism

Hilton House,
Alloa Business Park
Whins Road
Alloa FK10 3SA
Tel: 01259 720044
Advice line: 01259 222022
Twitter: @scottishautism
Email: autism@scottishautism.org
Website: www.scottishautism.org
Twitter: @scottishautism
Facebook: @scottishautism

The Scottish Society for Autism is a registered charity established in 1968. They aim to work with individuals of all ages with autism spectrum disorder (ASD), their families and carers, to provide and promote exemplary services and training in education, care, support and life opportunities.

Sense – The National Deafblind Charity

101 Pentonville Road
London N1 9LG
Tel: 0300 330 9250
Textphone: 0300 330 9252
Fax: 0300 330 9251
Email: info@sense.org.uk
Website: www.sense.org.uk
Twitter: @sensecharity
Facebook: @sensecharity

Sense is the leading national charity that supports and campaigns for children and adults who are deafblind. They provide expert advice and information as well as specialist services to deafblind people, their families, carers and the professionals who work with them. They support people who have sensory impairments with additional disabilities.

Services include on-going support for deafblind people and families. These range from day services where deafblind people have the opportunity to learn new skills and Sense-run houses in the community – where people are supported to live as independently as possible. They provide leading specialist advice, for example on education options and assistive technology.

Shine

42 Park Road
Peterborough PE1 2UQ
Tel: 01733 555988
Fax: 01733 555985
Email: info@shinecharity.org.uk
Website: www.shinecharity.org.uk
Twitter: @SHINEUKCharity
Facebook: @ShineUKCharity

The new name for the Association for Spina Bifida and Hydrocephalus (ASBAH). Europe's largest organisation dedicated to supporting individuals and families as they face the challenges arising from spina bifida and hydrocephalus. Advisers are available to explain the problems associated with spina bifida and or hydrocephalus and may be able to arrange visits to schools and colleges to discuss difficulties. Has a Facebook page and you can follow them on Twitter.

Signature

Mersey House
Mandale Business Park
Belmont
Country Durham DH1 1TH
Tel: 0191 383 1155
Text: 07974 121594
Fax: 0191 3837914
Email: enquiries@signature.org.uk
Website: www.signature.org.uk
Twitter: @SignatureDeaf
Facebook: @SignatureDeaf

Association promoting communication with deaf and deafblind people.

SNAP-CYMRU

Head Office
10 Coopers Yard
Curran Road
Cardiff CF10 5NB
Tel: 02920 348 990
Helpline: 0808 801 0608
Textphone: 0345 120 3730
Fax: 029 2034 8998
Email: enquiries@snapcymru.org
Website: www.snapcymru.org
Twitter: @SNAPcymru
Facebook: @SNAPCymru

An all-Wales service for children and families, which provides: accurate information and impartial advice and support for parents, carers, and young people in relation to special educational needs and disability; disagreement resolution service; casework service; independent parental support service; advocacy for children and young people in receipt of services; training for parents, carers, young people; training for professionals in relation to SEN/disability. Has a Facebook page.

Spinal Injuries Association

SIA House
2 Trueman Place
Oldbrook
Milton Keynes MK6 2HH
Tel: 01908 604 191
Adviceline: 0800 980 0501
Text: 81025
Email: sia@spinal.co.uk
Website: www.spinal.co.uk
Twitter: @spinalinjuries
Facebook: @SpinalInjuriesAssociation

Set up to provide services for people with spinal cord injuries.

The Ace Centre

Hollinwood Business Centre,
Albert Street
Oldham OL8 3QL
Tel: 0161 358 0151
Fax: 0161 358 6152
Helpline: 0800 080 3115
Email: enquiries@acecentre.org.uk
Website: www.acecentre.org.uk
Twitter: @AceCentre
Facebook: @AceCentre.uk

The centre offers independent advice and information, assessments and training in the use of assistive technology for individuals with physical and communication disabilities across the north of England.

The Alliance for Inclusive Education

336 Brixton Road
London SW9 7AA
Tel: 020 7737 6030
Email: info@allfie.org.uk
Website: www.allfie.org.uk
Twitter: @ALLFIEUK
Facebook: @ALLFIEUK

National network campaigning for the rights of disabled children in education.

The Brittle Bone Society

Grant-Paterson House
30 Guthrie Street
Dundee DD1 5BS
Tel: 01382 204446
Fax: 01382 206771
Email: bbs@brittlebone.org
Website: www.brittlebone.org
Twitter: @BrittleBoneUK
Facebook: @brittlebonesociety

A UK registered charity providing support for people affected by Osteogenesis Imperfecta (OI).

The Disability Law Service

The Foundry, 17 Oval Way,
London, SE11 5RR
Tel: 020 7791 9800
Fax: 020 7791 9802
Email: advice@dls.org.uk
Website: www.dls.org.uk
Twitter: @DLS_law
Facebook: @disabilitylawservice

The Disability Law Service (DLS) offers free, confidential legal advice to disabled people in the following areas: benefits; children; community care; consumer/contract; discrimination; further and higher education; and employment.

In some cases they are able to offer legal representation. The Disability Law Service is made up of solicitors, advisers and trained volunteers who provide up-to-date, informed legal advice for disabled people, their families, enablers and carers.

The Fragile X Society

Rood End House
6 Stortford Road
Great Dunmow,
Essex CM6 1DA
Tel: 01371 875 100
Fax: 01371 859 915
Email: info@fragilex.org.uk
Website: www.fragilex.org.uk
Twitter: @fragilexuk
Facebook: @thefragilexsociety

The aims of The Fragile X Society are to provide support and comprehensive information to families whose children and adult relatives have fragile X syndrome, to raise awareness of fragile X and to encourage research. There is a link network of family contacts, national helplines for statementing, benefits and family support for epilepsy. They publish information booklets, leaflets, a publications list, video and three newsletters a year. There are also national conferences four times a year. Family membership (UK) is free. Welcomes associate membership from interested professionals.

The Guide Dogs for the Blind Association

Hillfields
Burghfield Common
Reading
Berkshire RG7 3YG
Tel: 0118 983 5555
Fax: 0118 983 5433
Email: guidedogs@guidedogs.org.uk
Website: www.guidedogs.org.uk
Twitter: @guidedogs

Blind Children UK and Guide Dogs have fully integrated into one charity to become The Guide Dogs for the Blind Association, building on their existing services to support more children with sight loss and the issues they face. The Guide Dogs for the Blind Association provides guide dogs, mobility and other rehabilitation services to blind and partially sighted people.

The Haemophilia Society

Willcox House,
140 – 148 Borough High Street
London, SE1 1LB
Tel: 0207 939 0780
Email: info@haemophilia.org.uk
Website: www.haemophilia.org.uk
Twitter: @HaemoSocUK
Facebook: @HaemophiliaSocietyUK

Founded in 1950, this registered charity has over 4000 members and a network throughout the UK providing information, advice and support services to sufferers of haemophilia, von Willebrand's and related bleeding disorders. You can follow them on Twitter.

The Hyperactive Children's Support Group (HACSG)

71 Whyke Lane
Chichester
Sussex PO19 7PD
Tel: 01243 539966
Email: hacsg@hacsg.org.uk
Website: www.hacsg.org.uk

Support group. Will send information pack if you send a large SAE.

The Makaton Charity

Westmead House
Farnborough
Hampshire GU14 7LP
Tel: 01276 606760
Fax: 01276 36725
Email: info@makaton.org
Website: www.makaton.org
Twitter: @MakatonCharity
Facebook: @TheMakatonCharity

Makaton vocabulary is a language programme using speech, signs and symbols to provide basic means of communication and encourage language and literacy skills to develop in children and adults with communication and learning difficulties. Training workshops, courses and a variety of resource materials are available and there is a family support helpline too.

The Planned Environment Therapy Trust (PETT)

Archive and Study Centre
Church Lane
Toddington
Cheltenham
Gloucestershire GL54 5DQ
Tel: 01242 621200
Fax: 01242 620125
Website: www.pettrust.org.uk
Twitter: @pettconnect

Founded to promote effective treatment for those with emotional and psychological disorders.

The Social, Emotional and Behavioural Difficulties Association (SEBDA)

c/o Goldwyn School
Godinton Lane
Great Chart
Ashford
Kent TN23 3BT
Tel: 01233 622958
Email: admin@sebda.org
Website: www.sebda.org
Twitter: @SebdaOrg

SEBDA exists to campaign on behalf of and to provide information, training and a support service to professionals who work with children and young people with social, emotional and behavioural difficulties. Please note: they do not provide any services to parents.

The Stroke Association

Stroke House
240 City Road
London EC1V 2PR
Tel: 020 7566 0300
Helpline: 0303 3033 100
Fax: 020 7490 2686
Email: info@stroke.org.uk
Website: www.stroke.org.uk
Twitter: @thestrokeassoc
Facebook: @TheStrokeAssociation

More than 250,000 people in the UK live with the disabilities caused by a stroke. The association's website provides information and advice for free.

The Talent Development Programmes

Brunel University
School of Sport & Education,
Kingston Lane
Uxbridge, Middlesex UB8 3PH
Tel: 01895 267152
Fax: 01895 269806
Email: catherina.emery@brunel.ac.uk
Website: www.brunel.ac.uk/cbass/education/research/bace

Conducts research into all aspects of identification and provision for able and exceptionally able children. The centre has been involved in supporting the education of able children in inner city schools for a number of years. A number of courses are run for teachers to train them to make effective provision for able pupils.

The Thalidomide Society

Tel: 020 8464 9048
Email: info@thalidomidesociety.org
Website: www.thalidomidesociety.org
Twitter: @ThalSociety

Created in 1962. A support group for impaired adults whose disabilities are a result of the drug Thalidomide.

Together for Short Lives

New Bond House,
Bond Street
Bristol, BS2 9AG
Tel: 0117 989 7820
Helpline: 0808 8088 100
Email: info@togetherforshortlives.org
Website: www.togetherforshortlives.org.uk
Twitter: @Tog4ShortLives
Facebook: @togetherforshortlives

The new name for the Association for Children's Palliative Care (ACT). Helps families with children who have life-limiting or life threatening conditions.

Tourette's Action

The Meads Business Centre,
19 Kingsmead, Farnborough,
Hampshire, GU14 7SR
Tel: 0300 777 8427
Email: admin@tourettes-action.org.uk
Website: www.tourettes-action.org.uk
Twitter: @tourettesaction
Facebook: @TourettesAction

Registered charity offering support and information about Tourette's.

U Can Do IT

1 Taylors Yard
67 Alderbrook Road
London SW12 8AD
Tel: 020 8673 3300
Fax: 020 8675 9571
Website: www.ucandoit.org.uk
Twitter: @ucdit

U CAN DO IT is a London charity providing blind, deaf and physically disabled children and adults with the skills they need to utilise the internet. Tuition is one to one at home with costs starting from £1 per lesson.

WheelPower – British Wheelchair Sport

Stoke Mandeville Stadium
Guttman Road
Stoke Mandeville
Buckinghamshire HP21 9PP
Tel: 01296 395995
Fax: 01296 424171
Email: info@wheelpower.org.uk
Website: www.wheelpower.org.uk
Twitter: @wheelpower
Facebook: @wheelchairsport

The British Wheelchair Sports Foundation is the national organisation for wheelchair sport in the UK and exists to provide, promote and develop opportunities for men, women and children with disabilities to participate in recreational and competitive wheelchair sport.

Young Minds

Suite 11
Baden Place
Crosby Row
London SE1 1YW
Tel: 020 7089 5050
Parent Hotline: 0808 802 5544
Fax: 020 7407 8887
Website: www.youngminds.org.uk
Email: ymenquiries@youngminds.org.uk
Twitter: @youngmindsuk
Facebook: @youngmindsuk

National charity committed to improving the mental health of young people and children in the UK. Their website has advice, information and details of how you can help.

WEBSITES

www.abilitynet.org.uk

Ability Net is a charity that provides impartial, expert advice about computer technology for disabled people. You can follow them on Twitter.

www.abilityonline.net

Disability information and news and views online.

www.actionondisability.org.uk

Formerly HAFAD – Hammersmith and Fuham Action for Disability. Campaigning for rights of disabled people, the site is managed and controlled by disabled people.

www.amyandfriends.org

Website set up to support those families affected by Cockayne Syndrome in the UK.

www.cae.org.uk

Centre for Accessible Environments is the leading authority on providing a built enviroment that is accessible for everyone, including disabled people.

www.choicesandrights.org.uk

CRDC – Choices and Rights Disability Coalition. Run for and by disabled people in the Kingston upon Hull and East Riding of Yorkshire area.

www.deafcouncil.org.uk

UK Council on Deafness. Has interesting list of member websites.

www.disabilitynow.org.uk

Disability Now – award winning online newspaper for everyone with an interest in disability.

www.direct.gov.uk/disabledpeople

The UK government's web page for disabled people..

www.focusondisability.org.uk

Focus on Disability – resource of general information regarding disability in the UK.

www.heartnsoul.co.uk

Heart 'n' Soul Music Theatre – a leading disability arts group. Has a Facebook page.

www.ncil.org

National Centre for Independent Living. A resource on independent living and direct payments for disabled people and others working in the field.

www.peoplefirstinfo.org.uk

WELDIS – an online information resource of services in and around Westminster for older people, adults and children with disabilities and their carers.

www.qef.org.uk

Queen Elizabeth's Foundation – a national charity supporting over 20,000 physically disabled people annually.

www.revitalise.org.uk

Revitalise (formerly The Winged Fellowship Trust) provides respite care for disabled children, adults and their carers.

www.ssc.education.ed.ac.uk

Scottish Sensory Centre – for everyone who is involved in the education of children and young people with sensory impairment.

www.theark.org.uk

A registered charity set up to enhance the lives of people with multi-sensory impairment, learning difficulties and physical disabilities.

www.tuberous-sclerosis.org

Tuberous Sclerosis Association of Great Britain. Website provides information and support for people and families affected by TSC.

www.youreable.com

Information, products and services for the disabled community including news, shopping, pen pals and discussion forums.

Glossary

ACLD	Autism, Communication and Associated Learning Difficulties
ADD	Attention Deficit Order
ADHD	Attention Deficit and Hyperactive Disorder (Hyperkinetic Disorder)
AdvDip SpecEduc	Advanced Diploma in Special Education
AFBPS	Associate Fellow of the British Psychological Society
ALAN	Adult Literacy and Numeracy
ALCM	Associate of the London College of Music
ALL	Accreditation of Lifelong Learning
AOC	Association of Colleges
AQA	Assessment and Qualification Alliance/ Northern Examinations and Assessment Board
ASC	Autistic Spectrum Conditions
ASD	Autistic Spectrum Disorder
ASDAN	Qualifications for 11-16 age range
ASP	Asperger syndrome
AUT	Autism
AWCEBD	now SEBDA
BA	Bachelor of Arts
BDA	British Dyslexic Association
BESD	Behavioural, Emotional and Social Difficulties
BMET	Biomedical Engineering Technologist
BPhil	Bachelor of Philosophy
BSc	Bachelor of Science
BSL	British Sign Language
BTEC	Range of practical work-related programmes; which lead to qualifications equivalent to GCSEs and A levels (awarded by Edexcel)
C & G	City & Guilds Examination
C(Ed) Psychol	Certificate in Educational Psychology
CACDP	Council for the Advancement of Communication with Deaf People
CAMHS	Child and Adolescent Mental Health Service
CB	Challenging Behaviour
CD	Communcation Difficulties
CertEd	Certificate of Education
CF	Cystic Fibrosis
CLAIT	Computer Literacy and Information Technology
CLD	Complex Learning Difficulties
CNS	Central Nervous System
COPE	Certificate of Personal Effectiveness
CP	Cerebral Palsy
CPD	Continuing Professional Development
CRB	Criminal Records Bureau
CReSTeD	Council for the Registration of Schools Teaching Dyslexic Pupils
CSSE	Consortium of Special Schools in Essex
CSSIW	Care and Social Services Inspectorate for Wales
CTEC	Computer-aided Training, Education and Communication
D	Deaf
DDA	Disability Discrimination Act
DEL	Delicate
DfE	Department for Education
DIDA	Diploma in Digital Applications
DipAppSS	Diploma in Applied Social Sciences
DipEd	Diploma of Education
DipSEN	Diploma in Speial Educational Needs
DipSpEd	Diploma in Special Education
DT	Design and Technology
DYC	Dyscalculia
DYSL	Dyslexia
DYSC	Dyscalculia
DYSP	Dyspraxia
EASIE	Exercise and Sound in Education
EBD	Emotional, Behavioural Difficulties
EBSD	Emotional, Behavioural and/or Social Difficulties
ECDL	European Computer Driving Licence
ECM	Every Child Matters (Government Green Paper)
EdMng	Educational Management
ELC	Early Learning Centre
ELQ	Equivalent or Lower Qualification
EPI	Epilepsy
EQUALS	Entitlement and Quality Education for Pupils with Learning Difficulties
FAS	Foetal Alcohol Syndrome
FLSE	Federation of Leaders in Special Education
FXS	Fragile X Syndrome
GLD	General Learning Difficulties
HA	High Ability
HANDLE	Holistic Approach to Newuro-DEvelopment and Learning Efficiency
HEA	Higher Educaiton Authority/Health Education Authority
HI	Hearing Impairment
HS	Hospital School
ICT	Information Communication Technology

Glossary

IEP	Individual Education Plan
IIP	Investors in People
IM	Idiopathic Myelofibrosis
ISI	Independent Schools Inspectorate
IT	Information Technology
KS	Key Stage
LA	Local Authority
LD	Learning Difficulties
LDD	Learning Difficulties and Disabilities
LISA	London International Schools Association
MA	Master of Arts
MAPA	Management of Actual or Potential Aggression
MBA	Master of Business Administration
MD	Muscular Dystrophy
MDT	Multidisciplinary Team
MEd	Master of Education
MLD	Moderate Learning Difficulties
MS	Multiple Sclerosis
MSc	Master of Science
MSI	Multi-sensory Impairment
NAES	National Association of EBD Schools
NAS	National Autistic Society
NASEN	Northern Association of Special Educational Needs
NASS	National Association of Independent Schools & Non-maintained Special Schools
NATSPEC	National Association of Specialist Colleges
NOCN	National Open College Network
NPQH	National Professional Qualification for Headship
NVQ	National Vocational Qualifications
OCD	Obsessive Compulsive Disorder
OCN	Open Course Network
ODD	Oppositional Defiant Disorder
OT	Occupational Therapist
P scales	method of recording the achievements of SEN students who are working towards the first levels of the National Curriculum
PACT	Parents Association of Children with Tumours
PACT	Parents and Children Together
PCMT	Professional and Clinical Multidisciplinary Team
PD	Physical Difficulties
PDA	Pathological Demand Avoidance
PE	Physical Education
PECS	Picture Exchange Communication System

PGCE	Post Graduate Certificate in Education
PGCertSpld	Post Graduate Certificate in Specific Learning Difficulties
PGTC	Post Graduate Teaching Certificate
PH	Physical Impairment
PhD	Doctor of Philosophy
Phe	Partially Hearing
PMLD	Profound and Multiple Learning Difficulties
PNI	Physical Neurological Impairment
PRU	Pupil Referral Unit
PSHCE	Personal Social Health, Citizenship and Economics
RE	Religious Education
SAT	Standard Asessment Test
SCD	Social and Communication Difficulties
SCLD	Severe and Complex Learning Difficulties
SEAL	Social and Emotional Aspects of Learning
SEBD	Severe Emotional and Behavioural Disorders
SEBDA	Social, Emotional and Behavioural Difficulties Association
SEBN	Social, Emotional and Behavioural Needs
SEMH	Social, Emotional and Mental Health Needs
SLCN	Speech, Language and Communicational Needs
SLD	Severe Learning Difficulties
SLI	Specific Language Impairment
SLT	Speech and Language Teacher
SP	Special Purpose/Speech Processing
SpEd	Special Education
SPLD	Specific Learning Difficulties
SP&LD	Speech and Language Difficulties
STREAM	Strong Therapeutic, Restoring Environment and Assesssment Model
SWALSS	South and West Association of Leaders in Special Schools
SWSF	Steiner Waldorf Schools Foundation
TAV	Therapeutic, Academic and Vocational
TEACCH	Treatment and Education of Autistic and related Communication Handicapped Children (also sometimes written as TEACHH)
TCI	Therapeutic Crisis Intervention
ToD	Teacher of the Deaf
TOU	Tourette syndrome
VB	Verbal Reasoning
VIS	Visually Impaired
VOCA	Voice Output Communication Aid

Index

Index

Index